Rhetorical Ecologies

Rhetorical Ecologies

Edited by

Sidney I. Dobrin
University of Florida

Madison P. Jones
University of Rhode Island

National Council of Teachers of English
340 N. Neil St., Suite #104, Champaign, IL 61820
www.ncte.org

Staff Editor: Cynthia Gomez
Manuscript Editor: Michael G. Ryan
Interior Design: Jenny Jensen Greenleaf
Cover Design: Adrian Morgan
Cover Image: iStockphoto/The Nature Notes

ISBN (print): 978-0-8141-0189-6
ISBN (EPUB): 978-0-8141-0191-9
ISBN (PDF): 978-0-8141-0192-6

It is the policy of NCTE in its journals and other publications to provide a forum for the open discussion of ideas concerning the content and the teaching of English and the language arts. Publicity accorded to any particular point of view does not imply endorsement by the Executive Committee, the Board of Directors, or the membership at large, except in announcements of policy, where such endorsement is clearly specified.

NCTE provides equal employment opportunity (EEO) to all staff members and applicants for employment without regard to race, color, religion, sex, national origin, age, physical, mental or perceived handicap/disability, sexual orientation including gender identity or expression, ancestry, genetic information, marital status, military status, unfavorable discharge from military service, pregnancy, citizenship status, personal appearance, matriculation or political affiliation, or any other protected status under applicable federal, state, and local laws.

Every effort has been made to provide current URLs and email addresses, but because of the rapidly changing nature of the web, some sites and addresses may no longer be accessible.

Library of Congress Control Number: 2024936699

CONTENTS

CONTENTS

CHAPTER ONE

Ecologies of Rhetoric

SIDNEY I. DOBRIN AND MADISON P. JONES

In 1866, the German zoologist Ernst Haeckel coined the term "ecology" in his paper "General Morphology of Organisms" to describe the bespoke relationships between organisms and their respective environments. He describes a holistic "whole science" that studies "the organism's relationship with the surrounding outside world, which includes in a broader sense all 'existential conditions'" (Haeckel 4). He drew from the ancient Greek word *oîkos*, meaning "house," to characterize the study of the relationships between organisms and their home places. Since then, the concept of ecology has traveled far beyond its original context, place, and usage, and today the term finds purchase in thousands of applications across disciplines, philosophies, and cultures. As Erich Hörl (2017) explains, "There are thousands of ecologies today: ecologies of sensation, perception, cognition, desire, attention, power, values, information, participation, media, the mind, relations, practices, behavior, belonging, the social, the political" (1). Hörl contends that ecology has been denaturalized and removed from its original connections with nature and environment and semantically redefined to occupy any field where it might find utility—or, at least, convenience. From the origins of home economics to Rachel Carson's *Silent Spring* and the long tradition of environmental politics to iconic works like Marvin Gaye's iconic song "Mercy Me (The Ecology)," ecology has undoubtedly had a profound and pervasive cultural and multidisciplinary influence. Félix Guattari discusses this proliferation of applications in his 1989 book *The Three Ecologies* and, like Hörl, extends the term to social relations, subjectivity, and mediation. Following this work and gaining inertia from key theoretical works like Gilles Deleuze and Guattari's *A Thousand*

Plateaus: Capitalism and Schizophrenia, ecology became an influential concept beyond the "hard" sciences, influencing a wide range of disciplines and reaching peak usage as a concept in the late 1990s. To the extent that Google's Ngram Viewer search can provide an accurate indication of the concept's meteoric rise in English usage, its uptick in circulation noticeably began in the mid-1960s and reached a high-water mark in 1994 (see Figure 1.1).

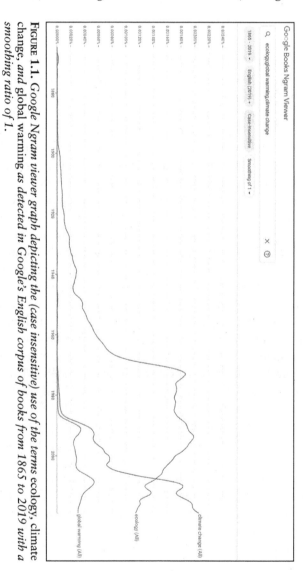

FIGURE 1.1. *Google Ngram viewer graph depicting the (case insensitive) use of the terms ecology, climate change, and global warming as detected in Google's English corpus of books from 1865 to 2019 with a smoothing ratio of 1.*

As this graph depicts, ecology began to dip in usage in the early 2000s, coinciding with the growing popularity of "global warming" as a term and then following a dramatic spike in the use of "climate change." This loss of rhetorical velocity suggests that today the "existential conditions" Haeckel refers to are changing rapidly, due in no small part to anthropogenic impacts of carbon emissions at the planetary scale, and those changes are only expected to accelerate by orders of magnitude in the coming decades. This marks not only a change to conditions in the material environment but also a rhetorical change in environmental discourse. This means that ecology not only helps us to articulate and respond to our current environmental, political, and rhetorical conditions but also that those discursive conditions are revising and reshaping ecology as a concept.

This ongoing discursive and political change coincides with the recent landmark Sixth Assessment Report by the UN's Intergovernmental Panel on Climate Change (IPCC) that underscores the urgent need for global action on drastically reducing carbon emissions to avoid or diminish the direst consequences of global warming. The report highlights the irreversible consequences of anthropogenic climate change and demonstrates the necessity of immediate and large-scale action to mitigate the ecological impacts of a warming world. In recognition of this call for change, we come together as scholars and teachers of rhetoric who are deeply concerned with ecology as a fundamental element of environmental justice. As climate change becomes a central matter of concern for science and environmental communicators, we seek to reinvigorate the conversation around the concept of rhetorical ecologies to bring the rich, complex, and sometimes contradictory disciplinary history and contemporary practices of ecology into greater conversation with rhetoric and writing studies.

Recent scholars working at the intersections of the environmental humanities, the digital humanities, and media studies have begun to discuss the need for a richer engagement with the specific disciplinary histories and social contexts of environmental concepts. For instance, Thomas Patrick Pringle illustrates the various ways that, within different contexts, "environments have been conceived as media technologies and vice versa" (Pringle 2021), producing what Hörl terms "an ecology of a natural–technical continuum" (2013, 128). This continuum makes ecology a complex and sometimes conflicting concept to analogize, as its conceptual history is shaped by rhetorical movements that resemble a pendulum's swing. Furthermore, these specific ideological and historical contexts have important political implications for ecology. In this case, Pringle discusses the "ecosystem" concept, coined by Arthur Tansley in 1935, which he regarded as in direct conflict with "the idea of holism propounded by Jan Smuts, the South African political leader, general, ecologist, and one of the philosophical architects of apartheid" (Pringle 2021, par. 2). By drawing from systems theory, Tansley offered a way to conceptualize environments without relying on abstract holism. Still, Pringle demonstrates the connections between Smuts's ecological holism and racist apartheid philosophy and the many troubling ways that his philosophy "pervasively and innocuously . . . persists." As ecosystems ecology emerged from Tansley's work in the 1960s and 1970s, it undercut Smuts's pernicious holism by focusing on the study of specific systems. Drawing from cybernetics, Howard T. and Eugene Odum revolutionized ecosystems ecology and helped shift the field toward more complex, scalar, and data-driven methods and models (Woods 2019). Yet these models were developed with methods and supported with funding directly tied to the US Army's nuclear testing in the Marshall Islands where the Odums carried out their groundbreaking ecological tests (Martin 2018; Jones 2021). These brief examples demonstrate that ecology's relationship to colonial ideologies across space and time requires careful context for its application to the study of rhetoric, writing, and communication.

The impetus for this collection, then, grows from rhetoric's "ecological turn," which has posed a need to closely examine how the concept of ecology informs methodological, theoretical, pedagogical, and practical approaches to writing, rhetoric, and communication. As such, contributors to this collection—as well as other writing scholars working within the penumbra of ecology—seek to critically examine the pasts, presents, and futures of the concept less as an analogy or metaphor and more as a *diagram*, as defined by Deleuze and Guattari. Diagrams are more than representations or scaled models—they are themselves systems of meaning making. In *Difference and Repetition*, Deleuze discusses how a "structure or an Idea is a 'complex theme', an internal multiplicity—in other words, a system of multiple, non-localizable connections between differential elements which is incarnated in real relations and actual terms" (183). Recent scholarship has connected "diagrammatic approaches to rhetoric" to understand how circulation and materiality, as well as motion and energy, pose important challenges and opportunities for rhetorical inquiry (Halm 2023; Hawk 2018). Rather than treating ecology as an abstract metaphor, or even as a scaled model, contributors to this collection instead endeavor to undertake what Noah Roderick refers to as "a project of critical analysis of analogical invention, which addresses the social conditions that underlie the creation and argument of knowledge in a world of complex systems" (Roderick par. 1). As such, this collection works not to simply recount the history of writing and rhetoric studies' adoption of ecology but to situate that history in rich discussions regarding the potential ecology holds for rhetoric and writing studies moving forward, fostering more inclusive, equitable, and justice-oriented approaches to rhetorical inquiry.

A Brief History of Rhetorical Ecologies

Over the last two decades, ecology has gained velocity as a key-word in rhetoric, as it has achieved significant traction across humanities disciplines. Its popularity stems, at least in part, from its capaciousness as a concept. Before discussing the specific history of rhetorical engagements with ecology, it is necessary to briefly situate that history in its broader context. Ecology indexes a wide range of relational systems, crossing what Guattari's "three ecologies" establishes as a trifold approach to ecology ranging from complexity theory and media studies to the spatial humanities and environmental justice. As such, it offers a loose framework that can help bridge work across disciplinary foci. *The Three Ecologies* argues that humans are being manipulated by way of the production of a collective, mass-media subjectivity and that there is a need for a mental ecology that accounts for the manner in which "Integrated World Capitalism (IWC)" has achieved social control via mass media as a means of governing human thought. Guattari contends that there are numerous components that converge to create the sense of who we think we are— subjectivity—but that the singularity of subjectivity is repressed by the dominant mass-media subjectivity and has nothing to do with individuals. That is, Guattari ties the idea of subjectivity to ecological relationships within a system, importing the concept of ecology into considerations of cultural systems that generate our understandings of identity and subjectivity. Guattari's notion of ecology, then, becomes paramount to understanding the pervasiveness of rhetorical network/systems and the ways in which mediated subject formations render the notion of subjectivity as indistinguishable from encompassing mechanisms that form the collective, mediated subjectivity. *The Three Ecologies*, thus, provides an ecological approach to comprehending that which mediates. That is, *The Three Ecologies* alleges that subjectivity should be understood as an ecology that enfolds subjectivity and environment into a single approach.

In *The Three Ecologies*, Guattari proposes an ecosophy, or ethico-political articulation between three "ecological registers": the environment, social relations, and human subjectivity. These registers can be rethought within a framework of rhetoric to understand environments more broadly as writing and communication, social relations as all relations, and human subjectivity as agents of a part/whole relation. Ecosophy leads to a reinvention in how we examine the relations of rhetorical systems to networks embodied by individual agents. For Guattari, traditional views of environment/culture dualisms oversimplify what amounts to complex relationships. Ecosophy, then, constitutes an attempt at formulating a non-scientific theory of complex ecology, which might be understood as an ecological rhetorical theory. Despite Guattari's social liberation agendas and his links with Marxist philosophies that generally espouse economic methods couched in economic metaphors, ecosophy encourages unfolding rhetoric as ecological. Of course, we should acknowledge that *The Three Ecologies* is an anomalous work for Guattari as its call for systems of interconnectedness seems counter to the resistance to holism that is evident in much of his collaboration with Gilles Deleuze, notably in work regarding difference and multiplicities in theories of rhizomatic structure forwarded in *Anti-Oedipus* and *A Thousand Plateaus.*

The Three Ecologies works away from individual subjects toward a more complex notion of subjectification, wanting to make explicit the distinction between individuals and subjectivity, exploring what can be clearly termed as a whole-part relation between subjectivity and the concepts that form subjectivity, what Guattari calls "processes of subjectification" (36). Guattari proposes developing ecological methods that are rid of scientific references and metaphors to instead develop an ecology of ethics. To do so, Guattari introduces what amounts to a posthuman approach to ecological/ethical thinking:

> I want to uproot them from their post-structuralist ties, from a subjectivity anchored solidly in the individual and collective past. From now on what will be on the agenda is a "futurist" and "constructivist" opening up of the fields of virtuality. The unconscious remains bound to archaic fixations only as long as there is no investment [*engagement*] directing it toward the future. This existential tension will proceed through the bias of human and even non-human temporalities such as the acceleration of the technological and data-processing revolutions, as prefigured in the phenomenal growth of a computer-aided subjectivity, which will lead to the opening up or, if you prefer, the unfolding [*dépliage*], of animal-, vegetable-, Cosmic, and machine-becomings. (38, emphases in original)

Guattari's approach suggests much about the ubiquity of writing and about rhetoric—if we take writing to encompass the digital, new media formations to which Guattari alludes, as well as the implications for artificial intelligence (AI) and the ubiquity of rhetoric therein—and the interrelations between agents, writing/rhetorical systems, and relations with the networks with which writing interacts. As he suggests:

> The question of subjective enunciation will pose itself ever more forcefully as machines producing signs, images, syntax and artificial intelligence continue to develop. Here we are

> talking about a reconstruction of social and individual practices
> which I shall classify under three complimentary headings, all
> of which come under the ethico-aesthetic aegis of an ecosophy:
> social ecology, mental ecology, and environmental ecology. (41)

In mapping out these three ecologies, then, Guattari explains that
it is crucial to dispense with any pseudo-scientific approaches to
established ecologic paradigms. This is because the ecologies of
The Three Ecologies propose to examine entities that are vastly
more complex than those that scientific ecologies examine and
for the fundamental fact that "the three ecologies are governed
by a different logic" (44). This is a crucial point in that when
dealing with complexities to the degree found in systems like
rhetoric and writing, scientific approaches can no longer provide
the degree of complex observation required—nor can the logics of
scientific paradigm or even entrenched rhetoric provide the needed
approaches for considering the ecologies of writing. Guattari's
recognition of system and ecology, then, encourages developing
ecological rhetorics from/in which to extend complex theories
about writing-as-system.

Theorizing rhetorical ecology, then, is not an inherent move
to formulate rhetorical theories that work toward consensus but
instead to cultivate a dissensus (Guattari's term) that perpetually
disrupts what we can "know" about rhetoric to the end of an
ever-increasingly complexifying view of rhetoric. Borrowing
again from *The Three Ecologies*, these new ecological practices
must articulate themselves within tangled and heterogeneous
spaces toward the objective of locating and making visible the
relations that lend themselves to rhetoric's velocity across and
among integrated systems. As Guattari suggests, this dissensus will
inevitably lead to new forms of eco-logics that might be thought
of in terms of the proverb "the exception proves the rule," only in
the new eco-logic, the "exception can just as easily deflect the rule,
or even re-create it" (52). Such an eco-logic—which seemingly
echoes Richard M. Coe's eco-logic, addressed below—underlies
the very notion of rhetorical ecology.

The numerous and tangled relations that draw together
around ecology suggest the wide scope it holds as a touchstone
for rhetorical inquiry. Yet the convenience of ecology's diverse

conceptual range also threatens to leave ecology as an empty signifier, a buzzword for rhetoric. Further, its popularity might suggest that it is a trend (in the negative sense of the word) and may someday become passé—a terrifying possibility in a time of escalating social and ecological crises. At the same time, the vitality of ecology lies, in part, in its nascence. To suggest that ecology be codified into a singular definition would only serve to diminish its conceptual momentum. As such, the contributors to this collection offer ecology, not as a convenient term but as one with a rich and complex intellectual history that must be mapped and counter-mapped across disciplinary, social, ecological, and intellectual histories. With these limitations and possibilities in mind, we offer here a brief history of the divergent strands that ecology weaves together in its disciplinary engagements with rhetoric and writing studies as we discuss the emerging possibilities for the concept in future scholarship.

For writing studies, ecology first entered the disciplinary conversation in 1974 when Richard M. Coe published "Rhetoric 2001" in *Freshman English News* (FEN) (the precursor to *Composition Studies*), which would be named the winner of FEN's annual essay contest, signifying its anticipated impact on the field. He followed this essay in 1975 with the influential article "Eco-Logic for the Composition Classroom" in *College Composition and Communication*. However, it wasn't until the mid-1980s that ecology really took root in rhetoric and composition with the publication of Marilyn M. Cooper's (1986) article, "The Ecology of Writing," in *College English*. These three pioneering texts stand as foundational to the evolution of rhetorical ecology.[1]

In "Rhetoric 2001," Coe establishes, well ahead of his time, a context in which ecological methodologies and concern for environmental crises, as well as the interactions between writers and computer technologies, would become dominant aspects of both composition instruction and the very understanding of writing itself. Coe anticipates ecological methodologies in rhetorical studies and writing studies as emerging as a fundamental school of thought as he links ecological crises to "three determining factors: (a) technological progress, (b) population increase, and (c) certain outmoded attitudes and thought patterns" (1). He shows us the need to take up systems theories and complexity theories, the very theories that would become critical to the development of ecocomposition, place-based composition, and ecological rhetoric thirty years following the publication of "Rhetoric 2001"—as accurately predicted in his title. At the time, Coe's work offered enormous potential for developing ecological understandings of writing, the foremost of which is the need to look at wholes rather than parts. His 1975 publication "Eco-Logic for the Composition Classroom" critiques composition pedagogy for seeking rhetorical approaches that work to break wholes into manageable parts. The problem Coe notes is that such methods only work when wholes can be attributed as the sum of all of their parts but are inefficient for addressing more complex phenomena—such as rhetoric and writing—and seem to anticipate Guattari's *The Three Ecologies*, as noted earlier. Coe explains that rhetorical traditions reflect the dominant logics of Western science, logics that are contradictory to eco-logic, a logic that scrutinizes wholes over the reduction of wholes to parts, which could be ordered, named, and managed. What Coe calls for, then, is a systems approach to writing that accounts for whole systems rather than subsystems.

More than a decade after the publication of "Rhetoric 2001," Marilyn M. Cooper's "The Ecology of Writing" anointed ecology as a critical component of research in rhetoric and composition, and it is often cited as the preeminent work in initiating considerations of rhetorical ecologies. In that foundational article, Cooper critiques composition studies' process movement. Cooper argues against composition studies' pedagogical theories (turning to James A. Berlin's taxonomy as a way of identifying those theories) as reliant upon a concept of the individual writer writing, instead proposing that writing is, indeed, a social act. Along with Kenneth Bruffee's 1981 article "Collaborative Learning," James A. Reither's "Writing and Knowing: Toward Redefining the Writing Process" (which summarizes the ideas of Gary Larson, Lee Odell, Patricia Bizzell, and John Gage), "The Ecology of Writing" really stands as a primary signaling moment that the cognitive process model was to be dethroned by the social epistemic vision of writing and writing pedagogy, a theory that inherently relies on ecological methodologies of systemic relationships.

Cooper presents an ecological model of writing "whose fundamental tenet is that writing is an activity through which a person is continually engaged with a variety of socially constituted systems" (367). In this thinking, Cooper reacts against understanding systems as stable and forwards a different kind of systems theory, one that does not embrace a social epistemic model but a hyper-circulatory concept of system in which agents become indistinguishable from the system itself, and thus, identify that both subject and system "determine and are determined by" characteristics of each or choose to accept the system as the predominant feature of the ecology, rendering the agent indistinguishable from the system. Cooper proposes that "the ecological model postulates dynamic interlocking systems which structure the social activity of writing" (368), a notion that allows us to develop a more direct understanding that ecological postulate dynamic interlocking systems that are themselves the structure of and structured by writing. Cooper forwards a now cliched metaphor for thinking about writing: the web, "in which anything that affects one strand of the web vibrates throughout the whole" (370). From Coe and Cooper, we can trace the origins of systems and ecological perspectives on rhetoric, writing, and discourse, as well as a focus on holism and complexity.

Following this initial foray into the ecologies of writing, Louise Wetherbee Phelps's (1988) *Composition as a Human Science: Contributions to the Self-Understanding of a Discipline* argued that discourse operates within "complex systems" that undermines the "static model" that composition studies traditionally applied to writing and communication (139). She deploys an "ecological strategy" for situating composition studies within its "specific cultural field of meaning" (3). Her important contribution to the "ecology of composition" highlights the tension between "differentiated, elaborated, hierarchical" structures of a general theory and the importance of "'division' or difference" in opening room for "continual self-transformation [and] novelty" (4). That is, in her discussion of the "contextualist paradigm" for writing, she demonstrates (building from Stephen Pepper) the important relationship between "(1) process or change, and (2) context," with context connoting "system, field, whole, ecology, relation" (32). This highlights the important agonism that must exist within disciplinary systems, in which divisions and changes function creatively, and sometimes transformatively, within the hierarchies of their contexts. While Phelps is sometimes ignored in contemporary disciplinary histories of ecologies of writing and rhetoric, her project sets the stage for ecological work that resists the Social Darwinism implicit in general or unified theories of both rhetoric and ecology, an imperative to which we will return. As Phelps defines the ecologies of writing, we take up her imperative to study both context and change as they affect ecology as a concept for rhetoric.

In the decades that followed these early contributions, ecology slowly began to gain traction as a means of understanding writing and rhetoric as complex, relational activities. Building in part from Phelps, Margaret Syverson's (1999) *The Wealth of Reality: An Ecology of Composition* applies systems thinking to enrich rhetoric and composition's engagement with place and context beyond the more simplistic "rhetorical triangle" model, which was prevalent at the time. She identifies the ways that the rhetorical triangle "of writer, text, and audience [. . .] has tended to single out the writer, the text, or the audience as the focus of analysis" and offers ecology as a concept through which to engage with "dimensions of composition" that "are distributed embodied emergent and enactive" (23). Following this work, Jenny Edbauer's (2005) influential article "Unframing Models of Public Distribution: From Rhetorical Situation to Rhetorical Ecologies" forwards the concept of "distributed rhetorical ecologies" (20) against Lloyd Bitzer's concept of "the rhetorical situation" as a way to "tune to a model of public rhetoric that sets its sights across a wider social field of distribution" (13). These texts bring together some of the key concepts that Coe and Cooper introduce into rich engagement with the need for place-based scholarship to engage with rhetorical ecologies as complex contexts and sites of change.

Other ecologically and environmentally influenced work in writing studies fed much of the thinking behind ecocomposition. In 1991, M. Jimmie Killingsworth and Jacqueline S. Palmer published the groundbreaking book *Ecospeak: Rhetoric and Environmental Politics in America*, the first book to apply ecology as a rhetorical methodology. In *Ecospeak*, Killingsworth and Palmer turn to rigorous rhetorical analysis of texts ranging from the literary to the legal to identify the ways in which the rhetorics used in those texts perpetuate an oversimplified vision of the conflict between economic and evolutionary progress. They call this oversimplified rhetoric "ecospeak," echoing Orwell's doublespeak, and explain how ecospeak paralyzes our ability to engage with ecological and environmental crises. Killingsworth and Palmer instead propose a more holistic ecological view of the rhetorics that inform environmental politics.

Likewise, Randall Roorda's 1998 book *Dramas of Solitude: Narratives of Retreat in American Nature Writing* asked as to the relationship between nature writing and social purposes of solitude. In doing so, Roorda began to inquire as to how we perceive nonhuman nature and the ways that such perceptions inform the ways in which we write about nature. Roorda's synthesis of narrative theory, nature writing, and social/ethical approaches to solitude opens doors to considerations of the ways in which we write about nature, environment, and ecology. In many ways, it initiated thinking about the dynamic relationship between "nature" and writing. Similarly, just before the publication of *Dramas of Solitude*, Roorda formed a Conference on College Composition and Communication (CCCC) Special Interest Group (SIG) that brought together writing specialists whose work actively engaged environmental, ecological, and nature writing through the Association of the Study of Literature and the Environment (ASLE). The ASLE-CCCC SIG began meeting officially at CCCC conferences in 1996. Roorda's efforts in his scholarship and his service to ASLE-CCCC established a critical relationship between ecocriticism and writing studies. Ecocriticism, reductively, is a literary criticism that examines the ecological and environmental properties of a text much as feminist literary criticism takes up the feminist aspects of a text or a Marxist criticism takes up matters of production and economy in a text. Ecocriticism has grown to be one of the most important forms of literary criticism currently studied; its roots solidified in 1992 with the first ASLE conference meeting and the publication of Cheryl Glotfelty and Harold Fromm's landmark collection *The Ecocriticism Reader* in 1996. Roorda's influence in bringing this—at the time—emerging literary criticism into conversation with writing studies would initiate a rich marriage between the two areas of study that would ultimately be as influential to the evolution of ecocomposition and rhetorical ecology as any other work. Such influence is easily identified in Dobrin's 2000 CCCC talk "On the Very Discourse of Nature, or Why Composition is Ecological" and his 2001 ASLE Plenary Address, "Ecocomposition."

Around the same time, Dobrin and Christian R. Weisser introduced "ecocomposition" to describe the distributed actions that produce writing, discourse, and literacy from an ecological perspective by attending to the relationships of places, contexts, and environments with discourse using postprocess and systems theories. Rather than treat ecology as a metaphor, or to focus exclusively on environmental ethics and politics, ecocomposition uses an ecological model to connect discourse and environment. Through a 2001 edited book, *Ecocomposition: Theoretical and Pedagogical Approaches*, and followed the next year by "Breaking Ground in Ecocomposition: Exploring Relationships between Discourse and Environment," an article published in *College English*, and a monograph the following year, *Natural Discourse: Toward Ecocomposition*, Dobrin and Weisser laid the foundation for ecocomposition as a subfield of writing studies. In forwarding ecocomposition, they build from Coe and Cooper's work, but they also engage directly with the field of ecocriticism, bridging important divides between literary criticism, environmental rhetoric, and composition studies. Since then, ecology has become a landmark concept for rhetoric and writing studies. While the brief summary we outline here does not fully account for ecocomposition's important influence on the disciplinary ecologies of rhetorical ecologies, nor do we seek to codify such a singular history, it begins to demonstrate the rich intellectual history that shapes the contemporary conversation.

While it is well beyond the scope of our brief introduction to fully account for any complete disciplinary history, or contemporary proliferation, of the ecological turn(s) in rhetoric and writing studies, we offer an abbreviated timeline in order to further augment our discussion of rhetoric's many engagements with the concept of ecology (Figure 1.2).

A Timeline of Rhetoric's Ecological Turn(s)

Dustin Edwards
"Critical Infrastructure Literacies..." (2021)

Louis M. Maraj
Black or Right (2020)

Dan Ehrenfeld
"Sharing a World with Others'" (2020)

Caroline Gottschalk Druschke
"A Trophic Future for Rhetorical Ecologies" (2019)

Madison Jones
"A Counterhistory of Rhetorical Ecologies" (2021)

Hannah J. Rule
Situating Writing Processes (2019)

Bridie McGreavy, & al.
Tracing Rhetoric and Material Life (2017)

Chris Mays
"Writing Complexity, One Stability at a Time" (2018)

Nathan Stormer & B. McGreavy
"Thinking Ecologically About Rhetoric's Ontology" (2017)

Asao B. Inoue
Antiracist Writing Assessment Ecologies (2015)

Gabriela Raquel Ríos
"Cultivating land-based literacies and rhetorics" (2015)

Angela Haas
Femrhet Keynote (2015)

Robin E. Jensen
"An Ecological Turn in Rhetoric of Health Scholarship" (2015)

Noah Roderick
"Analogize This!" (2012)

Nathaniel A. Rivers & Ryan P. Weber
Ecological, Pedagogical, Public Rhetoric (2011)

Douglas Eyman
Digital Rhetoric (2015)

David Grant
"Toward Sustainable Literacies" (2009)

Paul Lynch
"Composition's New Thing" (2012)

Collin Gifford Brooke
Lingua Fracta (2009)

Byron Hawk
A Counter-History of Composition (2007)

Sidney I. Dobrin & Sean Morey
Ecosee (2009)

Kristie Fleckenstein, & al.
"The Importance of Harmony" (2008)

Jenny Edbauer
"Unframing Models of Public Distribution" (2005)

Clay Spinuzzi
Tracing Genres through Organizations (2003)

Nedra Reynolds
Geographies of Writing (2004)

Marika Seigel
"One Little Fellow Named Ecology" (2005)

Stuart Blythe
"Agencies, Ecologies, and the Mundane Artifacts in Our Midst" (2007)

S. Dobrin & Christian R. Weisser
Ecocomposition (2001)

Margaret Syverson
The Wealth of Reality (1999)

S. Dobrin
ASLE Plenary Address (2001)

Randall Roorda
Dramas of Solitude (1998)

R. Roorda
Formation of the ASLE-CCCC SIG (1996)

M. Jimmie Killingsworth & Jacqueline S. Palmer
Ecospeak (1991)

George A. Kennedy
"A Hoot in the Dark" (1992)

Louise Wetherbee Phelps
Composition as a Human Science (1988)

Marilyn Cooper
"The Ecology of Writing" (1986)

Karen Burke LeFevre
Invention as a Social Act (1987)

Richard Coe
"Rhetoric 2001" (1974)

Richard Coe
"Closed System Composition" (1975)

Richard Coe
"Eco-Logic for the Composition Classroom" (1975)

FIGURE 1.2. *A timeline portraying some of rhetoric's ecological turn(s) and connections. This figure is not meant to represent rhetorical ecologies in its totality, nor as a unified concept, but rather to offer a cross-section of its intellectual development within rhetoric and writing studies, especially in relation to Richard Coe's early work applying systems theory to composition. There are many other works that have contributed to rhetorical ecologies, and in presenting this timeline, we hope to begin to contribute to a wider engagement with rhetorical ecology across and beyond disciplinary traditions and constraints.*

In doing so, we recognize that—like mapping out an ecosystem—rhetorical ecologies resist such conceptual boundary markers, and the task of fully accounting for the field(s) that have participated in the formation and propagation of rhetorical ecologies would be a deeply fraught endeavor, a point which we will return to in the next section. Instead, we hope to demonstrate the productive agonism and dissensus that characterizes rhetorical ecologies. As we examine the rich connections that rhetorical ecologies index, we encounter the First Law of Ecology as defined by Barry Commoner's 1971 book *The Closing Circle*, "everything is connected to everything else" (33).

We choose to include this representation because it helps visualize the complex circulation and development of ecological inquiry. However, such a timeline is linear rather than ecological, and as such it is necessarily limited, offering only some of the many highlights that make up the rich disciplinary story of rhetorical ecologies. One clear example of these limitations is in this timeline's focus on publications, especially print books. It would be difficult to include the many important conference presentations and keynote lectures that have helped to forward rhetorical ecologies and to expand and challenge its development as a concept. While we trace one ecological thread through Coe, we likewise acknowledge that there are numerous other strands that converge, like the intricate latticework of a spider's web, in the complex entanglements of rhetoric with ecology.

For instance, there is a long history of environmental rhetoric scholarship that crosses into conversations with the projects we have discussed, as well as in environmental history, communication studies, media studies, and science and technology studies, to name but a few. Like a field ecologist attempting to isolate an ecosystem, we quickly find that the boundaries we draw are more like permeable membranes, and rather than try to demarcate disciplinary boundaries, we engage with rhetorical ecologies as a way to embrace the pluriverse of nondisciplinary inquiry that ecologies open up or what Casey Boyle writes in his contribution to this collection, "A Wealth of Realities" (riffing off of Syverson). While we examine one series of examples, the contributors to this collection take up rhetorical ecologies through what Byron Hawk refers to in his contribution to this collection as "counter-traditions," resisting singular disciplinary definitions or constraints. While we have primarily discussed how ecology enters into rhetorical inquiry through composition studies, others have examined the history of ecology through its connections to communications theory, specifically discussing the conversations around *in-situ* (or place-based) and participatory rhetorics as well as activism, constitutive rhetorics, field methods, posthumanism, and new materialism. One keen example of other counter-traditions that emerge in the conceptual (counter)histories of rhetorical ecologies is Bridie McGreavy, Justine Wells, George F. McHendry, Jr., and Samantha Senda-Cook's edited collection *Tracing Rhetoric and Material Life: Ecological Approaches*, which discusses the connections between ecology and the field of Environmental Communication. Building from these and other works, we engage with rhetorical ecologies through methods that align with Natasha N. Jones, Kristen R. Moore, and Rebecca Walton's use of antenarrative, a storytelling technique that seeks to "destabilize and unravel aspects of the tightly woven dominant narrative" (212). They demonstrate how "antenarrative allows the work of the field to be reseen, forges new paths forward, and emboldens the field's objectives to unabashedly embrace social justice and inclusivity as part of its core (rather than marginal or optional) narrative" (212).

Just as the ASLE-CCCC SIG helped to forge important early connections between ecocriticism and writing studies, so have cultural rhetoricians more recently bridged other gaps between feminist and decolonial approaches at conferences and in symposia, and these important turning points may not be as evident in timeline form as they should be. For example, Angela Haas's 2015 plenary address at the 10th Biennial Feminisms and Rhetorics Conference, "Toward a Decolonial Feminist Operating System for Digital Rhetoric Studies," offers an important point of critique for the ways that privileging certain ecologies in writing studies has elided feminist and Indigenous perspectives. Along similar lines, the Rhetoric Review symposium "Perspectives on Cultural and Posthumanist Rhetorics" engages with ways that rhetoricians interested in these approaches "might work through productive tensions to produce pluriversal possibilities that are not totalizing" ("Perspectives" 375). These scholars introduce important areas of ecological inquiry that we will return to in the next section.

Furthermore, a linear temporal approach to representation offers a less-than-ecological view of rhetoric's engagement with ecology. There are many other ways to structure these relationships beyond a linear progression. For instance, using the digital application Connected Papers, we can map the papers which cite Coe's "Eco-Logic for the Composition Classroom," revealing a range of other studies that have emerged over the last forty plus years (Figure 1.3).

This visualization offers another way to think about the relationships that exist between conversations both within and outside of rhetorical ecological scholarship through Coe, which adds additional layers to the complex concept. As such, this collection responds to this conceptual history as well as its increasingly widespread usage in rhetoric, communication, and writing studies scholarship. While *ecology* has seen a marked decline in interest (at least according to Google Trends) over the last two decades (Figure 1.4), *rhetorical ecologies* has seen a more sporadic change in interest over the last few decades (Figure 1.5). We see this as an exigency for increased engagement with the concept, mobilizing its growing interest in rhetoric scholarship to help reinvigorate its more widespread use.

Just as we hope to add to the concept's velocity, we also see ecology as an important point of connection between what C. P. Snow famously termed the "two cultures" in his 1961 book *The Two Cultures and the Scientific Revolution*. He names a divide between humanists (whom he referred to as "literary intellectuals") and scientists. As such, rhetorical ecologies are a dynamic space to engage with both the rhetoric of ecological science and the science of ecological rhetoric. Yet, to date, no anthology has sought to treat this truly expansive concept in one collection. Likewise, little work exists placing the concept within its wide range of scholarship and disciplinary relations. *Rhetorical Ecologies* works to these ends.

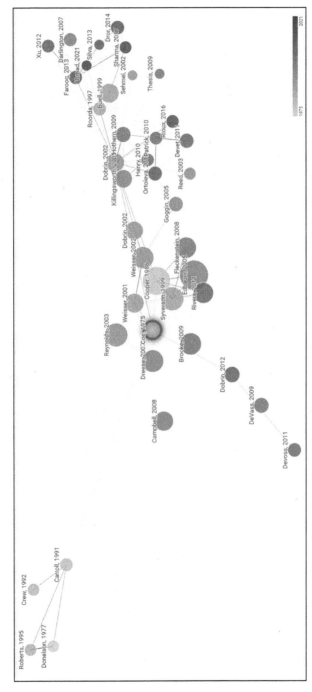

FIGURE 1.3. *A force-directed graph produced through Connected Papers portraying scholarship that cites Coe's 1975 essay "Eco-Logic for the Composition Classroom." This graph visually clusters similar papers and separates less similar papers.*

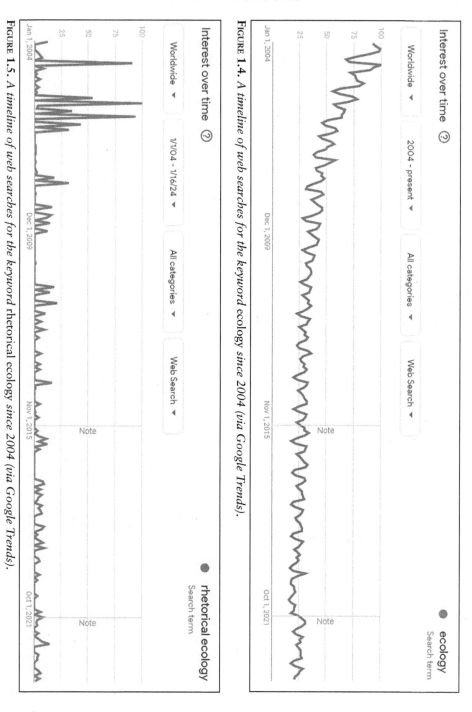

FIGURE 1.4. *A timeline of web searches for the keyword ecology since 2004 (via Google Trends).*

FIGURE 1.5. *A timeline of web searches for the keyword rhetorical ecology since 2004 (via Google Trends).*

Toward and Away from a General Rhetorical Ecology

We recognize that rhetoric's ecological turn suggests connections between general theories of both rhetoric and ecology, but we remain wary of the codification of a unified theory of general rhetorical ecology. It is thus useful to briefly discuss the distinctions that shape a general rhetorical ecology, building from the ontological-historical and disciplinary relations that converge around the concept. In his introduction to *General Ecology*, Erich Hörl (2017) builds from Bataille and Derrida's contrasts between general and restricted economy to distinguish "between general and restricted ecology" (46 n4). He argues that, as it has become a general concept, ecology "is increasingly denaturalized" (1) and suggests that what Timothy Morton refers to as "ecology without nature" identifies how technics have circumvented the "dogmas of authenticity" that have bound ecology to "Nature" as a signifier (2). Along similar lines, Madison Jones offers a "counterhistory of rhetorical ecologies" to trace its "successive rhetorical moves away from empirical naturalism toward theoretical, qualitative, and then quantitative approaches to studying environments" (336). These studies suggest the important social and historical dimensions of ecology's shifting relationship with nature and technics that become codified in the concept as it is taken up in contemporary theory. Without engaging with these elements, we risk not an "ecology without nature" but an ecology without science, without history, without its social and ecological context, without communities, without practice. In other words, ecology without its ecology.

Hörl identifies how a growing shift in the nature/technics divide has produced a "technoecological condition" (2). This ecological shift has led to "a fundamentally different value to the question of relation" that "does not turn relations into minor and derivative entities but considers them to be originary" (8). These systems of relation evoke an array of different power dynamics at play in ecology, from the swaying pendulums of governmental regulation to the widespread influence of algorithmic information control to the shifting landscapes of neoliberal-capitalism. Following Hörl's illustration of the technoecological condition as a teleology between technosphere and biosphere, we engage here with what he calls the "problematic of general ecology" as it intersects with notions of a general rhetoric. In this, he names the converging collection of situations and circumstances that shape ecology as a unified theory and master concept. This problematic offers an important starting point for the work of this collection, which engages with the constellation of theories, methods, disciplines, and histories that converge in rhetorical ecological inquiry, as well as demonstrates some of the various and divergent applications of rhetorical ecologies in practice.

Just as ecology has undergone a shift toward unification as a theory, so has rhetoric experienced, at least according to George Kennedy, an "evolution" towards a "more general theory of rhetoric" (2). In his landmark essay, "A Hoot in the Dark," he argues that rhetorical inquiry has been significantly restrained by a limited focus on specific linguistic systems of human communication. In response, he offers a broader definition of rhetoric as "energy" and as "code" and proposes steps toward tracing a "comprehensive history of its development" (20). One way to characterize the shift he proposes is through the same applications of "general" and "restricted" modifiers that Hörl applies to ecology. He offers eight theses that proceed from his "axiom that rhetoric is a form of energy," and from this starting point he aims to describe the advancement of a general theory of rhetoric (4). While Kennedy's notion of a "general rhetoric" opens up important and productive spaces for post/nonhuman and ecological approaches to rhetoric, in doing so, it also surfaces some of the perils of a general, universal, and unified theory of rhetoric along the same nature/technics lines that Hörl applies to a general theory of ecology. Likewise, unified theories tend to homogenize knowledge production, thereby limiting areas of inquiry and neutralizing other perspectives.

Throughout the essay, Kennedy draws upon evidence and examples from evolutionary and social biology, as well as linguistics, to make the case for a more universal definition of rhetoric. He argues that rhetorical features "of animal communication are analogies to what has developed in different species" and indicate "some possible parameters of rhetoric, of what nature has favored in particular environments, and perhaps of some of its basic features of communication" (9). It is here that the teleology of the nature/technics divide becomes particularly important for understanding the problematic, in Hörl's terms, of a unified theory of rhetorical ecology. He defines rhetoric as a "mechanism" that allows an organism to adapt to its environment (10). That is, as Kennedy defines rhetoric as a "mechanism for survival" for "an organism to environmental change," he glosses over the importance of the bespoke and autochthonous relationships that drive evolutionary adaptation in favor of a universalizing analogy for rhetoric. Justine Wells discusses how this application of Social Darwinism to define rhetoric supports a "general rhetoric of whiteness and white supremacy" (Wells). Against this general rhetoric, Lou Maraj situates "deep rhetorical ecology" or "deep ecology" to describe an "evolving series of rhetorical situations in which communication occurs, which are interrelated through bodies, spaces, cultures, and contexts with specific regard to power dynamics and race relations" (7). Maraj identifies key points of resistance to a general rhetorical ecology, focusing instead on "instances of fracture" (8). By similarly resisting a generalized unification, Wells demonstrates how "whiteness can be dismantled not only as a category of human identity, but as a way of being with the world" (Wells). Furthermore, such essentialist approaches to a unified rhetoric erase some of the precision that more situated engagements with rhetoric might produce.

With this in mind, the contributors to *Rhetorical Ecologies* do not seek to outline a complete map of rhetorical ecologies as a unified concept. Rather, we are interested in ecologies *plural*, understanding and acknowledging that rhetoric's ecologies are multiple, divergent, and highly situated knowledge-making practices. As Bridie McGreavy, Justine Wells, George F. McHendry, Jr., and Samantha Senda-Cook put it in their introduction to *Tracing Rhetoric and Material Life*, "the trope of ecology is neither singular nor static" (4). As such, we approach ecology in its many dynamic and conflicting forms and relations. In doing so, we follow the work of recent scholars like Aja Martinez (2020) who forward the concept of "counterstory as methodology" as a way to "disrupt erasures embedded" in our disciplinary histories (3). To return to the example of Arthur

Tansley's response to Jan Smuts's ecological holism, the ecosystem model encourages ecologists to focus on specific systems, even as it relies on the cybernetic metaphors at the heart of the technics/nature divide. That is, as we acknowledge rhetorical ecologies as multiple, we also understand that they are fragmented and dynamic, deeply situated in rich social, historical, and cultural contexts. In fact, we hold that in fragmentation lies its vibrancy as a concept. We are interested in unearthing and disrupting the ways that eco-logic informs contemporary rhetorical practices by examining ecological traditions and countertraditions in rhetoric, communication, and writing studies, as well as in its complex relations with other disciplines across the sciences and humanities.

In *Pollution Is Colonialism*, Max Liboiron engages with some of the ways that colonial practices shape scientific inquiry. As Liboiron demonstrates, much of modern scientific research is "based on colonial land relations, the assumed access by settler and colonial projects to Indigenous lands for settler and colonial goals" (5). Understanding these complex inheritances and relations are important because they offer ways to both "acknowledge and address" the "unmarked power dynamic" that is at play in the ways that settler and colonial land relations both produce and in turn are maintained by environmental crisis (12). For ecology, examples of the key points that Liboiron identifies abound. Following the turns from Smuts's holism to Tansley's ecosystems approach, Howard and Eugene Odum used complex trophic mapping to move ecosystems ecology beyond abstract models and to become a "hard" science. In 1953, Eugene and Howard Odum's *Fundamentals of Ecology* was born out of a growing need for the emerging discipline of ecology to define itself as distinct from the field of biology. The book was the field's only textbook for over a decade. Introducing a holistic approach to the study of biological systems, the Odums helped popularize the concept of ecosystem and to cement modern ecology as we know it today.

Yet as the Odums applied trophic mapping techniques to test the ecosystem hypothesis, they did so by working at sites that had been exposed to nuclear radiation, such as the Enewetak Atoll in the Marshall Islands. They also directly participated in releasing radiation into the environment in the Luquillo Experimental

Forest located within El Yunque National Forest in Puerto Rico. Because the Odums were broadly interested in creating sustainable energy flows through both natural and human ecosystems (Madison 1997), they chose to harness nuclear power to reveal the movement of energy through systems. This case implicates ecosystem ecology's development in the extractive politics of energy, power, and coloniality (de Onis 2023; Vega 2020) in Puerto Rico, as well as growing conversations around rhetoric, ecology, and nuclear colonialism (Endres 2018; Endres 2023; Jones 2020). In addition, it highlights the need for rhetoric to engage with what Justin Hosbey, Hilda Lloréns, and J. T. Roane refer to as "black ecologies" (Roane and Hosbey 2019) from a global perspective (Hosbey, et al. 2022) and specifically with the lived experiences and ecological knowledge of the communities directly impacted by this colonial history (Lloréns 2021; Walker 2022).

In her essay "A Land-Based Digital Design Rhetoric," Kristin L. Arola engages with the history of rhetorical ecologies and ecocomposition to demonstrate how "digital writing and rhetoric are always already part of our ecology and vice versa" (202). There, she forwards an important critique of rhetorical ecologies that reverberates with Liboiron's discussion of settler land relations and the Odums's example. Building from Gabriela Raquel Rìos's essay "Cultivating Land-Based Literacies and Rhetorics," she discusses the ways that ecology can abstract and obscure specific land relations. She engages with Matthew Ortoleva's critique of rhetorical ecologies, which argues that some scholars tend to "adopt ecological concepts in very broad ways, often wholly metaphorical" (Ortoleva 68 qtd. in Arola 202). As Arola explains, Ortoleva sets up a distinction between rhetorical ecologies (including Cooper; Dyehouse et al.; Edbauer; Syverson) and environmental rhetoric (including Killingsworth and Palmer; Stevens). However, Arola discusses how ecocompositionist approaches advanced by Dobrin and Weisser complicate these divisions by combining biosphere and semiosphere. As such, they offer a place to bridge divides in rhetorical ecological inquiry, especially by engaging more directly with land-based perspectives. Engaging with land, as opposed to more abstract ecological models, calls us to account for the complex relations that compose both digital and material spaces. That is, land relations call us to actively attend to the "actual lived experiences in and on the land [that] are co-constituted with our lived experiences of all things" (202). In doing so, we must turn from a unified theory of rhetorical ecologies toward land-based perspectives that situate us in specific and dynamic spatiotemporal contexts, as well as the ways that recent work in the Blue Humanities extends our focus to include the oceanic imperative for ecocriticism (Dobrin 2021; Oppermann 2023).

Just as Hörl cautions against approaches to general ecological thinking that ignore "the history of control and the corresponding rationality of power," so does this example remind us that power-relations are always present and that no version of ecology is either politically neutral or separate from its disciplinary inheritances and relations (8). In the case of the Odums, power indexes the interwoven history of nuclear colonialism with methods like trophic mapping that undergird the ecosystems model. As they received direct funding from the Atomic Energy Commission, the Odums's research both responded to and helped to produce and maintain a settler colonial approach to ecosystems, even as they reacted against the racist holistic models forwarded by Smuts. These examples underscore the need for rhetoric, writing, and communications scholars to engage critically with the important multidisciplinary histories and counterhistories that constellate ecology as a concept and a practice for social and environmental justice (Vega 2020). Following this disciplinary inheritance, *Rhetorical Ecologies* responds by situating rhetorical ecologies in a diverse array of historical, methodological, and disciplinary contexts to suggest how the term might provoke and inform the theories, methods, and practices of writing, rhetoric, and communication in the world to come.

Gathering Ecologies

Contributors to *Rhetorical Ecologies* extend this expansive and multidisciplinary conceptual history into work that richly engages with the interwoven pasts, presents, and futures of rhetoric, writing, and communication studies. Rather than offering limiting definitions of rhetorical ecologies, the contributors to this collection locate the concept in its disciplinary contexts to engage with its dynamic possibilities for the future. While contributors may not share particular key sources, approaches, methodologies, or even exact definitions or applications of ecology, these selections suggest the dynamic and provocative spaces that ecology opens up for rhetorical inquiry. Just as the word "anthology" comes from the Greek ἀνθολογία, meaning "gathering flowers," so do we intend to bring together a wide range of innovative scholars in this book to both uncover and upset ecological traditions in rhetoric and writing studies. Geared toward scholars, teachers, and practitioners in writing studies, generally, and the Humanities more broadly, *Rhetorical Ecologies* brings together conversations in rhetoric, communication, and writing studies with professional, technical, and scientific writing to examine rhetorical ecologies in relation to emerging and intersecting interests in systems and complexity theory, decolonial methods, Traditional Ecological Knowledge (TEK), science and technology studies, new materialism, ecocomposition, land-based perspectives and field work, participatory methods, posthumanism and the more-than-human world, circulation studies, digital rhetoric, ecocomposition, ecofeminism, and social justice. To illustrate ecology's potential for rhetorical inquiry, as well as how the concept might serve as a framework for rhetoric, the scholars gathered here discuss the use of ecological methods across their research, teaching, and public advocacy work. As such, the chapters in this book are divided into four parts and organized in a cumulative and sometimes recursive manner, with each section building on and departing from the themes discussed elsewhere. While each chapter shares focuses and points of convergence, they also demonstrate the wide array of practices and disciplines indexed by rhetorical ecologies.

The first section focuses on counter-ecologies. These chapters serve to interrupt the idea that we can trace any form of singular history of rhetorical ecology and by extension no single or unified definition, but instead introduce various provocations that situate ecology and rhetoric across various contexts, places, times, and practices. Opening the collection with Byron Hawk's "Counter-Traditions in Ecologies of Composition: Three

Models of Futurity" suggests the many different kinds of starting points we face in undertaking projects that engage rhetorical ecologies. Hawk demonstrates that rhetorical ecologies served as a countertradition in composition to the social turn of the 1980s and 1990s. Engaging with this counter-tradition, Hawk demonstrates, "necessitates an orientation toward the future" including "counter-futures." Across three different potential models, he traces futurity as it is enacted in the present, setting the stage for the work that will unfold across the other chapters and sections.

If Hawk suggests counter-traditions and futures for rhetorical ecologies, Chris Ingraham and Matthew Halm's "Acknowledging Some Challenges of Thinking Ecologically about Rhetoric" complicates rhetorical inquiry's ecological present by taking up the question of what we owe our rhetorical relations and how we acknowledge them in both material and discursive practices. They journey through the rocky terrain of rhetorical ecological inquiry across three important commonplaces of rhetoric—anthropocentrism, relationality, and circulation—to carefully engage with the ways that these elements of rhetorical theory might confound ecological approaches. Closing the first section, David Grant's "Nature Also Writes: On Rhetorical Thermodynamics" counters rhetoric's focus on living things, taking up Derrida's concept of life-death and Leroi-Gourhan's *grammè*. Grant connects energy flow to rhetoric's ecologies through Kennedy and Coe, establishing a countertradition of posthuman and new materialism that interact with the movement of rhetorical energy in systems.

Section two focuses on social and ecological justice. These chapters bring together these imperatives as they offer provocations for contemporary rhetoric. In the opening chapter, "Leah Heilig's "Distressed, Irrational, Disordered: Mad Design Thinking for Complex Systems" examines the relations between, among, and within "ecological madness" to frame and inform design thinking for the complexity of accessibility. Heilig traces the shared and conflicting histories of cognitive process and ecological models have had for rhetoric and design and demonstrates how this area opens space to disrupt inaccessible approaches to design thinking.

While Heilig highlights the productive disruptions of ecologies, Jennifer Clary-Lemon's "Between Hope and Failure: Cruel Optimism and Rhetorical Ecologies of Violence" examines the failures of human conservation of chimney swifts and the violent ecological relations they evidence between humans and nonhumans. Clary-Lemon refuses to turn away from the colonial violence that not only threatens the extinction of the chimney swift but also threatens to elide human responsibility and the failures of our responses, interpreting the rhetoric of hubris that often frames our relationships with nonhumans in the hope that we may learn from these failures in the future. Closing the second section, Candice Rai, Anselma Widha Prihandita, and Nolie Ramsey's "Toward Critical Ecological Methodologies: Stories and Praxes of Transformation in a Writing Program" takes up social and ecological justice within the context of writing program administration, examining the linguistic justice and antiracist imperatives through "a critical ecological methodology" that applies "storytelling as a vital way to illuminate complexities and possibilities for doing transformational equity work." Their study discusses the transformation of their writing program in an effort to create space for other programs to participate in transformative programmatic work.

Section three focuses on the ecologies of place. These chapters connect the importance of land and relations with environmental ethics and social justice. Opening this section, Jason Collins, Kristin L. Arola, and Marika Seigel's "Land-People Rhetorical Ecologies" apply frameworks from TEK to rhetorical ecologies in order to acknowledge and better understand the relations formed between people and land. They develop a land-people framework that critically engages with land as an imperative that has often been ignored in rhetorical ecological inquiry but leads to richer engagement with the specific places and agential relations of rhetoric. In Bridie McGreavy, Anthony Sutton, and Gabrielle Hillyer's "Tidal Ethics: Knowledge, Relations, and Writing" they reflect on rhetorical ecologies as they describe their approaches to field work in places shaped by tidal forces. Based on their place-based case study, they discuss "a tidal ethics approach" by deeply engaging with the ways that place participates in producing knowledge and/as relation. Their project offers a model for richly emplaced and embodied work combining science and environmental ethics with rhetorical field methods for engaged research. Closing this section, Samantha Senda-Cook's "*Mottainai* and Everyday Ecology at the Asian Rural Institute" discusses ecology through the Japanese concept of *mottainai*, which roughly translates to "Don't be wasteful." As embodying this concept, Senda-Cook describes a case study of a holistic approach to sustainable farming at the Asian Rural Institute, which connects human and nonhuman systems to develop a sustainable community. Through this study, she demonstrates the importance of ecology's mundane place-making practices and offers strategies for building resilient ecological communities through *mottainai*.

The fourth and final section looks at how we write worlds and relations through the pasts, presents, and futures of rhetoric. These chapters take up the ways that relationality and futurity transform contemporary practices of rhetorical ecology. This section opens with Laurie E. Gries's "We Parentheses: An Onto-Rhetorical Tale about Circulating Visual Marks of Hate," which uses a critical-creative approach to apply rhetorical ecologies to understand the circulation and distribution of white supremacist images online. Combining biographical narrative with rhetorical criticism, Gries discusses how white supremacist consequentiality circulates between the scales of personal and collective life. In John H. Whicker's "Becoming the Same: Ecologies and Writing-Objects," he discusses the ways that the circulation of rhetorical ecologies as a commonplace both identity and process "often strips the concept of its more disruptive, posthuman, and postcompositional force." By carefully attending to the problems of individual agents and subjects, Whicker offers an ecological perspective on the relationship between thinking and writing.

Following this discussion, Denise Tillery's "Environmental Communication in a Polluted Ecosystem: Challenges in the Age of Social Media" turns a critical eye toward the digital ecosystem, arguing "that the current social media landscape is extensively polluted, perhaps even hopelessly toxic." She offers a brief history of how information ecosystems reached this point and offers a narrative reflection on her own work, tracing "how some of that initial promise" she once saw in digital discourse has taken a dark turn. This important contribution offers salient perspectives on the limits of digital discourse, and it emphasizes the need for greater engagement with specific places and groups in order to cultivate better synergies between digital discourse and participatory action. In the closing chapter for this collection, Casey Boyle's "A Wealth of Realities" turns to the utopian and dystopian perspectives of futurity that can help us "attune to how dominant environmental imaginaries collapse the very complexity that systems thinking pursues." Boyle turns to fictional and futurist engagements with NewSpace imaginaries of deep space colonization to understand how these perspectives shape our world. Building from Syverson's *Wealth of Reality*, this chapter offers an engagement with a plurality of realities, revealing rich and multidimensional elements of rhetorical ecological inquiry that we can draw upon in imagining the futures of our many multiple presences.

Together, the selections gathered here offer provocations in ecological inquiry geared toward not only tracing conceptual counterhistories and countertraditions of this emerging sub-field but also suggesting some of the opportunities and limitations that ecologies present for rhetorical theory. Unfolding across these conversations, these chapters consider the possibilities that ecology holds for rhetoric to cross disciplinary lines and engage more meaningfully with contemporary ecological science and social justice. Bringing together a collection of disparate topics and potential applications of this concept itself functions in an ecological way. Therefore, the edited book format itself can reveal some of the advantages of ecology as a concept in rhetoric. This book brings together several lines of inquiry to demonstrate and test the capacity of ecology as a term currently circulating in rhetorical theory. While one might assume its applicability lies specifically with environmental criticism, this collection illustrates how ecological thinking can be employed to a number of cumulative and recursive ends. We hope to contribute to understandings of how rhetorical ecologies can not only better understand and engage with its disciplinary past(s) but also influence the future of scholarship, teaching, and advocacy in writing, rhetoric, and communication studies.

Note

1. For a more expansive consideration of Coe and Cooper's writing, see Dobrin, *Postcomposition*, Chapter 5.

Works Cited

Arola, Kristin L. "A Land-Based Digital Design Rhetoric." *The Routledge Handbook of Digital Writing and Rhetoric*, edited by Jonathan Alexander and Jacqueline Rhodes, Routledge, 2018, pp. 199–213.

Bataille, Georges. *The Accursed Share: An Essay on General Economy.* Translated by Robert Hurley, Zone Books, 1988.

Bitzer, Lloyd F. "The Rhetorical Situation." *Philosophy & Rhetoric*, vol. 1, no. 1, 1968, pp. 1–14.

Bruffee, Kenneth A. "Collaborative Learning and the 'Conversation of Mankind'." *College English*, vol. 46, no. 7, 1984, pp. 635–52.

Coe, Richard M. "Eco-Logic for the Composition Classroom." *College Composition & Communication*, vol. 26, no. 3, 1975, pp. 232–37.

Commoner, Barry. *The Closing Circle: Nature, Man & Technology.* Random House, 1971.

Cooper, Marilyn M. "The Ecology of Writing." *College English*, vol. 48, no. 4, 1986, pp. 364–75, https://doi.org/10.2307/377264.

de Onís, Catalina M. *Energy Islands: Metaphors of Power, Extractivism, and Justice in Puerto Rico.* U of California P, 2021.

Deleuze, Gilles. *Différence et Répétition.* Translated by Paul Patton, Presses Universitaires de France, Columbia University Press, 1968.

Deleuze, Gilles, and Félix Guattari. *Anti-Oedipus: Capitalism and Schizophrenia.* Translated by Robert Hurley, et al., U of Minnesota P, 1983.

———. *A Thousand Plateaus: Capitalism and Schizophrenia.* Translated by Brian Massumi, U of Minnesota P, 1987.

Derrida, Jacques. "From Restricted to General Economy: A Hegelianism without Reserve." *Writing and Difference.* Translated by Alan Bass, Routledge, 2001, p. 317–50.

Dobrin, Sidney I. *Blue Ecocriticism and the Oceanic Imperative.* Routledge, 2021.

Dobrin, Sidney I., and Christian R. Weisser. "Breaking Ground in Ecocomposition: Exploring Relationships between Discourse and Environment." *College English*, vol. 64, no. 5, 2002, pp. 566–89.

———. *Natural Discourse: Toward Ecocomposition.* State U of New York P, 2002.

Dyehouse, Jeremiah, et al. "'Writing in Electronic Environments': A Concept and a Course for the Writing and Rhetoric Major." *College Composition & Communication*, vol. 61, no. 2, 2009, pp. 330–50.

Edbauer, Jenny. "Unframing Models of Public Distribution: From Rhetorical Situation to Rhetorical Ecologies." *Rhetoric Society Quarterly*, vol. 35, no. 4, 2005, pp. 5–24.

Endres, Danielle. "The Most Nuclear-Bombed Place: Ecological Implications of the US Nuclear Testing Program." *Tracing Rhetoric and Material Life: Ecological Approaches*, edited by Bridie McGreavy, et al., Palgrave Macmillan, 2018, pp. 253–87, https://doi.org/ 10.1007/978-3-319-65711-0_10.

———. *Nuclear Decolonization: Indigenous Resistance to High-Level Nuclear Waste Siting.* Ohio State UP, 2023.

Glotfelty, Cheryll, and Harold Fromm, editors. *The Ecocriticism Reader: Landmarks in Literary Ecology.* U of Georgia P, 1996.

Guattari, Félix. *The Three Ecologies.* Translated by Ian Pindar and Paul Sutton, Athlone Press, 2000.

Haas, Angela. "Toward a Decolonial Feminist Operating System for Digital Rhetoric Studies." Women's Ways of Making, 10th Biennial Feminisms and Rhetorics Conference, Oct. 2015, Arizona State University, Tempe. Plenary Address.

Haeckel, Ernst. *Generelle Morphologie der Organismen: Allgemeine Grundzüge der Organischen Formen-Wissenschaft, Mechanisch Begründet durch die von Charles Darwin Reformirte Descendenz-Theorie.* Georg Reimer, 1866.

Halm, Matthew. "Molten Circulation and Rhetoric's Materiality." *Enculturation: A Journal of Rhetoric, Writing, and Culture*, 2023, https://enculturation.net/molten_circulation.

Hawk, Byron. "A Diagrammatics of Persuasion." *Circulation, Writing, and Rhetoric*, edited by Laurie E. Gries and Collin Gifford Brooke, Utah State UP, 2018, pp. 308–14.

Hörl, Erich. "A Thousand Ecologies: The Process of Cyberneticization and General Ecology." *The Whole Earth: California and the Disappearance of the Outside*, Sternberg Press, 2013, pp. 121–30.

Hörl, Erich, and James Burton, editors. *General Ecology: The New Ecological Paradigm*. Bloomsbury Publishing, 2017.

Hosbey, Justin, et al. "Global Black Ecologies," *Environment and Society: Advances in Research*, vol. 13, no. 1, 2022, pp. 1–10, https://doi.org/10.3167/ares.2022.130101.

Jones, Madison. "A Counterhistory of Rhetorical Ecologies." *Rhetoric Society Quarterly*, vol. 51, no. 4, 2021, pp. 336–52, https://doi.org/10.1080/02773945.2021.1947517.

Kennedy, George A. "A Hoot in the Dark: The Evolution of General Rhetoric." *Philosophy & Rhetoric*, vol. 25, no. 1, 1992, pp. 1–21.

Killingsworth, M. Jimmie, and Jacqueline S. Palmer. *Ecospeak: Rhetoric and Environmental Politics in America*. Southern Illinois UP, 1991.

Liboiron, Max. *Pollution Is Colonialism*. Duke UP, 2021.

Lloréns, Hilda. *Making Livable Worlds: Afro-Puerto Rican Women Building Environmental Justice*. U of Washington P, 2021.

Madison, Mark Glen. "'Potatoes Made of Oil': Eugene and Howard Odum and the Origins and Limits of American Agroecology." *Environment and History*, vol. 3, no. 2, 1997, pp. 209–38, https://www.jstor.org/stable/20723041.

Martin, Laura J. "Proving Grounds: Ecological Fieldwork in the Pacific and the Materialization of Ecosystems." *Environmental History*, vol. 23, no. 3, 2018, pp. 567–92, https://doi.org/10.1093/envhis/emy007.

Martinez, Aja Y. *Counterstory: The Rhetoric and Writing of Critical Race Theory*. National Council of Teachers of English / Conference on College Composition and Communication, 2020.

McGreavy, Bridie, et al., editors. *Tracing Rhetoric and Material Life: Ecological Approaches*. Palgrave Macmillan, 2018.

Odum, Eugene P. *Fundamentals of Ecology*. W. B. Saunders, 1953.

Odum, Howard T. "Rain Forest Structure and Mineral-Cycling Homeostasis." *A Tropical Rain Forest: A Study of Irradiation and Ecology at El Verde*, edited by Howard T. Odum and R. F. Pigeon, U. S. Atomic Energy Commission, 1970.

Oppermann, Serpil. *Blue Humanities: Storied Waterscapes in the Anthropocene.* Cambridge UP, 2023.

Ortoleva, Matthew. "Let's Not Forget Ecological Literacy." *Literacy in Composition Studies*, vol. 1, no. 2, 2013, pp. 66–73.

Phelps, Louise Wetherbee. *Composition as a Human Science: Contributions to the Self-Understanding of a Discipline.* Oxford UP, 1988.

Pringle, Thomas Patrick. "The Tech Ecosystem and the Colony." *Heliotrope*, 12 May 2021, https://www.heliotropejournal.net/helio/the-tech-ecosystem.

Roane, J. T., and Justin Hosbey. "Mapping Black Ecologies." *Current Research in Digital History*, vol. 2, 2019, https://doi.org/10.31835/crdh.2019.05.

Roderick, Noah. "Analogize This! The Politics of Scale and the Problem of Substance in Complexity-Based Composition." *Composition Forum*, vol. 25, 2012, http://compositionforum.com/issue/25/scale-substance-complexity.php.

Roorda, Randall. *Dramas of Solitude: Narratives of Retreat in American Nature Writing.* State U of New York P, 1998.

Sackey, Donnie Johnson. "Perspectives on Cultural and Posthumanist Rhetorics." *Rhetoric Review*, vol. 38, no. 4, 2019, pp. 375–401, https://doi.org/10.1080/07350198.2019.1654760.

Snow, C. P. *The Two Cultures and the Scientific Revolution.* Cambridge UP, 1961.

Stevens, Sharon McKenzie. *A Place for Dialogue: Language, Land Use, and Politics in Southern Arizona.* U of Iowa P, 2007.

Syverson, Margaret A. *The Wealth of Reality: An Ecology of Composition.* Southern Illinois UP, 1999.

Tansley, A. G. "The Use and Abuse of Vegetational Concepts and Terms." *Ecology*, vol. 16, no. 3, 1935, pp. 284–307, https://doi.org/10.2307/1930070.

Vega, Karrieann Soto. "Colonial Causes and Consequences: Climate Change and Climate Chaos in Puerto Rico" *Enculturation: A Journal of Rhetoric, Writing, and Culture*, vol. 32, 2020, https://parlormultimedia.com/enculturation/colonial_causes_consequences.

Walker, Kenneth. *Climate Politics on the Border: Environmental Justice Rhetorics*. U of Alabama P, 2022.

Weisser, Christian R., and Sidney I. Dobrin, editors. *Ecocomposition: Theoretical and Pedagogical Approaches*. State U of New York P, 2001.

Wells, Justine. "The Energy of Whiteness." 20th Biennial Conference of the Rhetoric Society of America, 27 May 2022, Baltimore. Conference Presentation.

Woods, Derek. "Scale in Ecological Science Writing." *Routledge Handbook of Ecocriticism and Environmental Communication*, edited by Scott Slovic, et al. 1st ed., Routledge, 2019, pp. 118–28.

I

COUNTER-ECOLOGIES

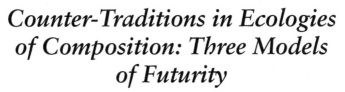

CHAPTER TWO

Counter-Traditions in Ecologies of Composition: Three Models of Futurity

BYRON HAWK

In Nathan Stormer and Bridie McGreavy's "Thinking Ecologically about Rhetoric's Ontology: Capacity, Vulnerability, and Resilience," they do an excellent job of developing a model for rhetorical ecologies as an orientation to patterns and relationships in the world, showing how the model shifts emphases from agency to capacity, violence to vulnerability, and recalcitrance to resilience as key theoretical orientations of rhetorical ecologies. In doing so, they offer Jenny Edbauer's "Unframing Models of Public Distribution: From Rhetorical Situation to Rhetorical Ecologies" (2005) as a beginning point for this work in communication studies. But this more disciplinary starting point skips over a much longer tradition in rhetoric and composition that lays the grounds for Edbauer's work. There is a longer counter-tradition in the field that begins with Richard Coe's "Eco-Logic for the Composition Classroom" (1975) as one of the first pieces in rhetoric and composition to articulate a need for thinking ecologically in composition. In "The Ecology of Writing" (1986), Marilyn Cooper jumps off from Coe's work to offer a more detailed attempt to see composition's object of study through the processes of ecology. While Cooper's piece is most widely recognized as a beginning point in rhetoric and composition, even more so than Edbauer's, two other works from the 1980s, Karen Burke LeFevre's *Invention as a Social Act* (1987) and Louise Wetherbee Phelps's *Composition as a Human Science* (1988), have gotten less uptake but provided other important detailed accounts. In many ways, their calls to see composition ecologically were overshadowed by the social turn as the field's dominant paradigm during the 1980s and 1990s. It took nearly a decade for various takes on the social turn to play out through the disciplinary debates before ecology could reach a more central position of exploration in Peg Syverson's *The Wealth of Reality: An Ecology of Composition* (1999).

In other words, the concept of ecology, initially, occurred outside of what LeFevre calls clusters of resonance, where peaks of economic, social, and political conditions overlap historically to make the development, circulation, and uptake of ideas and practices intensify and take hold. Each cycle has four stages (formative, developed, fluorescent, and degenerated) and rotates through these stages at different speeds. Innovation occurs when the developed and fluorescent stages of all three cycles coincide—economic, social, and political. Eventually, these forces start to align in composition, and the concept of ecology slowly intensifies and garners increased attention and elaboration in the 2000s. By the end of the 1990s and Syverson's book, the field is primed for an intensification of work that further develops this counter-tradition and moves it to the forefront of rhetoric and composition. This resurgence of the concept of ecology begins with Syverson's *The Wealth of Reality* and expands to create a cluster of resonance for Edbauer's article: Kristie Fleckenstein's *Embodied Literacies* (2003) turns Bateson's ecology of mind toward an ecology of embodied meaning, image, and word; Clay Spinuzzi's *Tracing Genres through Organizations* (2003) turns genre theory and activity theory into an analysis of genre ecologies; Cynthia Haynes's "Writing Offshore" (2003) deploys an ecological metaphor of a ship at sea to rethink composition as a contingent practice in relation to the movement and force of waves; and Jenny Edbauer's "Unframing Models of Public Distribution" (2005) turns rhetorical situation toward Deleuzian rhetorical ecologies.

All of this background work develops new ways of seeing composition from an ecological view that emphasizes relationality, circulation, and co-emergence as key aspects of rhetorical practice, which allows Edbauer to map out this circulation in a given case. Following this counter-tradition, Edbauer argues that rhetorical ecologies are spaces where affective and embodied experiences circulate and operate as an emergent system—like the weather, they can be predictable in some ways but unpredictable in others because they are in a continual process of change, and every encounter with other variables changes the conditions of possibility of the system throughout the life of a text's circulation. Her case study, the "Keep Austin Weird" campaign, started as a bumper sticker to support local businesses then migrated to T-shirts of other businesses; transformed over the course of a number of years to pledging campaigns for public radio, various tote bags, mugs, and billboards; and then it began to shift to other causes—becoming a central focus of a white paper on city politics; functioning in support of UT liberals arts; and, by the end of its circulatory life, ironically ending up as an advertising slogan for Cingular Wireless. Following Deleuze and Guattari's conceptual metaphor of a virus migrating between baboons and cats and evolving in an aparallel manner, she argues that what is carried through the rhetorical life of "Keep Austin Weird" is not the same text "but certain contagions and energy" (14). Edbauer brings to light multiple ecological encounters that co-produce and transform the text and its shifting materiality, the difficulties any author would have producing consistent effects and, by implication, the complexities researchers need to address in order to trace these transformations and produce an account.

What Edbauer's model makes most clear, however, is that ecologies are temporal, which necessitates an orientation toward the future. Counter-traditions, in other words, necessarily include counter-futures. What actants do in a relational space of encounter in the present is also a function of the space of encounter between the present and the future. This chapter examines three potential models of futurity by reading Louise Wetherbee Phelps's take on ecology in relation to Jacques Attali's structural take on futurity; Aristotle's circulatory notion of periodicity in relation to Afrofuturism's approach to futurity; and finally Paul Lynch's take on the apocalyptic turn in rhetoric and composition in relation to Benjamin's philosophy of history and messianic futures. I argue that these are three ways futurity might operate in rhetorical ecologies—emerge from the margins as in Attali's structural model, emerge from a disturbance or intervention as in Eshun's resonant model, or emerge from the future-anterior as in Benjamin's messianic model. The future in these approaches is not a problem to be solved but an orientation to be enacted. The three models provide orientations toward potential futures within the context of ecological models of composition. Any of them may be enacted in any combination to co-produce versions of the future.

Looking to Past Margins

For much of its early history, ecological approaches to composition functioned as a counter-tradition in composition and rhetoric—a conversation that ran counter to dominant models and theories of composing processes. While Cooper became a touchstone for ecology, LeFevre and especially Phelps are rarely cited in this regard and remain pushed to the margins. But Phelps's take on ecology and composition shows how counter-traditions are a necessary part of the process and become the source of novelty and innovation in an ecological system. Phelps uses the concept of ecology to organize both her conceptual understanding of composition as a discipline and her phenomenological understanding of composition as a practice. Her first two chapters, collectively titled "Constructing an Ecology of Composition," are based in the concept of a field—a clearing or open ground—that is "a self-organizing system, a kind of system that is dynamically capable, through its openness to the environment, of innovation and unpredictable evolution" (x). Resonance appears as a key factor in this process of innovation: the resonances between writer and field as they develop symbiotically; the resonances among composition and other fields; and the resonances between writer and the larger cultural and material world. The problem of inventing a discipline is necessarily tied up within these ecological resonances. Phelps writes:

> An ecological perspective treats entities like disciplines as systems within larger systems. An ecology is constituted through interdependence and transactions among all levels of the system both horizontally (the relations of parts within the whole at a

given level of organization) and vertically (the relations among elements at different levels). (3)

Developing an ecology of composition as a discipline, then, requires bringing forth the field as a system through its relations to other fields horizontally and larger cultural movements vertically. So, rather than shy away from composition's tendency to draw on multiple theories and methodologies, Phelps's method is to draw widely on work in the humanities and social sciences, from cognitive science, linguistics, education, and psychology to literary theory, philosophy, hermeneutics, and rhetoric in the context of the emerging cultural moment of the late '80s in order to develop the theoretical grounds for the advancement of composition as a distinct field.

Of course, this (inter)disciplinary ecology of composition only comes into being through composition as an ecology of practice that generates novelty through these open relations. Theories and practices must be held in constant relation and tension; their interplay, or mutual relation and difference, constitutes a field as a self-organizing system. "Such a system is a dynamic process rather than an equilibrium structure," Phelps writes. "[I]t maintains its integrity through continual self-transformation and possesses the capacity for novelty" (4). The task of an ecology of composition as a discipline, therefore, is to co-produce this continual transformation through resonant ecologies of practice. All local practices are events that participate in these systemic movements: they are temporal, they are configured through fields within fields, their elements are context dependent, their novelty is inexhaustible, and their meanings and interpretations are always open to new encounters or co-productions. Ecologically speaking, it is the constant entanglement of these variables through practice that produces domains, niches, purposes, and variations. In an ecological paradigm, "all parts are not only interdependent but mutually defining and transactive, so that through their shifting relationships they continually constitute new parts or elements as well as new structures" (32). For Phelps, these transactions are embedded in all horizontal relationships and at all vertical levels, making change resonate, reverberate, circulate, and disseminate through the entire system. At its core, an ecology is these resonances that both connect and co-produce. Her concluding definition of ecology is unequivocal: "This is the full measure of an ecology: a total interrelatedness and reciprocity of change for all parts at all levels. Within such a system emergent novelty, unpredictable new orderliness, becomes possible" (33). Such a system is multidimensional, where effects have multiple causes and causes have multiple effects. Disciplinary knowledge in this system is always partial and constantly changing, producing both unities and excesses, centers and margins, paradigms and novelties.

This connection between larger disciplinary ecologies and continual practices situates human individuals as multidimensional systems inseparable from social and environmental systems. Like LeFevre, Phelps draws on Gregory Bateson, who argues that human messages, learning, and minds are all functions of larger systems. Bateson writes:

> [I]n the communicational works, this dichotomy [between inside and outside] is irrelevant and meaningless. The contexts have communicational reality only insofar as they are effective as messages, *i.e.,* insofar as they are represented or reflected . . . in *multiple* parts of the communicational system we are studying; and this system is not the physical individual but a wide network of pathways of messages. Some of these pathways *happen* to be located outside the physical individual, others inside; but the characteristics of the *system* are in no way dependent upon any boundary lines which we may superimpose upon the communicational map. (qtd. Phelps 34)

As Phelps puts it: "Indeed the individual as such is an open system constantly evolving through the exchange of energies with the world, though *interactions* (the interdependence of relatively distinct entities and processes) and *transactions* (their interpenetration and inseparability)" (34; emphasis added). Interactions and transactions are not a binary opposition or mutually exclusive but co-constitutional. In a position reminiscent of Cooper's, Phelps argues that composition as a discipline and a practice is "prereflectively" already attuned to this ecological model because this is the larger disciplinary context and cultural ground in which it operates. In short, the constant entanglement and co-production of this ecology and its practices produce counter-traditions at a discipline's margins that can become acknowledged innovations in the future.

As Jacques Attali argues, noise at the margins of a historical or social system often pre-figures its future modes of organization, and looking to those counter-traditions can allow scholars to project those futures. Attali looks to the emergence of activity at the margins of a social system and turns it toward broader historical movements and the transformative potential of music, where marginalized noise becomes a creative force of change. Music is "the organization of noise" (4): it literally puts pitch and rhythm to noises and sounds. Noise is a mutation in the social, and music's enaction in the social (re)organizes this marginal social activity to establish new relations of thought, signs, and people. Attali argues, for example, that innovative eighteenth-century classical music carries with it a desire for harmony and order that emerges in nineteenth-century political thought and leads to forms of twentieth-century political and economic organization. Such ideas or values are organized, amplified, and sustained via musical practices, which can affect future organizational transformations. Turning this historical insight to his present, Attali sees the music industry as repressing noise and difference through mass-produced commodities. Black blues and jazz music at the margins gets turned into a reductive commodity for white audiences, but the demand for these marginalized musics by the youth culture also creates a desire to resurrect them beyond their commodity forms. Just as Mozart and Bach dream of harmony before nineteenth century political theory and twentieth century political organization, Joplin and Dylan, for Attali, dream of liberation from music as a norming commodity, organizing and amplifying this counter-value (31).

While Attali's model of stages outlines a structural sequence— ritual, order, silence, composition—his model culminates in a new practice of composition that more explicitly or actively draws on marginal noise to disrupt order and usher in a new system. For Attali, the popular music of the '60s shifts toward gift exchange rather than commodity and reconnects to an emphasis on change, if not revolution. He connects this kind of practice to composition, which is a kind of ecological practice that generates and cultivates novelty. Musicians in the late '60s and early '70s are looking for a new way of making music to create their own relations with the world, invent a new language, play for their own pleasure with no telos, no code. Composition as a process, not an end, becomes a free act that fuses production and reception and structures noise at the margins against normalcy and stasis (134–35). Composition in Attali's sense lies beyond repetition of the same and aims toward freedom, a musical practice that heralds arrival of new social relations, an interplay of concepts and organization that heralds new political strategy: "noise destroys order to structure a new order." 1960s popular music, however, still gets commodified, but the emergence of digital recording technology and distribution in the 2000s taps into its early ethos and extends it into a new gift-exchange model that both disrupts the music industry and leads to new forms of social organization.

Phelps can be seen as such a musical or compositional figure, drawing from the margins of multiple fields to articulate and amplify the concept of ecology, bringing forth composition as a discipline through its relations to other fields horizontally and larger cultural movements vertically. Cooper and LeFevre were read in the field but primarily in terms of the social, which elided their emerging emphasis on ecological models as a part of the marginal cultural context of the late '80s that Phelps also inhabited. But while Cooper became a touchstone for ecological approaches, LeFevre continues to be read in terms of the social, and Phelps largely remains relegated to the margins, partly because her book didn't fit neatly into the paradigm of the social turn and partly because it is detailed, complex, and continues to be difficult to pin down to a blurb that can easily circulate.[1] Ultimately, it took over a decade for various takes on the social turn to play out through the disciplinary debates before ecology could reach a more central position of exploration in Peg Syverson's *The Wealth of Reality: An Ecology of Composition* (1999). By the time composition and rhetoric reaches the 2000s, the clusters of resonance begin to coalesce and open a space for a more intensive engagement with the concept of ecology in the discipline that took off from Edbauer's "Unframing Models of Distribution"; my own *A Counter-History of Composition* (2007), which links ecology to a history of vitalism and complexity; Collin Brooke's *Lingua Fracta* (2009), which turns the rhetorical canons toward media ecologies; and Sid Dobrin's *Postcomposition* (2011), which turns his prior work with ecocomposition toward complexity. In the 2010s, as new materialism built on these works in ecology, resonant intensification set the stage for the circulation and spread of ecology in rhetoric more broadly and the emergence of works such as Stormer and McGreavy's.

But scholars can also take up this strategy historiographically by looking to other past margins of our own field. Rhetoric scholars are now in a position to go back to *Composition as a Human Science,* for example, and draw even more out of her work than scholars at the time were able to see. As early as 1998, Michael Bernard-Donals recognizes that as challenging and daunting as Phelps's work is, "there are good reasons to pay close attention to Phelps's project"; her aim is to critically examine "the ways language and social practice function in the material world" (*The Practice of Theory* 131). In addition to ecology, in other words, there is also a burgeoning new materialism in her work, another future residing noisily at the margins of her book. If scholars in the field see composition as a function of horizontal and vertical ecologies entangled through practice, then ecology's operations as an open system can serve as a basis for continuing the invention of future counter-traditions like those that Phelps foreshadows. What futures for new materialism might we find in Phelps's work? The implication, of course, is that scholars don't have to simply wait for all of the cycles of resonance to align. As Attali suggests, scholars can more explicitly look to the historical margins and write the future histories of the discipline now in their formative stages, co-producing the conditions for their future emergence. Futures are always in the process of forming at the margins and can be picked up, sustained, and amplified to resonate through the ecology and resound into the future.

Intervening in the Present

Aristotle's take on the period is not exactly a counter-tradition but doesn't get talked about as one of his primary rhetorical strategies. It is well known but often forgotten, marginalized in almost the opposite way as Phelps's take on ecology. But a closer look at the concept of the period shows that it is more than a grammatical footnote and opens a way onto contemporary takes on rhythm and futurity. The most traditional definition of "period" in the OED, which comes from *peri* - around and *hodos* - way or course, is from the Greek and into the Latin for going around, way around, revolution, cycle of years, recurrence, or course, traditionally referring to phenomena such as the orbits of heavenly bodies or the course of a disease. The OED breaks its discourse into four more specific senses: a course of chronological time; the completion or end of a course; in grammar, rhetoric, and music; and belonging to a style or culture. It is the third— grammar, rhetoric, and music—that points to a specific connection to rhythm, which is largely implicit in the other three. A sample sentence from 1837 reads: "He was the first . . . who replaced the rude structure of periods by some degree of rhythm" (559). This potential connection between periods and rhythm goes back, at least, to Aristotle's *Rhetoric*. Chapter 8 of Book 3 is Rhythm in Prose and is followed by Book 3 Ch. 9 Periodic Style. In his opening gloss on Ch. 9 in *Rhetoric*, Kennedy notes that it is a point of debate over whether or not Aristotle assumes this connection to rhythm. On the one hand, Aristotle says that the period has magnitude, is limited, has number, and is connected to verse, much of which shows up in Ch. 8 with regard to rhythm. On the other hand, he does not speak specifically of rhythm in the chapter on periods and instead focuses largely on structure.

Kennedy points to scholars who take up each of these positions but leaves the question open and focuses primarily on Ch. 9 and a structural approach to the period (*Rhetoric* 239). The period for Aristotle is not the contemporary sentence but combinations of clauses or phrases with a specific dual structure. In "Aristotle on the Period," Kennedy defines a period as composed of two colons or *kola*, which is even closer to a grouping of words than the clause or phrase of today. There are essentially two kinds—divided and antithetical. The divided need not be a complete sentence, as in "those gathering together the public festivals and instituting the gymnastic games" (Kennedy 284). The antithetical similarly brings together two *kola* but that are opposites in some way, such as, "You spoke of him in life meanly and now you write of him meanly" (*Rhetoric* 243). So, the period is a twofold statement that is divided into parts, complete in some logical sense, and is easily said in one breath, all of which increases clarity and is much more memorable for listening audiences. This definition of the period, for Kennedy, is much more specific than the usages that came after Aristotle, but it aligns well with the antithetical style of Antiphone and Gorgias in the fourth century, and it connects well with the general notion of antistrophe as "that which has been turned over, around, or back . . . a statement which goes one way and comes back again in a twofold motion" (Kennedy 283). The back and forth or cyclical motion invokes rhythmic movement but also relationality, which is at the heart of most approaches to ecology in rhetoric and composition.

While Kennedy's discussion of the period primarily emphasizes its structure and limits itself to Aristotle's Ch. 9, Thomas Fleming, in "The Origin of the Period," argues in favor of reading Aristotle's chapter on periods in the light of his previous chapter on rhythm. For Fleming, the term period was used in both rhetoric and metrics, and these uses "have enough in common to suggest a common origin" (95). Thrasymachus is often credited with the invention of the periodic sentence, though Fleming argues it was in use earlier, but Thrasymachus's best-known contribution to rhetoric is his use of *paeonic* rhythm that draws on the affective power of rhythm in music (96)—the *paeonic* is one of the three types of rhythm that Aristotle takes up in Ch. 8 based on differing combinations of long and short syllables. Fleming shows how it makes more sense to read Aristotle as connecting rhythm to period rather than limiting it to structure through Aristotle's discussion of balanced antithetical structure and an analogy to the type of *circuitus* race course implied by the term period (98). Rather than imagine a racecourse that is linear with a single beginning and end, Fleming argues that Aristotle implies a back-and-forth race called the *diaulos*, which has a turning-post that runners cycle around in laps. Rather than keeping the end goal of the overall discourse in view, the period's smaller structure keeps a more immediate sensible connection in the forefront, which helps bring audiences along by having a shorter-term goal as they listen. Aristotle's emphasis on the dual nature of antithesis in periods and the rhythmic balance among a period's clauses or phrases suggests this reading. This back-and-forth rhythmical movement to the discourse, for Fleming, seems to largely be the point of the analogy and makes it reasonable to think that Aristotle assumes this connection between the two chapters is an enthymeme that his audience will supply.

Current work on rhythm can provide further insight into this rhythmic nature of the period and point toward its relation to futurity. In *The Rhythmic Event*, Eleni Ikoniadou notes that the Greek term *rythmos* means "order of movement, [or] any regular, recurring movement or measured motion of time" (10). But it was also associated with "to flow" in the Heraclitean sense of the "uninterrupted flux of matter" (11). For her, then, rhythm means both unpunctuated flow and punctuated regularity or sustained movement as well as disruptions of that movement. This dual nature comes through in a musical sense of rhythm as well, which sees rhythm as the relationship been the length of one note, the length of another note, and the pause or break between them. This connection between rhythm and period as both a course and its ending is there in Aristotle, who defined rhythm in relation to the lengths and combinations of syllables in groupings of words. Ikoniadou, however, turns Aristotle's linear relationship between movement and structure into a recurrent one. For Aristotle, she argues, the punctuated nature of rhythm leads to an essentialist notion of structure—one that could be read into the relationship between Aristotle's Ch. 8 on rhythm and Ch. 9 on the period where rhythm produces a definitive form of the period. Aristotle's approach organizes time into a stable, humanly sensible form, which developed into the modern notion of time as measured and subordinated to space and privileges form overflow (11–12). But Ikoniadou is interested in what rhythm can do when this essentialism is resisted. Following Serres, she sees the uninterrupted flow of rhythm as primary rather than universal structure, which makes the punctuated, periodic nature of rhythm a local event that cuts into the movements of matter and redirects it, cyclically folding back into co-producing that flow. Rhythmic movement transforms matter rather than universalizes it. This conception allows her to theorize sensation "from a nonanthropocentric standpoint" (24). Rhythmic movement conditions bodily experience at a tacit level rather than determines recognizable forms that frame conscious experience; rhythm "becomes the very building material of the event as it self-generates independently of human action and perception" (87).

This more Deleuzian conception of rhythm is what Kodwo Eshun calls the "futurhythmachine," which sees music as something that can break into present ecological materiality. In *More Brilliant than the Sun*, Eshun seeks a music criticism that performs versions of these sonic disruptions and rhythmic breaks, one that is commensurate with the Afrofuturist musics he writes about in the book. In his chapter titled "Mutantextures of Jazz," for example, Eshun reviews key works from 1968–1975, an era that he notes turned jazz into an "Afrodelic Space Program." For each album he reviews, he writes in short rhythmic bursts though aphoristic vignettes of one or two paragraphs broken up by headings and strung with metaphors. In one of his vignettes on George Russell's '68 album *Electronic Sonata for Souls Loved by Nature*, Eshun writes, "jazz must move through the cyclone, implode and be reassembled as electronic dub" (01/002). This reassembly operates through "the simultaneous future-past time of the mix": "At 3 mins, Rypdal's guitar crashes in < > is sucked into the maw of ring modulation." Eshun substitutes arrows that point to the past and future < > for a period. I imagine this brief play with punctuation is an attempt to connect the cycle of the period with the simultaneous past-future of Afrofuturism. This alternate use of punctuation continues throughout the chapter and is inter-spliced with attempts to find language that accounts for and enacts rhythm. Rhythm is characterized as "gravity" that pulls players, listeners, and sound into a song's "tonal center" (01/003); these "cyclical rhythms are in sync but out of phase"; amplified instruments "transmolecularize" sounds into a "continental drift." Futuristic electronically manipulated sounds from Hendrix's fuzz to Moog tape-delayed dub "destratify" and "dissolve" the sounds of the instruments into noise in such a way that "effects defect from cause" (01/006–007). Rhythm ultimately becomes, for Eshun, a "biotechnology" that coproduces the "parahuman"—"natural evolution [as] a computational process of adaptation to an ever changing environment" (01/007–008).[2] By the end of the chapter, Eshun concludes that this era of "Atlantic Futurism is always building Futurhythmachines, sensory technologies, instruments which renovate perception, which synthesize new states of mind"; molecular components of rhythm are mobilized "across the communication landscape" and "cross pollinates the eager fan," ultimately "transmaterializing their sensorium" (01/012). Rhythm, for Eshun, produces a temporal disturbance that creates competing futures in the present of embodied listeners.

Eshun's later article "Further Considerations on Afrofuturism" explains and defends what his early book performs. In it, he argues that since Western, imperial Enlightenment has written African American subjectivity out of history and excluded it, the primary historical and cultural response has been to recover it to demonstrate its presence and contributions. These assembled counter-memories, however, ultimately situate the collective trauma of slavery as the founding moment, which leaves displaced Africans less empowered by being tied to a determining and reductive past. Afrofuturism does not seek to deny counter-memory but to extend it through a reorientation toward potential futures. For Eshun, it is never simply about forgetting this trauma but turning all of the efforts at recovery toward new futures, "towards the not-yet, towards becoming" (289). Eshun is primarily interested in the crossover of two vernacular expressions of these counter-futures: science fiction and music. Sun Ra's self-created cosmology based on the past-future confluence of Egyptology and science fiction, for example, leapfrogs the colonialist and Christian eras to break into their deterministic hold on new potential futures. Similarly, Eshun argues that sound technology disrupts the ability to assign pre-determined racial identities to sounds and voices. Synthesizers and vocoders create sounds that don't fit stereotypes associated with voice and genre and evoke a future when these boundaries are blurred, nonexistent, or remade. For him, this "human-machine interface became both the condition and the subject of Afrofuturism" (296). In each case, science fiction and sound coordinate with each other to enact a "distortion of the present" that puts a mutation into circulation, intervenes in current situations, disrupts linear time, and (re)conditions potential futures rather than determining them (297).

Extending this connection through to Ikoniadou's and Eshun's contemporary discourses on rhythm and music suggests the potential for an expanded sense of the period as regular rhythmic endings that condition (re)beginnings. The rhythmic nature of even the grammatical period breaks into larger flows of discourse and entrains readers, bringing them into its new flow, event, and world. The period opens up the potential for the new and, along with the disruptive potential Eshun is after, can break into deep histories and complex ecologies in ways that are not just conceptually structural but also materially embodied. For Eshun, periodic intervention would be something that is a function of each instance or enaction. Perhaps there is also a connection between Aristotle's initial sense of the period as the turning post in the race that keeps a more immediate sensible connection in the forefront rather than the long-term point, goal, or end of the race, and the more immediate sonic aims of Afrofuturist sound artists that intervenes in the present and leaves more extended futures open. Rhythmic breaks—breaks in but also breaks from—are central to circulation and ecology. They are ways to inhabit and enact this futurity that are ultimately a non-anthropocentric and non-teleological progressivism. Eshun is nonessentially committed to black identity, whatever that might be in the future. In other words, being committed to an open system where intervention into the present sends rhythmic resounding into the future.

Projecting the Future-Anterior

In "Composition's New Thing: Bruno Latour and the Apocalyptic Turn," Paul Lynch identifies an emerging counter-tradition in composition and rhetoric that he calls the "apocalyptic turn," which is concerned with the ways potential economic, social, or environmental collapse has started impacting our "disciplinary and pedagogical imagination" (458). By tracing a number of authors in the field, he shows how their disparate and marginalized takes on the contemporary moment are coalescing and should begin to occupy a more prominent place in our research and teaching, ultimately forcing us to reexamine what composition is and whether or how it can speak to these ecological exigencies.

Blitz and Hulbert, for example, note that the polluted planet, unequal global economy, racism and sexism, and media meant to dull its consumers are ills that pedagogy should begin to face, arguing that our pedagogies should address these problems but may not be up to the task. Owens, concerned with environmental collapse, proposes a "pedagogy of sustainability" but wonders if it is "already too late" (461). Spellmeyer argues that the litany of mostly human-made disasters at hand overwhelms our linguistic and conceptual resources. And Worsham wonders whether the personal narrative and critical approaches typical of composition and rhetoric will be enough to respond to these challenges. For Lynch, critique of these various problems that could lead to collapse or apocalypse doesn't go far enough toward addressing the concerns. Many versions of critique or even critical thinking are grounded in revelation, or the unmasking of the problem, rather than moving forward toward responses to them, especially when problems are vast and interconnected. Ironically, he points out, revelation is imbedded in the notion of apocalypse, but the apocalyptic turn, which Lynch is the first to identify and name as an emerging counter-tradition, moves beyond this critical logic and instead "urge[s] composition to face the apocalypse itself" (459).

Rather than close, critical analysis to outline, if not create, technical problems, Lynch turns to Latour's notion of composition as a way to orient the field toward the many problems that are readily available. Latour uses the concept of composition to develop a post-critical approach to such complex ecological concerns, and Lynch takes it up as a way to compose responses to the coming collapses. Composition, as we know for Latour, is about composing with others, putting things together in all of their heterogeneity, cultivating new entities that are large enough and complex enough to address and respond to coming catastrophes. For Lynch, "if we assume a dire future as a given, we risk reducing issues to facts. Latour's composition would have us avoid this division by doing the opposite" (467). Rather than assume the future is given or predestined, composition acknowledges our roles in building alliances across differences and divisions in ways that open up potential futures and give them the capacity to speak and be heard in the present. Latour's approach is irreductionist—it doesn't exclude anyone or anything from co-participating in composition, even critique. Rather it aims to not stop at assuming exposure of the problem is all that can be done. Being critical is looking at various ways to compose a collective response to a matter of concern. Plastic pollution, as a problem, is becoming clearer and clearer. Much scientific research and public-facing journalism is exposing the depth and breadth of the problem. Composition would continue to connect this work to various stakeholders—consumers, government agencies, scientists and chemists, and corporations—to various practices—cleaning up, recycling, and reducing plastic production—and to various systems—infrastructures, regulations, finances, and chemical processes—all as a part of a collective, multifaceted response needed to take on such a multifaceted problem. Continually recomposing these compositions is the task that always lies ahead.

Latour's "Compositionist Manifesto" ultimately concerns itself with these future prospects and how compositionists might orient toward them, situating himself in response to Walter Benjamin. In his section titled "No Future but Many Prospects," Latour addresses the Modern notion progress and the "direction of the flow of time" (485). He agrees with Benjamin's take on the angel of history, which looks back rather than ahead, as a figure for Modern approaches to history. But for Latour, Benjamin sees the angel as witnessing past catastrophes and ignoring the future, whereas he sees the angel as co-producing if not creating the destruction as he looks back. Latour writes, "The ecological crisis is nothing but the sudden *turning* around of someone who had actually *never before* looked into the future, so busy was He extricating Himself from a horrible past" (485–86). Moderns looked back to critique and dismantle the past tradition, whether it was religious, social, or philosophical, and set about the production of new knowledge based on the objectivity of nature but ignored the effects of their actions and innovations. And when they finally did turn to look forward, it was with a utopian notion of progress. For Latour, Moderns had a utopian future but never a real chance to achieve it. Instead, he calls for us to "*break for good* with our future, turn our back, finally, to our past, and explore our new prospects . . ." (486). When we orient toward the future, it will not be a beautiful, harmonious, well-composed cosmos: it will be messy, unclear, difficult, and complicated. Composition, then, would require realistic looks at future prospects in order to have a chance at composing them. It would require innovations but would deploy them with caution and an eye toward their potential effects. And it would require patience to slowly compose a collective world that everyone and everything shares. Compositionists don't yet know fully how to fulfill these potentials but have to start looking toward a livable and breathable home for the masses.

But Latour doesn't leave us with much more to go on, even though some prospects for how to do so might be found in Benjamin. Latour never mentions, in other words, the role of the messianic in Benjamin's analysis. In "On the Concept of History," Benjamin contrasts his notions of history and time with both traditional history and historical materialism. Traditional history values the victors and writes the progression of their linearly unfolding victories, which creates an eternal, universal image of the past. Its historiography is not theoretical, just an additive procedure that gathers up data to fill empty time with a causal chain of moments. In this universal history, the present is empty, just a vessel for the progressive movement of victors, which is ultimately the history of fascism. Historical materialism writes against this traditional history of the victors and documents its barbarism—fascism is always tainted by the toil of others. Consequently, historical materialism always "calls into question every victory, past and present, of the rulers," defaulting to critique and looking for the next revolution (390). Its sense of time isn't empty but is filled with conflicts that arrest thought. Its notion of the present is always in transition, in which "time takes a stand and comes to a standstill"; "thinking comes suddenly to a stop in a constellation saturated with tensions" (396). It is a unique experience of the past from this specific present. But for historical materialists, there is a continual danger of being a tool of the ruling class, and they must always be on guard and fight against it. Historical materialism places faith in politicians to fight fascism only to see those politicians become fascists because they still subscribe to progressive history—if they defeat fascism in any instance, then they are the victors, and the politicians betray the people and are complicit with progressive history.

Traditional history and historical materialism, then, are both anticipatable; the past is marshaled as evidence for a claim or progressive narrative that anoints a victor, a foreseeable outcome in the present and the future.

Benjamin builds his sense of messianic time out of historical materialism but seeks to leave its sense of progressive history behind. For Benjamin, progressive history piles up past wreckage to push victors to the forefront and into the future. Therefore, he seeks a history that turns away from the past and from progress. Messianic time, like historical materialism, fills time with action and sees it as an event. Historical materialism is filled with the present, reads the past from the present, and leaps into the past for fragments to tell a history of and from the present; it is a dialectical leap Marx called revolution. But messianic time doesn't see history as a causal chain of moments or a clash of class struggle. Messianic time is shot through with the future. A messianic future is not empty or homogenous, either, but it sees every moment as a small gathering through which the messiah *might* come. Traditionally, the messiah is not only the redeemer but also the ultimate victor over the anti-Christ. Even though the enemy, whether the anti-Christ or the ruling class, is potentially victorious in any present clash, the messiah *will* eventually come. This position made it possible to wait passively for the emergence of a revolutionary situation. But in messianic time, every moment carries with it its revolutionary chance, opportunity, or potential—a chance for "a completely new resolution to a completely new problem" (Benjamin, Paralipomena 402). Political action becomes messianic when classless society is not a final goal of progress but is frequently miscarried and interrupted or is constantly in transition. Messianic time prepares for the messiah whether he comes or not. It is open in anticipation for what is to come, is prepared to accept whatever comes, and is ready to intervene again in the present.

The crucial difference between historical materialism and messianic time is a particular understanding of the present in relation to this futurity. Before we have learned to deal with things in a given present moment, "it has changed several times"; therefore, the present is always fractured and "we always find out too late what is happening" (Turgot, qtd. in Benjamin,

Paralipomena 405). Since we can never fully understand the present from past causes or present conditions, politics has to *foresee the present*. The angel of history turns back from the present to look at the past, but the messianic makes the present visible by looking to the future to understand the present, not simply as a now that is perpetually moving but as some future point. We enact history in the present through an orientation toward the future anterior. The future anterior is an event that will be completed prior to some future time but hasn't been completed yet. Since we can't see the present in the present—because the present is fractured, never fully present, and is always changing—we can only see a present retroactively from its future, projecting into the far future to look back at a more recent future to see what will have been, looking forward to turn and look back at another futural point. Historical evidence is emergent and is not marshaled in the service of a preexisting narrative or claim as in traditional or progressive history. It is a revolutionary gesture without revolution as pure violence or dominating power that results in a victor. It is a dialectical image that leads to a flash of insight but doesn't lead to a necessary outcome.

Lynch connects Latour to Burke's casuistic stretching—extending and remaking old principles to address new conditions and concerns, a kind of continual composing and linking together through ongoing experimentation with an eye toward a (post) apocalyptic future. What Latour's, and our, foray in Benjamin provides is a different way to imagine and make possible those futures—look forward to a future time and turn to look back to a more recent future point to see what has transpired and imagine how and why, imagine future conditions where an event has come to pass to then look back and see how it could have come about. What modes of composition will have happened? How did those things and worlds coalesce into that composition? "What will have been" is ultimately a historiographic approach to the future as a past that hasn't happened yet. That is how to figure out prospects for how things would get or be better. We imagine the potential future consequences and evaluate present conditions on whether they will have been well or badly composed from that future anterior orientation. In short, the apocalyptic turn can't be addressed by a linear or progressive sense of temporality. A messianic sense of temporality disrupts this but not through a purely open sense of futurity either. The future anterior anticipates potential futures but understands that they may never come. This orientation toward the future is what we need to address and respond to the coming crises, one that intervenes in the present toward an uncertain future that we've nevertheless partially anticipated. It is open but open in anticipation of what has been projected to come through the future anterior.

These three approaches to futurity, emerging from three different ways to think about ecology, form three different counter-traditions—the marginal, the periodic, and the futural—and offer a heuristic starting place for thinking about temporality in ecologies of composition:

- ◆ "Looking to Past Margins" is about identifying and structuring past marginal noise that already exists to create new futures;

- ◆ "Intervening in the Present" is about breaking into present order to create marginal noise as a basis for possible futures; and

- ◆ "Projecting the Future-Anterior" is about looking forward to potential orders and then looking back to a more recent future to create noises that could lead to those orders.

Futurity is not a problem to be solved; it is an orientation to be enacted. The three models provide orientations toward the future within the context of ecological models of composition. Any of them may be enacted to co-produce versions of the future. Compositionists should look realistically at the prospects in order to have a chance at composing them. They can't flee the future like Moderns did, so we have to confront it in stark or at least pragmatic terms and compose it with the full meaning of the term—"compromise, care, to move slowly, with caution and precaution" (487).

Notes

1. See John Schilb's critique of Phelps from a Marxist social perspective ("Cultural Studies"; Lisa Ede's take on Phelps that her "analysis remains at a fairly high level of abstraction" [*Situating Composition* 123]; and

Michael Bernard-Donals note that Phelps was reviewed with responses from "hostility" to "utter incomprehension" [*The Practice of Theory* 131]).

2. See my *Resounding the Rhetorical* for more on the parahuman as parasitic on material ecologies and the energy that drives them (14, 53, 64, 119, 129–30, 142, 257n6–7).

Works Cited

Aristotle. *On Rhetoric: A Theory of Civic Discourse*. Translated by George Kennedy, Oxford UP, 1991.

Attali, Jacques. *Noise: The Political Economy of Music*. Translated by Brian Massumi, U of Minnesota P, 1985.

Beiner, Ronald. "Walter Benjamin's Philosophy of History." *Political Theory*, vol. 12, no. 3, 1984, pp. 423–34.

Benjamin, Walter. "On the Concept of History." *Walter Benjamin: Selected Writings, Volume 4, 1938–1940*. Translated by Edmund Jephcott, edited by Howard Eiland and Michael W. Jennings, Belknap Press of Harvard UP, 2003, pp. 389–400.

———. Paralipomena to 'On the Concept of History.'" *Walter Benjamin: Selected Writings, Volume 4, 1938–1940*. Translated by Edmund Jephcott, edited by Howard Eiland and Michael W. Jennings, Belknap Press of Harvard UP, 2003, pp. 401–11.

Bernard-Donals, Michael. *The Practice of Theory: Rhetoric, Knowledge, and Pedagogy in the Academy*. Cambridge UP, 1998.

Brooke, Collin. *Lingua Fracta: Towards a Rhetoric of New Media*. Hampton Press, 2009.

Coe, Richard. "Eco-Logic for the Composition Classroom." *College Composition & Communication*, vol. 26, no. 3, 1975, pp. 232–37.

Cooper, Marilyn. "The Ecology of Writing." *College English*, vol. 48, no. 4, 1986, pp. 364–75.

Dobrin, Sidney. *Postcomposition*. Southern Illinois UP, 2011.

Edbauer, Jenny. "Unframing Models of Public Distribution: From Rhetorical Situation to Rhetorical Ecologies." *Rhetoric Society Quarterly*, vol. 35, no. 4, 2005, pp. 5–24.

Ede, Lisa. *Situating Composition: Composition Studies and the Politics of Location.* Southern Illinois UP, 2004.

Eshun, Kodwo. "Further Considerations on Afrofuturism." *CR: The New Centennial Review*, vol. 3, no. 2, 2003, pp. 287–302.

———. *More Brilliant than the Sun: Adventures in Sonic Fiction.* Quartet Books, 1998.

Fleckenstein, Kristie. *Embodied Literacies: Imageword and a Poetics of Teaching.* Southern Illinois UP, 2003.

Fleming, Thomas. "The Origin of the Period." *Quaderni Urbinati di Cultura Classica*, vol. 82, no. 1, 2006, pp. 95–102.

Hawk, Byron. *A Counter-History of Composition: Toward Methodologies of Complexity.* U of Pittsburgh P, 2007.

———. *Resounding the Rhetorical: Composition as a Quasi-Object.* U of Pittsburgh P, 2018.

Haynes, Cynthia. "Writing Offshore: The Disappearing Coastline of Composition Theory." *JAC*, vol. 23, no. 4, 2003, pp. 667–724.

Ikoniadou, Eleni. *The Rhythmic Event: Art, Media, and the Sonic.* The MIT Press, 2014.

Kennedy, George. "Aristotle on the Period." *Harvard Studies in Classical Philology*, vol. 63, 1958, pp. 283–88.

Latour, Bruno. "An Attempt at a 'Compositionist Manifesto'." *New Literary History*, vol. 41, no. 3, 2010, pp. 471–90.

LeFevre, Karen Burke. *Invention as a Social Act.* Southern Illinois UP, 1987.

Lynch, Paul. "Composition's New Thing: Bruno Latour and the Apocalyptic Turn." *College English*, vol. 74, no. 5, 2012, pp. 458–76.

Novak, David. "Noise." *Keywords in Sound*, edited by David Novak and Matt Sakakeeny, Duke UP, 2015, pp. 125–38.

"Period." *The Oxford English Dictionary*, 2nd ed., Oxford University Press, 1991, pp. 558–60.

Phelps, Louise Wetherbee. *Composition as a Human Science: Contributions to the Self-Understanding of a Discipline.* Oxford UP, 1988.

Schilb, John. "Cultural Studies, Postmodernism, and Composition." *Contending with Words: Composition and Rhetoric in a Postmodern Age*, edited by Patricia Harkin and John Schilb, Modern Language Association, 1991, pp. 173–88.

Spinuzzi, Clay. *Tracing Genres through Organizations: A Sociocultural Approach to Information Design*. The MIT Press, 2003.

Stormer, Nathan, and Bridie McGreavy. "Thinking Ecologically about Rhetoric's Ontology: Capacity, Vulnerability, and Resilience." *Philosophy & Rhetoric*, vol. 50, no. 1, 2017, pp. 1–25.

Syverson, Margaret. *The Wealth of Reality: An Ecology of Composition*. Southern Illinois UP, 1999.

CHAPTER THREE

Acknowledging Some Challenges of Thinking Ecologically about Rhetoric

CHRIS INGRAHAM AND MATTHEW HALM

What challenges beset ecological thinking about rhetoric? Consider the following.

This chapter was written from the traditional and ancestral homelands of the Shoshone, Paiute, Goshute, and Ute Tribes. It was also written from lands taken from the Muscogee (Creek) and Cherokee people. As a remote collaboration between Salt Lake City and Atlanta, we relied upon several telephone calls that required an infrastructure of wireless cellular towers crossing the country (often on other Indigenous lands) while emitting electromagnetic radiation that may disrupt the reproductive wellbeing of local flora and the migration patterns of nearby fauna (Karipidis et al.). By sharing documents online, we also utilized undersea internet cables whose installation disturbed aquatic ecosystems, as well as cloud storage servers that require enormous energy to cool (Starosielski). Our mobile devices and laptops meanwhile contained tantalum mined on aboriginal lands in Australia and cobalt mined in the Congo, likely by child laborers, among other rare earth minerals such as praseodymium, dysprosium, and neodymium, probably extracted from Mongolia and India. Occasionally, we took notes with No. 2 hex pencils. These were made with logged Chinese basswood trees and graphite from quarried gneiss rock. The paper we wrote on, like the paper you might be reading from now, probably came from the pulp of conifers in the pacific Northwest of America and Canada.

Land acknowledgments are important ways of recognizing the violence and oppression that are otherwise elided in the maintenance of a status quo. But why stop there? In the oft-romanticized maxim of ecological thought—that all things exist in relation to one another—it makes some sense also to acknowledge that a chapter like this could not have been produced without a whole assortment of interdependent relations that made it possible. Those relations are not only numerous; they also stretch back into the past (via ancestral lands taken from Indigenous people, for instance, or the ages-old carbon desequestrated from earth to cool the cloud servers), and they reach far into the future (via the lifelong lung disease of those exposed to cobalt mining, say, or the irreparable damage being done to the planet itself). Beyond a gesture, there is an important ethic in acknowledging what has been or will eventually be lost in order to make possible something else—even something like a book chapter. And yet (leaving aside the occasionally false moral exhibitionism of such acknowledgments), trying to identify all the salient relations that helped produce the words you're reading would be a fool's errand. Any "rhetorical ecology" is simply too vast to account for in its entirety.

So, what to do?

It might seem, at least in terms of this chapter's "content," that citations and bibliographies exist to do some of this important acknowledgment work. And well enough they do. But how to account for all those unplaceable yet lingering things we've read or all the indirect influence of our teachers, students, and colleagues? What about personal experience? Then there's the due dates. Word counts. A sore back. A sick child. A hot room. A broken pencil. Such influences must certainly have found their way into our thinking bodies, at least obliquely, and perhaps even been put into language, perhaps now into print. It's not just that all the relations making up an ecology around this chapter and this book are too numerous to name or too dispersed across time and space to capture, though they are. It's also that the relations are not all the same. Why or how they matter, and for whom, just differs and depends.

What if "rhetoric" is a name to describe the material-discursive energy that makes some relations matter and others seem less consequential?

To begin with, it would be worth noting that all relations, like the ecologies that comprise them, are both material *and* discursive—never just one or the other. *Discursivity* in that sense would simply name the mechanism of something's capacity to have relevance to another. The qualitative effect of that relevance would then be a *relation*. And we'd also want to note that the constitutive form of all discourse is its *materiality*, from the sound waves of a voice vibrating an eardrum to the shards of graphite that a pencil leaves on paper. It would be worth saying, too, that the rhetorical energy behind these material-discursive relations often results in persuasion, though sometimes in violence, sometimes loss, survival, joy, or many other things besides. Rhetoric in this sense would neither be creative nor destructive, composition nor decomposition, though it might do all these things and more. In this chapter, the array of dynamic factors that influence what rhetoric does—and to what effect—are what we mean when we talk about "ecological rhetoric."

Our aim here is accordingly to identify and explore some of the challenges implicit in understanding rhetoric as ecological in nature. Scholars studying rhetoric in English, Writing, and Communication departments alike have, for some decades now, been noticing that rhetoric's force functions in ecological ways. We won't endeavor a history of this turn here or even a tidy lit review thereof, though we are compelled by the argument of Justine Wells and her collaborators that ability for humans to exert "geological force" on the planet means that an "ecological orientation . . . is needed for our profoundly ecological times" (8; also see Ingraham 2023). With this in mind, we hope to sketch out some of the ways that contemplating an ecological ontology of rhetoric requires that those of us studying rhetoric adapt to a radical and, we argue, necessary shift in what one takes rhetoric to be and do. Because this shift in thinking is so extreme, however, the challenges of accepting and operationalizing it to critical and productive ends are hard to meet. Our modest goal is therefore to describe a few of these challenges by identifying their potential and their perils, with our emphasis landing squarely on the benefits of embracing the former.

Acknowledgment where acknowledgment's due: this project owes a particular debt to Stormer and McGreavy's important

2017 article, "Thinking Ecologically about Rhetoric's Ontology," which set out to do something similar. Their work sought to show that "rhetoric teems with ecologically inclined thoughts" which, if followed, demand revisions of three concepts that have long been taken for granted as "commonplaces of theory" in rhetorical studies (3). Specifically, instead of treating agency, violence, and recalcitrance as among such rhetorical commonplaces, they offered that an ecological approach invites us to emphasize capacity, vulnerability, and resilience in their place. This work has been influential in our own thinking about the stakes implicit in accepting rhetoric's ontology as ecological. And these stakes are high. As we explore in what follows, the stakes of accepting rhetoric's ecological basis include revising at least three more major commonplaces in ways of understanding rhetoric: first, its anthropocentrism; second, its relationality; and third, its circulation. After sections devoted to each of these, we conclude briefly by reflecting upon some of what's lost if, by clinging to hoary notions of "good men speaking well," we neglect to embrace rhetorical ecologies more wholeheartedly.

Anthro-Decentrizing Rhetoric

Human storytelling, especially in dominant Western traditions, has long relied upon recurrent archetypes to explain the course of humankind on earth. The Hero, the Warrior, the Savior, the Genius. Across fictions, histories, religions, and various nationalisms, these and other familiar character types recur. They are alike in speaking to a human (alas, all too human) conceit: namely, a deeply ingrained supposition that it is individual human actors—specific people with names and lifespans that eventually fit astride a dash—whose actions change the course of history. Granting that there are many alternative traditions, whole cosmologies even, that refuse this story of great individualism in favor of more collective ways to understand how change occurs through an entanglement of human and more-than-human actors alike, the archetypes should at least be familiar enough. These archetypes are central to the dominant understanding of rhetoric dating to antiquity, and they are, above all else, what thinking ecologically about rhetoric challenges us to abandon.

One of the quickest ways to exemplify how entrenched human agency and individualism have been to rhetorical studies since its outset is through Quintilian's well-known *vir bonus*, the notion of rhetoric being encapsulated by "the good man speaking well" (Quintilian Book XII, 1.1). It has long been fashionable, among those of us who bother with such things, to look at least slightly askance at such a notion. A certain "anti-Quintilianism," stemming from the *vir bonus*, dates at least to the Italian Renaissance (Monfasani) but also extends to Victorian-era critiques (Lares) and forward through more recently raised eyes at Quintilian rhetoric's extreme masculinity (Gunderson; L'Hoir; Vaught) and intrinsic moralizing (Brinton; Winterbottom), among other concerns. But the most illustrative way to demonstrate the incompatibility of the *vir bonus* idea with ecological understandings of rhetoric is simply to consider the classic rhetorical act: an individual speaker addressing a bound audience, whether a good man does it or not.

In such a "situation," the audience is positioned as passive receivers, bound to the declamations of the speaker, whose supposedly ensorcelling speech is—as Gorgias put it centuries before Quintilian—"a powerful lord" ("Encomium of Helen"). Today, the notion of a "powerful lord" doesn't play well against centuries of slavery, conquest, colonialism, and other forms of subjecting unwilling others to domination, through persuasive speech or otherwise. There is very well a *relation* being enacted between speaker and audience in this prototypical scenario, but it is not all that reciprocal. In other words, the speaker is the one presumed to have the meaningful agency, not the audience. We shouldn't need to reiterate how quaint and limiting this model now sounds—even if it's merely a caricature—particularly in a digital age of such information overload and communicative freedoms that, conceivably, at any given moment, we are all rhetor *and* audience, simultaneously, in different directions.

But even if the "good man" or "powerful lord" version of rhetoric were to fall completely into disregard, including all the archetypes of individualisms that follow it, that would still leave an enormous, irreconcilable gap between ecological approaches to rhetoric and its precedents. The reason is that a truly ecological rhetoric refuses to accept the human, let alone individual human actors, as the origin or basis for the rhetorical. This isn't to say that ecological thinking doesn't acknowledge that, yes, individual people can be persuasive rhetors or exert influence on what matters to others. Humans aren't out of the picture in rhetorical ecologies; we're just no longer in the center. Indeed, such is the essence of the challenge ecological thinking proposes: What would it take to anthro-decentrize our understanding of rhetoric?

To approach an answer, it may help first to know that, notwithstanding ecological concepts having had ample time to be squirreled away across a broad tradition of study that is 2,500 years old, explicit attention to rhetorical ecologies developed only recently, more or less in-step with an ongoing "ecological turn" across the humanities at large. This is important because the shift in thinking was in some ways galvanized by a growing awareness that our planet's natural environments are imperiled—and that this imperilment has inordinately been caused by humans. The recent forms that the ecological turn in rhetoric has taken, as in other fields, can accordingly be seen as a reactive measure to the disproportionate influence of humans on the geological, biological, and climatic features of our shared planet. In this sense, the ecological turn is both a *retreat from* the myth of heroic humanism and, having caught a whiff that actual end times could be nigh, a desperate *movement toward* more environmentally conscientious figures of thought.

One of the major challenges that follows may perhaps now be coming into view. How can it be that, in one breath, we're given to understand that human actions are causing extinction-level harm to the planet on a geological scale while, in the next, we're led to reject the powerful lordship of humanity and accede that we're just one part of a broader planetary ecology? From this standpoint, it can sometimes seem as if the "ecological turn" is, paradoxically, a way of entrenching confidence in humanity's absolute dominion, including our ability to solve any problem we ourselves created; and, at the same time, a clever workaround to let us off the hook by distributing blame more "ecologically" all around. Whatever the case, the shift to thinking ecologically about rhetoric is—and should be recognized as—far more than a topical call for rhetoricians to study "environmental issues."

An ecological line of thinking about rhetoric does not ask that everyone wave the flag of environmentalism (though that's always welcome), but it does ask that many of the most longstanding and taken-for-granted precepts about rhetoric be exchanged for a wholly different ontological basis.

The anthropocentric default of rhetoric, with its strong bias toward the human tendency for symbolic action, is not easy to shake. To begin with, the only beings that ponder or discuss rhetoric are people. And even if we weren't alone in that interest, we would still be up against the limitations of our human bodies as our only perceptual interface for empirically encountering others. What if birds or deer are also rhetorical actors, as George Kennedy proposed in 1992? Many others have since agreed that "creaturely rhetorics" are real (Davis), and have even been part of rhetorical thought since antiquity (Hawhee). And what about the "sylvan rhetorics" of trees (Jones), the rhetorical movement of tumbleweed (Gries), the material and social rhetorics of beer (Pflugfelder; Rice), or the heliotropism of plants at large (Muckelbauer)? An anthro-decentric rhetoric, unfortunately, can't be achieved through a tidy plug-and-pop switch in emphasis—from human animals to nonhuman ones, or even from humans to plants or rocks. It also isn't enough to shift in scale, say, from studying "FDR's rhetoric" to "presidential rhetoric" in general, nor even to shift in agency from "FDR's rhetoric" to "the rhetoric of FDR's wheelchair." The move isn't an either/or; it's a both/and. Rhetoric needs to be understood not as *either* the work of an individual human *or* the work of something else but always *both* the work of an individual human *and* the work of something else. What's being asked by the ecological wager, in other words, is that rhetoricians rethink the relationship of rhetoric to relationality itself.

Relationshipping Rhetoric

Thinking about relations, and good relations in particular, is part of what land acknowledgments ask people to do. Statements like the one with which we began this chapter seek to recognize that nothing is without a history of accomplices. Whatever possibilities or new relations might be unfolding now are themselves made possible by many lingering others that typically go unnoticed or forgotten. Often, though, even the work of acknowledgment falls back upon the default of an implied or sometimes explicitly named actor held responsible for given acts—good ones and bad. Traditionally, these actors are taken to exert their *agency*, whereby *rhetorical agency*—like the kind involved in writing a book chapter—has been regarded as "the act of effecting change through discourse" (Herndl and Licona 134). Because it goes without saying, it must be said that the agent or agents effecting such change are almost invariably assumed to be humans. Ecological thinking about rhetoric challenges us to think otherwise.

Just as the taking of ancestral homelands was actuated by smallpox on blankets, by lead balls in muskets, and by no shortage of guile and cunning, so too does what we've composed in this chapter exceed our limited human role as the bounded agents presumed to have made it possible. No doubt, it was we, acting as Author Chris and Author Matt, who conceived of the chapter's content and composed it into a readable form. When we used a pencil, our hands conducted its course. When we used a laptop, our fingers pressed the keys, as sure as it was other specific people who once loaded their muskets with ammunition or laced their blankets with disease. This chapter simply would not exist without our human and controlling touch. But that's obvious. That's uninteresting. Thinking ecologically about rhetoric doesn't mean denying human agency or refusing to concede a human's often-commanding role in rhetorical invention. But an ecological commitment to "both/and" figures of thought does call for acknowledging that, while something like this chapter wouldn't be possible without certain of our decisive authorial actions, neither would it be possible without the wood that made the pencil, without the tantalum inside the laptop, and so on. And that's *not* obvious. That's interesting. It's also a huge impediment to a more widely adapted practice of studying rhetoric ecologically.

What makes mobilizing "both/and" figures of thought for rhetoric so challenging, in other words, is not just the tacit threat to anthropocentrism that such thinking poses. The challenge is that, even if one grants that rhetoric relies on an array of other-than-human relations to achieve its force-effects, it creates a slippery slope. How can we possibly know where to cut off the innumerable relations and phenomena without which no rhetorical force could exist? In the effort to understand or critique rhetoric's force in the world, that is, how does one constrain the many accomplices of rhetoric to only the most salient and decisive? Where does an "agential cut" get made? The bald answer, however hopelessly unsatisfying, is that in practice, it just depends. But the stakes exceed mere rhetoric. As Karen Barad has shown in their research on how theoretical physics is studied among scientists, agential cuts are implicated in no less than how we understand the universe itself.

Barad's work could well be the flag that ecologically inclined rhetoricians wave to rally their kind. In their notion of a universe composed of "intra-action" (as opposed to "interaction"), independent entities cannot be assumed *a priori* because they come to be what they are, they come to matter, through the ways they come into relation:

> It is through specific agential intra-actions that the boundaries and properties of the components of phenomena become determinate and that particular concepts (that is, particular material articulations of the world) become meaningful. (*Meeting* 139)

This would imply a radical shift in how the longstanding study of rhetoric has typically done its business. Conventional approaches to rhetoric more or less reduce rhetoric to a formula with variables that include some combination of Rhetor + Audience + Text, perhaps with Context as a denominator. In this caricatured understanding, rhetoric is an *interaction* between variables regarded as independent and already formed prior to the rhetorical act. The Speaker is so-and-so, their Text says such-and-such to an Audience invested in this-and-that. Applying Barad's notion of intra-action to rhetoric, however, would mean we cannot know the variables until they come into relation with one another. The relation itself is what makes a speaker this speaker, a text this text, an audience this audience. Indeed, the emergent relation may be such that these aren't even the appropriate variables in play. The salient variables might rather be the pencil, the tantalum, the blankets, the gunpowder.

For Barad, "all matter makes itself felt" through a "host of material-discursive forces—including ones that get labeled 'social,' 'cultural,' 'psychic,' 'economic,' 'natural,' 'physical,' 'biological,' 'geopolitical,' and 'geological'" ("How Things" 810). Or, we could add, "rhetorical." As Jennifer Charteris and her collaborators have noted, Barad emphasizes that agential cuts are produced in the assemblage of these forces, not independent of their relationality (Charteris et al. 911). Barad, that is, understands agential cuts as "boundary-drawing practices" that aren't created by "willful individuals" (Barad, *Meeting* 140) but rather through the wider "material arrangements of which we are a part" (178). To understand rhetoric ecologically is to see it as an analogous boundary-drawing practice: both material and discursive, both human and not, but always generating its force through its embedded relations.

Perhaps it's time for an example. We've discussed how, even in a simple land acknowledgment, bearing witness to the many material-discursive accomplices that have made something possible in the present can soon spiral out indefinitely. The long trail of relations coalescing to bring about any new encounters are just too manifold. But that tells us little about the differential force of these relations or the ways, to paraphrase Barad, *different relations yield different relata*. So, consider a different example. Consider the moment, in 1881, when Friedrich Nietzsche first began writing on a typewriter. By then, he had been writing effectively with a pen for years, in a fluid, protracted style that accommodated nuanced and developed thoughts. But, almost immediately, with the typewriter his writing became more aphoristic. More punchy, more jolted. Literally, we could say, the typewriter wrote differently than his pen. This, too, is a matter of the "intra-action" whereby different relations don't just yield different results—as in a formula—but where the relata themselves become constituted by their different relationality.

For Nietzsche, that is, what happened was that when the material form for mediating his thought and written language changed—from pen to typewriter—this enacted an entirely new *relationship* between his thought and writing. In other words, the ball typewriter he used revealed itself as intrinsically complicit in *thinking* his writing, not just in executing it. As Nietzsche himself put it, "Our writing tools are also working on our thoughts" (quoted in Kittler 200). And, of course, that suggests that, why not, mustn't the pen and page have earlier been complicit in his philosophizing, too? And if them, then what else? His desk perhaps? His mustache? You can see how it's easy to approach a *reductio ad absurdum* with this line of thought. Not wanting to do so is one reason ecological approaches to rhetoric can stall before they even begin. When it comes to thinking ecologically about rhetoric, then, we might say that rhetoric seems to operate *both* as a process of making agential cuts *and* as an expression of the agential cuts that occur irrespective of willful human intention.

Though the example of Nietzsche's typewriter is conventionally "rhetorical" in that it concerns written invention (persuasive language, a good man writing well, etc.), and though Nietzsche was evidently the willful individual punching the letters on the keytops, the typewriter example shows that the manifestations of rhetoric's force are not just a product of human will but of a whole assemblage of material-discursive relations that actualize that force in perceivable force-effects. The bounding of that assemblage through agential cuts that enables it be comprehensible as an instance of things-in-meaningful-relation is both part of what rhetoric *does* and part of what rhetoric *is*. Rhetoric both bounds and acts as a boundary. Both/and. Insofar as agential cuts mark ontic-semantic boundaries—"self" and "other," say, or "inside" and "outside"—they provide what Barad calls "a contingent resolution of the ontological inseparability within the phenomenon" (*Meeting* 348). Truly ecological thinking about rhetoric will necessarily be committed to such ontological inseparability. Relata cannot be separated from the relationships that actualize them. It's not, "Nietzsche thought . . ." or even "Typewriter thought . . ." but "Nietzsche-Typewriter thought . . ."

Decomposing Rhetoric

Thus far, we've been arguing that ecological approaches to rhetoric offer radically new opportunities to revise time-tested tenets of rhetoric that have tended to focus on the actions of individual rhetors and the means of persuasion available for them to influence an audience in any given situation. But this traditional approach has not just been destabilized by the introduction of ecological thought. Since Lloyd Bitzer first theorized "rhetorical situations" in 1968, several adjustments have been made to his emphasis on "those contexts in which speakers or writers create rhetorical discourse" (1). Many readers here may know this story, but it merits a quick recap. In 1973, Richard Vatz offered a formulation opposite to Bitzer's yet equally as tenable. Instead of "rhetorical discourse [coming] into existence as a response to a situation" (Bitzer 5), Vatz describes rhetoric as "a creation of salience," producing the situation rather than responding to it (158). In face of this living *dissoi logoi*, with one argument and its counterargument being directly opposed on nearly every claim, Barbara Biesecker suggested in 1989 that there wasn't much reason to see either side coming out on top. Instead, she argues, a deconstructive approach is more appropriate: "the 'rhetorical dimension' names both the means by which an idea or argument is expressed and the initial formative intervention that, in centering a differential situation, makes possible the production of meaning" (112). Both/and. Since then, the floodgates have opened.

Biesecker's deconstruction of the rhetorical situation has, in any case, been followed by more recent moves toward depictions of rhetorical "ecologies." Marking a distinct contrast from the comparatively static and bounded character of rhetorical situations, such moves tend to acknowledge the interconnectedness of entities that may have once been presumed to be discrete. Rather than study individual components of a rhetorical situation, an ecological frame suggests that everything that was previously considered stable is actually in flux, circulating and varying in intensity. As Jenny Edbauer puts it in the article that likely did more than any other to popularize the use of ecological terminology in the study of rhetoric, an ecological approach sees rhetoric as both "a process of distributed emergence and as an ongoing circulation process" (13). Again, witness the both/and in action. An ontology of rhetoric premised upon the circulation of entities in complex systems is especially important yet difficult to take on because by nature such circulation recurrently actuates new compositions and interactions, rhetoric and writing included, though these new compositions can neither be located in a single part of the ecology nor equated with its totality. We want to suggest that—alongside rhetoric's anthropocentrism and relationality—this process of *circulation* is one of the other major challenges that ecological thought poses to rhetorical studies.

Laurie Gries has called circulation an "emergent threshold concept," arguing that the "complex and plural" nature of the concept has transformative potential for rhetorical studies ("Introduction" 5). While circulation, as Gries points out, has informed the study of rhetoric since its origins, its naming as a discrete concept of inquiry is a relatively recent development. In many ways, that impulse to name circulation as a locus for rhetorical studies is a product of the same ecological tendencies discussed in this chapter. Because of its emphasis on movement within a discourse community, circulation lends itself to ecological perspectives on rhetoric, but it also encounters similar challenges. In particular, the entity "doing" the circulating is displaced by a more-than-human ecological approach to rhetoric. Rather than see circulation as an autonomous entity moving (or causing something to move) within an ecology, a more-than-human perspective suggests that circulation is movement of the ecology itself (the aggregate motion of innumerable constituent entities and the relationships tying them together), carrying entities with it over its shifting terrain. If circulation is signal- or feedback-transmission across ties in a network, it is the flux of the contours of the network itself that is circulation.

To produce a pencil, for example, matter must move. Raw materials must be harvested, extracted, synthesized, and combined into new compositions. Concepts must also move, themselves owing their existence to material processes. The idea for the production of pencils, as well as the cultural practices of which they are a part, must be created from constituent parts of the greater planetary ecology. Many of these actions do not presuppose the existence of "pencilicity" in advance. The production of the pencil's material-conceptual form is a consequence of the intra-active circulation of matter and energy within ecologies. Circulating material draws on existing compositions that must be broken down. All of the matter and energy involved in the production of rhetorical effects has to come from somewhere—it has to be disassembled and decomposed before it can be recomposed as something new.[1]

The reciprocal connection between circulation and decomposition is a critical outcome of ecological thought in rhetoric. Not only does all circulation require that an environment yield components of itself for the production of new compositions, but all compositions eventually decompose, extending lines of circulation that re-enter the environment long after any human-centric "rhetorical effect" might have been said to occur. The act of using a pencil is another form of circulation. Put very simply, pencils are tools for rearranging graphite. Taken together with the processes involved in their manufacture, pencils take graphite from one part of the planet and distribute it to many others. When this distribution results in recognizable symbols used for communication, it is generally called writing. Even in this basic sense, where certain arrangements of graphite hold conceptual significance, the conceptual and the material are intertwined, if they are distinguishable at all. The material of the world is/are concepts, shifting (circulating) through various permutations, some of which are more easily recognizable within human frameworks than others.[2]

The vast majority of an entity's circulation will take place *after* it has had whatever effect it might have been intended for—this circulation is what an ecologically and ethically minded rhetoric should prepare for. Ecologies do not produce permanent compositions. Nothing lasts forever, but true ecologies know this in advance. The products of ecologies always break down—decompose—to produce raw materials for the next cycles of production. Everything in the ecology is the medium for the next iteration of the ecology.

In his article "Politics of Edibility," Joshua Trey Barnett focuses on a project to devise a method of decomposing one's own body after death with a fungus grown specifically for the task. The goal of this project is to come up with a more environmentally aware burial process, but its implications extend toward a broader understanding of one's place in the world that resituates the human's place in an ecology and inverts what we might mean by circulation within that ecology. The project allows Barnett to reevaluate the "eater/eaten" dichotomy, which he demonstrates is a politically motivated distinction. Unpacking the ethics of eating leads Barnett to describe decomposition as "radically social" (229). To decompose

> is also to be lost, to be distributed, to be digested, to be transformed into something else. And, then again, it also suggests that one is a part of something larger, part of an ecological life-world, part of a web of relations in which the human is neither wholly sovereign nor capable of maintaining a sense of wholeness in life or death. (229)

Barnett clarifies that such an integration does not suggest a "dissolution of agency" but instead highlights the importance of agency as a process of decision making within an ecology. His "ethics of edibility" is an ethics of decomposition. What we are today (bodily, culturally, materially, and so on) will decompose and form part of the future. The choice to act on that knowledge invokes planetary ethics.

Land acknowledgments are an attempt to foreground this sort of ethical dimension. They do not declare ownership or lineage, but recover the threads of decomposed circulation still present in the world. The history they draw attention to remains part of the world (how could it not?) and has material effects on the world's continual ecological circulation. In part, they are a corrective, but circulation is always corrective, always in flux and never finished. Decomposition exposes that transience; everything works by breaking down.

Rhetorical Ecosophy

By way of conclusion, we want to return to the environmental exigence that, in many ways, has been spurring more interest in ecological rhetoric. The "geological force" that Wells, et al. argue humans exert in the Anthropocene is an extreme description of actions that have consequences enabled by an always preexisting relationality. An ecological understanding of writing and rhetoric suggests by extension that the planet itself has always existed in a "profoundly ecological" way. An ecological orientation is thus not a new requirement of inhabiting the planet, though it is one that has been given insufficient attention. In this chapter, we have accordingly suggested that some key points on which to focus more attention might include rhetoric's longstanding anthropocentrism, its relationality, and its circulation. These, however, are far from a comprehensive list of those fundamentals that ecological thinking about rhetoric demands—indeed, such thinking might reject the idea of fundamentals in the first place. To even approach a more comprehensive set of factors pertinent to the rhetoricity of our earthly coexistence, the scale of focus needs to expand to even broader registers. We close, then, with some broader reflections about these registers and the stakes of thinking ecologically in these most "ecological" of times.

In 1989, Félix Guattari—known for his work with Gilles Deleuze but prolific in his own right beyond those collaborations—published a concise but powerful argument about the threefold nature of ecology. Though it wasn't translated into English until 2000, the ideas were as pertinent then as they are now. For Guattari, the question of "living on this planet" is only approachable from a multiplicity of "registers," represented by the eponymous *Three Ecologies* discussed in his book: the environment, social relations, and human subjectivity (19–20). Each of these registers cannot be considered apart from their relation to the others (and the choice of "three" ecologies is merely an ontological conceit; he concedes that there are multitudes of ecologies, some yet to be). Still, these three provide a sturdy basis for Guattari's whole "ecosophy"—a philosophy he defines as developed from attention to the three major ecologies whose "disparate domains constantly engage one another" (Genosko 84). In this sense, a Guattarian ecological reconciliation accounts not only for the "natural" wildness of global ecosystems but also for the social, technical, and mental spaces constructed through embodied inhabitation of the planet.

If we wish to take seriously rhetoric's ecological nature, we will need to acknowledge that it doesn't just manifest through rhetoric's anthropocentrism, relationality, and circulation. As we've tried to show, that's a tough ask already. But it gets harder still, because rhetoric also both creates and operates within the three larger ecologies that Guattari identifies. These ecologies are not interchangeable or indistinguishable, but they are intertwined and enmeshed. Ecologies like rhetoric or writing—as Guattari's ecosophy emphasizes—are fundamentally connected to the ecologies of plants, animals, tantalum, smallpox, subjectivity, and so much more, such that a truly planetary ecology must take all of these and more into consideration. If the distinction between human and nonhuman action on the planet matters for environmental conservation, it is not because of some ontological or typological hierarchy. No, it is precisely because human actions are so intricately interwoven with nonhuman actions that they can have profound effects on the latter. And if our human actions are destroying the very planet that makes such actions possible in a process of mutual constitution, then it is urgent to attend to those actions that impede more mutual flourishing.

For anyone studying writing or rhetoric, this means that the writing subject or the rhetor cannot be separated from the larger composition they form through writing or rhetoric (which are each natural and energetic components of the world). The very capacity for subject formation is a function of the ecology formed by writing, rhetoric, the planet, and everything else. Attending to the ecological, then, means treating each of these things as parts of the others: both composing and decomposing worlds that better suit their immanent mutuality. A critical feature of ecologies is that the "end" of any of their constituent parts is the "beginning" of another. Of course, if one end is another beginning, when all of the entities in question are wrapped up in each other the very concept of ends and beginnings decomposes. We're left to live in the unfolding present, with both one and the other.

Notes

1. The "trophic" character of rhetoric is another way to approach this set of problems, particularly regarding the nested interdependency of rhetoric's many de/compositions. See Gottschalk 2019; Keeling & Prairie 2018.

2. For more on the material and planetary nature of rhetorical circulation, see Halm 2023.

Works Cited

Barad, Karen. "Posthumanist Performativity: Toward an Understanding of How Matter Comes to Matter." *Signs: Journal of Women in Culture and Society,* vol. 28, no. 3, 2003, pp. 801–31.

———. *Meeting the Universe Halfway: Quantum Physics and the Entanglement of Matter and Meaning.* Duke UP, 2007.

Barnett, Joshua Trey. "Politics of Edibility: Reconceptualizing Ecological Relationality." *Environmental Communication,* vol. 12, no. 2, 2018, pp. 218–31.

Biesecker, Barbara A. "Rethinking the Rhetorical Situation from within the Thematic of *Différance.*" *Philosophy & Rhetoric,* vol. 22, no. 2, 1989, pp. 110–30.

Bitzer, Lloyd. "The Rhetorical Situation." *Philosophy & Rhetoric,* vol. 1, no. 1, 1968, pp. 1–14.

Brinton, Alan. "Quintilian, Plato, and the 'Vir Bonus.'" *Philosophy & Rhetoric,* vol. 16, no. 3, 1983, pp. 167–84.

Charteris, Jennifer, et al. "Posthumanist Ethical Practice: Agential Cuts in the Pedagogic Assemblage." *International Journal of Qualitative Studies in Education,* vol. 32, no. 7, 2019, pp. 909–28.

Davis, Diane. "Creaturely Rhetorics." *Philosophy & Rhetoric,* vol. 44, no. 1, 2011, pp. 88–94.

Druschke, Caroline Gottschalk. "A Trophic Future for Rhetorical Ecologies." Enculturation: A Journal of Rhetoric, Writing, and Culture, 20 Feb. 2019, https://enculturation.net/a-trophic-future.

Edbauer, Jenny. "Unframing Models of Public Distribution: From Rhetorical Situation to Rhetorical Ecologies." *Rhetoric Society Quarterly,* vol. 35, no. 4, 2005, pp. 5–-24.

Genosko, Gary. *Félix Guattari: A Critical Introduction.* Pluto Press, 2009.

Gorgias. "Encomium of Helen." *On Rhetoric: A Theory of Civic Discourse,* by Aristotle. Translated by George Kennedy, Oxford UP, 2007, pp. 251–56.

Gries, Laurie E. "Introduction: Circulation as an Emergent Threshold Concept." *Circulation, Writing, and Rhetoric,* edited by Laurie E. Gries and Collin Gifford Brooke, Utah State UP, 2018, pp. 3–24.

———. *Still Life with Rhetoric: A New Materialist Approach for Visual Rhetorics*. Utah State UP, 2015.

Guattari, Félix. *The Three Ecologies*. Translated by Ian Pindar and Paul Sutton, Continuum, 2008.

Gunderson, Erik. *Staging Masculinity: The Rhetoric of Performance in the Roman World*. U of Michigan P, 2000.

Halm, Matthew. "Molten Circulation and Rhetoric's Materiality." *Enculturation*, 9 Aug. 2023, https://enculturation.net/molten_circulation.

Hawhee, Debra. *Rhetoric in Tooth and Claw: Animals, Language, Sensation*. U of Chicago P, 2017.

Herndl, Carl G., and Adela C. Licona. "Shifting Agency: Agency, *Kairos*, and the Possibilities of Social Action." *Communicative Practices in Workplaces and the Professions*, edited by Mark Zachry and Charlotte Thralls, Baywood Publishing, 2007, pp. 133–53.

Ingraham, Chris. "Ecological Rhetoric." *Oxford Encyclopedia of Communication*, 19 July 2023, https://doi.org/10.1093/acrefore/9780190228613.013.1388.

Jones, Madison. "Sylvan Rhetorics: Roots and Branches of More-than-Human Publics." *Rhetoric Review*, vol. 38, no. 1, 2019, pp. 63–78.

Karipidis, Ken, et al. "What Evidence Exists on the Impact of Anthropogenic Radiofrequency Electromagnetic Fields on Animals and Plants in the Environment? A Systematic Map Protocol." *Environmental Evidence*, vol. 10, no. 39, 2021, pp. 1–9.

Keeling, Diane M., and Jennifer C. Prairie. "Trophic and Tropic Dynamics: An Ecological Perspective of Tropes." *Tracing Rhetoric and Material Life: Ecological Approaches*, edited by Bridie McGreavy, et al., Palgrave Macmillan, 2018, pp. 39–58.

Kennedy, George. "A Hoot in the Dark: The Evolution of General Rhetoric." *Philosophy & Rhetoric*, vol. 25, no. 1, 1992, pp. 1–21.

Kittler, Friedrich. *Gramophone, Film, Typewriter*. Translated by Geoffrey Winthrop-Young and Michael Wutz, Stanford UP, 1999.

Lares, Jameela. "Arguments in Quintilian against Rhetoric: John Milton and 'Regenerative Reason.'" *Quintiliano: Historia y Actualidad de la Rétorica*, Volume 3, edited by Tomás Albaladejo, et al., Instituto de Estudios Riojanos, 1998, pp. 1373–380.

Monfasani, John. "Episodes of Anti-Quintilianism in the Italian Renaissance: Quarrels on the Orator as a *Vir Bonus* and Rhetoric as the *Scientia Bene Dicendi.*" *Rhetorica: A Journal of the History of Rhetoric*, vol. 10, no. 2, 1992, pp. 119–38.

Muckelbauer, John. "Implicit Paradigms of Rhetoric: Aristotelian, Cultural, and Heliotropic." *Rhetoric, through Everyday Things*, edited by Scot Barnett and Casey Boyle, U of Alabama P, 2016, pp. 30–41.

Pflugfelder, Ehren Helmut. "Rhetoric's New Materialism: From Micro-Rhetoric to Microbrew." *Rhetoric Society Quarterly*, vol. 45, no. 5, 2015, pp. 441–61.

Quintilian. *The Orator's Education* [*Institutio Oratoria*]. Translated by Donald A. Russell, Harvard UP, 2001. 5 vols.

Rice, Jeff. *Craft Obsession: The Social Rhetorics of Beer*. Southern Illinois UP, 2016.

Starosielski, Nicole. *The Undersea Network*. Duke UP, 2015.

Stormer, Nathan, and Bridie McGreavy. "Thinking Ecologically about Rhetoric's Ontology: Capacity, Vulnerability, and Resilience." *Philosophy & Rhetoric*, vol. 50, no. 1, 2017, pp. 1–25.

Vatz, Richard. "The Myth of the Rhetorical Situation." *Philosophy & Rhetoric*, vol. 6, no. 3, 1973, pp. 154–61.

Vaught, Jennifer C. *Masculinity and Emotion in Early Modern English Literature*. Ashgate, 2008.

Wells, Justine, et al. "Introduction: Rhetoric's Ecologies." *Tracing Rhetoric and Material Life: Ecological Approaches*, edited by Bridie McGreavy, et al., Palgrave Macmillan, 2018, pp. 1–36.

Winterbottom, Michael. "Quintilian and the *Vir Bonus.*" *The Journal of Roman Studies*, vol. 54, nos. 1–2, 1964, pp. 90–97.

CHAPTER FOUR

Nature Also Writes:
On Rhetorical Thermodynamics

DAVID M. GRANT

While the science of ecology may be centered on the life of organisms, that term also extends beyond life and its affectability to the non-living *oikos*, the home on which those lives depend. As *The Homer Encyclopedia* details, an *oikos* "consists of the house itself . . . land for agriculture, orchards, and vineyards, livestock (cattle, sheep, goats, and pigs) grazed on uncleared or marginal land, and its human members: the nuclear family at its head (husband, wife, sons, and daughters), slaves and such other types of dependent laborers as there might be . . . and higher-status 'retainers'" (373). Clearly, ecology is concerned with much more than just the living but also with those things that support life—the house, the labor, and the land, including its quality as uncleared, fertile, or marginal, a quality dependent on nonhuman activities. While rhetorical ecologists like Marilyn Cooper have viewed agency and activities as distributed and decentered from the human[1], my question here concerns how, perhaps, our *oikos* has centered on an active *bios* without adequately explaining the activities of inert, physical matter.

Bruno Latour raises a similar specter in his interview with Lynda Walsh. He cites his own dissatisfaction with rhetoric as not knowing "What allows for continuity, so that you can go on talking about . . . how do you proceed on smoothly into the nitrogen cycle and that sort of thing? Whatever is your term to cover that enterprise, we need a term that doesn't break down at the limit of consciousness" (417). What Latour seems to suggest here is that for a fully coherent ecological rhetoric, we must specify how persuasion happens across domains of the noetic and anoetic, not just the sapient and the sentient. That is, Latour doesn't see how rhetoric can encompass the difference between thinking and non-thinking or between sensing and non-sensing. For Latour, rhetoric seems inadequate because persuasion works through some form of thinking or affect, no matter how limited we configure those operations.

Without a minimal consciousness necessary for the response a general theory of rhetoric might entail, we are left to either keep physical mechanics outside the scope of rhetoric or to explain them *as if* physical mechanics were a series of persuasions. Clearly, new materialist and object-oriented philosophies have generated new views on agency for rhetoricians, but their explanations of non-living agency have relied on models of living beings. There is a sometimes tacit, sometimes overt, view of objects acting from some interior space of being or of making intentional choices through some panpsychist "black box" that extends a limited notion of vitality to all things. If we accept that things act without a subjective interior, what is left of persuasion except force? To what degree, for example, can we say that nitrogen's movement through the soil, the bodies of plants and animals, water, and air is rhetorical? Does nitrogen have a rhetoric, and would it have a rhetoric even if living organisms did not work upon it?

The task for ecological rhetorics, then—if Latour's objection is to be answered (and there is always the question of whether rhetorical ecologists would even want to answer it)—is to think of rhetoric before life and the living. In posing the question in this manner, I am not suggesting we neglect life or reduce life to brute mechanics. Rather, I follow those who have pointed out before me that any conception of the living depends on the non-living. Derrida's *la vie-la mort*, or "life-death," is a notable example. Francesco Vitale argues that because Derrida did not consider life and death as opposed binaries, he "lays the premises for the question of the survival, '*survie*' or '*survivance*,' to which the bearing of the deconstruction of the traditional notion of life is linked" (33). By taking up ecological rhetorics in this way, perhaps Latour's question acquires a new dimension in which we might conduct an inquiry.

To sketch this out, I briefly review this Derridean sense of life-death through Leroi-Gourhan's concept of *grammé,* which has been influential to ecocomposition and rhetorical ecologists alike. In Derrida's thought, *grammé* becomes something of a minimal unit of informational *différance*. *Grammé* are bits of difference that both mark and inform. They are information: a change, an endurance, a modulation. Such information is never objective but informational in relation to a subject embedded in a spatiotemporal and ecological matrix. As material and ontic objects, *grammé* can be speculatively understood from within thermodynamic relativity rather than epistemic relativism. Because *grammé* are encountered by living and non-living alike through relative movement without center or foundation, each *grammé* is an occasion and invitation for rhetoric without epistemology, noesis, or affective sensory stimuli.

I explain this in light of ecological rhetorics focused on energy, since according to information theorist Rolf Landauer, mass, energy, and information can all be converted into the other (Landauer 1996). That is, following Einstein's equation on relativity, Landauer's principle adds information because information is difference; it is a writing as *différance*. Both George Kennedy and Richard Coe look to rhetoric as a kind of energy, though each makes different characterizations. I argue that rhetorical energies are not ontically separate from the system in which they flow. That is, they are not anything to be wielded or applied to a situation but to be considered as thermodynamic "information" (Coe "Rhetoric"). Prior to interior/exterior or living/non-living is a physical structuring that in*form*s the system. By relying more on physics than biology, I situate in*form*ation within posthuman and new materialist rhetorical ecology in order to argue for a sense of ontic relativity whereby we might work among others with consideration toward objects in their own being rather than in accordance with our own thinking.

Interior Equivocations

Animal and creaturely rhetorics have made forays into nonhuman persuasion, though they bring an emphasis on meaning making. Ian Bogost's *Alien Phenomenology* and Steven Shaviro's *The Universe of Things*, for example, both inquire into the interior life of things. For Bogost, "[t]he phenomenologist who performs carpentry creates a machine that tries to replicate the unit operation of another's experience" (100). Bogost asserts that things have an experience, and while he is clear about a further operation representing or replicating the what-it's-like, his premise begins with things having a what-it's-like we might be able to know. Shaviro follows Graham Harman's argument that aesthetics are not cognitive structures of beauty applied to things, but precognitive responses of feeling and, thus, "the root of all relations . . . including causal relations" (Harman, quoted in Shaviro 156). Yet Shaviro arrives here after opening things up to a panpsychism where "all entities have insides as well as outsides, or first-person experiences as well as observable, third-person properties" (104). With notions of "experiences" and "insides," pure physical materiality must be discussed metaphorically *as* discourse or *like* persuasion, at which point most scientists balk and insist on this as a deformation of empirical observation. Nitrogen molecules don't "talk" with other molecules through ionic bonds, nor do they assume configurations that "feel" right; they really and actually bond because they absolutely must. Anything else is romantic poetry.

Less romantic, some ecological treatments of rhetoric deal with what Louise Phelps called "contextualism" or a process that "assumes a flow of information/energy in an open system" (53). Rather than formulate a rhetoric based on the interior thoughts or feelings of things, Phelps's ecology is more cybernetic and, therefore, more mutable and attuned to contingency within regularity. Cybernetics has, since Norbert Wiener, been an approach that sheds distinctions between biology and technics, requiring neither outside nor inside, only a flow of information in a medium. As Wiener put it, "Instead of building a wall between the claims of life and those of physics, the wall has been erected to surround so wide a compass that both matter and life find themselves inside it" (38). Nitrogen, as much as people, is moved by energetic flows of information throughout the *oikos*.

Information is not to be thought of as separate from sender or receiver but as continuous throughout a system—as energy. Carolyn Gottschalk Druschke uses a trophic metaphor[2] from biology to critique the tendency of theorizing "rhetoric (construed as symbolic language) [that] emerges epiphenomenally, divided off from originary reality" (Druschke). Symbols, sounds, and movements are themselves material and need full consideration as such. For Druschke, this entails seeing rhetoric not "as ecological thought or orientation or comportment. But rhetoric *as ecology*. And ecology *as rhetoric*." (emphases in original). That is, all beings are equally participating in rhetorical work through their relations. Druschke forwards "controlled equivocation: the active co-creation of knowledge between researcher and researched (human animal, other-than-human animal, spirit, mineral, and otherwise) that emerges from always-only-partial connections across ontological difference" as the rhetorical-ecological structuring of emergence. Things have a way of feeling out their responses through their relations and always within relations themselves.

While controlled equivocation shifts the center of intentionality and gets closer to rebutting Latour's qualm—Druschke quotes the same reservation I do above—I am not sure it adequately responds to his question. If we understand Latour's attention to "consciousness of some kind" in his own expansive sense—that is, separate from questions of agency—then must we follow that rhetoric requires *intent* in the sense of its Latin and Husserlian etymology, as a stretching out of one's being? Paul Lynch and Nathaniel Rivers note the appearance of "intelligence" for Latourian rhetoric, a sense of holding relations together—again an act of will or intent (4). Such intent, as protention and retention, could also be found in the actions of animals, or in Druschke's formulation, anything from "the non-discursive and non-logocentric, to human animality via animals that don't behave like humans, to the most basic relations: the flows of energy transferred in forms of relationality between beings through hunting and eating and fucking and decomposing." It seems only the last items in her series of actions is generally without "intent," at least intent of the organism discussed, though not the millions of decomposing scavengers, bacteria, and fungi whose labor of decomposing is their own eating. That difference seems to be what Latour points to—if not agency, then some biotic activity, attentiveness, or responsivity independent of mechanistic force seems to creep into the heart of rhetoric. In short, intent.

Grammé as Non-Hermeneutic Information

The idea of *grammé* is something of a basic unit of difference, operating as a condition of possibility not just for further meaning, but further mattering, of a "program." The term was coined by anthropologist Andre Leroi-Gourhan, though it famously appears in *Of Grammatology* as that which ultimately provides Derrida with the justification to declare "there is no outside-text [*il n'y a pas de hors-texte*]" (158). Derrida was not pointing merely to constructions within discourse but to all phenomena, be they material or ideal, that must be encountered as *grammé*, as marks of difference pro-grammatically woven together into texts whose "reading" can only happen through contrasting differences and deferrals of meaning. This is the basis for both Gergory Ulmer's electracy and Bernard Stiegler's philosophy of technics. John Tinnell argues that "Stiegler, even more than Derrida, professed to see life in the world—human becoming, historical change, social organization—as the evolution and play of *grammé*" (135). We might consider *grammé* as the basic unit of difference.

Ψ*Grammé* are at the limit of knowing and the epistemic, an entanglement with an ontic trace through which any and all response-ability can occur. Diane Davis points this out through Derrida's discussion of Alice in *Through the Looking Glass*, where what distinguishes human from nonhuman utterance are never clear and independent criteria,

> as if the specifically human response were fully intentional and reasonable, an authentic response distinct from reaction or instinct or an unplumbable psychodrama— as if these distinctions were obvious and clear; in any case, as if "I" would be in a position to discern among them, and as if that capacity were the key to communication. (*Inessential* 161)

Any mark of différance, even the registration of two moments containing the same state of affairs, is encountered only as *grammé*, a something *there* that we cannot help but encounter from a *here* and a *now* as an "I," already woven and participating in the weave. Biochemistry is as much based on the *grammé* as are computer programming languages; archaeological marks from early hominids are *grammé* left behind for others to encounter as a trace and compose into meaning. *Grammé* only supplement (*supplément*) the meaning of an already-there whose being exceeds any ability to totally grasp. *Grammé* defer resolution and are the materiality of différance. *Grammé* are a trace of something else that has already passed by, like the odor of a strong cologne lingering in an elevator, a spoor.

While *grammé* are not alive and do not exhibit the kind of protention and interiority that mark phenomenology, they do, according to Derrida, aid life and help structure it, given the capacity they hold for marking time, for retention and recording. According to Francesco Vitale, Derrida provides an "interpretation of différance as the structural condition of the life of the living, from its elementary biological structure to the psychic system that presides over the relationship between the living and alterity in general" (27). In Vitale's terms, we must understand "life" as a text "not constituted by itself, independently from its transmission/translation, according to the classical relation signifier/signified" but life as arising

> in the effect that produces its transmission/translation; the sense therefore refers to another, different text; it necessarily and irreducibly bears within itself its differing from itself, according to the structural and temporal dynamic of différance and thus *is never accomplished and established by itself*, beyond the network of references in which it is inscribed. (Vitale 105; emphasis added)

We live only because of our situation within a network of differences. If this is so, then we have an opening onto an ecology that includes abiotic and non-living physical mechanisms. At some point within the network, inert and non-living things are incorporated into the living and the living pass into the inert.

This is what Latour invites us to more deeply consider in our rhetorics—"the nitrogen cycle and that sort of thing." Bacterial fixing of nitrogen in the soil is a kind of microbial trace or *grammé* left as a writing that plants "read" and respond to as part of the nitrogen cycle. Microbes do not *intend* to leave nitrogen in forms such as ammonia or ammonium nitrate (NH_4NO_3). Even further, some nitrogen fixation occurs abiotically as a secondary reaction of lightning, so no prior life is even necessary for this writing (Downie). Such chemical processes leave behind nitrogen as *grammé*, which is then available for other uses independent of any intention. While Plato attacked this promiscuous availability as a *pharmakon* of texts, Derrida celebrates it as the only truth there is. As a matter of pure matter, nature also writes.

With this description we have a very powerful urge to think rhetorically and to do so without reference to mentality. It is only through an openness toward différance between the living and the dead that we might consider the non-living more fully as part of our rhetorical ecology. Inert bodies react in surprising ways. Etymologically, inert means "without art" or, rhetorically, *atechnic,* as in the manner of some proofs. With cybernetic ecologies encompassing the technical along with the biological, what manner of ecological technics might describe proof-making among and between *grammé?* To consider this further, I leave aside the various treatments of the interior life of things because asking "what is it like to be a thing?" is an attempt at resurrection or reanimation of something that is always already at work. While both Bogost and Shaviro make persuasive arguments, I share with Diane Davis a framework that does not posit a "world of shared horizons—the fantasy of 'intersubjectivity' really is toast—nor exactly to Heidegger's (for me) still too tidily gathered world as fourfold but to a horizonless and ungatherable 'world' opened each time in the address of the other" ("Rhetoricity" 434). Each "ungatherable world" approaches the nitrogen cycle a bit differently, not as a unitary thing but as phenomena thermodynamically relative within its own informational flow. The phenomenon of nitrogen may itself be the same, but it is encountered differently (as *grammé*) through relations, such that some organisms excrete nitrogen compounds as waste while others ingest them as food. Nitrogen becomes different in different worlds, not different minds; its multiple dimensions of being disclosed in relation.

Rhetoric and/as Thermodynamic Energy

Thermodynamics is a highly practical area of study widely applicable to the sciences, including the fundamental operations of ecology. It is highly capacious in its scope, and as Bill Poirier defines it, "thermodynamics is the science that addresses how matter behaves at the macroscopic scale (i.e., at the ordinary scale of everyday human experience), and also how this behavior relates to the molecular scale (i.e., of individual molecules, nanoparticles, etc.)" (1). It thus includes not only the behavior of matter but also energy, motion, work, and how to measure such activities and flows through a system. As such, thermodynamics is helpful to view how nature writes—what sort of trophic work and energy transfers happen with respect to particular *grammé* and their encounters with particular weavers.

George Kennedy's definition of rhetoric as a kind of energy has been taken up by new materialist, animal, and affective rhetorical scholars to think about parts and wholes and how rhetoric may be part of nature rather than separate from it. As Kennedy put it in "A Hoot in the Dark: The Evolution of General Rhetoric," this "rhetoric, as an energy, has to *exist in the speaker* before speech can take place" (4; emphasis added). The thermodynamics here are clear. As a general form of energy, rhetoric is not just prior to speech but prior "in biological evolution" (4). He provides numerous examples of animal communication, and while he makes clear that animals do communicate in various ways, what is less sure "is the extent of their intentionality and consciousness of sending and receiving messages and the resulting question of whether some animals have a sense of self and of mental individuality" (6). Such intentionality and lack of self-consciousness might take rhetoric outside ethics, though Kennedy reintroduces the ethical dimension with his consideration of audience in Thesis II. As he notes, "A speech that is not successful at the moment may affect future conditions indirectly" (8). In all this, Kennedy retains a sense of rhetorical energy that exists as an energy possessed by a subject and an instrument to be used given a rhetorical exigence. One may use that energy wisely or unwisely, productively or unproductively, thus imbuing it with an ethical dimension.

Kennedy is careful to argue that "rhetoric is not a 'substance' in the logical sense" and looks to locate "a 'genus' of which the various historical meanings of rhetoric are 'species'" (1). Energy fits his criteria. However, while his analysis is systemic, his language is highly biological in the sense of Linnaean morphology. He looks for taxonomies of an overall rhetoric whose limits might be contiguous with that of life itself. Where Kennedy does foray into physics, in his Thesis VII, he does so speculatively, wondering if "rhetoric is perhaps a special case of the energy of all physics as known from subatomic particles" (13). This leaves the question of a rhetoric before life or *bios* an open one, though with unresolved movements from biological taxonomies to the physical and non-conscious thermodynamics of physics.

A year before "Hoot in the Dark," in the first edition of his translation of Aristotle, *On Rhetoric: A Theory of Civic Discourse*, Kennedy argues that rhetoric encompasses both animals and human beings since both "have a natural instinct to preserve and defend themselves" (1991, 3). Kennedy describes rhetoric "in the most general sense . . . the energy *inherent* in emotion and thought, transmitted through a system of signs, including language, to others to influence their decisions or actions" (1991, 3; emphasis added). Kennedy amends his formulation slightly in his second edition preface, where he revises his sentence to "Rhetoric, in the most general sense, can be regarded as a form of mental or emotional energy *imparted* to a communication to affect a situation in the interests of the speaker" (2007, 7; emphasis added). Here, the energy is "imparted" rather than "inherent," which makes it amenable to some control or modulation by an intentional, thinking, and communicating agent. This helps clarify Aristotle's distinction between rhetoric and sophistry in Book One, Chapter One of *Rhetoric*, where "sophistry is not a matter of ability but of deliberate choice [*proairesis*] [of specious arguments]" (Kennedy 2007, 36; emphasis in original). Through judgment, perception, or similar faculty, a subject comes to possess some energy and use it in ways that we may examine to understand rhetoric. Whether that energy be inherent or imparted, it requires a consciousness, awareness, or interestedness that, alongside the dangers of sophistry, allows for rhetoric's connection to ethics. A conscious subject is always at the heart of rhetoric and makes a choice to use it for good or ill.

This makes some sense given that Aristotle himself was an ardent biologist, and his method of approaching the life sciences has been praised by philosophers and scientists alike (Leroi 2014; Owen 1992). Moreover, as Dobrin and Weisser note, Aristotle's conception of rhetoric was "in essence an ecological conception of rhetoric" (*Natural* 168). Even further, it is Aristotle's rhetoric that comes back to us in the form of Heidegger's ontology of being, since "when approached as [a] work of ontology, the *Rhetoric* reveals itself to be nothing less than an exploration of *logos* as the condition of possibility for human being-there" (Barnett 90). But I want to point out Kennedy's shift as perhaps a wrong turn in our thinking—from Aristotle to Heidegger, energy is not, strictly speaking, a possession.

A very different take on rhetorical energy comes from Richard Coe's "eco-logic" for composition studies. Coe does not limit himself to *bios* as Kennedy does. He begins not with classification and division as his method of invention but with an exigence in "more complex phenomena which are increasingly relevant to contemporary realities," like "ecological difficulties" ("Eco" 232). Coe decries the "fallacy to discuss a subsystem without considering the whole system or to discuss anything out of context" ("Eco" 233). As his examples demonstrate, "Human beings do not perceive data," but we do perceive patterns ("Eco" 235)[3]. Such patterns are relative, though Coe does not chalk up such relativism to the usual suspects like culture, structure, or ideology. Unstated, but still there, is an emphasis on time. He gives an example of prior backpacking advice to bury any "non-burnable garbage" until "the number of backpackers per acre reached a level where cans were being buried faster than steel can decompose" and the rule had to be changed ("Eco" 235). The energy in the rhetorical act of advising one to bury garbage is not its message or content. It is not in the materiality of discourse itself, but in the play of difference—of *différance*. A temporal difference changes how things mean, how data are made, and what their consequences may be. As Coe says elsewhere, "information is not matter, it is difference" ("English" 21). This difference is the same as that between any writing and its reading. As Coe also succinctly puts it, "Information is in*form*ation only when it is in-formation" ("2001" 15; emphasis in original). Unlike Kennedy's energy, which exists "in the speaker" or is "inherent in emotion or thought," Coe's energy comes from the openness of difference in the spatial and temporal surround—as part of the overall ecological patterning of a system.

Where Kennedy uses biology as paradigm to work out rhetoric as energy, then, Coe uses physics. This results not only in a more expansive set of connections to place and ecology but a sense of rhetoric that exceeds the living. In "Closed System of Composition," Coe notes the familiar modes of teaching writing as a series of "techniques for effecting separations of knowledge and none (save for perhaps analogy) for making complex connections" ("Closed" 406). His remedy is a more holistic approach that looks at communication as an ecology of interlocking systems, and he uses an example of billiards to demonstrate his meaning. Player, cue stick, billiard balls, and table constitute a closed system in which the pool player's striking of the ball with the cue effects "a transfer of energy" ("Closed" 408) that is completely predictable. Yet, Coe explains,

> If I make exactly the same motion with the same stick, but strike a person, the predictive process becomes more complex. Unlike a billiard ball, the person will respond not to the transfer of energy, but to the information which is carried by that energy. The energy for the response will come from that person's own energy system and the nature of the response will depend primarily on how that information is evaluated (i.e., on its perceived meaning). ("Closed" 408)

He thus draws out the "marker/meaning distinction (i.e., the distinction between the mass-energy or absence thereof and the information it carries)" ("Closed" 409). The information is not exhausted in difference itself but in all the ways that difference is received, rendered, and relayed as it co-labors through other bodies. There is, then, not only the original difference but a play of difference among other differences in a wider system of relations, some of which impinge into consciousness and some of which do not.

Coe's example demonstrates Druschke's sense that information is "not only" epistemic, and not only ontic, but open to different entanglements. We have the same *grammé*, or mark, whose existence provides a potential energy to be tapped or not depending on the relations of a system. This energy is only differentially existent, and it remains not a possession to be wielded but a potential to be unlocked, affected as much by the overall system's thermodynamics as by any particular interaction. In short, *grammé* are transduced: converted from one message or bit of information into something else[4]. When light enters an eye, it hits the retina and is transduced from visible light energy into the electric impulses of neurons: same "message," different media. In grammatology, not only do signs mark a trace of something that has already passed, but that sign may also operate transductively since, as *grammé*, they have no inherent meaning. This allows a sign to be differently appropriated and re-composed for different purposes. Imagine the hoof print of a deer in soil that marks its passing and is to a hunter a sign for deer. That same sign, through transduction, holds different significations for other things: a spanse for a spider to weave her web, an obstacle for ants, a catchment for rainwater.

Systems organize themselves according to their energies in a transductive multiplicity rather than as a set of discrete objects. In Coe's example, a system restricted to purely physical objects and atomic forces is in*form*ed by the pool cue whose energy is transferred to the billiard ball to make it roll. Not all of the energy transfers directly to the ball, however, since some fraction is released as sound and a little bit more absorbed in friction and in the ball's resistance, which sends some energy back up the pool cue. The ball, the table, the air, and the cue respond to the new in*form*ation according to the description of energy in Newtonian physics, $F = ma$. In Coe's other system, a person is in*form*ed by the pool cue, their body's atoms relaying energetic force to neuronal structures that transduce that into ionic and chemical reactions of sense perception. Other parts of the person's body absorb the energy according to their own structures, so that capillaries may stress, break, and bruise. One event with multiple, branching, systemic effects.

The point here is that with the more open system of person, the sense impression of being hit with a cue—with enough force to cause pain or not—cascades into a search for meaning: "Why did someone do that?" or "What is that other person thinking?" From our point in relativity, we have the in*form*ation as a *grammé* of pain and sensation, which not only unfold in time but which are energy transduced from non-conscious physical effects to conscious epistemic ones. This is not, as Casey Boyle explains in *Rhetoric as a Posthuman Practice*, an understanding of information as something sent and received, as a letter or email. Instead, "information is a transductive, not transmitted activity" (73). In*form*ation transduces, or alters from one kind of material trace into another in a ceaseless flow. Boyle points out that information "cannot be reduced to a message formed by a medium but must instead be mobilized as an ongoing structuring process wherein the form of any given structure matters much less than its capacity to enact and to become differently formed" (75). In*form*ation both moves and is the relative movement of matter in thermodynamic formation.

Without naming it as such, what Coe asks us to attend to are what physicists call inertial frames. From a relativistic standpoint, with all physical objects moving in time and no point of absolute rest, we have to specify the inertial frame used to describe other things. It is not that specifying frames allows us to understand epistemic differences, nor that differences arising out of subjective apprehensions can be objectively corrected. As physicist Richard Muller argues, "you have probably read that different observers, moving at different velocities, 'disagree.' That's nonsense" (28). There is not a disagreement in any epistemic sense but in the ontic sense that "Observers disagree in relativity only to the extent that they would also disagree on the velocity of someone flying in an airplane. They all know velocity is relative, and the number depends on the reference frame" (28). Things like clocks or GPS satellites might "appear" to tick more slowly, but this isn't just an appearance, as Muller explains, "Not only does it *appear* to be ticking more slowly, but it *is* ticking more slowly—measured in your proper frame" (30). And there is no absolute to proper frames, which "are just things used for reference; pick any one you want" (29). Since any measurement is an encounter with *grammé* in its movement, every encounter within the flow of energetic difference is fraught with rhetorical implications.

Understanding Inertial Frames

Karen Barad's agential materialism makes a similar argument with its emphasis on quantum agential cuts as an entanglement of meaning and matter. While agential materialism is a powerful analytic, I remain agnostic about its claims. Barad draws skillfully from Neils Bohr, the main developer of quantum mechanics, where states of matter and energy can only be probabilistically determined through matrices and strange topologies. But to convince scholars of rhetoric, not to mention scholars beyond rhetoric like Latour, we need a demonstration within classical dynamics. This does not simply mean "at scale" nor does it involve what Muckelbauer notes "is simply an argument for an even bigger sense of big rhetoric" (40). It has nothing to do with size but with scope and extent. This is why I turn to relativity in a thermodynamic sense. Relativity, as explained below, is an implication of a universe in constant motion. Such continual movement precludes any hermeneutic grounding, upending stasis as a means to adequately navigate life, the cosmos, and all our measures. If *grammé* are material markings that have their own relative movements, then encounters with them are subject to the relativistic effects of thermodynamics.

Let's say we are driving to the beach in a bus. I am at the front of the bus, behind the driver, and you are in the back. The bus is traveling at sixty miles per hour. Being absent-minded, I forgot my sunscreen, so I yell back to you to please toss yours up to me. You do, and someone sitting in the middle happens to use a stopwatch to record the time it took the sunscreen to travel the distance. Knowing the distance between us, that middle person measures the sunscreen's speed—say, twenty miles per hour. Let's also suppose that at the same moment, a police officer points her radar gun at the bus, but it glitches and focuses on the sunscreen instead of the bus (just bear with my improbability on this), thus adding the two speeds. The bus gets pulled over because, the officer says, her radar gun displayed a speed of eighty miles per hour. The driver insists it is a mistake because he had the cruise control set to sixty. The passenger in the middle overhears this, notes the difference is twenty miles per hour, and the misunderstanding gets straightened out. Yet the fact remains that in one measurement, the sunscreen moved at twenty miles per hour while in another, it moved at eighty. Both are true statements and must stand as "facts" to be reckoned with. This is relativity in a nutshell.

On the bus, our frame of reference is already in motion, so we intuitively discount it. We, along with the sunscreen, are already moving at sixty miles per hour. We share the same inertial frame. But to the radar gun, the inertial frame of reference is the road, not the bus. Most of us understand the road as stationary, and we, too, intuitively measure motion relative to it when we are positioned outside the bus. However, in doing so we make the same error of not specifying our inertial frame. This has far-reaching implications, especially as we widen scope. The earth, for example, rotates at about 1000 miles per hour and orbits around the sun at about 66,000 miles per hour (Howell). No piece of road nor the ground upon which it is laid is *absolutely* stationary. Move a perspective far enough away—view the scenario from the moon, perhaps—and the sunscreen moves faster than 1000 miles per hour. Once again, if we simply adopt the same inertial frame—that of the Earth's surface—we find ourselves in complete agreement.

If we accept this, not only is speed relative but all of physics. As Muller puts it, Einstein "concluded that not only does the time between two events depend on the reference frame (ground, airplane, satellite) but so also does the length of objects" (38). One way to explain the glitched radar gun's reading is that because the bus was moving, its length was shorter. Relativity posits that faster objects both flatten and increase mass. As Jeffrey Bennett sums up, "objects in moving reference frames have 1) slower time, 2) contracted length, and 3) increased mass" (56). The very *grammé* through which we interface the world, then, will take different forms and properties depending on our relative speeds and distances. While this is a matter of measurement, it is not a matter of deciding which is correct. Bennett reminds us "that motion is always relative and all viewpoints are equally valid" (53). There is no "outside inertial frame" just as there is no "outside-text." Relativity does not make the sunscreen speed up or slow down, nor does it allow for simply *any* measurement to be valid. It simply asserts that encounters with *grammé* are conditioned by thermodynamics, by the energetic velocities and relative movements whose differences create the necessity for rhetoric.

This has at least two implications. First, objects can react to other objects not because they "experience" each other in certain ways, but because they exist differently in respective frames of spacetime. Time, distance, and mass are not uniform but thermodynamically relative. Like Collin Brooke's ecology of new media practices, what matters are "the strategies and practices that occur at the level of interface" (28). Grammatology allows rhetoric to work smoothly across a full ecology and perhaps even demands such a rhetoric, given relative interfaces with *grammé*. The second implication I note is how this rhetoric gets at Druschke's "use of ecological understandings *not only* metaphorically and *not only* to point towards relationality with the things of the world" since no material or mechanical phenomenon can be objectively totalized. Such "not only" can be read as a move toward ethics and I take this up by way of conclusion.

Topoi, Trophe, and Oikos

We have seen how information is not thought of as separate from sender and receiver but as continuous throughout a system, modulating and arranging it formatively as much as conceptually. Information is *différance* constituted through specific relations and whose residue, or *grammé*, interact according to the thermodynamics of physics. While we can see how objects react to one another in relative ways, it leaves open the question of whether or not they can choose to do otherwise. This is the ethical dimension of force and persuasion that differentiates rhetoric from physics. We might have agentive encounters between inert things that occur *not only* according to how we might measure, but can we have encounters between inert things that happen *otherwise* than what physics tells us?

Megan Foley's work on the force of rhetoric reads Aristotle

in a way that feels pertinent to both Derridean force and rhetorical energy. Much of this hinges on what is meant by "available" in, as Kennedy and others translate Aristotle, "the available means of persuasion" (37). The precise term referenced is "endekhomenon," which can also mean "possible," though "available" indicates not just purely possible but a possibility for *someone* or *something* to realize. In other words, it is to be understood in a relativistic and relational sense rather than a pure condition we might locate in the acting subject. In short, rhetoric's persuasiveness (peitho) always admits some degree of force (bia). While one can have force without rhetoric, one cannot fully theorize rhetoric or persuasion without accounting for some force being applied. In every *endekhomenon pithanon* or every kind of availability for persuasive action a rhetor can ascertain, an element of force will inhere.

Foley sees this force in two ways. In the first instance, it is the force that works "'*para phusin,*' or contrary to that body's nature" (175), an external force that makes something into another thing or causes it to act in some way contrary to its immanent being, absent the introduction of *bia*. The other instance, Foley explains, works through *kata phusin*, or in accordance with that nature of the thing that force is applied to. Here, this "*dunamis* activates potentialities that the body had already, rather than forcing it to actualize forms against the grain of its latent potential. By this definition, *bia*, or force, makes a body do or become something that it is incapable of doing or being on its own" (175). There are, then, relative senses of *bia*. Force cannot be said to be independent of its object. Rather, from the start it is an ethical relation to the nature of that which it acts upon. Force can, through *para phusin*, sunder a window to glassy dust, or, through *kata phusin*, solidify liquid when one opens a supercooled container. Yet if I shatter a window, isn't its change to glassy dust still a change according to its nature? It doesn't fundamentally change in any other way, such as turning into slime or fire, without a host of extraneous conditions transducing their own inscriptive forces. Foley follows Antonio Agamben to note that there is an "aporia in the character of potentiality itself" (176). It is, perhaps, the reason for Derrida's pause at the moment of *différance*. It also points to another way to parse rhetoric and physics: between what *can* happen and what *must* happen.

Physics concerns what *must* happen according to nature and entelechy, while rhetoric concerns what *may* happen according to availability and *endekhomenon*. That is, they ask two different questions. Even though they may observe the same phenomena, the questions differ. For the physicist, everything must happen as physics describes it. Given enough information, physics can supposedly predict the future. Yet Foley notes Derrida's meditation on *endekhetai*, the question of what is possible or available, also concerns "the possibility of the impossible" (176). More simply put, a rhetoric's question about potential is not merely the ability to do something; it is also the ability to *not* do so. Any positive conception of potentiality, or of availability in the case of rhetoric, requires its refusal. Foley puts it this way: "If potentiality did not contain an element of impotentiality, everything potential would actually happen. If possibility did not contain an element of impossibility, everything possible would come to pass" (176). Following from this, Foley reasons that "if potentiality by Aristotle's own definition must contain impotentiality, then every actualization harbors an element of force" (177). Within each moment of *différance*, the impotentials are realized as much as the potential. The impossible is held at bay at the same moment the possible comes to pass.

Such an ecology of potential puts a heady and heavy ethical burden on the rhetor—be they concerned with human speech or the ways in which they co-write a planetary ecosystem through their own energetic exchanges and dependence on greenhouse gas emissions. At any moment, the rhetorical tables can be turned. There is always the inevitable potential for our own lives to be taken up in a trophic exchange and our own possibilities to be forcefully ended. Perhaps this can happen in a way that pleases some because they can call it some measure of "progress." But such measures may be approached more openly and as multiple instantiations of being rather than through an epistemological relativism that simply prioritizes one mode of consciousness over another, as Latour worried.

Notes

1. See Cooper (2019). While I do not disagree with her work, I do take her title as a starting point for my own.

2. See also Keeling and Prairie for a discussion of trophic energy in/as rhetoric.

3. See also Hong (2020) who argues that data are not found but made via measurement.

4. See also Boyle, Brown, and Ceraso (2018) for a treatment of transduction in rhetorical technics.

Works Cited

Aristotle. *On Rhetoric: A Theory of Civic Discourse.* Translated by George Kennedy, 1st ed., Oxford UP, 1991.

———. *On Rhetoric: A Theory of Civic Discourse.* Translated by George Kennedy, 2nd ed., Oxford UP, 2006.

Barnett, Scot. *Rhetorical Realism: Rhetoric, Ethics, and the Ontology of Things.* Routledge, 2017.

Bennett, Jeffrey. *What Is Relativity? An Intuitive Introduction to Einstein's Ideas, and Why They Matter.* Columbia UP, 2014.

Bogost, Ian. *Alien Phenomenology, or What It's Like to Be a Thing.* U of Minnesota P, 2012.

Boyle, Casey. *Rhetoric as Posthuman Practice.* Ohio State UP, 2018.

Boyle, Casey, et al. "The Digital: Rhetoric behind and beyond the Screen." *Rhetoric Society Quarterly,* vol. 48, no. 3, pp. 251–59.

Brooke, Collin. *Lingua Fracta: Towards a Rhetoric of New Media.* Hampton Press, 2009.

Coe, Richard. "Eco-Logic for the Composition Classroom." *College Composition & Communication,* vol. 26, no. 3, 1975, pp. 232–37.

———. "Closed System Composition." *ETC: A Review of General Semantics,* vol. 34, no. 4, 1975, pp. 403–12.

———. "'Rhetoric 2001' in 2001." *Composition Studies*, vol. 29, no. 2, 2001, pp. 11–35.

Cooper, Marilyn. *The Animal Who Writes: A Posthumanist Composition.* U of Pittsburgh P, 2019.

Davis, Diane. *Inessential Solidarity: Rhetoric and Foreigner Relations.* U of Pittsburgh P, 2010.

———. "Rhetoricity at the End of the World." *Philosophy & Rhetoric*, vol. 50, no. 4, 2017, pp. 431–51.

Derrida, Jacques. *Of Grammatology*. Translated by Gayatri Spivak, Johns Hopkins UP, 1997.

Dobrin, Sidney, and Christian Weisser. *Natural Discourse: Toward Ecocomposition*. State U of New York P, 2002.

Downie, J. Allan. "Legume Nodulation." *Current Biology*, vol. 24, no. 5, 2014, pp. R184–90.

Druschke, Carolyn Gottschalk. "A Trophic Future for Rhetorical Ecologies." *Enculturation: A Journal of Rhetoric, Writing, and Culture*, 20 Feb. 2019, http://enculturation.net/a-trophic-future. Accessed 12 Dec. 2021.

Foley, Megan. "*Peitho* and *Bia*: The Force of Language." *Symplokē*, vol. 20, nos. 1–2, 2012, pp. 173–81.

Hong, Sun-ha. *Technologies of Speculation: The Limits of Knowledge in a Data-Driven Society*. New York UP, 2020.

Howell, Elizabeth, and Doris Urrutia. "How Fast Is Earth Moving?" *Space.com*, 2019, www.space.com/33527-how-fast-is-earth-moving.html. Accessed 12 May 2021.

Keeling, Diane, and Jennifer Prairie. "Trophic and Tropic Dynamics: An Ecological Perspective on Tropes." *Tracing Rhetoric and Material Life: Ecological Approaches*, edited by Bridie McGreavy, et al., Palgrave Macmillan, 2017, pp. 39–58.

Kennedy, George. "A Hoot in the Dark: The Evolution of General Rhetoric." *Philosophy & Rhetoric*, vol. 25, no. 1, 1992, pp. 1–21.

Landauer, Rolf. "The Physical Nature of Information." *Physics Letters A*, vol. 217, nos. 4–5, 1996, pp. 188–93.

Leroi, Armand M. *The Lagoon: How Aristotle Invented Science.* Bloomsbury Circus, 2014.

Lynch, Paul, and Nathaniel Rivers. "Introduction: Do You Believe in Rhetoric and Composition?" *Thinking with Bruno Latour in Rhetoric and Composition*, edited by Paul Lynch and Nathaniel Rivers, Southern Illinois UP, 2015, pp. 1–20.

Muckelbauer, John. "Implicit Paradigms of Rhetoric: Aristotelian, Cultural, and Heliotropic." *Rhetoric, through Everyday Things*, edited by Scot Barnett and Casey Boyle, U of Alabama P, 2016, pp. 30–41.

Muller, Richard. *Now: The Physics of Time*. W. W. Norton & Company, 2016.

Owen, Richard. *The Hunterian Lectures in Comparative Anatomy, May and June 1837*, edited by Phillip Reid Sloan, U of Chicago P, 1992.

Phelps, Louise W. *Composition as a Human Science: Contributions to the Self-Understanding of a Discipline*. Oxford UP, 1991.

Poirier, Bill. *A Conceptual Guide to Thermodynamics*. Wiley, 2014.

Shaviro, Steven. *The Universe of Things: On Speculative Realism*. U of Minnesota P, 2014.

Thalmann, William G. "Household." *The Homer Encyclopedia*, edited by Margalit Finkelberg, vol. 2, 2011, pp. 373–75. *Wiley Online Library*, https://doi.org/10.1002/9781444350302.wbhe0613.

Tinnell, John. "Grammatization: Bernard Stiegler's Theory of Writing and Technology." *Computers and Composition*, vol. 37, 2015, pp. 132–46.

Vitale, Francesco. *Biodeconstruction: Jacques Derrida and the Life Sciences*. Translated by Mauro Senatore, State State U of New York P, 2018.

Walsh, Lynda, et al. "Forum: Bruno Latour on Rhetoric." *Rhetoric Society Quarterly*, vol. 47, no. 5, 2017, pp. 403–62.

Wiener, Norbert. *Cybernetics: or Control and Communication in the Animal and the Machine*. 2nd ed., The MIT Press, 1961.

II

SOCIAL AND
ECOLOGICAL JUSTICE

CHAPTER FIVE

Distressed, Irrational, Disordered: Mad Design Thinking for Complex Systems

LEAH HEILIG

When I think of what it means to be Mad in our complex, networked world, my first thoughts go to cocoons. In their fantastic book *Mobile Interfaces in Public Spaces* (2012), authors Adriana de Souza e Silva and Jordan Frith talk about how the experiences of public and private are modulated by technology in space. Among other examples, they illustrate how reading a book in public, such as in a coffee shop or public transit, creates a "controlled experience of the space" (60) that is "consisting of different ways of self-presentation and co-existence . . . the book becomes part of the experience of the public for the reader, not as a way to fully privatize or remove oneself from the public, but instead as a way to negotiate the (sometimes awkward) experience of being in public" (61). I'm intrigued by how the agency in the action of reading a book (or wearing headphones, or looking at your phone, etc.) creates ownership of the space and experience apart from the one that's being shared publicly and how relationships are modulated through the interface, as users draw boundaries around themselves. Design in these scenarios is protective, a means of redirecting constant, networked activity, a way of layering reality and its demands.

In my experience, being Mad has always meant living in these experimental boundaries between what is private and what is public and the degree of control that exists within them when interacting with the world outside of my head. While the definitions of what it means to be Mad differ from person to person, scholar to specialist, there is a central tenet that is true regardless of context or field or experience: Madness is socio-relational and often centers on feelings of public discomfort—mainly centering the feelings of those who do not understand or who stigmatize Mad interaction. One might think of Madness as existing purely in atypical cognition or processing, but the reality is Madness is created by systems and imaginary boundaries that govern behavior—in the (failed) regulation of private and public. It is defined by how "disordered" thoughts influence "disordered" behaviors and how those do not "conform to dominant, psychiatric constructions of 'normal'" (Liegghio, "Denial" 122). It can also be defined by the effect of "distress" or the social, external factors that affect mental states such as triggers, stigma, and oppressive or abusive environments (Sapey, Spandler, and Anderson). The act of passing while Mad, as it is defined by and lives within ecologies, is not unlike the act of reading a book in public space, in the cocoon to maneuver private and public: this "controlled experience" is simultaneously a barrier of protection and a wall that stops something new from emerging.

The removal of barriers—from environments, technologies, interactions, and so on—is the widely known goal of accessibility. As a Mad scholar who studies accessibility, I am drawn to questions of autonomy and equity not only as they exist in technological and environmental designs but in the interactions and relationships that surround them. The bulk of research has set a precedent for accessibility as strictly a material or adaptive problem. However, this approach is limited in two major ways: 1) it often excludes those with non-physical disabilities and, as this chapter focuses on, particularly those with psychiatric/ mental disabilities or Madness, and 2) it doesn't account for wider issues of complexity and the social or environmental realities of disability (Heilig).

Complexity is often positioned as the lack of control a designer has over the environment they are designing within, due to interactivity being "open-ended, multidimensional, and dynamic" (Still and Crane 36). Frustration therefore exists for designer and user alike in a "world of avalanches" where "thresholds as systems suddenly tip from one state to another" (Urry 30). This frustration is more intensely felt when said systems are rife with accessibility barriers, making disability not something residing in individual bodies but "in built environments and social patterns that exclude or stigmatize" (Kafer 6). And, arguably, this frustration is further compounded for those with psychiatric disabilities, which have been treated as "a side-issue" (Sapey, Spandler, and Anderson 2) to disability instead of a set of experiences and barriers deserving of separate narratives and attention. Of importance is that Madness is inherently social, defined by the deviance from normalized behavior and social interactions in public environments. Price's (2013) inequities of interaction and Prendergast's (2001) recounting of schizophrenic storytelling have addressed other people's discomfort in socially interacting with those who have disruptive thinking, moving, feeling, and being. This discomfort ultimately results in discrimination, stigma, and distress—turning human interactions into sites of ecological oppression.

Much like Cooper (1986) argues to situate writing in its socio-relational ecologies outside of individual cognition, this chapter addresses the undeniable need for accessibility to do the same. Due to its stigmatized interactions within ecologies, I posit Madness as one way to address this need, embracing divergent ways of thinking and relating to better inform design practice. Marrying the ambiguity and rhetoricity of design thinking (Greenwood et al.) to psychosocial models of disability, this chapter therefore offers "Mad design thinking" as a critical methodology for accessibility in the design and study of complex systems. Mad design thinking broadens accessibility through its acknowledgment of complexity, moving beyond single-context, single-technology practice to considerations of distress, irrationality, and disorder. These considerations emphasize accessibility as socio-relational and located in ecological activity, causing productive—and needed—disruption to the increasingly naturalized process of design thinking and best practices of accessibility.

To begin, I will first address how epistemic violence is perpetrated against the Mad to include stigmatized interactions and devaluing Mad ways of knowing and behaving. I will then identify and discuss the presence of Madness in traditional "eco-logic" (Coe) to include approaches toward and for systems thinking and complexity. Finally, I will apply Mad thinking to design, establishing three frames for driving a deeper understanding of accessibility and design practice (distress, irrationality, and disorder) as well as identifying the inherent saneism and naturalization in current approaches to design.

"Rendered Out": The Disqualification of Mad Knowing

Madness is not a universal condition but rather a construction of various historical or cultural contexts, and there "is no real basis of inherent or natural characteristics that define an eternal Mad subject" (Diamond 74). That said, the Mad experience is often defined by the systemic and symbolic violence at the core of psychiatric systems (Menzies, LeFrancois, and Reaume 3). These violences manifest in various ways, from curative models to involuntary hospitalization, to other forms of distress such as trauma. While the forms of oppression against those who identify as Mad, mentally ill, psychiatrically/mentally disabled, and onwards are varied and continuous, I find it important to investigate the effects of systemic and symbolic violence on rhetoricity and epistemology in the study of Madness and the ecology of mind—or the ways of being and knowing.

Symbolic violence "is difficult to recognize because its practices are deeply ingrained in everyday activities" and "it shows the subtlety of violence, its possibility of occurrence without actors' intentions and/or realization" (Lee 106). Prominent modes of symbolic violence against the Mad are disqualification and stigmatization (Crossley 172), which have the far-reaching consequences of isolation/alienation, distress, powerlessness, self-doubt, and public doubt or fear. Of note for this contribution is the effect Madness has on *ethos,* as "the cultural stigmatization of mental disability guarantees that the challenge to a speaker's credibility begins the minute she reveals her condition" (Uthappa 165). With such stigma, the very rhetoricity of a Mad person is called into question, as is the ability of the Mad person to create and translate meaning. As disqualified individuals, a defining element of Mad people are that they are "deeply discredited in a particular culture at a particular time" (J. Johnson 464), and their believability and ability to connect persuasively to an audience is compromised. As Catherine Prendergast succinctly states: "to be disabled mentally is to be disabled rhetorically" (57).

Rhetorical disablement can be seen as a form of epistemic violence or the treatment of "knowledge and ways of knowing as something other than knowledge and other than legitimate" (Liegghio 124). Epistemic violence can have a person "rendered out of existence by the assertion that their experiences are 'disordered,' or the symptoms of a 'mental illness'" (Liegghio 125). Mad people, as disqualified knowers, have their ideas, perspectives, and experiences institutionally, systematically, and publicly ignored or ridiculed. Common social attitudes toward Mad thinking are often positioning its knowledge as incompetent or dangerous (Liegghio) and a threat against psychiatrically ascribed norms. Hard boundaries exist around what counts as epistemology, and it is an issue of social justice to "bring persons back into existence" (Liegghio 127).

The call to resist epistemic violence begins with denouncing "the institutional assaults . . . against nonconforming narratives, knowledges, and ways of knowing" (Liegghio 127). It means granting legitimacy toward Mad ways of moving and being in the world as well as unpacking the dominant attitudes and ways meaning is constructed (Price, "Defining"). It is the (potentially) uncomfortable action of challenging rationality as the de facto way of understanding, as "Madness and the madman stubbornly refused to yield to reason and to science" (Starkman 27). And, most importantly, it is the process of making meaning "not in spite of our mental disabilities, but *with* and *through* them" (Price, "Mad at School" 8).

This chapter is my attempt to think *with* and *through* Madness as it relates to complexity, to find the joy and importance of disorder and disruption. Because, as the next section addresses: ecologies are completely crazy.

Locating Madness in Ecologies

In 1988, alternative rock band the Pixies posed a rhetorical question that has haunted the entire drafting of this chapter:

Where is my mind?

Madness has always had a role in ecology—one that is understudied in writing and design. In rhetoric, the location of thought is in flux at best, existing somewhere in the complex relationships between cognition, activity, and environment. As early as *Phaedrus*, "*mania*," or the divine madness, "literally takes one 'outside oneself'" (Thompson 362). Cooper (1986) offers up the web, "in which anything that affects one strand of the web vibrates through the whole" (370), to depict the ecological model of writing—one that is based in socio-relational elements aside from individual cognition, where meaning, much like Madness, emerges from interaction. Even earlier, ecology is used as a driving metaphor for what Gregory Bateson (1975) calls "the stuff" (24) of the mind, wherein "ideas are interdependent, interacting, that ideas live and die" in a "cooperating tangle" (24) of layers and networks from which ways of knowing and behaving emerge.

As an accessibility researcher and as a Mad person, I am fascinated by "the stuff" that gets ignored in the study of design— the "ideas that die" (Bateson 24) because they don't fit within networks. I am curious as to what knowledges are affected by "the various layerings of your mind" (Bateson 24), how our non-linear, complex, *crazy* continuum of a world is organized into systems of meaning and how these systems are studied to understand—and sometimes control—behavior. In this section, I begin by first presenting a few ways in which ecologies are thought through: eco-logic, systems thinking, and complexity. I then demonstrate how these ways of knowing are not divorced from Madness and that Madness is created in ecologies through the drawing of artificial boundaries on complex systems.

Eco-logic, Systems Thinking, and Complexity

"Implicit in any rhetoric is a logic and a way of perceiving," writes Richard M. Coe (233) in his foundational article "Eco-Logic for the Composition Classroom." As the title of the piece suggests, Coe's work introduces what he calls "eco-logic" into writing studies or: "1. A logic designed for complex wholes. 2. Any logic which considers wholes as wholes, not by analyzing them into their component parts. 3. *Esp.*, a logical model appropriate for ecological phenomena" (Coe 232). Eco-logic emphasizes that meaning is relative to context and that it's important to evaluate "systemic interrelations instead of analytic separations" (Coe 237) when attempting to understand meaning and how knowledge emerges from tradition. While eco-logic can be a way to position writing as part of a larger set of contexts and relations, it also can be applied as a broader philosophy of rhetoric and, arguably, epistemology.

The way knowledge is created and understood through eco-logic is like the epistemology of systems thinking or the study between structure and behaviors. Systems thinking is grounded in identifying patterns of behavior over time between interconnected items or agents and is applied across a wide range of disciplines from computer science to politics. While seemingly driven by algorithmic understandings, systems thinking recognizes the somewhat manufactured quality of rationality when trying to understand our larger world: "On the one hand, we have been taught to analyze, to use our rational ability, to trace direct paths from cause to effect, to look at things in small and understandable pieces, to solve problems by acting on or controlling the world around us . . . on the other hand, long before we were educated in rational analysis, we all dealt with complex systems" (Meadows 3). Systems thinking encourages a critical exploration of what designers have deemed "wicked problems" (Buchanan) or systemic issues that transcend disciplinary boundaries, such as poverty or illness, by using an understanding of systems to radically restructure them: "Obvious. Yet subversive. An old way of seeing. Yet somehow new. Comforting, in that the solutions are in our hands. Disturbing, because we must *do things,* or at least *see things* and *think about things,* in a different way" (Meadows 4). Like eco-logic, systems thinking challenges analytical and categorical separations by observing large networks of agents, creating knowledge from relationships and behaviors.

Further connecting both eco-logic and systems thinking is the focus on complexity or "a slap in the face for traditional reductionist approaches to understanding the world" (N. Johnson 17). Complexity has no set definition but investigates "emergent, dynamic, self-organizing and interdependent systems that interact in ways that influence later probabilities" (Urry 30). Complex systems are open, making it hard to study specific areas in isolation and can be influenced by their environments (Still and Crane). Complex systems are also alive, "driven by an ecology of agents who interact and adapt" (N. Johnson 14). Adding a layer of difficulty to understanding complex systems is that they are often categorized by non-linear responses (Albers) and exhibit mixtures of ordered and disordered behavior (N. Johnson). Complexity exists in networked environments with potentially limitless factors, ensuring that "in the end, disorder rules" (N. Johnson 24). Eco-logic, systems thinking, and complexity are lenses in which epistemology emerges from interconnections or "the relationships that hold elements together" (Meadows 13) within ecologies.

Boundaries for Sanity: The Inherent Madness of Ecology

In visual media, a common way to physically represent Mad reasoning takes shape in the form of a person standing in front of a wall or bulletin board. The surface is covered with items, usually photographs or handwritten notes. And the stereotypical Mad person is transfixed, obsessive as they connect the items on the wall together in physical space using dark arrows and red thread, attempting to solve something or unearth a conspiracy only they can understand. They may externalize their thoughts as they move, but if they do, they are half-uttered, disjointed, or too quick to be interpreted by the "sane" onlooker—they are unknowable to the outside audience. Instead of knowledge to be shared, Madness takes form in how the person begins to draw connections between ideas and agents that only they can see. I argue that this depiction of Madness is 1) really annoying, and 2) demonstrates a need to flip the script for what counts as knowledge. It's not that the Mad person is creating something unintelligible in their connections but that the rigid, homogenized boundaries that define thinking (and the dreaded "rational thought") prevent new ways of understanding. To draw on the beginning metaphor of this chapter, privileged approaches to epistemology force us to cocoon ourselves in.

How we study and understand ecology is not entirely separate from how society constructs Madness. If complexity encompasses the tension between order and disorder, Madness represents embracing disruption. So, what is the catalyst between knowledge that is legitimate (logic) and disordered thinking (Madness) in the study of systems? Ultimately, a logical system is one that can be understood in terms of predictability and, by extension, control. If "the Holy Grail of Complexity Science is to understand, predict, and control [such] emergent phenomena" (N. Johnson 5) of complex systems, there needs to be boundaries for what constitutes the limits of observable study. In a non-linear, complicated world that exists in states of constant flux, the boundaries of ecologies are drawn to make rational sense: "There is no single, legitimate boundary to draw around a system. We have to invent boundaries for clarity and sanity" (Meadows 97).

The metaphorical constraints of ecologies become problematic when "we forget that we've artificially created them" (Meadows 97), as the behavior of complex systems becomes surprising when it fails to operate within said boundaries. This juxtaposition between what is expected and what can occur within interconnections and relationships speaks to the systems thinking principle of self-organization or "the power to add, change, or evolve system structure" (Meadows 159). Being surprised by behavior indicates a lack of control over said system—disorder. But for an ecology to diversify and evolve, disruptive behavior is needed: Madness needs to occur.

In actual ecologies, logic (reason, predictability, patterns) and Madness (disorder, non-linearity, irrationality) exist symbiotically, where new ways of doing, learning, and growing depend on "freedom and experimentation" (Meadows 80). Ecologies are Mad in that they can defy the boundaries of what constitutes acceptable (predictable) behavior, and Madness is the result of drawing constraints upon interconnections, relationships, activity, and knowing to organize understandings of complex systems. Acknowledging this connection recenters Madness as necessary and needed for growth and expansion as well as emphasizes that the stigmatization of Madness is created by socio-relational and contextual governance.

Moving toward Mad Design and Complex Accessibility

One of the first books I ever read on design was Alan Cooper's (1999) *The Inmates Are Running the Asylum: Why High-Tech Products Drive Us Crazy and How to Restore the Sanity*. The cover features a distressed man holding on to lines created by traces and pads meant to simultaneously represent a microchip and prison bars. The title on the inside page is created with a font that looks like something that wouldn't be out of place in a haunted house, like a message scratched on a wall. I remember my first impression of this foundational, popular introductory text was: "this is shitty" and then: "this makes me feel like shit."

While this book makes the connection between saneism and design blatant, framing like this (and general resistance to deviations or struggles in thinking) is pervasive throughout traditional approaches to user experience, usability, and occasionally even human-centered design and accessibility. Expediency is privileged in thought and action: in research, tasks are timed, "efficiency" is a metric, and stock phrases established by earlier scholarship are often circulated like "don't make me think" and "keep it simple, stupid (KISS)." There is also the goal to design rationally, to make sense of predictive patterns and construct experiences based on that sense-making. In the consistent practice of these approaches and use of these perspectives, the "messy and beautiful" (Jen) gets ignored or displaced, labeled as an outlier or removed from significance. Recently, there has been gaining momentum in countering these perspectives, as designers further social justice approaches in research and practice. Such movements include but are not limited to design justice (Costanza-Chock), the slow design movement (Strauss and Fuad-Luke), identifying and abolishing white supremacy in design (Benjamin), resisting capitalist and exploitive design practices (Monteiro; Wizinksy), and addressing equity and sustainability in user experience (Rose et al.). What I contribute with this chapter is a more direct addressing of the inherent saneism in design praxis and scholarship as well as how we need Madness to formulate approaches to complex accessibility.

An ecological understanding of Madness can help designers address the significant hurdle of furthering complex accessibility.

In scholarship and practice, there is an absence of accessibility work that centers the Mad—a historically underserved and oppressed population. As Madness is manufactured by socio-relational activity, and the Mad are therefore disabled by built environments and social interactions that exclude, how we approach the practice of accessibility needs to change. With calls to expand practices of accessibility at large (Zdenek) and to find ways to integrate "psychological inclusion" in design (Kett and Wartzack 215), it's important to consider how Mad knowledges and experiences might be heard, valued, and incorporated into accessible design.

An important first step toward Mad designing is to view accessibility as socio-relational and located in ecological activity, as opposed to an action that takes place in single contexts and often with single technologies. A severe limitation of accessibility is how it is often treated like a closed system, in which there is only one way of removing barriers. Instead, accessibility should be treated as a complex, open system in which there are multiple avenues for problem solving. We should focus on "changing *spaces*" rather than trying to achieve "the nearly impossible task of understanding the complex causes of the response in that one person" (Ford par. 8). While situating accessibility as a complex system is important, what I want to move toward is seeing Madness as an avenue to identify *specific* accessibility barriers within ecologies and potentially use a Mad design thinking to approach these barriers.

Mad Design Thinking

Design thinking in a general sense is an iterative approach to problem solving, one with an end goal of understanding the user, thinking through assumed knowledge, and redefining existing problems to come up with alternative solutions and strategies that we might not be able to draw from our own understanding (Dam and Siang). Design thinking usually consists of five general steps: empathize with users; define problems, needs, and insights; ideate or create ideas; prototype; and test. In contemporary discussions, design thinking has drawn criticism for being a "buzzword" that has a "complete lack of criticism" and perpetuates linear conceptions of design (full of Post-its) (Jen). Design thinking is also seen as an inadequate approach for addressing social issues, as it neglects to identify existing design inequalities as a source for potential problems (Costanza-Chock).

Design thinking on its own is not an inclusive practice, but there are ways it can still be used to promote dissensus, encourage divergent thinking, and embrace ambiguity as a central goal (Greenwood et al.). I want to complicate design thinking by troubling the waters of the "thinking" part, working against the increasing naturalization of the design process. I offer Mad design thinking not as a replacement and certainly not as a universal or even permanent approach but as a way of *resituating*. Through Mad design thinking, I want Madness to be considered as part of a larger ecology and what that means for traditional notions of "good" design solutions.

So, what is Mad design thinking?

Mad design thinking is defined by epistemic violence. It draws from discredited ways of looking at the world and knowledges that have been delegitimatized. It is about finding "ways to move" (Price, "Mad at School") within complex systems that enact violence toward those with divergent thoughts and behaviors. Mad design thinking considers how disqualification and stigmatization serve as *fundamental design questions* that can guide understandings of how ecologies operate within prescribed boundaries, and how oppression arises out of interactivity within built environments.

How do we use Mad design thinking?

Having discussed the open-ended nature of complexity, as well as the importance of ecological Madness in promoting growth and diversity, it feels counterintuitive to provide a how-to list or a toolbox full of what is and isn't Mad design thinking. Much like deep accessibility (Ford) and design justice (Costanza-Chock), Mad design thinking is concerned with changes in systems rather than trying to master complex relationality. As what counts for Madness is dependent on historical and cultural contexts, what counts as Mad design thinking is also subject to evolving social relationships and networks. It's intentionally frustrating, open to evolution, and above all else, not defined by a fixed or linear state.

To conclude this chapter, I am going to introduce three frames—as they exist right now—that could constitute a Mad design thinking as it relates to problems of complex accessibility. These frames are distress, irrationality, and disorder. In the following sections, I provide a brief definition of the frame as I've arrived at it and its relationship to design. I then identify design problems that could be understood through said frame.

Distress

Distress can be most simply understood as the situational impacts of Madness or the result of the oppression created within ecologies. Distress is not equivalent to impairment, as it is important to understand its relationship to Madness in a way that does justice to the Mad experience (Russo and Shulkes). Mental distress is, at least in part, socially constructed "and infused with a continuing legacy of oppressive and exclusionary power relations" (Tew 80), necessitating that "making some sort of sense of distress experiences may be a prerequisite for re-establishing agency—and the agency that one establishes may need to take account of the context, content and meaning of one's impulses and experiences" (Tew 76). Sources of distress might include stigma, trauma, and pain caused by environments and systems that privilege the normative minds, normative bodies, normative ways of behaving, and/or in social relationships that support epistemic and symbolic violence. Public space on its own can be a source of distress due to the stigmatization of ways of thinking, moving, and being.

When considering design, distress is manifested through the presence of factors such as triggers, sensory overload, affective influences, and actions that harm emotional well-being such as abuse or self-harm. It can also take the form of panic or anxiety in the face of social situations in which behavioral norms aren't clearly defined. As a tool for Mad design thinking, distress is the principal way to determine where and how ecological systems cause harm. Returning to the metaphorical cocoon, distress is what emerges from failed negotiations with the public, when those who experience it are unable to redirect constant, networked activity.

Concrete ways of applying distress to design might include improving flexibility and customization in the interfaces meant to regulate public spaces. We might consider how a thorough understanding of distress can help us build environments that reduce the chances of panic attacks, for example, or how considering the distress of the socially anxious could improve issues of crowding or traffic flows. Distress can help us, as designers, think about accessibility barriers as existing in socio-relational spaces.

Irrationality

I draw irrationality as an intentional opposite of the interactive design principle of rationality or the creation of processes that are understandable and reasonable, such as defined by participatory designers Löwgren and Stolterman (2004):

> We usually consider a process to be rational: (1) when it is possible to understand—that is, when we can see why the process has been enacted in a specific way, and (2) when the enactment is in line with our own values. This means that in order to declare a process to be rational it has to be possible to understand the actions and decisions in the process as based on reasons, and that these reasons coincide with our own means of assessing actions. (49)

When an agent within a system is irrational, it is unable to be positioned as reasonable or understandable, and "any expressions of irrationality may be seen as potentially subversive to the very fabric of social relations" (Tew 71). The presence of irrationality identifies where epistemic power is lacking in ecologies, and as a Mad design thinking principle, it can both draw attention to issues of stigma and disqualification *as well as* pivot to where those within an ecology are limited by "bounded rationality" or the action of when "people make quite reasonable decisions based on the information they have. But they don't have perfect information, especially about more distant parts of the system" (Meadows 106).

Bounded rationality refers to the inability to have "the full range of possibilities," and it results in being unable to "foresee

. . . the impacts of our actions on the whole system" (Meadows 106). Irrationality can be a way to acknowledge and address the unpredictability of interactions and environments in complex systems, to avoid "analytic separations" (Coe 235), recognize the inherent Madness that exists within ecologies, and design better for complexity. A Mad design thinking that considers irrationality can identify areas of epistemic inequality in ecologies, as well as map out possibilities and futures for larger complex system interaction. Becoming comfortable with the irrational and "being less surprised by complex systems is mainly a matter of learning to expect, appreciate, and use the world's complexity" (Meadows 111).

Disorder

Disorder can be seen as a blanket term for anything that does not ascribe to linear activity, but in the case of Mad design thinking, I am curious as to how disorder changes perceptions of time as part of an ecology. Those of us Mad people often live within what Alison Kafer (2013) calls "strange temporalities" (37), in that the mental states of depression, panic, mania, trauma, and so on fundamentally change how time is experienced and related to. Normative, linear chronology discounts the "strange temporalities" formed through the mental states that fundamentally change how time is experienced and related to in ecologies—such as how mania affects processing, trauma induces flashbacks, or panic attacks "seem simultaneously to speed up and slam shut, leaving one behind" (Kafer 38).

Disorder as part of Mad design thinking might allow us to explore crip time more definitively as a design solution. From disability studies, crip time (shorthand for cripping time) can be most succinctly defined as "a flexible approach to normative time frames" (Price, "Mad at School" 62). I primarily see crip time as an exercise of consideration or making efforts to disrupt the naturalization of time when thinking of things like schedules, appointments, processes, and routines. This concept can be illustrated by examples such as respecting that someone with social anxiety might need more time to arrive at a conference, that depression can make an hour feel like a week, that some people cognitively process conversation slower, or that someone in the throes of a panic attack is going to experience hours of stress in the span of seconds.

In interaction design, there's a gap in practice for this type of flexibility. This gap is most clearly evidenced in map APIs, like Google Maps, that not only create constricting travel narratives but also allow no room for customization of route planning other than by mode of transportation: on foot, by public transit, by car, or, recently, by wheelchair. It also manifests in how we facilitate design research, such as sequenced task analysis or "time on task" as a measurement of effectiveness in usability. The sequences in designs construct naturalized chronologies through the ordering of experience—mobility and time become linear, efficiency becomes the driving (and sometimes only) factor for designing a positive user experience.

Conclusions

This chapter explores how Madness is inherently socio-relational, existing in public relationships and as a resistance to psychiatric constructions of normal thinking, behaving, feeling, and being. My work further contends that Madness has always had a role in ecology and that ecologies are inherently Mad, as an ecology requires disruption and disorder to diversify and evolve. I argue that an ecological understanding of Madness can help designers create complex approaches to accessibility, as the social construction of Madness locates accessibility barriers in interactions and experiences. I offer Mad design thinking to promote complex accessibility, as Mad legitimacy and ways of knowing are often subjected to epistemic and symbolic violence, resulting in disqualification and stigmatization. Mad design thinking broadens accessibility through its acknowledgment of complexity, moving beyond single-context, single-technology practice to include considerations like distress, irrationality, and disorder. These considerations emphasize accessibility as socio-relational and located in ecological activity, causing productive—and needed—disruption to the increasingly naturalized process of design thinking.

Works Cited

Albers, Michael J. *Communication of Complex Information: User Goals and Information Needs for Dynamic Web Information.* Routledge, 2004.

Bateson, Gregory. "Ecology of Mind: The Sacred." *A Sacred Unity. Further Steps to an Ecology of Mind,* edited by Rodney Donaldson, Bessie/HarperCollins, 1991.

Benjamin, Ruha. *Race after Technology: Abolitionist Tools for the New Jim Code.* Polity Books, 2019.

Buchanan, Richard. "Wicked Problems in Design Thinking." *Design Issues,* vol. 8, no. 2, 1992, pp. 5–21.

Coe, Richard M. "Eco-Logic for the Composition Classroom." *College Composition & Communication,* vol. 26, no. 3, 1975, pp. 232–37.

Cooper, Marilyn M. "The Ecology of Writing." *College English,* vol. 48, no. 4, 1986, pp. 364–75.

Costanza-Chock, Sasha. *Design Justice: Community-Led Practices to Build the Worlds We Need.* The MIT Press, 2020.

Crossley, Nick. "Not Being Mentally Ill: Social Movements, System Survivors and the Oppositional Habitus." *Anthropology & Medicine,* vol. 11, no. 2, 2004, pp. 161–80.

Dam, Rikke F., and Teo Y. Siang. "What Is Design Thinking and Why Is It So Popular?" *Interaction Design Foundation,* www.interaction-design.org/literature/article/what-is-design-thinking-and-why-is-it-so-popular. Accessed 16 Mar. 2022.

de Souza e Silva, Adriana, and Jordan Frith. *Mobile Interfaces in Public Spaces: Locational Privacy, Control, and Urban Sociability.* Routledge, 2012.

Diamond, Shaindl. "What Makes Us a Community? Reflections on Building Solidarity in Anti-Sanist Praxis." *Mad Matters: A Critical Reader in Canadian Mad Studies,* edited by Brenda LeFrançois, et al., Canadian Scholars' Press, 2013, pp. 64–78.

Ford, Star. "Deep Accessibility." *Star Ford: Essays on Lots of Things since 1989,* 6 Sept. 2013, https://ianology.wordpress.com/2013/09/06/deep-accessibility/. Accessed 16 Mar. 2022.

Greenwood, April, et al. "Dissensus, Resistance, and Ideology: Design Thinking as a Rhetorical Methodology." *Journal of Business and Technical Communication*, vol. 33, no. 4, 2019, pp. 400–424.

Grieco, Margaret, and John Urry, editors. *Mobilities: New Perspectives on Transport and Society*. Routledge, 2016.

Halberstam, Judith. *The Queer Art of Failure*. Duke UP, 2011.

Heilig, Leah. "Silent Maps as Professional Communication: Intersections of Sociospatial Considerations and Information Accessibility." *Business and Professional Communication Quarterly*, vol. 81, no. 4, 2018, pp. 421–39.

Jen, Natasha. "Design Thinking Is Bullshit." *YouTube*, uploaded by 99U, 19 Mar. 2018, www.youtube.com/watch?v=_raleGrTdUg&ab_channel=99U. Accessed 16 Mar. 2022.

Johnson, Jenell. "The Skeleton on the Couch: The Eagleton Affair, Rhetorical Disability, and the Stigma of Mental Illness." *Rhetoric Society Quarterly*, vol. 40, no. 5, 2010, pp. 459–78.

Johnson, Neil. *Simply Complexity: A Clear Guide to Complexity Theory*. Oneworld Publications, 2007.

Kafer, Alison. *Feminist, Queer, Crip*. Indiana UP, 2013.

Kett, Susan G., and Sandro Wartzack. "Considering Emotional Impressions in Product Design: Quality of Life Theory and Its Impact on Design Strategy." *DS 84: Proceedings of the DESIGN 2016 14th International Design Conference*, The Design Society, 2016, pp. 1719–728.

Lee, Ji-Eun. "Mad as Hell: The Objectifying Experience of Symbolic Violence." *Mad Matters: A Critical Reader in Canadian Mad Studies*, edited by Brenda LeFrançois, et al., Canadian Scholars' Press, 2013, pp. 105–21.

Liegghio, Maria. "A Denial of Being: Psychiatrization as Epistemic Violence." *Mad Matters: A Critical Reader in Canadian Mad Studies*, edited by Brenda LeFrançois, et al., Canadian Scholars' Press, 2013, pp. 122–29.

Löwgren, Jonas, and Erik Stolterman. *Thoughtful Interaction Design: A Design Perspective on Information Technology*. The MIT Press, 2004.

Meadows, Donella H. *Thinking in Systems: A Primer*. Chelsea Green Publishing, 2008.

Menzies, Robert, et al. "Introducing Mad Studies." *Mad Matters: A Critical Reader in Canadian Mad Studies*, edited by Brenda LeFrançois, et al., Canadian Scholars' Press, 2013, pp. 1–22.

Monteiro, Mike. *Ruined by Design: How Designers Destroyed the World, and What We Can Do to Fix It.* 2019.

Prendergast, Catherine. "On the Rhetorics of Mental Disability." *Embodied Rhetorics: Disability in Language and Culture*, edited by James Wilson and Cynthia Lewiecki-Wilson, Southern Illinois UP, 2001, pp. 45–60.

Price, Margaret. *Mad at School: Rhetorics of Mental Disability and Academic Life.* U of Michigan P, 2011.

———. "Defining Mental Disability." *The Disability Studies Reader*, edited by Lennard Davis, Routledge, 2013, pp. 298–307.

Rose, Emma J., et al. "Social Justice in UX: Centering Marginalized Users." *SIGDOC '18: Proceedings of the 36th ACM International Conference on the Design of Communication*, Association for Computing Machinery, 2018, pp. 1–2, https://doi.org/10.1145/3233756.3233931.

Russo, Jasna, and Debra Shulkes. "What We Talk about When We Talk about Disability: Making Sense of Debates in the European User/Survivor Movement." *Madness, Distress and the Politics of Disablement*, edited by Helen Spandler, et al., Policy Press, 2015, pp. 27–42.

Sapey, Bob, et al. Introduction. *Madness, Distress and the Politics of Disablement*, edited by Helen Spandler, et al., Policy Press, 2015, pp. 1–9.

Starkman, Mel. "The Movement." *Mad Matters: A Critical Reader in Canadian Mad Studies*, edited by Brenda LeFrançois, et al., Canadian Scholars' Press, 2013, pp. 27–37.

Still, Brian, and Kate Crane. *Fundamentals of User-Centered Design: A Practical Approach.* CRC Press, 2017.

Strauss, Carolyn, and Alastair Fuad-Luke. "The Slow Design Principles: A New Interrogative and Reflexive Tool for Design Research and Practice." *Proceedings of the Changing the Change Conference*, Allemandi Conference Press, 2008, pp. 1–14.

Tew, Jerry. "Towards a Socially Situated Model of Mental Distress." *Madness, Distress and the Politics of Disablement*, edited by Helen Spandler, et al., Policy Press, 2015, pp. 69–82.

Thompson, Claud A. "Rhetorical Madness: An Ideal in the *Phaedrus*." *Quarterly Journal of Speech*, vol. 55, no. 4, 1969, pp. 358–63.

Uthappa, N. Renuka. "Moving Closer: Speakers with Mental Disabilities, Deep Disclosure, and Agency through Vulnerability." *Rhetoric Review*, vol. 36, no. 2, 2017, pp. 164–75.

Wizinsky, Matthew. *Design after Capitalism: Transforming Design Today for an Equitable Tomorrow*. The MIT Press, 2022.

Zdenek, Sean. "Reimagining Disability and Accessibility in Technical and Professional Communication." *Communication Design Quarterly*, vol. 6, no. 4, 2018, pp. 4–11, https://readingsounds.net/wp-content/uploads/articles/Zdenek-guest-editor-intro-reimaginingdisability-CDQ2018.pdf.

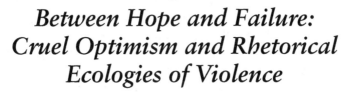

CHAPTER SIX

Between Hope and Failure: Cruel Optimism and Rhetorical Ecologies of Violence

JENNIFER CLARY-LEMON

I read from my field notes of late May at the Chalk River decommissioned nuclear reactor: "Rainy, 16–19 degrees Celsius, mosquitos nearly killed both of us." Such a comment reflects the second time in my life that I have seen chimney swifts, following a mad dash off the side of the highway, scrambling down a grass-slicked power line corridor in the nearing dark. As I round down a curve in the path, panting from exertion, I stop when I'm greeted with the sight of eight hundred birds chittering and careening their way into the round top of a tall chimney stack. As I get closer to the bottom of the stack, attached to an abandoned trailer but still blinking with aerial antennae, my eyes and neck are trained on the black cyclonic mass of swifts circling the chimney. I take frantic notes in the rain, my ink mixing with water on the page while mosquitos bite every available surface of skin I have—hands, neck, face. I note how the chittering of hundreds of swifts completely blocks out the sound of the Chalk River immediately behind them; how each time the swifts circle the chimney, 10–20 disappear inside; how watching them roost is like watching the reversal of smoke going inside of a chimney. The entire spectacle takes only 35 minutes, and then it is quiet, and I am left feeling like I have just experienced a fireworks display but am not quite sure I've watched the end.

Such an experience is one out of time, where sixteen feet underneath the marvel of hundreds of birds flying into a 150-foot chimney—all designated as "vulnerable" by the International

Union for the Conservation of Nature's (IUCN) Redlist and "threatened" by Canada's Species at Risk Act—lies uranium, thorium, and plutonium. The abundance of birds on this contaminated site sits, for a second, in a place kind of like hope. Of course, as Michelle Bastian reminds us, it is "easier to negotiate with the time of the living, perhaps, than with the time of ghosts" (161). It is easier to reflect on swifts' agencies and capacities when I see them for myself, easier to deny their threatened status. Yet this is a kind of cruel optimism, an attachment growing out of impossible conditions, an "ecology out of time," as Madison Jones has it (341). It is easier to believe in a vision of a broken world made whole—when the birds will always return—than contend with relations of violence—our extinction stories. It's no wonder that those who have grown attached to swifts are also attached to the structures that fail to house them.

As an aerial insectivore, the chimney swift population, known as *Chaetura pelagica*, has declined over 90 percent in the last forty years, primarily due to decline in insect biomass, human disturbance, habitat loss, and climate change (Gauthier, Richardson et al.). As a result of contemporary forestry practices decimating original habitat of old-growth hollow trees, the chimney swift now shares common habitat with humans—the chimney swift is now primarily an urban bird. Action plans legislated by the Species at Risk Act in Canada guide the building of particular infrastructures when critical habitats of threatened species are damaged. For chimney swifts, this means building artificial chimneys for the birds each time a critical habitat, in the form of historic masonry chimneys, is destroyed.

Yet the swifts do not tend to inhabit human-built fake chimneys; these are generally a failed experiment in Canada, though they show some success in the US (see Finity and Nocera; Kyle and Kyle). These mitigations, refused by the swifts, serve as monuments to both the absence and presence of species extinction and to the human difficulty of approaching alterity affectively—getting close enough, for example, to mark either loss of species or desire for future reconciliation, for turning toward or turning away. Taken together—bird, landscape, structure, human—the case of the chimney swift is a tricky rhetorical ecology, and one that I have argued elsewhere as approaching the rhetorical trope of *alloiostrophos* (*strophos*, bending/turning; *alloio*, otherwise/ differently; see Sutton and Mifsud; Clary-Lemon, "Examining'"; *Nestwork*). These empty simulacra, in relation to both bird and human, act as complex architectural superpositions of the *zoe* and *bios* (see Braidotti, "The Critical") that cannot be examined apart from the rhetorical ecologies in which they emerge. In doing so, they provide sites for intervention and reflection on the Anthropocene. They also act as an invitation into considering the very real places of absence and violence wrought by species loss and force us to contend with the limits that human-centered hubris offers attempts to mitigate such violence. To that end, every case of species decline is also a rhetorical-ecological problem, a blending of the material and discursive, of the affective and the physical.

As Bridie McGreavy et al. argue, engaging with rhetorical ecologies turns our attention to the articulation between rhetorical elements (as opposed to imagining them as separate and static) and to transhuman ways of meaning making, often drawing from processual and systems thinking stemming from contemporary movements in composition studies (5). Rhetorical ecologies turn beyond the linguistic and toward the material-discursive and affective, underscoring the importance of bodies, objects, and matter in acts of suasion. This turn is reflected in, as McGreavy et al. note, "engaged rhetorical practice" (5) that uses fieldwork specifically as a site of rhetorical being-in-the-world. More than this, however, ecological-rhetorical study underscores the notion of ecological *care* in turning focus to potentials for "change, ethics, and justice" (5). These ideas are echoed in the work of Jones, who argues for an emplaced vision of rhetorical-ecological thinking that force us to contend with colonial violence, and of Caroline Gottschalk Druschke, who underscores the importance of fieldwork and physicality in particular in moving toward relational thinking with the ecologies in which we live.

In this chapter, I focus on two particular field sites of failed chimney swift mitigations in Canada. These sites sit as rhetorical ecologies that emphasize human failure and violent relations with nonhumans in service of cruel optimism about the possibility of species recovery. As I detail, chimney swift structures have far more symbolic potential for humans than true utility for chimney swifts, and they organize stories of human violence in their assembly and perseverance. They function instead as a kind of desire-object that organizes behavior and feeling—as Lauren Berlant would say, such towers offer "a cluster of promises we want someone or something to make to us and make possible for us" (23).

In *Cruel Optimism*, Berlant suggests that optimism becomes cruel when objects of attachment promote ways of being that are unsustainable and damaging but are nonetheless artificially promising and affirming. Artificial swift towers are such objects because they sit somewhere between memorial and monument, somewhere between hope and despair. Given the massive global decline of chimney swifts, each artificial chimney or stand-alone tower might symbolically stand in as a collective grave marker or at least a place for "material solemnizing" for chimney swifts (Blair 279). Yet unlike true memorials, they resist what is necessary for mourning such loss because they avoid what public memorials do: give space and names for those deemed lost, missing, or unrecoverable. The artificial swift constructions also resist a transparent semiotic monumentalizing; as Krzyżanowska notes, monuments exist as a "traditional carrier of collective memory in the material space of the city" (467). As failures without swifts to fill them, such towers have no referring subject to value, turn to, or commemorate—yet they are still objects representing this desire. They sit as structures of ambivalent attunement, encouraging humans to both turn toward and turn away from the nonhumans they are built to entice. In some cases, they continue the fantasy of the environmental "fix"; in others, they invite us to closely listen to bird bodies in their complete absence.

In all cases, I argue, these particular rhetorical ecologies are embedded with violence, with the creation of a precarious subjectivity that such mitigations construct. As Kathryn Yusoff argues, "subjectivity declared through precarity prepares an ontological field for the subject in which dependence is already inscripted in the material conditions of emergence; the orangutan declared in the midst of deforestation is already an abandoned being. Its presence, its proximity, is a preparation for death" (586). Or as Helen Macdonald eloquently states in *H is for Hawk*, "the rarer they get, the fewer meanings animals can have. Eventually rarity is all they are made of" (181). As I outline in the next section, uncharismatic and mysterious birds like the chimney swift are particularly vulnerable to this characterization.

Storying the Anthropocene: Rhetorical Ecologies of the Chimney Swift

The textual evidence of chimney swifts' presence and disappearance on landscapes shows a complicated human narrative predicated on swifts' shadowy, secretive existence emerging commensally with urban development. Their Latin name speaks to both their looks and mystery, *chaetura* for "bristly" or "spiny tail" and *pelagica*, which translates to "of the sea" but is thought to refer instead to the nomadic Pelasgi Greeks, underscoring chimney swifts' enigmatic and dynamic behavior. Unlike other aerial insectivores who fly by day and may be easily spotted by humans, chimney swifts by their very design are elusive. Swifts are in the *Apodidae*—or "feetless"—family of birds, with legs so short that they cannot perch or walk on horizontal surfaces like other birds. Instead, swifts spend their entire lives in flight, stopping only to rest vertically on the dark hidden insides of columnar structures with appropriately rough surfaces for traction. In other words, swifts, more than other birds, suffer from a kind of absenting presence, given their chosen habitat of the inside of tall, dark human-made columns when they are not in constant flight. Most humans will never catch a glimpse of a chimney swift.

From the very first sightings of swifts, humans have thought they were something else—swallows, martins, bats. Even today, the Vaux's swift (*Chaetura vauxi*), a western aerial insectivore that is not currently listed as endangered by any international body, is often mistaken for the chimney swift, who migrates in the east and is listed as endangered. Such confusion has so surrounded exactly what kind of bird chimney swifts are that until 1886, when an account of the swift was published in *The Code of Nomenclature and Check-List of North American Birds*, it was known by a variety of other names and given two separate Latin names. At first thought to be another kind of swallow, the chimney swift was known interchangeably as a house swallow, chimney swallow, aculeate swallow, chimney-bird, diveling,

American spine tail, and American swift (Graves 303–4). Those first records of experiences emerge steeped in the fact that, via the decimation and clear-cutting of millions of acres of forests by European settlers to the Americas, chimney swifts became visible through their adaptation to urban sites by being forced from their originary habitat. As one of the earliest ornithological accounts of swifts naively states in its observations in 1776, "it is a natural question to ask: where did the swallows build their nests before the Europeans came and made houses with chimneys? It is probably that they formerly made them in great hollow trees" (Graves 303). While this account is correct, it also overlooks that what made chimney swifts visible to Eurowestern humans was their synonymous "emergence" with colonization. It was European colonization of North America that lead to a near-100 percent overhaul in swifts' breeding ecology. As Graves (300) observes, between 1672 and the late 18th century—in fewer than 150 years—chimney swifts, forced out of forest habitats, opted to nest exclusively in human-built structures, preferring instead historic columns built of roughly textured substrates, whether chimneys, silos, air shafts, tobacco sheds, wells, or concrete sewer pipes (Richardson et al.). Today, there are fewer than two dozen known cases of chimney swifts roosting in trees in North America, to the point that when such behavior is noted, it is a cause for observation and scholarship (Graves; see also Hines, Bader, and Graves). In other words, chimney swifts' commensality with humans uniquely coincide with colonization. Or to think about it another way, *Chaetura pelagica*, the "spiny tails of the sea" or "bristly-tailed nomad," *became* chimney swifts, became real to Eurowestern humans, during the act of colonization. Thus, the case of the chimney swift also offers some insight into what Jones terms "the colonial history of Anthropocene ecology" (338).

What stands out in the case of chimney swift decline is its close connection to human urban development; chimney swifts are quite picky about which structures they might choose to either nest or roost within. Because chimney swifts settle so closely to urban humans, habitat disturbance and intrusion is listed as a primary reason for their decline (Richardson et al.). This might take the form, in some cases, of development and demolition of historic buildings. In others, it might take the form of capping chimneys to keep birds and other critters out of them. In still others, such disturbance is the common fault of property owners or chimney sweeps—although the birds nest in summers when chimneys are not usually in use, they may be disturbed either by the occasional off-season fire or seen as a fire risk and nuisance and destroyed if caught nesting in warmer months by chimney sweeps. Too, the changeover from fireplace to electric heat in the last century means there are far fewer chimneys that exist for swifts to nest in, and those that do often have been upgraded with interior metal liners that dissuade the birds, are too small (smaller than twelve inches when the birds prefer at least twenty inches), or have been capped.

Because of their primary choices of chimneys in which to roost and nest, chimney swifts are also far more likely to be exposed to contaminants and pollutants than other birds. Similarly, temperature fluctuations inside chimneys represent a threat to the success of their nesting behaviors; below 55 degrees Fahrenheit, the birds will abandon nests, and above 108 degrees, nestlings will perish. As such, chimney swifts most prefer chimneys that are connected to an internal source of warmth, like a basement (or a nuclear sub-building), to modulate the internal temperature of the stack itself (11). Chimney swifts show extreme site fidelity and return to nest in the same places year after year. In other words, chimney swifts are demanding about where they roost and nest: they prefer tall stacks that extend upwards of nine feet above a roofline and have an internal area of about three square feet, making non-residential chimneys their pick beyond smaller residential chimneys. They also want to return to the same chimney each year. Thus, the place one might find the contemporary chimney swift tends to be in large, older (usually 19th century) chimneys attached to factories, schools, and churches.

Despite the fact that chimney swifts are so choosy about their roosting and nesting habitat (that is, a chimney does not guarantee a chimney swift), nonetheless the mitigation of habitat loss continues to be the erection of chimney-like structures. Both artificial chimneys and free-standing towers in Canada have been modeled after successful American versions put forward by Paul and Georgian Kyle, self-taught swift conservationists who donated ten acres of property to become the Travis Audubon Chaetura Canyon Bird Sanctuary. The couple literally wrote the book on how to construct swift towers (see Kyle and Kyle), building seventy towers in the Austin area where they live, which have had remarkable success in attracting nesting swifts. Their designs have spurred the building of over 179 towers in the US and Canada (Graham).

However, the simple act of exporting a tower design has not traveled well across country borders. Across Canada, both artificial chimneys and free-standing towers have been built to try to attract chimney swifts; however, only ten known structures have attracted swifts across the country (two roosts in New Brunswick and Quebec and eight nesting sites: one in Manitoba, one in Ontario, and six in Quebec) (Bumelis, personal communication). Experts infer that it is the colder weather and the fluctuations in internal tower temperatures that result in so much more success in the US than in Canadian towers. Nonetheless, both artificial chimneys and free-standing towers continue to be built as mitigations for the destruction of habitat.

This offers quite the conundrum: where mitigations are the most successful (in the southern US), chimney swifts are not listed as a threatened species and are generally more abundant. Where the mitigations are needed (in the birds' northern migration routes where they are listed as threatened), they are not used and are generally considered failures. This discrepancy points our attention to the impossibility of determining rhetorical-ecological relations of precarity using human-based national boundaries. It seems that at least in Canada, the propositions that these unused structures are making only ever result in one answer by chimney swifts, despite their varied approaches in manufacture and location by humans. I next take up two cases of such failure.

Timothy Street Park: Failure and Cruel Optimism

The Timothy Street Park tower sits on a lot-sized residential greenspace in Mississauga, Ontario, located between a small multi-unit housing development and some power lines (see Figure 6.1). It is a donation to the city of Streetsville by a longtime

FIGURE **6.1.** *Timothy Street Park Chimney Swift Tower.*

resident Chester Rundle, who lived across the street. Alongside the eighteen-foot-tall freestanding masonry chimney are other collectibles of Rundle's: a decommissioned windmill and water pump with a memorial plaque about him, a set of wagon wheels, a small birdhouse on a pole, and seven boulders carted from Niagara, two of which have glued-in marbles for eyes. Upon first glance, the park reads rather as a mish-mash of a yard extension of the housing next to it, less a park than where someone has dumped their nice historic detritus. In many ways, the greenspace is a memorial to a local resident who passed away in 1996.

The chimney tower itself, however, has nothing at all to do with Chester Rundle. As a plaque on the chimney tells me, it is a testament to a local conservationist who noticed swifts inhabiting the nearby Streetsville United Church and lobbied the city to build an independent masonry swift tower (Stewart). It reads, "Dedicated to Bill Evans and the Chimney Swift Action Team in recognition of their efforts to protect and conserve the chimney swift species." As I observe the well-built structure and put my ear up to the iron cleanout in early June, it is absent of any interior scufflings that might indicate the presence of chimney swifts.

Like the thirty-foot windmill to its right, the masonry tower is just one more item in the park's strange collection, neither a home for swifts nor a working chimney. As the short write-up in a neighborhood paper asserts, it is a tribute to "one man's struggle to save the chimney swifts," storied by a lifetime resident of the city of Streetsville and a self-taught naturalist Bill Evans, who worked with a local conservation group, a former Ontario Ministry conservation officer, a local councilor, and local apprentices at a masonry training center to erect the tower. As the local interest piece says of the tower, "There are not too many projects that you can say are 100 per cent one guy's idea. But this one certainly was" (Stewart). To encounter this particular swift tower is not so much about encountering either birds or a structure built for birds; it is instead a monument to men.

I say this not to denigrate the work of committed individuals in conservation or the attention such a citizen-driven initiative might bring to the plight of a threatened species like the chimney swift—after all, swifts are "named" on this masonry chimney. Yet actions such as the Timothy Street Park tower embody current public narratives about species loss, in which focusing on problems of extinction are often future-oriented and terrifyingly dystopic, but reflections on current solutions are optimistic (see Randall). In a turn toward the optimism of conservation in erecting a stand-alone tower, the recognition of the loss of chimney swifts as a species—the "efforts to protect and conserve"—are overshadowed by the celebration of the "dedication" of the humans that prompted the structure's construction. Yet chimney swifts themselves, as absent from the structure, are propagated as both rare and mysterious in such absence. To return to Yusoff's assertion, the precarity of the chimney swift invoked by the tower's construction already inscripts the birds' dependence on humans in the material argument made by the structure itself. It directs attention not toward the loss of chimney swifts, where it might have had an educational or memorial impact. Instead, the Timothy Street Park tower acts as a material object of epideictic rhetoric, a column of praise for human individuals doing the work of conservation, even as that work has very little-known success. Such a celebratory object not only constructs nonhuman precarity—here the swift is already an abandoned being in favor of overdetermined human hubris and confidence in its preservation—but it also prevents real human acknowledgment of species loss-in-progress.

In Rosemary Randall's work with citizen action groups that focus on climate change, she suggests that solution-focused narratives of baby steps or green consumerism often are optimistically vague. Such positivity not only makes the present feel safe but also ignores loss as something to be projected into the future (119). The outcome, for Randall, are parallel narratives in which loss is split. Loss gets moved from the present into a version of a horrific future while current, real, and lived losses become impossible to both recognize and mourn. What we are left with, as in the case of the Timothy Street Park tower, are ineffectual monuments to optimism that do not allow us to do the work of grief effectually. The Timothy Street Park tower, as an optimistic solution, suffers from the kind of self-referentiality noted by Carole Blair of structures like the Gateway Arch in St. Louis (283): the tower refers only back to itself via the work of human volunteers and its own construction, doing little to truly recognize the nonhumans implicated by its presence or offer up cultural values that might intervene in their decline. Blair turns to the questions of such structures by invoking James Young, who asks

> whether an abstract, self-referential monument can ever commemorate events outside of itself. Or must it motion endlessly to its own gesture to the past, a commemoration of its essence as dislocated sign, forever trying to remember events it never actually knew? (1992, 54–5)

When a passerby first comes across the Timothy Street Park tower, there is absolutely no way they would otherwise know its purpose or intent, stuck as it is amongst the park's other peculiar debris. It is in this way abstracted even further from its already abstracted purpose, given the abysmal success rate of independent swift towers in Canada, and dislocated from the real series of ecological events that have led to biodiversity loss on a mass scale. As a self-referential abstraction, in Young's words, the tower simply celebrates itself. It sits as a commemoration of human ingenuity without fully allowing engagement and recognition of a strange present, precisely because it withholds the truth of what is *ceasing to be*, in Braidotti's terms ("Theoretical" 36). Although the tower is strange on the landscape and whispers, perhaps, at alloiostrophos by virtue of its brick almost-chimneyness, in this case it still functions to underscore a metaphoric system: the chimney is at once *like* other useless structures on this landscape—the windmill, the wagon wheel. It fails to secure the assent of contact with the nonhuman other, itself a metaphoric proposition, as Sutton and Mifsud remind us. Instead of opening up possibilities, this tower closes them down, its nonhuman subjects already abandoned. Instead, it sits as an object of cruel optimism, urging passersby to maintain an attachment to it that is no doubt problematic. The Timothy Street Park tower, as quasi-monument, completely excises nonhuman loss even as it appears to be a conservation object.

Neither an impossible future in which building a swift tower successfully attracts the birds (despite research suggesting otherwise) nor a present that simply erects free-standing masonry towers in the middle of a neighborhood greenspace allow for an acknowledgment of real loss. Without the ability to move beyond an intellectual acceptance of species extinction and instead toward a lived, emotional experience of the reality, humans are stuck in a kind of optimistic waiting place about our own, and others', demise—one littered with cheerily "eccentric" items (Stewart). As such, the Timothy Street Park swift tower's rhetorical-ecological proposition on the landscape is not oriented toward swifts, who have already refused it. The tower, by virtue of its focus, doesn't really even function as a memorial to biodiversity loss or the loss of the what-was-once-common encounter of humans watching swifts entering and exiting urban chimneys. Such a recognition would represent the network of loss that Ryan notes as the "emotional and material connections" (130) that people develop to a variety of species. Instead, the tower's existence is a simple monument to a man in a huddle of other monuments to another man, divorced from meaningful engagement with other humans and nonhumans, and devoid of acknowledgment of historic settlement.

At best, the Timothy Street Park tower is an ambivalent quasi-monument to nonhuman loss, reading more to the uninformed as an obelisk dedicated to a human individual than a meaningful object of relation. Though for some it might stand as an object of hope, instead, I argue, the ecology in which it functions provides a cruel optimism, a proposition of precarity. As scholars of hope note, "the conditions that make it possible to hope are strictly the same that make it possible to despair" (Marcel 101). It is the threatened nature of chimney swifts that makes mitigation actions hopeful and possible in the first place, an "indeterminate, *not-yet-become*" (Anderson 733, emphasis added) of complete extinction. As Anderson notes, and what my next case shows of the rhetorical swift-human-landscape ecology, "some types of hope can also feed back to *continue* relations that diminish even as we are attached to them" (743, emphasis added).

Queen's University Chimneys: Thinking-With Violence

The four artificial chimneys on two university buildings at Queen's University in Kingston, Ontario, are complex examples of rhetorical ecologies that circulate between chimney swifts and humans. As I discuss, they mark what happens when we listen to the disappointment inherent in hope by allowing nonhuman bodies to story their own demise at the hands of humans. They are rhetorical-ecological objects that invite us to think about what now seem impossible about the relationships invoked by the term *commensality*: that in living together, we harm none.

The four artificial chimneys are on the roofs of two separate buildings on Queen's nearly 100-acre campus, two chimneys located on the roof of Fleming Hall (home of administrative offices, Campus Security, IT, Human Resources, and Marketing and Communications) and two on Craine Hall (which houses the campus Physical Plant). The Queen's chimneys are the only artificial chimneys on urban buildings—as opposed to stand-alone towers—listed of all the coordinates I've been given by Bird Studies Canada. I know in advance from Chris Grooms, head of the Kingston Field Naturalists' Chimney Swift Project, that the artificial chimneys at Queen's are unoccupied and have never been used. I am struck powerfully by both the inaccessibility of the chimneys and the urban nature of the chimney swift for the first time, as my main mode of observation becomes craning my neck to the sky and trying to decipher one chimney from another. The reminder of swifts' secretive existence—and my own distance from them—has never felt plainer as I strain and squint skyward.

All four of the chimneys built on Queen's buildings emerged from historic sightings of chimney swifts in a variety of campus chimneys since 1928 (see Bowman). The large populations of swifts were so noteworthy that the university was a location of a large-scale swift banding initiative lasting over fifteen years and banding anywhere between 200 and 4000 chimney swifts in a given year (Greer). As of a 2012 Ontario Swiftwatch report, only one nesting/roosting chimney has been identified as active in Kingston (Bird Studies Canada). These statistics suggest just how ambivalent an attunement the Queen's chimneys urge in humans: at once a site of both mass bird bodies and a functioning heating system, they now sit empty on both counts. While various campus chimneys have been capped and then uncapped in response to preserving swift habitat over the years as the species has declined, Chris tells me that this has resulted in only a few swifts nesting on campus in any given year—an average decline of 6 percent a year. Despite the fact that all four campus chimneys were part of a large research survey that monitored the success of artificial chimneys in Canada (complete with 24-hour video cameras wired through ethernet cables), in the five years of the study, no swifts were known to nest or roost in them. Now, Chris says, the artificial chimneys are falling into disrepair and will likely be removed as the campus responds to building maintenance.

Of the four chimneys, the Fleming Hall artificial chimneys are a bit more observable, in part because at four stories the building is not that tall and in part because Fleming Hall houses a huge original gray Kingston limestone chimney, clear on the roofline, that once was responsible for coal-powering not only the Queen's campus but much of Kingston's downtown and hospitals. While the large main stack has since been decommissioned, the building still contains a large amount of boiler infrastructure in the basement, which steam-powers many nearby campus buildings. It is the artificial chimneys that sit on either side of the large round stack that contribute to a comparative sense of scale for swift habitat while showcasing the tension between visible structure and invisible appeals to swifts (see Figure 6.2).

Built in 1904, Fleming Hall burned down in a fire and was rebuilt in 1933. From 1933 to 1993, the main chimney in the building was open to roosting and nesting swifts, and the chimney was capped in 1993. Based on the advocacy of biologists and naturalists, in 2009 the chimney was uncapped, and a few swifts began to roost in it the next year (PEARL), though they have not regularly returned. When the Fleming Hall chimney was uncapped, workers found sixty years' worth—over six feet—of chimney swift guano inside. Researchers working in paleoecological environmental assessment, usually reserved for sediment core sampling of soil and rock, were quick to see the

FIGURE **6.2.** *Fleming Hall Artificial Chimneys (left and right). Note the original chimney in building's center.*

guano deposit inside Fleming Hall chimney as one with a story to tell. Each layer of guano showed a chronostratified change—a marking of time based on diet. Grooms was one of the researchers on the project, and he toured me around the bowels of Fleming Hall, warm from the boiler still encased in the basement.

What the researchers found in the sixty-year evidence of chimney swifts who returned, again and again, to this chimney, was not what I would have expected. The story that those droppings contained was a ghost story. It is an archive of the historic diet of chimney swifts, a story of insect remains. The researchers examined the guano for the remains of insects, pesticides, and carbon and nitrogen, and what they found was yet another story. Based on the concentrations of pesticides found in the guano and the amount of bug remains and beetle remains (beetles being one of the main sources of food for chimney swifts), the scientists found a major shift in the diet of the swifts between 1940 and 1950, from beetles to bugs. The increase of bugs from beetles, as well as DDT and DDE measurements in the guano samples, coincided with large scale DDT use in the late 1940s. DDT was known to have a disastrous effect on Coleoptera (beetles), yet beetles remain one of the chimney swifts' primary high-calorie value foods. While acknowledging that habitat loss and environmental stressors no doubt are in part responsible for chimney swifts' decline, the research team concluded that "their population declines are probably a product of the general decrease in relative abundance of Coleoptera from the early 1970s to 1992" (Nocera et al. 5).

This conclusion runs counter to the Committee on the Status of Endangered Wildlife in Canada's (COSEWIC) 2018 report on chimney swift nesting and roosting habitat. Yet it has been supported by other researchers of chimney swifts' decline, particularly those who have inventoried the use of urban chimneys, artificial structures, and relative populations of swifts. What has been found that runs counter to the building of the mitigations I observed is the fact that even suitable chimneys in urban areas lack swifts—there is a low occupancy rate (about 25 percent) even in the most suitable of original chimney sites (Fitzgerald 510). Other factors, such as prey decline and climate change, seem so much more at issue that it led a separate research team to "contend that the effort and expense of construction of artificial towers in southern Ontario may be better directed elsewhere" (511). In other words, those who study swift decline and artificial chimneys have declared the mitigation an epic failure.

Conservationists and governments are enamored of the artificial chimney as the hopeful "fix" of species decline, and their monumental appearance can often do the feel-good work of attachment to resolution-as-species-return. Yet the relation itself—between human and swift—continues to diminish. Such a relation suggests another, darker kind of hope, one that Berlant frames from the work of Anna Potamianou: "as a stuckness within a relation to futurity that constitutes a problematic defense against the contingencies of the present" (2011, 13). This is a kind of hope that we cannot bear creatively or hold uncertainty within; instead, it is a fantasy, a "set of dissolving assurances" (3), an ecology out of time, about the change that is not going to come.

The Fleming Hall chimney, thus, is not just a story of chimney swift decline, though it clearly offers a powerful reflection on nonhuman withdrawal from human infrastructural propositions. In close proximity to the fake chimneys built on either side that tell of the swifts' refusal, the Fleming Hall stack, through bird and insect bodies, shows us rhetorical-ecological conditions of diminishing hope and human violence. The memory of up to 4,000 birds returning yearly to this one place with the hope that they will again, filled with centimeter-by-centimeter fecal narratives of the use of human-made poison, sits side by side with empty wooden boxes still hooked up to abandoned ethernet cables. Here, at Queen's, chimney swifts have given us an archive of their own demise, of the role of pesticides on their bodies and the bodies of their prey. These three chimneys, side by side, are less openings to possibility than they are a showcase of the "difficult relations of loss and violence," as Yusoff (2012, 578) puts it. Here we are given an unfathomable scale of loss—up to 240,000 birds, millions more beetles, in a span of sixty years—seen both visibly (in the guano deposits in the large stack) and invisibly (in the absence cultivated by the swifts' non-return to any of the chimneys available when they used to return en masse).

Yet as Yusoff reminds us, *thinking with* such violence—colonial violence perpetrated by humans with the use of DDT on a range of creatures—might allow us possibilities for "more nourishing ties" (580) with the other. We cannot story the decline of the chimney swift as simply a matter of the destruction of historic urban buildings or the nebulous remembrance of long-gone old-growth forests. We must instead, as the Fleming Hall chimneys tell us, come to terms with the fact that humans' main mode of relating to the swift and its decline has been through "invisible ties that bind us to violence as a primary mode of relating" (582). It is a rhetorical-ecological lens, pairing the material and the discursive, that allows a realization of such relations. Swifts are declining not only because they don't have a place to roost, not only because of climate change, not only because their main food source has been decimated. Chimney swifts—as thousands of other plant and animal species—are declining because humans' main mode of relating to them has been, is, and continues to be, a violent one.

The Fleming Hall chimneys serve as a powerful reminder of precarity, of cruel optimism, of the once-present and now absent, and point to the complexities inherent in the failure of trying to make nonhumans visible. As Yusoff contends, a human-focused struggle for nonhuman visibility emerges "as a kind of haunting configured around a profoundly human sensibility" (585). In pointing to the possibilities for thinking with the violence inherent in such hauntings, Yusoff points again to turning our attention to "violence as part of the scene of our relations (so that we might work towards it being a less visible part of that relation)" (585). This scene of ghost birds, like that of the nuclear stack that began this chapter, is a violent one, but the violence is quiet and invisible and told through bones and sediment and isotopes and chemicals. Like the human failures lauded as successes marked by the Timothy Street Park tower, looking closely at the ways objects like these function in rhetorical ecologies provide sites for reflection about human and nonhuman relations. They show points of different temporal contact that material-discursive extinction stories hold: "seconds and microseconds," "years and decades," the "longue durée" of human history-telling "that entails a consideration of multiple centuries of trade, mobility, and colonialism," and "epochal time of thousands and millions of years" (Parreñas 8). They offer researchers ways in to thinking about what rhetoric about disappearing species really looks like in action and what interventions into these failures might reasonably look like in the Anthropocene future ahead.

Works Cited

Anderson, Ben. "Becoming and Being Hopeful: Towards a Theory of Affect." *Environment and Planning D: Society and Space*, vol. 24, no. 5, 2006, pp. 733–52.

Bastian, Michelle. "Encountering Leatherbacks in Multispecies Knots of Time." *Extinction Studies: Stories of Time, Death, and Generations*, edited by Deborah Bird Rose, et al., Columbia UP, 2017, pp. 149–86.

Berlant, Lauren. *Cruel Optimism*. Duke UP, 2011.

Bowman, R. I. "Chimney Swift Banding at Kinston, Ontario from 1928 to 1947." *The Canadian Field-Naturalist*, vol. 66, no. 6, 1952, pp. 151–64.

Braidotti, Rosi. "The Critical Posthumanities; or Is Medianatures to Naturecultures as *Zoe* Is to *Bios*?" *Cultural Politics*, vol. 12, no. 3, 2016, pp. 380–90.

———. "A Theoretical Framework for the Critical Posthumanities." *Theory, Culture & Society*, vol. 36, no. 6, 2019, pp. 31–61.

Bumelis, Kaelin. "Question about Successes of Artificial Swift Towers in Ontario." Personal communication, 2021.

"Chimney Swift Project High-Resolution Images." Paleoecological Environmental Assessment and Research Laboratory, 2012, www.queensu.ca/pearl/projects/Biovector/subprojects/swiftdiet/swiftphotos.php.

Clary-Lemon, Jennifer. "Examining Material Rhetorics of Species at Risk: Infrastructural Mitigations as Non-Human Arguments." *Enculturation: A Journal of Rhetoric, Writing, and Culture*, 10 Nov. 2020, http://enculturation.net/material_rhetorics_species_at_risk.

———. *Nestwork: New Material Rhetorics for Precarious Species*. Penn State UP, 2023.

Druschke, Caroline Gottschalk. "A Trophic Future for Rhetorical Ecologies." *Enculturation: A Journal of Rhetoric, Writing, and Culture*, 20 Feb. 2019, http://enculturation.net/a-trophic-future.

Finity, Leah, and Joseph J. Nocera. "Vocal and Visual Conspecific Cues Influence the Behavior of Chimney Swifts at Provisioned Habitat." *The Condor*, vol. 114, no. 2, 2012, pp. 323–28.

Fitzgerald, Trina M., et al. "Loss of Nesting Sites Is Not a Primary Factor Limiting Northern Chimney Swift Populations." *Population Ecology*, vol. 56, no. 3, 2014, pp. 507–12.

Gauthier, Jean, et al. *COSEWIC Assessment and Status Report on the Chimney Swift Chaetura pelagica in Canada.* Committee on the Status of Endangered Wildlife in Canada, 2007.

Graves, Gary R. "Avian Commensals in Colonial America: When did *Chaetura pelagica* Become the Chimney Swift?" *Archives of Natural History*, vol. 31, no. 2, 2004, pp. 300–307.

Greer, Kirsten. "Chimney Swifts Return to Queen's University." *Network in Canadian History & Environment*, 9 Apr. 2010. https://niche-canada.org/2010/04/09/chimney-swifts-return-to-queens-university/.

Hines, Richard E., et al. "Chimney Swifts (*Chaetura pelagica*) Nest in Tree Cavities in Arkansas." *Southeastern Naturalist*, vol. 12, no. 4, 2013, pp. N18–20.

Jones, Madison. "A Counterhistory of Rhetorical Ecologies." *Rhetoric Society Quarterly*, vol. 51, no. 4, 2021, pp. 336–52.

Kyle, Paul D., and Georgean Z. Kyle. *Chimney Swifts: America's Mysterious Birds above the Fireplace.* Texas A&M UP, 2005.

Macdonald, Helen. *H Is for Hawk.* Penguin, 2016.

Marcel, Gabriel. *Being and Having: An Existentialist Diary.* Harper & Row, 1965.

McGreavy, Bridie, et al., editors. *Tracing Rhetoric and Material Life: Ecological Approaches.* Palgrave Macmillan, 2017.

Nocera, Joseph, et al. "Historical Pesticide Applications Coincided with an Altered Diet of Aerially Foraging Insectivorous Chimney Swifts." *Proceedings of the Royal Society B*, vol. 279, no. 1740, 2012, pp. 1–7.

Ontario Swiftwatch: 2012 Summary Report. Bird Studies Canada, 2013. https://www.birdscanada.org/download/CHSWONReport.pdf.

Parreñas, Juno Salazar. *Decolonizing Extinction: The Work of Care in Orangutan Rehabilitation.* Duke UP, 2018.

Randall, Rosemary. "Loss and Climate Change: The Cost of Parallel Narratives." *Ecopsychology*, vol. 1, no. 3, 2009, pp. 118–29.

Richardson, Kristyn, et al. *COSEWIC Assessment and Status Report on the Chimney Swift (Chaetura pelagica) in Canada 2018*. Committee on the Status of Endangered Wildlife in Canada, 2018.

Stewart, John. "One Man's Struggle to Save the Chimney Swifts." *Mississauga.com*, 2015, www.mississauga.com/blogs/post/5474395-one-man-s-struggle-to-save-the-chimney-swifts/.

Sutton, Jane S., and Mari Lee Mifsud. "Towards an Alloiostrophic Rhetoric." *Advances in the History of Rhetoric*, vol. 15, no. 2, 2012, pp. 222–33.

Yusoff, Kathryn. "Aesthetics of Loss: Biodiversity, Banal Violence and Biotic Subjects." *Transactions of the Institute of British Geographers*, vol. 37, no. 4, 2012, pp. 578–92.

CHAPTER SEVEN

Toward Critical Ecological Methodologies: Stories and Praxes of Transformation in a Writing Program

CANDICE RAI, ANSELMA WIDHA PRIHANDITA,
AND NOLIE RAMSEY

To teach writing or to lead a writing program in a US university is to be entangled within ecologies that sustain racial violence, exclusionary language ideologies, and systemic inequities that perpetuate harm and often in the names of access, rigor, excellence, and the public good. It is to participate in reproducing the myriad ways, as Prendergast asserts, that "literacy has been managed and controlled . . . to rationalize and ensure White domination" (21); it is to contribute to the "ubiquity of structural racism" (4), as Condon and Young put it, that persists in our writing classrooms and programs. Given the pervasiveness of linguistic and racial injustice within university ecologies, this chapter asks: *What is required to envision and create long-term transformation toward equity and social justice within our writing program and broader university ecologies? What kinds of capacities, labor, practices, tools, and ethical relations must be developed to imagine, do, and sustain this work?*

Our chapter engages these concerns by articulating a *critical ecological methodology* for engaging in transformation labors within writing programs and other ecologies. As rhetorical-ecological perspectives emphasize, university (and all other) ecologies are sustained through the radically complex, pluralistic, dynamic, and tangled coming together of everyone and thing within an ecology. The reproduction of everyday institutional life is activated and reinforced at all levels, in all places, through every utterance and every mundane process and genre kept in motion, from the most intimate and personal interior inklings and lived experiences to the broadest structural participation in political and economic systems, in ways known and unknown, and too often through habit alone. This is all a way to say that our opening questions point toward ecological problems that require ecological, place-based capacities and responses.

In valuing story as a vital way to illuminate the complexities of and possibilities for doing place-based, transformational equity work, we draw inspiration from scholars like Jones, Moore, and Walton, who engage in "antenarrative" as a poly-vocal, fragmented, storytelling and sense-making practice that "seeks to destabilize and unravel aspects of the tightly woven dominant narrative" (2). Reflecting on and disrupting dominant narratives and histories through story can, they argue, open up space for the "working out of actionable knowledge" and can enable "different possibilities for the future" (2). Our chapter is grounded within stories that trace histories of and ongoing shifts (to program practices, policy, curricula, etc.) within a writing partnership (later discussed as our "stretch" composition program) designed to support first-generation, poverty-impacted, and BIPOC students as they navigate issues of equity and access at the University of Washington, a predominantly white institution. We trace our efforts through stories that draw on our experiences as writing program administrators and teachers and from qualitative research involving students, instructors, campus partners, and program archives.

Our stretch composition program, and the ecology of campus stakeholders supporting it, has continually served as a contested site for negotiating what access and what social, linguistic, and racial justice might mean in light of the ongoing legacies of discriminatory language ideologies and intersectional inequities endemic within our university and broader society. While our stories document some of our efforts to create large-scale transformation in our writing program ecology and to create more just and equitable learning environments, these stories equally demonstrate how the labors involved in transforming ecologies are intentional but often incremental, mundane, fleeting, and complicit. Most broadly, we hope our chapter will open up possibilities for others interested in engaging in equity-oriented institutional transformation.

On Rhetorical Ecologies
and Critical Ecological Methodologies

The "ecological turn" in writing and rhetorical studies brings attention to the radically diverse, complex, interconnected, dynamic, emplaced, contested, and situational nature of language and meaning making. Rhetorical-ecological orientations expand our understanding of rhetoric and attune us to the entangled constellations of language, materiality, living beings, ideologies, and all manner else that circulate within and shape everyday life. Edbauer's well-known conception of rhetorical ecologies foregrounds interrelation and fluidity wherein the "elements of the rhetorical situation simply bleed" and rhetoric is perceived as a "circulating ecology of effects, enactments, and event" (9). River and Weber conceive "rhetorical action" as "emergent and enacted through a complex ecology of texts, writers, readers, institutions, objects, and history" (188), and Dobrin highlights the complexities of writing as "so diverse and divergent" that it is impossible to "account for all the facets and functions of writing" within an ecology (143). Within ecological perspectives, agency is dispersed among and across all of the elements within an ecology, albeit unevenly, inequitably, and dynamically. Here, rhetoric is *not* conceived reductively (e.g., as static persuasive texts awaiting analysis) nor pejoratively (e.g., as specious language, empty sound bites, political B.S.), though it can include all these things.

Rather, rhetoric is a capacity for attuning to and acting within the constellations of meaning and agencies present and circulating within the world (Rickert). Rhetorical capacities, from an ecological perspective, can be imagined as something honed and practiced by individuals, yes, but it also points to environmental, system-wide capacities within an ecology/ institution/community that include but are beyond any one person or thing. In this way, rhetoric is fundamentally ontological, as Barnett and Boyle argue, in the sense that rhetoric is not just a "knowledge-making praxis" but also "constitutes ways of being and ways of being-with-others-in-the world" (9). For us, these insights mean that we don't just ask how we can revise this or that policy or craft this or that assignment to be more equitable (though we do that, too). Rather, we wonder: given the pervasiveness of systemic violence here, which we all participate in reproducing, how can we tilt the dynamics in this ecology to make it more likely that equity work will be sustained, discussed, critiqued, breathed to life anew, dynamically and creatively, by the people present over time but also beyond the people, on the level of institutional and ecological habits and structures beyond? It is to say, again, that if we face ecological problems (and we do), then we need ecological capacities, responses, and ethics.

Recognizing writing programs as "discursive and material ecologies" (4), Reiff et al. identify four "ecological attributes" of writing programs: interconnectedness, fluctuation, complexity, and emergence (9). While we agree that writing program ecologies are marked by complex and dynamic interrelationships of people, things, genres, discourses, and material conditions, the persistence of linguistic racism in our universities and broader culture illuminates how ecological attributes also include resistance, impasse, habits, and sustained, structural violence. As Megan Eatman argues, rhetorical ecologies are never "blank spaces" in which all "can move with ease"; rather, ecologies always "allow some groups to flourish, others to die, and many to struggle in a liminal space" (9). Eatman's critique of our field's fixation on mobility, flow, and dynamism in its uptake of rhetorical ecology is crucial. Centering power and structures of harm, she asks us to pay attention to "constraints on who and what can circulate" (11, fn12) and to the "cumulative effects of circulating violence, including how that circulation reinforces existing structures of power" (11). Eatman asks, how does "power inher[e] in everyday practices" and become "reinforced at multiple levels and through varied systems" (11)?

In writing program ecologies, these ideas translate to questions, such as: *How does linguistic racism and other oppressive logics inhere within our pedagogies, curricula, and teacher development initiatives and within our program practices? Given their pervasiveness at all levels, how do we begin to disrupt these logics and structures within our writing program?* How might our language policies and writing curricula better invite and sustain the knowledges and discourses from our students' lives so that they might circulate within and as a vital part of the university's knowledge production? Given the complexities of university and writing program ecologies and the all-encompassing ways that racism, colonial, and other harmful logics are reproduced through literacy education, any response to these questions requires ecological ways of thinking and acting. To perceive writing programs ecologically, we must view them as "more than collections of shifting, circulating elements," as Eatman puts it; rhetorical ecologies "also produce moods, dispositions, orientations toward people and the surrounding environment" that "have (and are) cumulative effects," which is "one way of understanding the cooperation of direct, structural, and cultural violence. Each is more than the sum of its parts because, through continued circulation, these forms of violence are world-making" (13).

Recent critiques by Jennifer Clary-Lemon, Louis M. Maraj, and others also call out the problematic tendency of some rhetorical-ecological scholarship to overlook important work by Indigenous, Black, and feminist scholars (Ahmed, Kimmerer, Sharpe, Tuck and McKenzie, and others) who offer ecological, place-based perspectives that foreground ethical and relational world-making practices and that resist, interrupt, and seek to transform Western, racial capitalist, and settler colonial orders. Building on this work, we forward a *critical ecological methodology* that centers questions of equity—and that encourages the ongoing collaborative work necessary to understand, disrupt, and transform harmful logics and structures reproduced within our writing program (or any other) ecology. Transformational equity work from a critical ecological perspective requires us to recognize, as Sara Ahmed puts it, that institutional ecologies develop "habits" over time that continuously replicate certain norms, structures, and logics and "assume certain bodies," spaces, and rhythms (*Willful* 146–47). While these habits are "not empty of intent or purpose," they do become naturalized and keep replicating throughout the ecology, in part, because they require little energy or attention (146). For example, later you'll hear an illustrative story about how a simple, mundane form replicated problematic habits of exclusion in our writing program for decades. Such habits of exclusion, animated through ordinary institutional genres, work to further erase already marginalized knowledges and subjectivities. Yet institutions proliferate such seemingly innocuous genres (and practices, attitudes, policies, criteria, and discourses) and through these, institutional habits are replicated in diffuse, pervasive, decentered, often ownerless and invisible ways, every day, everywhere, by everyone and thing.

Critical rhetorical-ecological perspectives help us conceive how these replications emerge from the dynamic and shifting yet habituated coming together of relationships, structures, rhetorics, knowledges, and practices over time. While institutionalized habits are necessary to sustain any community or collaborative effort and thus are not inherently problematic, the trouble arises when forms of structural violence are reproduced through habituated and largely invisible constellations. Critical ecological methodologies, as we discuss here, prompt ongoing, often modest, labor to make more visible, disrupt, and transform the "forms of violence" circulating with an ecology. Our work is also informed by Max Liboiron's anticolonial science research. Writing of orientations that might guide anticolonial, antiracist work, they argue that "[o]rientations [. . .] come out of obligations" and relationships (155), but ones that are never free from complicity (such untainted space, after all, is the dream of the colonist). To have an orientation "mean[s] that you are facing a particular direction with a specific horizon of possible action before you"— orientations are the "condition of possibility for some futures and not others" (155). Liboiron's wisdom about co-laboring toward collective orientations that are never fully reached but that "condition the possibility" for a future that might be otherwise is a helpful reminder that the ethical orientations guiding our work must emerge from existing spaces, relationships, and investments (which, again, is what makes this work necessarily place-based).

Critical ecological methodologies, then, offer an analytic and praxes for helping us better understand and transform complex rhetorical ecologies. Critical ecological methodologies prompt us to:

◆ understand all forms of communication, meaning making, and lifeways as always, already ecological, which means that our forms of response to and ethical orientations for addressing urgent problems must also be ecological;

◆ conceive ecologies as complex entanglements that are the dynamic, fluid, pluralistic, fragmented, emergent, and highly situated comings together of people, rhetorics, economic/historical/ sociopolitical contexts, ideologies, materialities, embodied knowledges, more- and other-than-human epistemologies and beings, and all manner else within a place;

◆ recognize that ecologies reinscribe habituated structures of violence and uneven conditions of survival in ways that are pervasive/climatological, which urges us to imagine ways to listen across difference, to resist easy solutions, to sit with/in ambivalence, incommensurability, multiplicity, and complicity;

◆ foreground questions of equity and justice (the content of which is always emergent, unstable, contested, negotiated) while actively working to resist and transform the logics of racial capitalism, settler colonialism, and other harmful systems and to co-labor toward a future that might be otherwise (more equitable, just, ethical, inclusive, sustainable) and one that we may never see/ can never be fully realized;

◆ accept that whatever we build or do toward social justice (no matter the care we practice) will harm someone or something, which is to say that we must be reflexive, practice humility, remain open to learning and change;

◆ create and nurture ecological agencies, capacities, and ethical orientations toward a more equitable and inclusive life in common; and

◆ attend to time, temporality, and embodiment by sitting with the ongoing-ness of ecological transformation work, which means sometimes slowing our rhythms, tapping out, attending to our and others' bodies, imaginations, and well-being; by remembering to love and be joyful; and by opening space for reflecting on and taking stock of our efforts.

A critical ecological methodology doesn't point toward a method one unrolls with neat steps to follow. Rather, it is an ongoing praxes and disposition, an ethical orientation that prompts inquiry and raises critical questions one might use to engage in transformational co-laboring in their own local ecologies. In our case, critical ecological methodologies help us better understand and transform the conditions that reproduce racial and linguistic inequity within our writing program. In our context, this has meant creating program statements and spaces for professional development, revising curriculum, and interrogating program discourses and practices to better orient toward our equity goals. In the following sections, we offer stories about modest transformations within our stretch composition and broader writing program ecology.

Rhetorical Ecologies and Critical Ecological Praxes in a Stretch Composition Program

Our stretch composition program is a micro-ecology within the Program for Writing and Rhetoric (PWR) at the University of Washington-Seattle (UW), a large primarily first-year writing program with a teaching staff of 75+ that supports 5000+ writing students annually. In most "stretch" writing programs, students take two or more courses that target the same learning outcomes as the general required university composition course(s) only "stretched" over more courses. According to Glau, stretch courses are generally for writers whose test scores or other indicators suggest they could "use more time and more directed writing experience [and . . .] more feedback" (31–2). Because stretch courses overwhelmingly serve multiple marginalized students, they are positioned within a complex institutional ecology and tend to reveal the fault lines of a university's claims to access and equity, to say the least here.

While it is well documented that stretch courses can increase student retention, learning, and sense of belonging (Glau; Peele), they also play an ambivalent role in centering dominant English and white cultural/linguistic norms as the key to university access and success. Reinforcing linguistic norms in this way, as Inoue argues, creates a "white racial habitus" that excludes and penalizes the "discourses of many students of color, working class students, and multilingual students" (17). This puts the onus on historically marginalized students to acclimate to institutional language norms rather than question the ways we need to transform university ecologies to be more inclusive, equitable, anticolonial, and antiracist (Guerra; Rendón, Jalomo, and Nora). Paris and Alim, for example, critique "White-gaze-centered" notions of access that fixate on changing students' language practices ("How can 'we' get 'these' working-class kids of color to speak/write/be more like middle-class White ones?") and not on changing oppressive educational ecologies (How might we "critique the White gaze itself that sees, hears, and frames students in everywhichway as marginal and deficient?") (3). In sum, discourses of remediation and monolingual ideologies are problematically commonplace in stretch composition ecologies. Like Davila and Elder, we advocate a model that is "dedicated to valuing linguistic diversity" and resisting practices of remediation (par. 23).

Our stretch courses (English 109/110) are part of a longstanding campus partnership that includes the PWR, the Education Opportunity Program (EOP), Student-Athlete Academic Services (SAAS), advisors, writing centers, students, and instructors. This partnership, which serves around two hundred students annually, has played a vital role of providing language support and advocacy for new students most at risk of leaving the university and who often experience various precarities, such as housing and food insecurity, health issues, and other safety concerns. The history of our program is especially tethered to the EOP, established in 1971 as a division of the Office of Minority Affairs & Diversity, to promote "academic success and graduation for under-represented ethnic minority, economically disadvantaged, and first-generation college students." Our stretch program, one of the oldest in the nation, emerged from an experimental basic-writing program established in 1968 and, from what we can gather, we began partnering with EOP near its inception. It's worth remembering 1968 as a significant year in the Civil Rights Movement—MLK was assassinated, the Fair Housing Act was signed, and student-led movements erupted at universities nationwide, urgently demanding social justice for poverty-impacted, Black, Indigenous, Latinx, and other marginalized peoples. EOP was created in response to these exigencies and local protests led by UW students and faculty. During these earlier years of our stretch partnership, the vast majority of UW's BIPOC students joined the university through EOP. Between

1978 and 1984, approximately 73–80 percent of UW's Black, Indigenous, and Latinx students were "special admits" through the EOP ("Registrar"), many of whom were placed in our stretch courses to increase academic access and success, in which literacy "proficiency" has figured as a longstanding, vexed linchpin.

For example, our archival research of program letters and documents from 1985[1] revealed familiar tensions around the gatekeeping role of literacy for historically marginalized students seeking to access the university. The letters were written in the context of a three-year+ "battle" to determine whether our stretch sequence was equivalent to the "so-called regular" writing classes. One letter, written by a UW dean, articulated the courses as "remedial" and designed to "remediate deficiencies" of EOP students who "lack adequate preparation for university-level study"—this definition, if accepted, meant the students would need to pay for and complete both stretch courses *before* taking the "regular" required writing classes. In response, the EOP faculty coordinator at the time, our field's own Victor Villanueva, counterargued that the courses should fulfill the composition credit because they were "designed for minority students [. . .] to meet or surpass the standards of so-called regular classes" and to provide "intensive academic writing practice in a coherent, ethnically sensitive curriculum" (Villanueva et al., Letter to Charles Schuster, 1985). This heated exchange reflects the still pervasive contests around language ideology that are unlikely to surprise anyone reading this. The successful outcome of this exchange (and one that we inherited) was that the stretch sequence would indeed fulfill the UW composition requirement.

Returning to our own efforts, beginning in 2018, PWR leadership (along with stakeholders in EOP and SAAS)[2], have actively worked to reconceive these stretch courses alongside program-wide equity work. These initiatives are guided by commitments that we articulated in our "Statement of Antiracist Pedagogy and Program Praxis[3]," which are underscored by translingual, antiracist, anticolonial, and feminist approaches. For example, in the statement, we articulate "[a]ntiracist pedagogical frameworks [. . . as] intersectional, which means that they center different forms of intersecting marginalizations as well as the power relations among race, class, gender, and other social, political, and cultural identities and experiences that may manifest in texts that we read and write, in students' and teachers' experiences, and in classrooms as well as broader social dynamics" ("PWR"). The statement advocates for pedagogy and assessment that foregrounds students "language choices and rhetorical effectiveness based on the writing occasion, genre, purpose, and audience rather than strictly on monolingual and dominant academic English norms and standards of correctness" and that "integrate[s] language justice work as part of writing courses in which we examine how systemic racism is often encoded in practices that uphold academic language or Standard English" ("PWR").

While we initially set out to focus on revising our curriculum to better align with these commitments, the interconnected nature of the transformations we were aiming for required a more ecological perspective, and we began laying the foundation to revise teacher training, program processes and documents, larger program structures and minutiae alike. To inform our work, we interviewed instructors, students, and administrators to learn more about peoples' experiences, assumptions, and understanding of our stretch partnership and courses. We quickly found ourselves caught within complex contradictions and entrenched monolingual language ideologies—including those we were circulating ourselves in our writing program ecology, despite decades of advocacy to the contrary. For example, interviews revealed that our stretch classes were still perceived by many students, most advisors, and some instructors as offering remedial language support that both advisors and students referenced as "slower," more "basic," or for writers who "needed more writing help" to "strengthen [Standard Academic] English."

One small but significant change we made was updating the course title, catalog descriptions, and requirements to align with our commitments. In addition to the redescription of the course, we advocated for English 109 to fulfill both the "W" (writing) and "DIV" (diversity) requirements and the "C" (composition) upon completion of both courses. Prior to this, students paid for and completed both and only received the "C" credit. As long as students had to take two courses that only counted for one requirement, it was hard to get out from under the sense that the course was remedial. Contrary to this perception, our own sense was that the stretch courses—which had lower enrollment caps, more institutional support, twice as much class time, and an explicit focus on critical language practices and public, transmodal writing—should be imagined as the gold standard of what our "regular" courses could only aspire toward. Moreover, students stressed the financial hardship of taking two rather than one course, even as they appreciated the community, curriculum, and instruction. In sum, these changes aimed to materially support students in their progress to degree; foreground critical aspects required of DIV classes; and center commitments to linguistic justice and culturally sustaining pedagogies.

Below, we share the spare original stretch course description used from 1977–2021 followed by the revised title and descriptions. The revisions reflect the antiracist, translingual orientations driving our program transformations, which insists that language difference is both the norm and also tied to power and uneven material conditions and, thus, our approaches must be "grounded in an antiracist critique of structural inequity and a decentering and decolonizing of normalized, White-supremacist, racist institutional structures, practices, and pedagogies" (Thu et al. 196–97). Echoes of other program commitments compressed in the course description include valuing writing as social action and as ethical communication across difference that draws on feminist theories of listening and collaboration (Ratcliffe); Indigenous and anticolonial work that foregrounds relational ethics tied to language, culture, materiality, and place (Haas, Kimmerer, Powell, Tuck and Mackenzie); and translingual, antiracist, and cultural sustaining pedagogical approaches (Baker-Bell, Guerra, Inoue, Matsuda, Paris and Alim, Thu et al.).

Original Course Descriptions

ENGL 109 Introductory Composition

Development of writing skills: sentence strategies and paragraph structures. Expository, critical, and persuasive essay techniques based on analysis of selected readings.

Revised in 2020–2021 to center commitments to culturally
sustaining pedagogies, linguistic and racial justice, and ethical
communication[4]

ENGL 109—Critical Composition I: Inquiry
This course understands writing as social action and language
as tied to identity, culture, and power. Centering students'
diverse language resources, knowledges, and goals, this course
builds rhetorical capacities and skills for composing ethically,
critically, and impactfully across different contexts, audiences,
and genres within and beyond the university. This is the first
course in a two-quarter sequence that fulfills the "C," "DIV,"
and "W" requirements.

This section outlined only a few stories of transformation
within our writing program ecology. While these changes—from
revising the curricula and course descriptions to overhauling
everyday program documents—may seem mundane, we stress
that transforming institutions entails working at all levels, in
all places, and on all things within the ecology, including, most
especially, working in the land of minutia.

In the following sections, we offer more stories of
transformation in our writing program, foregrounded by
translingual, antiracist, anticolonial, and culturally sustaining
approaches. These vignettes document changes to teacher
development and trace the institutional work of a humble genre
(the fifth-week report). These stories model critical ecological
methodologies in action and offer instances of micro-level changes
that build ecological capacities within and across our program
(and at various levels) for collective transformation work.

Reorienting the Orientation: Antiracist and Culturally Sustaining Writing Pedagogy in the Eurocentric University[5]

The university, as Cupples and Grosfoguel argue, is a "site where
learning and the production, acquisition and dissemination of
knowledge are embedded in Eurocentric epistemologies that are
posited as objective, disembodied and universal and in which
non-Eurocentric knowledges such as black and indigenous

knowledges are largely ignored, marginalized or dismissed" (2). What does it mean to grant "access" to the university for marginalized students, when the university itself reproduces white supremacist logics, Eurocentric norms, and monolingual ideologies that are linguistically and racially discriminative? Accessing the university—while beneficial and sometimes even life-saving—can also mean, especially for marginalized students, leaving parts of themselves behind that do not mesh well with the university's white Western norms as a precondition for entry and a requirement for success. As Guerra reminds us, "our bodies often find themselves in worlds not designed for them, especially when they are worlds that foreclose and block our language, culture, and, at times, our entire way of being. Under such circumstances, we may well want to call on [. . .] culturally sustaining pedagogies to provide our students with the tools they need to respond proactively to [. . .] conditions designed to dismiss them so that their bodies may, in turn, feel more at home in the world" (37).

We recognized that courses like English 109/110, which aim to grant "access to the university" for historically marginalized students, should *also* have an official and explicit agenda to scrutinize the conditions and cost of access. While our program builds on longstanding equity work and had already been working to center antiracist, translingual approaches, we experience(d) contradictory and harmful practices everywhere, and ongoing work remains to embed these ideas throughout our writing program ecology and to resist the assimilative dynamics that come with accessing the university. This is why we felt it necessary to *actively* enact culturally sustaining pedagogy, which, quoting Paris, seeks to "sustain—linguistic, literate, and cultural pluralism as part of the democratic project of schooling" (96).

I (Anselma) grapple with this problem as a teacher and administrator in our stretch partnership. When I first attended the instructor orientation in 2019, the role of stretch courses in accessing the university and providing students with a community of support was still heavily emphasized. Since then, we have redesigned our teacher orientation to emphasize culturally sustaining, antiracist pedagogies, and we explicitly reframed the courses as a space for students to think critically about the university and negotiate their place in it as historically marginalized students. In this section, I outline our writing program's strategies for enacting culturally sustaining pedagogy in our stretch program teacher orientation. First, both teachers and students need to denaturalize and critique the norms of the university so that whiteness, heteropatriarchy, capitalism, ableism, and other forms of structural inequity and oppression are not taken for granted as "normal" or as standards of excellence. Only after these norms are destabilized can we make room for linguistic practices and epistemologies that are historically marginalized and invalidated. Second, the teachers, classroom, and curriculum must be designed to actively tap into and sustain students' linguistic and cultural lifeways. One way this can be done, as I detail later, is through personal writing that invites students to connect with their own cultures and interests and draws on their diverse linguistic resources. Such writing also fosters students' confidence, because, too often, marginalized students have been told that their knowledges, experiences, and cultural and linguistic resources are less-than.

We introduced these strategies into the instructor orientation for our stretch courses in 2020. We substantially revised the orientation to align with and enact some of the commitments in our PWR Antiracist Praxes Statement through: (1) explicit discussions that question the university and how its Eurocentrism, racism, and coloniality structure teaching and learning and (2) encouraging the development of culturally sustaining and critical curricula. In thinking about critical ecological methodologies for transformation, we saw every document, professional development, interaction, and assignment as an opportunity for shifting the writing program ecology and building individual and system-wide capacities for more equity-oriented learning environments. The changes we made in our course orientation were attempts to allow the kinds of capacities, labors, knowledges, practices, and relationships necessary for antiracist work to circulate more explicitly within our writing program, while previously they might not have been as salient a part of our institutional ecology.

While only one node in the ecology, professional teacher development plays an important role because it establishes a foundation for supporting teachers in centering antiracist praxes and cultural sustainment, directly impacts on student learning, and facilitates capacities for equity-oriented work within the teaching community as more sample syllabi are created, workshops designed, and conversations supported. Beginning with the 2020 orientation, new and returning instructors gathered to discuss texts like Grande's "Refusing the University," Garcia and Baca's *Rhetorics Elsewhere and Otherwise*, Inoue's *Antiracist Writing Assessment Ecologies*, Ruiz and Baca's "Decolonial Options in Writing Studies," and Young's "The Indispensable Role of Critical Race Theory in Teaching Writing." We hoped these conversations on antiracist and anticolonial pedagogies would create ongoing space for instructors to think more critically about their pedagogies and invite such critical discourses into our program's ecology with the aims of disrupting dominant language ideologies and racially neutral writing instruction.

Building on this work, the 2021 orientation included a redesigned workshop space for instructors to grapple with the following questions:

- How have you and your fellow instructors taken up pedagogies that interrogate power and center diversity?

- In light of the readings we have discussed, how are you understanding antiracist and anticolonial teaching and your commitments to this teaching? What challenges are you facing in (re)designing your curriculum with these ideas and commitments in mind?

- How are you enacting these commitments in your curricula? Is there anything you might revise or would like to change in the future?

The session ended with a reflective freewriting exercise in which instructors summarized their orientations to and practices of antiracist and equity-oriented praxis and their future plans.

Furthering the shared commitments in our program's antiracist praxes statement, we also encouraged instructors to craft their curricula and praxes to challenge the Eurocentric university and deepen into culturally sustaining pedagogies, which we engaged through a two-layered strategy. First, we denaturalize the hegemonic norms and standards of excellence, disrupting the circulation of ideas and habits that affirm the white Western hegemony within the academy. Then, we invite marginalized knowledges and traditions into the classroom—both by including diverse scholarship and by inviting students to bring their own cultures, resources, and experiences—all of which, we feel, are crucial moves in disrupting dominant language ideologies in our writing program and in our university, more broadly. To facilitate this shift, I designed model syllabi for English 109/110 that intentionally questioned norms of whiteness and imagined a more inclusive learning environment that tapped into students' lived experiences and linguistic resources. Overall, the syllabi encouraged instructors to interrogate the politics of epistemology in the academia, work against the deficit framing that monolingual language ideologies construct about marginalized students, invite students' and diverse experiences into the classroom, and practice writing as social action. The syllabi included readings that disrupted hegemonic valuing of Standard Academic English (including Baker Bell, et al. and Flores and Rosa); critiqued the university's involvement in epistemic colonization and racism (e.g., Cupples and Grosfoguel); and centered diverse knowledge-making traditions (e.g., Simpson; Noe).

The writing assignments include weekly journal entries, in which students are invited to reflect on their educational experiences and any frictions that arise, and a rhetorical analysis of how authors framed their research while negotiating academic genre conventions and their own personal styles, experiences, and needs. Students also wrote positionality statements, literature reviews, and research proposals with questions informed by their own lived experiences, concerns about their communities, and scholarly conversations on their chosen topics (see Appendix for assignment excerpts). One assignment sequence features an autoethnographic research project[6] that invites students' experiences, cultures, interests, and concerns into the classroom, taking them up as valid research topics that offer valuable insights instead of bracketing them as not belonging in "standard, proper, objective" academic discourse.

The design of the writing assignments was particularly significant in our attempt to shift the ecology enacted through the kinds of writing we assigned in our classrooms. Writing included *both* traditional academic genres of power *and* genres that invite the personal and communal. As an act of culturally sustaining pedagogical practice, we believe students should be given the opportunity to experiment with academic genres of power—such as the research paper—and modify and mix them to also include subjectivities, genres, languages, and audiences that are traditionally excluded from academic knowledge-making. And so, these generic interventions can be seen as interruptions in the institutional and cultural knowledge-making habits instilled by traditional academic genres—every modification and mixing is an attempt to invite into the academic ecology those forms of knowledges and subjectivities usually marginalized in the university. At the same time, centering personal experiences fosters cultural sustainment by encouraging students to draw on their own linguistic and cultural resources as well as affirming the students' cultures and experiences by signaling that they offer valuable knowledge.

Some things I've mentioned here might seem basic, nothing new. But just as merely writing diversity or antiracist statements does not immediately relieve material oppressions of minoritized populations, we think these efforts are still important ways to work toward our commitments. Reading more materials on antiracism does not immediately make people antiracist, but structuring time for ongoing conversation and mutual learning sends a signal that this *is* indeed something urgent that must be prioritized, and it also helps build individual and ecological capacities for engaging in ongoing antiracist and equity-oriented praxes within our teaching community. While simply inviting students to bring their cultural and linguistic knowledges and lived experiences into the classroom does not immediately undo centuries of systemic erasure, it is one small step toward a sustained critique of power and toward more inclusive learning spaces.

After shifting our teaching orientations to emphasize antiracist and culturally sustaining pedagogies, we noticed that our instructors' course designs focused more on linguistic and racial justice and took a critical stance on standard language norms. While writing skills—such as summarizing, intertextuality, and rhetorical analysis—are still taught, they are taught in a way that

SOCIAL AND ECOLOGICAL JUSTICE

is interwoven with explicit discussions on broader power relations in writing practice and scholarship. Instructors have been eager to include materials from non-Western rhetorical and knowledge traditions, such as Indigenous and South American rhetorics. Rather than teaching writing, rhetoric, and research in apolitical ways or defaulting to uncritical centering of Standard Academic English and its genres of power, we have made deliberate attempts to include critical discussions on social justice issues and to model other ways of writing and languaging.

These curricular shifts and the way they center issues of power and diversity do seem to have a positive impact on the students, especially in fostering self-affirmation, self-acceptance, confidence, and resistance against oppression—things that work to ameliorate the effects of non-belonging and deficiency that the predominantly white, Eurocentric, colonial university often promotes, especially for historically marginalized students. In an interview[7], a student who completed our stretch sequence told us how course readings, such as Anzaldúa's "How to Tame a Wild Tongue," had powerfully connected with them and encouraged them to embrace their "true self and identity," something that was very important for them in light of their identity "as a minority in almost every way possible," a lesson that they would "remember and act upon when the majority decides to try and smother [them]." Another student remarked on how learning about writing and epistemologies from other knowledge traditions (in this case, from Indigenous Native American knowledges) was "validating" because it demonstrated that "intelligence has different definitions" and that learning can be "so vastly different from what [they] had spent most of [their] life conforming to."

While these changes are promising, the work to enact antiracist and culturally sustaining pedagogy is ongoing. This section details only a few shifts in our writing program ecology, but we hope it models how a critical ecological methodology encourages constant revision, interrogation, and intentional changes that accumulate over time in significant ways. Next, we offer another small window into how mundane shifts within our ecology can be meaningful by tracing the work of a humble form.

Reform and Forms: Attending to the Small and Mundane in Writing Program Ecologies[8]

We now turn our focus to a form that was used in our stretch composition courses for decades to consider how institutional minutiae can reproduce and sustain institutionalized racism within an ecology. Critical ecological approaches prompt us to take note of the mundane objects and texts that we create, inherit, and use in institutions and to see even a simple form as a potential site of harm and opportunity for transformation.

In bolded, size 14, Times New Roman font, the title is unassuming but clearly demarcated: "Fifth-Week Progress Report."

Fifth-Week Progress Report

Attention instructors: please complete this form for all of your students.

Date:	
Course #:	
Section:	
Instructor Name:	
Instructor Email:	
Student Name:	
Student UWID #:	
Student Advisor:	
Student Program (EOP or SAAS):	

A brief note about the student's performance:

Attendance:	
Participation:	
Quality of Work:	
Timeliness (meeting deadlines):	
Other Comments or Concerns:	
The instructor requests contact with the counselor? (yes or no):	

FIGURE 7.1. *Fifth-Week Progress Report.*

This is a perfectly ordinary form, politely (but firmly) telling instructors to provide information about students enrolled in their classes. Ordinary, really. Ahmed illuminates how ordinariness matters and demonstrates that objects are never free of the politics present in their construction or everyday uses. For Ahmed, objects "function as orientation devices" ("Orientations" 235). A table is far more than a table when linked to the history of invisible labor and the politics of women's housework, especially Black and working-class women (253). Just as a table is never just a table, a form is never just a form.

As an assistant director supporting our stretch program, not only had I (Nolie) personally filled out the "Fifth Week" form for my own students, but I also trained others to do so in my administrative role. Many of us found the form troublesome because of the way it prompted us to record and circulate students' "performance" to counselors and other program stakeholders. This form raised questions:

> What kinds of relationships, benefits, and harms are created by this form or from the activities it organizes and the values it upholds/dismisses?
>
> What exactly should be reported under "Other Comments and Concerns"? Should I mention that a student fell asleep in class or lacks adequate access to technology? Should concerns about students' food insecurity or personal safety go here?
>
> What do counselors do with this form once they read it? Do the well-meaning intentions of the form outweigh the possibility of violating students' privacy? Is there a better way to create support that doesn't bypass student agency?
>
> What does it mean that we only report on students in this program (e.g., first-generation students of color, economically impacted students)? Are we reproducing racist and classists attitudes and practices, like paternalism or surveillance?

The form did not make room for questions like these. By their nature, forms prompt and shape certain responses and relationships. Inherited texts contain residue of the ideologies and desires of the wider ecologies they circulate within; long after a genre is created and after all have forgotten its history and original function, genres continue orienting institutional practices. LeMesurier's examination of genre uptake and its capacity to circulate and shore up tacit racisms within an ecology is apt: "To realize how genre uptake can perpetuate tacitly coded racist behavior across contexts is to realize the limits of personal intention as a guard against racist ideologies" (20). Despite our best intentions and through our own participation in using ordinary genres, we may find ourselves perpetuating the recirculation of systemic power within the institutions in which we find ourselves.

As discussed earlier, as part of our transformation work, we started reviewing all of our program processes, practices, and documents. When we came around to questioning the function and origin of this form, no one in our writing program ecology had a clue as to its origin. *Isn't it yours? No, we thought it was yours? Nope. Hmmm. . . .* In fact, it wasn't until we began reading through program archives from nearly thirty years ago for this essay that we discovered a probable origin. Created by former EOP faculty dedicated to linguistic and racial justice, it seems the form was crafted to identify early signals that students needed support. The course operates with the understanding that the students who take English 109/110 often face systemic institutional barriers and a wide range of precarities, such as homelessness, food insecurity, personal safety concerns, mental and physical health issues, unstable home environments, and inequitable access to technology and healthcare. Our archival research revealed that PWR staff in the 1990s were wrestling with how to meaningfully support students by responding to these realities and their effects on students inside and outside of the classroom. In 1995, as a part of a reform effort in our stretch program, a "new progress report form" was created, facilitating a clear communication avenue between instructors and students' EOP and SAAS counselors that was intended to initiate a collaborative, holistic approach to student support. When I saw this 1995 form, I recognized it immediately.

```
                    EOP WRITING PROGRAM
                    THIRD WEEK REPORT

                              English 104, Section _____
                              Quarter/Year: _____
Student: _____        I.D.#: _____
Circle One:   EOP   SSS   SA    Advisor: _____
Note to Advisor: Please contact the student ___ the instructor __
```

	Very Good	Good	Average	Poor	Very Poor
Attendance					
Participation					
Quality of Work					
Timeliness					
Improvement					

```
Mid-Term Grade: _____
Instructor: _____        Extension: _____
     Any comments on reverse side of page?   Yes ___   No ___
```

FIGURE 7.2. *EOP Writing Program—Third-Week Report, 1995 version.*

The form we used until 2020 was clearly an iteration of this 1995 version. Through our inheritance and use of this form, we recognized that the very genre re-created problems we and our 1995 colleagues wanted to address—namely, it didn't foster ethical relationships, it overvalued instructors' and advisors' perspectives, and it did not initiate a clear procedure for student support. Perhaps most egregious, the form bypassed student agency and failed to make room for student perspectives on their learning. We decided we didn't like the orientation, to return to Ahmed's term, of the genre. We also didn't like that it made instructors feel like they were surveilling their students, that students didn't consent to sharing information about themselves, or that it was unclear how student information was used, stored, or acted on. So, we began to imagine alternative ways to honor the form's original intentions of activating networks of support without reproducing these concerns.

In 2019, in collaboration with our campus partners, instructors, and students, we began working on a protocol for communicating circumstances of student precarity requiring urgent action that begins by involving students in creating a plan of support for working with advisors. We also created a goal-setting assignment to replace the form's function of reporting "progress," in which students set writing and other goals early on and revisit them throughout both stretch courses; reflect on previous writing experiences and their learning; and decide how and when to share with advisors (who were encouraged to ask about but not demand access), among other things. For instructors, these goal-setting and reflective activities also open a generative space for conversation with students during conferences and provide opportunities for metacognitive reflection that can deepen students' learning.

While we feel that this goal-setting assignment results in a more just and equitable classroom practice, I acknowledge in the same breath that in thirty years, the document we created may become something utterly different, recognizable through genre conventions but not through its intended impact within the larger ecology. It has happened before. Our archive illuminated that, in 1995, our colleagues engaged in a year-long reform effort that included meeting with different campus stakeholders, establishing new procedures and policies, establishing community among instructors, developing a new handbook, and addressing curriculum and pedagogy issues.

The first time I read the list of reform efforts, I paused. An eerie sense of familiarity arose as I read a description of their equity work. With a few tweaks, it could describe our own. Humbling. Such is the reality of activism in an institution. Change is incremental, ongoing, and cannot be accomplished through a single act, reform, in a year, or in a lifetime. While abolishing a form cannot shatter an entire system of power, its removal did align with other changes we made that better oriented us toward a more equitable and inclusive writing program ecology. By no means is this reorientation enough; this type of work will never be satisfactory as long as the university exists "as an arm of the settler state" that reinscribes white supremacy (Grande 47). However, the form's story demonstrates a straightforward practice of reorienting toward a different vision of education. The practice is an unoriginal and simple one: things that do not align with justice and equity—even and especially objects that are seen as too foundational, embedded, or mundane—must be reimagined (or eradicated) to create space for more ethical relationships and inclusive learning ecologies.

Toward Conclusions

Our writing program is (just as all writing programs, English departments, and universities in this country are) built on colonialism, racism, and capitalistic exploitation (Viswanathan, Watts). We could spend our entire lives working to transform our writing program and university ecologies, and still, oppressive structural injustices that adversely affect Black, Indigenous, Latinx, first-generation, poverty-impacted, and others would persist in some form or another. In our case, we certainly hope that transforming our program ecology increases our collective capacities to create learning spaces that resist the structures of racism and colonialism reproduced in our universities and that allow students to critically reshape the classroom in ways that tap into their own interests, knowledges, lived experiences, and linguistic and cultural resources. But, as we've stressed throughout, one core insight of critical ecological methodologies is that institutional transformative work is ongoing, complex, and recursive. It is important to resist the sense that one can ever check off a box or roll out a curriculum or follow some process and finally arrive. As a praxes and ethical orientation grounded within commitments to equity and justice, critical ecological methodologies ask us to acknowledge the persistence of violence (and our own unavoidable complicity in reproducing harms despite our intentions and even through our social justice efforts). Violence changes form, yes, but it cannot be eradicated. We cannot do justice work from an untainted moral high ground (though we can be reflective and intentional in how we resist and reduce harm in ways that matter). Knowing all of this and yet persisting in transformational work is an ethical orientation—a painful and hard-to-sustain orientation that asks us to sit with profound complexity, interconnection, and incommensurability within our ecologies and that urges us to continue co-laboring and building capacities oriented toward (always and only toward) more just futures.

Notes

1. These letters are from the UW Program in Writing and Rhetoric's records (formerly known as the Expository Writing Program).

2. The coauthors served in PWR leadership positions and played central roles in the work described throughout. As PWR assistant directors, Anselma Widha Prihandita and Nolie Ramsey taught and helped coordinate the stretch composition courses/teacher orientations from 2020–2022 and 2019–2021, respectively. Candice Rai served as the PWR director from 2014–2021 and co-led the research and stakeholder conversations on our stretch program. PWR coordinator Jacob Huebsch played a key role in the institutional transformation described, and Taiko Aoki-Marcial contributed to the stretch orientation/program starting in 2021. We also acknowledge Alec Fisher, Brittney Frantece, Matthew Hitchman, Nanya Jhingran, Sara Lovett, and Patrick McGowan for their contributions to this transformation work.

3. See Thu, Malcolm, Rai, and Bawarshi for more on this statement.

4. Jake Huebsch, Anselma Widha Prihandita, Candice Rai, and Nolie Ramsey worked on these revisions.

5. Anselma Widha Prihandita is lead author of this section.

6. See Noe's work for more.

7. Alec Fisher and Anselma Widha Prihandita conducted these student interviews in 2021.

8. Nolie Ramsey is lead author of this section.

Works Cited

Ahmed, Sara. "Orientations Matter." *New Materialisms: Ontology, Agency, and Politics*, edited by Diana H. Coole and Samantha Frost, Duke UP, 2010, pp. 234–54.

———. *Willful Subjects*. Duke UP, 2014.

Baker-Bell, April, et al. "This Ain't Another Statement! This Is a DEMAND for Black Linguistic Justice!" *Conference on College Composition & Communication*, 2020.

Barnett, Scot, and Casey Boyle, editors. *Rhetoric, through Everyday Things*. U of Alabama P, 2016.

Clary-Lemon, Jennifer. "Gifts, Ancestors, and Relations: Notes toward an Indigenous New Materialism." *Enculturation: A Journal of Rhetoric, Writing, and Culture*, 12 Nov. 2019, http://encultura tion.net/gifts_ancestors_and_relations. Accessed 15 June 2020.

Condon, Frankie, and Vershawn Ashanti Young. Introduction. *Performing Antiracist Pedagogy in Rhetoric, Writing, and Communication*, edited by Frankie Condon and Vershawn Ashanti Young, WAC Clearinghouse / UP of Colorado, 2017, pp. 3–16.

Cupples, Julie, and Ramón Grosfoguel, editors. *Unsettling Eurocentrism in the Westernized University*. Routledge, 2019.

Davila, Bethany A., and Cristyn L. Elder. "Welcoming Linguistic Diversity and Saying Adios to Remediations: Stretch and Studio Composition at a Hispanic-Serving Institution." *Composition Forum*, vol. 35, 2017, https://compositionforum.com/issue/35/new-mexico.php. Accessed 20 Feb. 2019.

Dobrin, Sidney. *Postcomposition*. Southern Illinois UP, 2011.

Edbauer, Jenny. "Unframing Models of Public Distribution: From Rhetorical Situation to Rhetorical Ecologies." *Rhetoric Society Quarterly*, vol. 35, no. 4, 2005, pp. 5–24.

Flores, Nelson, and Jonathan Rosa. "Undoing Appropriateness: Raciolinguistic Ideologies and Language Diversity in Education." *Harvard Educational Review*, vol. 85, no. 2, 2015, pp. 149–71.

García, Romeo, and Damián Baca, editors. *Rhetorics Elsewhere and Otherwise: Contested Modernities, Decolonial Visions*. National Council of Teachers of English, 2019.

Glau, Gregory R. "Stretch at 10: A Progress Report on Arizona State University's Stretch Program." *Journal of Basic Writing*, vol. 26, no. 2, 2007, pp. 30–48.

Grande, Sandy. "Refusing the University." *Toward What Justice? Describing Diverse Dreams of Justice in Education*, edited by Eve Tuck and K. Wayne Yang, Routledge, 2018, pp. 47–65.

Guerra, Juan C. "An Embodied History of Language Ideologies." *Writing across Difference: Theory and Intervention*, edited by James R. Daniel, et al., Utah State UP, 2022, pp. 21–38.

Inoue, Asao B. *Antiracist Writing Assessment Ecologies: Teaching and Assessing Writing for a Socially Just Future*. Parlor Press, 2015.

Jones, Natasha N., et al. "Disrupting the Past to Disrupt the Future: An Antenarrative of Technical Communication." *Technical Communication Quarterly*, vol. 25, no. 4, 2016, pp. 1–19.

Kimmerer, Robin Wall. *Braiding Sweetgrass: Indigenous Wisdom, Scientific Knowledge, and the Teachings of Plants*. Milkweed Editions, 2013.

LeMesurier, Jennifer L. "Uptaking Race: Genre, MSG, and Chinese Dinner." *Poroi*, vol. 12, no. 2, 2017, pp. 1–23.

Liboiron, Max. *Pollution Is Colonialism*. Duke UP, 2021.

Maraj, Louis M. *Black or Right: Anti/Racist Campus Rhetorics*. Utah State UP, 2020.

Matsuda, Paul Kei. "The Myth of Linguistic Homogeneity in U.S. College Composition." *College English*, vol. 68, no. 6, 2006, pp. 637–51.

Noe, Mark. "Autoethnography and Assimilation: Composing Border Stories." *The Journal of the Assembly for Expanded Perspectives on Learning*, vol. 21, 2016, pp. 86–99.

Paris, Django. "Culturally Sustaining Pedagogy: A Needed Change in Stance, Terminology, and Practice." *Educational Researcher*, vol. 41, no. 3, 2012, pp. 93–97.

Paris, Django, and H. Samy Alim, editors. *Culturally Sustaining Pedagogies: Teaching and Learning for Justice in a Changing World*. Teachers College Press, 2017.

Peele, Thomas. "Working Together: Student-Faculty Interaction and the Boise State Stretch Program." *Journal of Basic Writing*, vol. 29, no. 2, 2010, pp. 50–73.

Perryman-Clark, Staci, and Collin Lamont Craig, editors. *Black Perspectives in Writing Program Administration: From the Margins to the Center*. National Council of Teachers of English, 2019.

Prendergast, Catherine. *Literacy and Racial Justice: The Politics of Learning after Brown v. Board of Education*. Southern Illinois UP, 2003.

"Registrar's Quarterly Ethnic Enrollment Survey." University of Washington, 1985. Reiff, Mary Jo, et al. "Writing Program Ecologies: An Introduction." *Ecologies of Writing Programs: Program Profiles in Context*, edited by Mary Jo Reiff, et al., Parlor Press, 2015, pp. 3–18.

Rendón, Laura I., et al. "Theoretical Considerations in the Study of Minority Student Retention in Higher Education." *Reworking the Student Departure Puzzle*, edited by John Braxton, Vanderbilt UP, 2000, pp. 127–56.

Rìos, Gabriela Raquel. "Cultivating Land-Based Literacies and Rhetorics." *Literacy in Composition Studies*, vol. 3, no. 1, 2015, pp. 60–70.

Rivers, Nathaniel A., and Ryan P. Weber. "Ecological, Pedagogical, Public Rhetoric." *College Composition & Communication*, vol. 63, no. 2, 2011, pp. 187–218.

Ruiz, Iris, and Damián Baca. "Decolonial Options and Writing Studies." *Composition Studies*, vol. 45, no. 2, 2017, pp. 226–29.

Sharpe, Christina. *In the Wake: On Blackness and Being*. Duke UP, 2016.

Simpson, Leanne Betasamosake. "Land as Pedagogy: Nishnaabeg Intelligence and Rebellious Transformation." *Decolonization: Indigeneity, Education & Society*, vol. 3, no. 3, 2014, pp. 1–25.

"Statement on Antiracist Pedagogy and Program Praxis." Program in Writing and Rhetoric, University of Washington, 2021, https:// english.washington.edu/diversity-equity-and-inclusion-pwr-and-pwac.

Thu, Sumyat, et al. "Antiracist Translingual Praxis in Writing Ecologies." *Writing across Difference: Theory and Intervention*, edited by James R. Daniel, et al, Utah State UP, 2022, pp. 195–217.

Tuck, Eve, and Marcia McKenzie. *Place in Research: Theory, Methodology, and Methods*. Routledge, 2015.

Viswanathan, Gauri. *Masks of Conquest*. 25th ed., Columbia U, 2014.

Watts, Richard J. *Language Myths and the History of English*. Oxford UP, 2011.

Young, Vershawn Ashanti. "The Indispensable Role of Critical Race Theory in Teaching Writing." Conference for Antiracist Teaching, Language and Assessment, 17 Sept. 2021, Oregon State University. Keynote Address.

Appendix 1: Rhetorical Analysis as Collective Annotation —English 109/110 Prompt Excerpt

This assignment asks you to do a rhetorical analysis of Simpson's "Land as Pedagogy: Nishnaabeg Intelligence and Rebellious Transformation." Rather than write a rhetorical analysis essay, we will analyze this article by annotating it together.

Here are questions to help get you started:

1. What genres are mixed in this autoethnographic text, and what arguments does this genre mixing help Simpson make? How might different audiences respond to this genre mixing?

2. What does genre mixing help Simpson do or communicate that she couldn't have if she had stayed rigidly within academic genre conventions? What are the effects of incorporating non-academic genre elements within this text? Would it be possible for her to write this autoethnography within the conventions of a traditional scientific article?

Appendix 2: Reflection on Positionality and Research—English 109/110 Prompt Excerpt

Please reflect on how your positionality can affect the way you conduct research. This is similar to the reflection Kathleen St. Louis and Angela Calabrese Barton do in their article, except you are reflecting before starting your research. 2–3 pages.

Consider:

1. What lived experiences and identity markers (such as race, gender, sexual orientation, socioeconomic status, education, or experiences) shape who you are, what you believe, and how you think? How do your identity and experience relate to your research topic?

2. What are some assumptions that you already hold regarding your topic and research? It's important to make these preconceptions visible early on, so that you can understand and mitigate your biases.

3. How do your positionality, assumptions, and biases inform your research, your interests, and what you value? How and why might these affect how you conduct every step of your research?

4. Given your subjectivity and positionality, how can you make sure that you're conducting ethical research? If you are interacting with people, what can you do to make sure that you are engaging and representing them ethically?

5. What are the stakes of your research for you and others? Who benefits from the knowledge you create? Who might lose something or be harmed?

III

ECOLOGY AND THE
IDEAS OF PLACE

CHAPTER EIGHT

Land-People Rhetorical Ecologies

JASON COLLINS, KRISTIN L. AROLA, AND MARIKA SEIGEL

In 2019, the three of us joined the Michigan Community and Anishinaabe Renewable Energy Sovereignty (MICARES) team, a project funded by the National Science Foundation's (NSF) Growing Convergence Research Program. MICARES—which includes engineers, social and natural scientists, community organizers, tribal leaders, energy policy specialists, Indigenous education experts, and technical communicators—works to understand the opportunities and barriers associated with renewable energy transitions and to help rural communities and Tribal Nations in Michigan make decisions about renewable energy that align with their values and priorities. As technical communicators and rhetoricians on the team, we have been active in community-engaged research, working to assess community values around renewable energy itself. While this project has taught us much about decision making and the ways it intersects with energy policy, community wants and needs, and technical affordances, in this essay we unpack how renewable energy strategic plans illustrate the ways land is positioned as part of decision making.

MICARES has six community partners—three tribal and three nontribal—across Michigan. In this essay, we focus specifically on the Keweenaw Bay Indian Community Lake Superior Band of Chippewa Indians (KBIC) as well as the city of Traverse City. KBIC, of which Kristin is a first-generation descendant through her mother, is a federally recognized tribe located along the shores of Lake Superior in Michigan's Upper Peninsula. Note that "Chippewa" is a variation of the word Ojibwe, and the Ojibwe along with the Odawa and Potawatomi peoples comprise the Three Fires Confederacy, a longstanding alliance between the tribes collectively known as the Anishinaabe. The KBIC has 1,200 members living on the reservation itself, and the county it is located in includes 8,000 people. Meanwhile, Traverse City, Michigan—located on Lake Michigan in the northern Lower Peninsula—while in some ways rural, is a city of 20,000 residents in a county of close to 100,000 people. Traverse City is quite near to two Anishinaabe communities—the Grand Traverse Band of Odawa and Chippewa Indians and the Little Traverse Bay Bands of Odawa—yet it is comprised of predominantly white settler-colonial residents.

In this chapter, we offer a comparative analysis of two renewable energy strategic plans—one from the KBIC and the other from Traverse City. We perform this analysis through the framework of a land-people rhetorical ecology. This framework provides the field of rhetoric a way of considering land as an agential force in our rhetorical acts. Additionally, it illustrates the value of attuning to land when working with tribal communities. Finally, it highlights how certain communication genres, like the strategic plan, make it difficult, but not impossible, to assert non-Western value systems.

Rhetorical Ecologies and Traditional Ecological Knowledge

To understand what we mean by a land-people rhetorical ecology, one that conceptualizes land as agential, in this section we describe how both rhetorical ecologies and TEK have positioned and understood land. As this collection affirms, ecological approaches to rhetoric and composition destabilize the centrality of the human rhetor and distribute rhetorical agency across various human and nonhuman actors, networks, and processes, opening the possibility of seeing nonhuman entities, including land, as agential. In 2005, Jenny Edbauer sought to destabilize the traditional Bitzerian rhetorical situation by introducing "a wider context of affective ecologies comprised of material experiences and public feelings" (5). While Edbauer's ecological approach has been taken up in numerous ways by the field, we call attention to how such an approach shifts attention to processes and events that extend beyond the limited boundaries of writer, text, and audience as discrete nodes in the rhetorical situation, distributing agency throughout a network of "forces, energies, rhetorics, moods, and experiences" (10). Edbauer's work asks us to consider the ways in which history, physical experience, perception, and institutional forces shape, influence, and constrain writers, audiences, and texts. Similarly, Marilyn Cooper (2019) has invoked ecology as a metaphor to account for the dynamic interaction and co-constitution of writers, their texts, and contexts. She writes, "all interlocuters act; all speak and listen and respond. And persuasion requires respect for and trust in interlocuters' responses, reactions, and inventions so that deliberations will be continuously renewed, not ending in silence, frustration, or resistance" (220).

Relatedly, for new materialist and posthuman rhetorical scholars (see also Barnett and Boyle; Grabill and Pigg; Herndl and Licona), there is a vibrant life to the world around us that warrants rhetorical investigation. Humans respond to the suasiveness of things similarly to the ways in which they respond to symbols. In addition, things and environments influence discourse, are the subjects of discourse, and discourse itself is materially constructed and experienced. What is being developed in the field of rhetoric is an interdependent, interconnected notion of epistemology and ontology, what Barad refers to as ontoepistemology (44). While some of these conversations afford the space for us to imagine land as agential, others, as Matthew Ortoleva has described, have a tendency to "adopt ecological concepts in very broad ways, often wholly metaphorical" (68).

Outside the field of rhetoric, the term *ecology* often includes concepts that very clearly understand land as agential. Fields like ecocomposition (Brown) and geology (Hunt) regularly use ecological concepts that emerge directly from Indigenous relations to land, sometimes referred to as Traditional Ecological Knowledge or TEK. The construct of TEK represents diverse spiritual and cultural land relations that Indigenous people, like the hundreds of federally recognized and many more unrecognized bands and tribes of Turtle Island, have maintained for thousands of years. Examples range from linguistic markers for weather patterns to herding and building techniques, many of which predate recorded history. One commonly cited TEK definition comes from ecologist Fikret Berkes, who claims that TEK is "a cumulative body of knowledge, practice, and belief, evolving by adaptive processes and handed down through generations by cultural transmission, about the relationship of living beings (including humans) with one another and with their environment" (7). Berkes' definition acknowledges the adaptive, transmitted nature of TEK while highlighting humans as only part of the relationships encompassed within TEK. In archaeology, Margaret Bruchac (Abenaki), defines "traditional indigenous knowledge as a network of knowledges, beliefs, and traditions intended to preserve, communicate, and contextualize indigenous relationships with culture and landscape over time" (3814). Whereas Berkes defines TEK as descriptive of or "about" traditional relations to land, Bruchac's inclusion of "preserve" recognizes responsibility as foundational to Indigenous people's relations to land. More than merely preserving, or conserving, species, TEK is the maintaining of traditional relations to a land that is living.

TEK and traditional Indigenous knowledge represent only two of the many terms used to describe a plurality of Indigenous knowledges. Other terms include but are not limited to traditional knowledge(s) (TK) (CTKW), Native Science (Cajete [Tewa]), and Indigenous and local knowledge (ILK) (IPBES). Kyle Whyte (Citizen Potawatomi Nation), notes that TEK (and its synonyms), in an academic context, is a collaborative term (similar to a boundary term or threshold concept in rhetoric and composition theory, e.g. Meyer, Land, and Baillie). TEK is often employed to illustrate how Indigenous communities approach the very question of the nature of knowledge and how this approach relates to environmental and natural resource governance rather differently than disciplines like ecology or biology (Whyte). That is, TEK as a term referencing a diverse range of peoples' knowledges invites coalitional engagements that elide simplistic assumptions about whose knowledges get to count as expert.

Geographers Larsen and Johnson, through their engagement with TEK, understand people's relations to an agential land as educational (17). Land's agency is made visible through the lessons land has to teach. Importantly, the educational relationships people have with land are pluriversal, meaning each educational relationship is contextually developed through the lessons specific to a place. In addition to being contextual, land's lessons, in Indigenous cosmologies like that of the Abenaki, are literal. Lisa Brooks (Abenaki) describes how Native leaders adopted writing as a tool to reclaim land and rights in the northeastern US. In describing how she, as Abenaki, understands land, she says, "What I am talking about here is not an abstraction, a theorizing about a conceptual category called 'land' or 'nature,' but a physical, actual, material relationship to 'an ecosystem present in a definable place' that has been cultivated throughout my short life, and for much longer by those relations who came before me" (xxiv). Brooks's focus is on the stories told in collaboration with land, by the "ecosystem present in a definable place" (xxxv).

The agency of land, for Brooks, Larsen, and Johnson, resides in the stories land tells and in the ways people are educated by the stories land tells. Some of land's stories include stories of removal (Deloria [Standing Rock Sioux]), stories of resistance (Brown), and, in the Anishinaabe tradition, stories of other-than-human relatives (Absolon). What is important to understand about the stories that land tells is that neither the stories nor the ability of land to tell stories are "mythic" tales of Indigenous fiction (Watts 22). The reluctance to engage something like an Anishnaabe creation story in the same way as a study published in the American Journal of Science, argues Vanessa Watts (Mohawk, Anishinaabe), is rooted in the Western tendency to separate ontologies and epistemologies. To illustrate how the separation of ontologies and epistemologies is artificial, Watts provides the creation examples of First Woman and Sky Woman. Sky Woman is said to have fallen from the sky to land on the back of a turtle, the two of which became the Earth. Watts offers the term "Place-Thought [as] an extension of her circumstance, desire, and communication with the water and animals—her agency" (23).

For many Indigenous communities, land is not merely the physical geography of a place; land is alive, not only with the flora and fauna living on it and the climate and natural movement of it, but land is alive in the way that it shapes the actions and lives of people. The ability of land to shape and organize human practices, practices like reading and writing for example, demonstrates land's suasive potential. Drawing from TEK, we offer here the term land-people ecology as a way of adding to discussions of rhetorical ecology and to represent TEK understandings of a living agential land that educates, organizes, informs, and persuades people through the stories that it tells.

Methods for Gathering, Harvesting, and Sense Making

Understanding community values and priorities around renewable energy is a key component of the MICARES research. When working with the KBIC, it is important to understand how their community relates to land and how those relations shape the tribe's approach to energy transition. Understanding these land relations was intended to inform MICARES methods and the project's overall approach to community-focused renewable energy transition. That is, our goal was not to lead with technical solutions. Rather, our goal was to learn what the community valued and then align the solutions with those values.

Originally, our team planned to conduct interviews with KBIC members and tribal representatives using a walkabout method, a method suggested by one of our KBIC community and team members. This method "entails 'going walkabout' with informants in the places that they consider to be important, and collecting social, historical and ecological data *in situ*. It observes that places not only reflect the physical materialization of cultural beliefs and values, they are also a repository and a practical mnemonic of information" (Strang 1). In addition to the devastating toll the COVID-19 pandemic took on the physical and mental health of people worldwide, the pandemic made many research methods, including the walkabout method, unrealistic given required safety protocols.

One of our team's many research pivots included forgoing walkabouts (which would have provided a literal enactment of land-people ecologies) and instead collecting internal and publicly available documents from and about our community partners. While the move from engaging with literal people and the land to gathering and assessing digital documents was not ideal, our goal remained the same: to understand community perceptions and priorities around energy generation and renewable transitioning.

We worked with Sarah Smith, the then CEO of the KBIC and a MICARES team member, to gather as many documents as we could find around the topic of renewable energy development on KBIC land. We gathered everything from meeting minutes to news articles to energy usage reports.

To facilitate a community-focused inquiry, the team established a heuristic that included basic genre information as well as targeted categories for which we coded each document in our corpus. Deductively, we studied the documents for things like community values, opportunities, barriers, and risks, categories that produced findings into each community's specific priorities. In the case of the KBIC, we gathered and analyzed thirty-seven documents. Because of the ways it represents many of the trends we saw across the tribe's documents, here we focus specifically on the KBIC Strategic Energy Plan, comparing and contrasting it to the Traverse City Climate Action Plan. By working with internal community documents and collaboratively sussing out things like community values and barriers to renewable energy transition, our team sought to express the pluriversality of Michigan communities' rhetorical relationships to land.

Strategic Plan as Genre

As a genre, "the strategic plan is written as a document that communicates an organization's strategy for the years to come" (Cornut, Giroux, and Langley 45). An extensive study of the generic features strategic plans have in common found they function to draw people together, illustrate "the importance of expressing collective consensus and collaboration," and assure readers (both within and without of the organization) that the strategic direction communicated in the document arose from a participatory, democratic process (45). That being said, the structures of such documents do not provide the sense that "planning is a rational process in which analysis leads to and justifies choice"; in other words, there is not frequently an explicit, and explicitly logical, connection between the contextual, vision, and process-oriented sections of the document and the sections that actually communicate the specific action items the organization will take to fulfill the strategic plan (46).

As Carolyn Miller argues in "Genre as Social Action," "[a] genre is a rhetorical means for mediating private intentions and social exigence; it motivates by connecting the public with the private; the singular with the recurrent" (163). As you'll see below, in a worldview that views the land-as-agential, these "private intentions" include not only those of humans but of the land itself. Meanwhile, in a worldview that views land as resource, these private intentions tend to conflate land with economic opportunity. Land mediates its intentions in the strategic plan genre through land-people relations as they are expressed in community values and future plans of action. That being said, the conventions of a strategic plan itself tend to promote economic values over land-people relations as the grounds for decision making.

Community-Values

To best understand how land-people relations function in a community where land is understood as agential, it helps to briefly unpack some key components of an Ojibwe worldview as contrasted to a more Western-Christian-based worldview. We do this acknowledging no worldview is static and that for the sake of argument we are somewhat flattening "Western" knowledge as contrasted to "Indigenous" knowledge. That being said, while there are commonalities across Indigenous worldviews, each tribe's worldview is unique. The KBIC are Ojibwe (part of the Anishinaabe), and so here we outline some key ways of understanding their community values as aligned with a land-people ecology. Our description is based on traditional "scholarly" academic citations, storytelling shared with us, and personal knowledge. We share this knowledge with a good heart. All mistakes are ours alone.

In traditional Ojibwe culture, there is a co-constitutive shaping between land and people. Ojibwe ontology is rooted in part in the concept of kinship (Awāsis; Johnston), in which land is understood as kin and as "an anchor to collective identity and ways of knowing. . . . The Anishinaabe learn from the land how to be human" (Schelly et al. 3). These lessons include learning how to live sustainably, which is taught through observation, behavior, and storytelling. This understanding of land varies from that in Christianity-based traditions whereby stories teach that Man has dominion over nature. Take, for example, Genesis 1:26–28, "let man have dominion over the fish of the sea, and over the flow of the air, and over the cattle, and over all the earth, and over every creeping thing that creeps upon the earth" (KJV). Critiques of this worldview's compatibility with environmentalism are common, going back to White's 1967 "The Historical Roots of our Ecological Crisis." While "dominion over nature" doesn't always translate into treating the environment as an extractive resource (in fact, it can result in seeing the land as an object to care for), it does envision the earth as separate from humans.

In traditional Ojibwe understandings, because the land is understood as kin, it is intimately connected to one's being. Take, for example, that in Anishinaabemowin (the Anishinaabe language), there is no understanding of the self without place. The closest one can get to a translation of "to be" is "ayaa" which means to be *in* a certain place (Freeland 45). One way of illustrating how this land-people sense of self contrasts with settler ontologies is through the ways 19th-century treaties were understood. Mark Freeland (Ojibwe) describes Article 13 of the 1836 Treaty of Washington that ceded lands in what is now the eastern portion of Michigan's Upper Peninsula and northern portion of the Lower Peninsula. Article 13, similar to many articles in treaties across the US, reads: "The Indians stipulate for the right of hunting on the lands ceded, with the other usual privileges of occupancy, until the land is required for settlement" (viii). Freeland, through a deep exploration of an Anishinaabe worldview and Anishinaabemowin, illustrates how for the Anishinaabeg at this time, there was no concept of an individual actor doing the hunting. Instead, the "the right of hunting on the lands ceded" includes the hunter, the hunter's community, and the land itself. In 1836, promising the Anishinaabeg the right to hunt would have meant, according to Freeland, that the land on which one would hunt will be cared for so that the animals continue to prosper. Separating out "the right to hunt" from a concept of understanding the land and her resources as kin, as agential, is inconceivable. The land is always already part of the action. It is part of being. This land-people way of being and knowing is always in relation.

Relationality is often cited as a key tenant of much Indigenous thought. For the Ojibwe specifically, as Absolon (Anishinaabe) describes, this involves a worldview in which people see themselves humbly within a larger web or circle of life: "Indigenous knowledge lives in the animals, birds, land, plants, trees and Creation. Relationships among family and kinship systems exist within human, spiritual, plant and animal realms" (Absolon, 31). Two important concepts from this Ojibwe worldview are seventh-generation thinking and mino bimaadiziwin, both of which are evident in the strategic plans that we analyze below. Therefore, we briefly explain these concepts so as to provide a framework for analyzing the documents through a land-people ecology, one rooted in local community values.

First, seventh-generation teachings are common in many American Indian communities. For the Ojibwe, this relational worldview asks humans to make decisions about all things, including land and harvesting, based on how it will affect seven generations in the future. Therefore, any choice you make today should be good both for the community of which you are currently a part and the community that will exist seven generations from now. As such, it ensures, as Patty Loew (Ojibwe) describes, "the growth and success of future generations. . . . It discourages 'me-first' instant gratification and instead reinforces unselfishness, community mindedness, and an ethic of sustainability" (xv). Second, mino bimaadiziwin, the good life, is a lifeway and a praxis, one that means living life, as Leann Simpson (Ojibwe) describes, "in a way that promotes rebirth, renewal, reciprocity, and respect" (132). It means living in close relationship with Anishinaabe Akiing (land) and the surrounding life in that land (Freeland 132). Seventh-generation thinking is part of mino bimaadiziwin, insofar as mino bimaadiziwin is marked by intergenerational continuity. It is an "intergenerational cycle of thought and action that is happening in many Anishinaabeg communities to push beyond survival into flourishing" (Freeland 133). To flourish as a community, in this case, means being attuned to the land as agential and making choices and actions with the seventh generation in mind.

Processing the Harvest: An Analysis

KBIC's Strategic Energy Plan (SEP) was first drafted in 2008 by CARE, the Committee for Alternative and Renewable Energy. CARE is comprised of representatives from various tribal government departments, committees, and Tribal Council, and serves as an advisory committee to the Tribal Council (KBIC's governing body) regarding the development of alternative and renewable energy sources. To understand the SEP, it helps first to understand the 2005 Integrated Resource Management Plan (IRMP). An IRMP is a tribal-specific document and initiative endorsed by the Bureau of Indian Affairs. It serves as an umbrella tribal policy document offering a long-range, strategic-level, comprehensive management plan for the tribe's natural resources. As a genre, IRMPs attempt to embrace Indigenous worldviews by incorporating social, cultural, environmental, and economic aspects of the tribe into management decisions. As such, they are relational in nature, as this type of planning "links all decisions that affect a tract of land together so that each decision's impact can be weighed against all others" (KBIC; IRMP). The vision statement for the 2005 IRMP is "To live in harmony while enhancing and sustaining the resources of the Keweenaw Bay Indian Community for the Seventh Generation." This commitment to the seventh generation, which, as described earlier, necessarily understands the land as part of all decisions, is seen both in the vision statement and throughout the document itself. As it is relational in nature, the IRMP traces the following tribal values—Strong Families, Sovereignty, Tradition/Culture, Employment/Business, Healthcare/Good Health, Education, Environment, Youth, Elders, Safety, Government/Leadership, and Respect—across fifteen different tribal endeavors ranging from cultural fisheries to recreation to economic development.

As an umbrella document, the IRMP was used in the 2008 creation, and subsequent 2015 revision, of the Strategic Energy Plan. The SEP begins with a robust introduction and vision, moves into a detailed technical description of current energy use across tribal buildings, and concludes with a less fleshed-out action plan. Similarly, Traverse City's 2011 Climate Action Plan (CAP) also functions as a strategic plan and follows a similar organizational structure (vision, current energy use, and action plan). Traverse City's CAP was supported by a Department of Energy Award, which in part helps explain why their action plan makes up a third of the document, as opposed to the KBIC's SEP where the action plan only exists in a bulleted list of hopes and questions, making up a small portion (one-tenth) of the total document. Part of MICARES' work with KBIC is to help identify the needed technical assistance and opportunities to move the KBIC vision into action.

As a point of comparison, we set aside the energy use and action plan sections of the documents here and instead offer an analysis of the Introduction and Vision Statements for both communities. Both strategic plans outline a clear set of priorities aligned with community cultural values. For example, the SEP begins with the following statement:

> The Keweenaw Bay Indian Community (KBIC), a federally-recognized Tribe, is located along the shores of Lake Superior in Michigan's Upper Peninsula and has a long tradition of environmental stewardship and planning for the future.

Contrast this opening from Traverse City's 2011 Climate Action Plan:

> The world is dependent on a consistent supply of energy to power nearly every aspect of life. The vast majority of this energy comes from fossil fuels that are limited in supply.

The KBIC immediately identifies themselves as an entity rooted in place and time. With their understandings of themselves as connected to a land-base, their people, and futures, the KBIC SEP embodies mino bimaadiziwin and seventh-generation values. Meanwhile, Traverse City does not locate themselves in a place. Instead, they begin with a defined need (energy) and a problem to solve.

The KBIC SEP goes on to describe their intent, which is "to provide a healthy and productive resources base to sustain the members of KBIC far into the future, as well as to enhance and perpetuate all of the traditional, cultural, and spiritual values which tie members to the land" (4). Again, mino bimaadiziwin and seventh-generation thinking are illustrated with direct connections to the land. Pursuing renewable energy, in this community's vision, will "utilize the natural gifts the Creator has given to educate and benefit endazhi-Ojibwewanishinaabeng (our Ojibwe people) and the next seven generations" (6). Such transitions are for the good of the people, who are always already tied to a land base. These commitments are also illustrated in the vision statement's reference to the IRMP environmental values, which include keeping the waters of Lake Superior clean and honoring "our traditions and culture through the preservation of our homelands." The people and the land are interconnected, and renewable energy goals and priorities are made with these values at the forefront.

Meanwhile, the land is not positioned as a key player in Traverse City's CAP. In fact, the 83-page document never once mentions Lake Michigan (upon whose shores Traverse City sits), and water is only mentioned in reference to the city's wastewater treatment plant. The land is only described in terms of a place where solar or wind may be sited. We do not mean to suggest that the authors of the Traverse City strategic plan do not care about the land; however, unlike the KBIC, they frame their rationale for renewable energy in terms of economic goals. Even when the Traverse City strategic plan mentions the environment, it never does so in isolation. Not once does the document mention the environment without also mentioning the economy:

- "It makes both economic and environmental sense to develop a plan to maximize efficiency and manage resource consumption" (1);

- "The plan promotes environmental stewardship and economic sustainability through resource conservation, responsible consumption, and energy efficiency efforts" (1);

◆ "... taking action to save costs on energy used by government operations is a clear win-win-win for local tax-payers, regional air quality, and the global environment today" (4);

◆ "Wanting to create a win for people, place, and planet; a focus was placed on making climate action economically viable, as well as socially and environmentally responsible" (5); and

◆ "In creating and following this action plan, a precedent will be set for the community and the surrounding region to responsibly manage resources and encourage environmental resilience along with economic sustainability." (5)

Lest it appear that we are critiquing Traverse City's focus on the economy, it is worth noting their claim that "[q]uick progress is made by first tackling energy efficiency projects that provide the strongest economic return" (1) has proven to be accurate for their community. While not the only factor in their success, the attention they give to economic goals (a priority for the community) has helped them make great progress toward 100 percent clean energy.

While the KBIC does not foreground economic opportunities, it is not accurate to say that they don't care about economic factors. For example, the SEP lists the following energy objectives:

◆ To create alternative and self-sustainable clean energy system that preserves the environment, conserves our natural resources, and lowers energy costs.

◆ Preserve and increase tribal self-sufficiency.

◆ Minimize environmental impact.

◆ Utilize local resources.

◆ Create economic benefit through job creation and lower energy costs.

◆ Increased knowledge and collaboration.

While you'll notice here the mention of economic goals, preserving and increasing tribal self-sufficiency through the use of local resources is less about economic goals as an end in itself and more as a means of supporting tribal sovereignty. Sovereign-nation status is an inherent component of tribal nations and guarantees both a type of self-sufficiency as well as a nation-to-nation relationship with the United States. As Bessette, et al, describe it,

> Tribal Nations, in particular, are increasingly focused on energy sovereignty as an assertion of self-determination, a mechanism for community autonomy and development (Powell; Royster; Stefanelli et al.), as well as an environmentally sustainable option for living in accordance with community values regarding relations among humans and nonhuman beings (McDonald and Pearce; Tsosie). (408)

For the KBIC, part of being a sovereign nation includes upholding the "traditional, cultural, and spiritual values which tie the members to the land" (SEP 4). As such, the goal of transitioning to renewable energy is focused less on economic outcomes, and more on tribal sovereignty. Legally speaking, the concept of sovereignty itself relies on a defined territory. For the Ojibwe and in the SAP itself, the land isn't merely a territory to be owned; it is an actor that ties people to tradition, to land, and to language. *Ayaa. To be in a place.* Transitioning to renewable energy is one way to achieve and/or enact sovereignty, and the pathway and vision for doing so must involve seventh-generation thinking and bimaadiziwin. In all of this, land is, for the KBIC, an agential force in decision making.

As mentioned earlier, a disconnect between the contextual sections of the strategic plan (those that focus on the organization's vision, background, and strategic planning process) and the actual action items is a common feature of the genre. In other words, the link between vision, process, and action is generally not made explicit. Instead, these contextual sections "play a largely informative and almost ritual role whose connection with the choices made is at best implicit, not explicit" (Cornut, Girroux, and Langley 46). Interestingly, Traverse City's CAP explicitly connects the contextual sections with the action sections, noting how the prioritized short- and long-term actions arose specifically from the strategic planning process and how they relate to the economic and environmental values articulated earlier in the plan:

> During the planning process the Green Team considered many ways to reduce the City's environmental impact. A great deal

of time was spent creating a comprehensive list of possible measures for reducing GHG emissions. This included studying the successes of many other climate action plans, energy audits, conservation literature, and the use of ICLEI's CAPPA action planning tool. These measures were analyzed, quantified, and narrowed based on economic and environmental benefits, as well as feasibility of implementation and City interest. (20)

Again, the value of the land, or environment, is explicitly linked to its economic value. As noted earlier, this emphasis on action in the CAP may be partially explained by its grant-funded status. The KBIC's SEP, in contrast, follows the more common generic convention of not explicitly connecting its action items to the plan's contextual sections. The action items are clearly meant for an internal audience who understands their context and are therefore presented with little context or additional information that is accessible to external audiences.

In both examples—the KBIC SEP and the Traverse City CAP—understandings of land influence the outcome of the genre. In Traverse City, where peoples' relations to land are often linked to economics, land ownership and land use often translate into economic opportunities, therefore the land is represented through economic-focused action items. For the KBIC, land-people relations are about preserving not only the land for this generation and for the seven generations to come but also preserving the relations themselves. Land acts through these relations in the strategic plan, shaping the values that drive the plan as well as the action items that are meant to preserve the land-people. Land-people here, as influenced by Watts and Freeland, connotes the inseparability of the two. A land-people ecology as illustrated by these two communities' visions for the future suggests land-people's entangled agency that shapes priorities and makes decision making possible.

Walkabouts and Valuing Frameworks for (Re)Seeing

We want to conclude by returning to our pivot, as briefly described in the methods, from walkabouts to document analysis. As described, originally our subteam, which focused on community-engaged research, planned to learn through a walkabout method in order to "learn about past, current, and prioritized future uses of energy activities in the communities," including KBIC and Traverse City.

The deliverable from these walkabouts was going to be "digitized cultural maps" in which the community members' stories about energy use could be linked to the places that brought forth those stories; these maps would provide sources of data both for the MICARES team and for the communities themselves. The MICARES project's goal was to not only learn from but to give back to the communities involved in the project; therefore, the communities involved would have co-constituted the project's goals and objectives. Because the walkabout method is centered in place, a land-people relationship in which land is agential would be very apparent—the land would be agential in shaping and drawing forth the stories that would have been told about energy use in this context. Researchers and community members would have been standing together on the land. But of course, technical documents like strategic plans also tell stories, and those stories are also, as evidenced by the documents we have analyzed here, shaped by the land that communities inhabit and by their different relationships to that land, even if the land might be further from our minds as we sit in our home offices, reading text on our computer screens, looking for traces of water, rock, and tree.

About a half-year into the MICARES project, the COVID-19 pandemic hit, rendering the walkabout method impossible, and document collection and analysis (once intended mostly for background information and context) became a central activity for the three of us. Technical communication genres such as proposals, reports, and strategic plans make up much of this collection. As technical communication scholars concerned with social justice such as Angela Haas, Natasha Jones, and Cana Itchuaqiyaq have pointed out, however, technical communication genres, as well as the academic spaces that study them, are entangled with histories of colonization: "Even in the most progressive spaces and places," Haas writes, "the colonial rhetorical detritus of racism and ethnocentrism remains, and if these worldviews and rhetorics go unchallenged, they will continue to influence who and what we think of when we consider issues of race and technological literacy and expertise" (287). Ultimately, the NSF panel that reviewed the MICARES project after the first two years decided not to renew the project for years three through five. While there are many complex reasons for this nonrenewal that likely have nothing to do with the project's centering of Indigenous knowledge, it also bears note that "centering of Indigenous knowledge" would never be given as an explicit reason for nonrenewal of any project or to not hire a job candidate and so on. The reasons that were shared with us for the nonrenewal included that our science wasn't adding any new knowledge to existing research and that our technological component wasn't seen as innovative. As Sarah Hunt has observed, "[t]he situatedness of Indigenous knowledge calls for the validation of new kinds of theorizing and new epistemologies that can account for situated, relational Indigenous knowledge yet remain engaged with broader theoretical debates" (31). What counts as science, technology, and as knowledge itself within academic spaces is still very much defined by a colonial, imperialist orientation, even (or maybe especially) in spaces that are explicitly looking for innovation and new approaches to knowledge creation.

If genre mediates private intention and social action, technical communication genres have historically often mediated the private intention to colonize land and people with the social actions of colonization and occupation. As Hunt describes, "[w]estern spatializations such as the frontier, the survey and the grid, played an important practical and ideological role in colonial expansion, legitimizing the displacement of Indigenous peoples from their territories" (30). Indeed, our attempt to read land as agential in these strategic plans could itself be seen as a colonizing move: here is a rhetorical strategy used in the strategic plan, something that can be extracted and exploited in other contexts. Yet we hope this analysis highlights the ways the perspective of land-as-agential differs from appeals to "environmental values" or understanding a text as part of a broader ecology. It means recognizing land, and land-people relations, as an agent that shapes rhetoric rather than simply being acted upon or invoked.

Works Cited

Absolon, Kathleen. "Decolonizing Education and Educators' Decolonizing." *Intersectionalities: A Global Journal of Social Work Analysis, Research, Polity, and Practice*, vol. 7, no. 1, 2019, pp. 9–28.

Awāsis, Sākihitowin. "Gwaabaw: Applying Anishinaabe Harvesting Protocols to Energy Governance." *The Canadian Geographer / Le Géographe Canadien*, vol. 65, no. 1, 2021, pp. 8–23.

Barad, Karen. *Meeting the Universe Halfway: Quantum Physics and the Entanglement of Matter and Meaning*. Duke UP, 2007.

Barnett, Scot, and Casey Boyle, editors. *Rhetoric, through Everyday Things*. U of Alabama P, 2016.

Brondizio, Eduardo, et al. *Global Assessment Report on Biodiversity and Ecosystem Services of the Intergovernmental Science-Policy Platform on Biodiversity and Ecosystem Services*. IPBES, 2019.

Brooks, Lisa Tanya. *The Common Pot: The Recovery of Native Space in the Northeast*. U of Minnesota P, 2008.

Brown, Stephen. "The Wilderness Strikes Back: Decolonizing the Imperial Sign in the Borderlands." *Ecocomposition: Theoretical and Pedagogical Approaches*, edited by Christian R. Weisser and Sidney I. Dobrin, State U of New York P, 2001, pp. 117–30.

Bruchac, Margaret. "Indigenous Knowledge and Traditional Knowledge." *Encyclopedia of Global Archaeology*, edited by Claire Smith, Springer, 2014, pp. 3814–24.

Cajete, Gregory. *Native Science: Natural Laws of Interdependence*. Clear Light, 2000.

Cooper, Marilyn. *The Animal Who Writes: A Posthumanist Composition*. U of Pittsburgh P, 2019.

Cornut, Francis, et al. "The Strategic Plan as a Genre." *Discourse & Communication*, vol. 6, no. 1, 2012, pp. 21–54.

Deloria, Vine, Jr. *Behind the Trail of Broken Treaties: An Indian Declaration of Independence*. U of Texas P, 1985.

Edbauer, Jenny. "Unframing Models of Public Distribution: From Rhetorical Situation to Rhetorical Ecologies." *Rhetoric Society Quarterly*, vol. 35, no. 4, 2005, pp. 5–24.

Freeland, Mark D. *Aazheyaadizi: Worldview, Language, and the Logics of Decolonization*. Michigan State UP, 2021.

Grabill, Jeffrey T., and Stacey Pigg. "Messy Rhetoric: Identity Performance as Rhetorical Agency in Online Public Forums." *Rhetoric Society Quarterly*, vol. 42, no. 2, 2012, pp. 99–119.

Haas, Angela M. "Race, Rhetoric, and Technology: A Case Study of Decolonial Technical Communication Theory, Methodology, and Pedagogy." *Journal of Business and Technical Communication*, vol. 26 no. 3, 2012, pp. 277–310.

Herndl, Carl G., and Adela C. Licona. "Shifting Agency: Agency, *Kairos*, and the Possibilities of Social Action." *Communicative Practices in Workplaces and the Professions: Cultural Perspectives on the Regulation of Discourse and Organizations*, edited by Mark Zachry and Charlotte Thralls, Routledge, 2007, pp. 133–54.

Hunt, Sarah. "Ontologies of Indigeneity: The Politics of Embodying a Concept." *Cultural Geographies*, vol. 21, no.1, 2014, pp. 27–32.

Itchuaqiyaq, Cana U., and Breeanne Matheson. "Decolonizing Decoloniality: Considering the (Mis)Use of Decolonial Frameworks in TPC Scholarship." *Communication Design Quarterly*, vol. 9, no. 1, 2021, pp. 20–31.

Johnston, Basil. *Ojibway Heritage*. U of Nebraska P, 1990.

Jones, Natasha N. "Coalitional Learning in the Contact Zones: Inclusion and Narrative Inquiry in Technical Communication and Composition Studies." *College English*, vol. 82, no. 5, 2020, pp. 515–26.

Larsen, Soren C., and Jay T. Johnson. *Being Together in Place: Indigenous Coexistence in a More than Human World*. U of Minnesota P, 2017.

Loew, Patty. *Seventh Generation Earth Ethics: Native Voices of Wisconsin*. Wisconsin Historical Society Press, 2014.

Meyer, Jan, et al., editors. *Threshold Concepts and Transformational Learning*. Sense Publishers, 2010.

Michigan Community & Anishinaabe Renewable Energy Sovereignty (MICARES). "Project Description." Michigan Community & Anishinaabe Renewable Energy Sovereignty (MICARES), 2019.

Miller, Carolyn R. "Genre as Social Action." *Quarterly Journal of Speech*, vol. 70, no. 2, 1984, pp. 151–67.

Ortoleva, Matthew. "Let's Not Forget Ecological Literacy." *Literacy in Composition Studies*, vol. 1, no. 2, 2013, pp. 66–73.

Schelly, Chelsea, et al. "Cultural Imaginaries or Incommensurable Ontologies? Relationality and Sovereignty as Worldviews in Socio-Technological System Transitions." *Energy Research & Social Science*, vol. 80, 2021, pp. 1–7

Simpson, Leanne Betasamosake. *Dancing on Our Turtle's Back: Stories of Nishnaabeg Re-Creation, Resurgence and a New Emergence.* Arbeiter Ring, 2011.

Strang, Veronica. "Mapping Histories: Cultural Landscapes and Walk-about Methods." *Environmental Social Sciences: Methods and Research Design*, edited by Ismael Vaccaro, et al., Cambridge UP, 2010, pp. 132–56.

Townsend, Solomon, et al. *City of Traverse City Climate Action Plan.* City of Traverse City 2011.

Watts, Vanessa. "Indigenous Place-Thought and Agency amongst Humans and Non-Humans (First Woman and Sky Woman Go on a European World Tour!)." *Decolonization: Indigeneity, Education & Society*, vol. 2, no. 1, 2013, pp. 20–34.

White, Lynn. "The Historical Roots of Our Ecologic Crisis." *Science*, vol. 155, no. 3767, 1967, pp. 1203–07.

Whyte, Kyle. "On the Role of Traditional Ecological Knowledge as a Collaborative Concept: A Philosophical Study." *Ecological Processes*, vol. 2, no. 1, 2013, pp. 1–12.

CHAPTER NINE

Tidal Ethics: Knowledge, Relations, and Writing

Bridie McGreavy, Anthony Sutton, and Gabrielle Hillyer

Pisipiqe (https://pmportal.org/dictionary/pisipiqe) is a Passamaquoddy-Maliseet word that names the place-verb where rivers and oceans meet (Francis and Leavitt). Also known as estuaries, pisipiqe are dynamic places that have long gathered water, sediment, people, animals, and plants into relations. Pisipiqe are situated within Wabanaki peoples' ongoing relationships that shape knowledge of what these places are and how they sustain ways of life, relationships that have persisted for, as Geo Soctomah Neptune (Niskapisuwin) describes, "time immemorial" (94) and that continue in the present. Essok (soft-shell clams), qahaks (quahogs), massols (blue mussels), and pahsapsq (oysters) seek the soft muddy or rocky substrates and tidal flows that characterize pisipiqe, becoming integral entities within intertidal ecosystems, coastal cultures, and shellfishing livelihoods. These are places where nit wen nukcihkuwa ess elomocokek (one goes right to the clams there on the mudflat) because ktoliyan elomocokek pawatomon essok (you go to the mudflat if you want to get clams) (Francis and Leavitt). One such place, Moneskatik, also known as Bar Harbor, situated near Acadia National Park, has long been a clam-gathering place. As an expression of a system of language that has learned to sense "place thought" (Watts 21), pisipiqe and these related concepts become ways of naming, attending to, and writing with emplaced relations between rivers, oceans, tides, mud, clams, people, languages, knowledges, and so on.[1]

As coauthors, our relations have been shaped within these tidally influenced places in ways that have also constituted how we create knowledge together. In this chapter, we describe how these ecological influences are formative for approaching knowledge as relation. Over the last decade of doing engaged rhetorical fieldwork, we have observed, asked questions about, and sought to co-create knowledge with pisipqe, elomocokek, intertidal ecosystems, shellfish harvesters, and many other partners. In the process, we have also been guided by an emergent sense of ethics about what is right and of mutual and yet unequal responsibilities and obligations to this place, to each other, and to partners. We refer to this sensibility as tidal ethics. Because relations matter, we start by briefly situating ourselves, describing how we came to be involved in these efforts, and some of the qualities of our relationships. As we did in our fieldwork, we then turn to scholarship influenced by tidal forces to describe a tidal ethics approach to knowledge as relation. Tidal ethics are shaped by rhythms of time, listening, breathing, and standing with and moving within ecologies. We describe practices within tidal ethics and conclude by discussing how tidal ethics influences our writing praxis for incommensurate and decolonial justice.

Knowledge as Relation: Tracing How We Gather

The three of us share an interest in creating knowledge in ways that challenge dominant systems of power, such as colonialism, capitalism, heteropatriarchy, and whiteness. The ways in which knowledge and power interconnect are complex and deeply tied to specific histories and ecologies within a place. For example, in Maine's shellfish comanagement system, clammers have an incredible depth of knowledge about conservation practices; the patterns of clam growth and abundance; how tides vary; interpersonal histories, dispositions, and local or Wabanaki cultures that shape how clammers negotiate and make shared decisions; and so on. However, the structure of the State of Maine's municipal shellfish comanagement program and other institutional forces that shape perceptions of expertise limit the ability to weave this knowledge into decision making about activities like conservation closures, shellfish license sales, or how to run a shellfish program. Further, municipal and state boundaries also limit knowledge sharing from one community to the next and reinforce exclusions and erasures of Wabanaki knowledge and long-term inhabitation on the coast. Despite this context specificity, academic scholarship and our own experiences also point to broader exclusionary patterns that recur, including the division of knowledge into discrete disciplines (Smith); worldviews that construct reality as singular and know-able and thereby grasp-able (Glissant); constructions of expertise that position some forms of knowledge as more valuable than others (Nadasdy; Whitt); and material barriers that deny access to academic knowledge, especially in contexts when that access is denied to those who helped create the knowledge in the first place (Simonds and Christopher).

Recognizing how knowledge-based patterns reconstruct disciplinary divides, epistemic hierarchies, and knowledge extractivism raises the question about how to create knowledge in ways that do not reproduce these patterns and instead challenge and transform them. For us, finding ways to connect rhetorical fieldwork (e.g., Middleton, Hess, Endres, and Senda-Cook; Rai and Druschke) with sustainability science's orientations to engaged research have offered ways of challenging dominant power in knowledge. Though sustainability science has been slow to recognize how sociopolitical forces like colonialism and racialized capitalism reinforce dominant patterns in science and knowledge production more broadly (Johnson et al.; McGreavy, Ranco et al.; Sze), we were each initially drawn to sustainability science's commitment to do knowledge differently and in more relational ways.

Oriented to sustainability science, rhetorical fieldwork, and knowledge as relation, McGreavy and Sutton began working together as graduate students in communication at the University of Maine in 2010 and have been in continual dialogue about what these commitments mean in practice. Over time, we began to get a grounded sense of the responsibilities associated with collaborative approaches to rhetorical fieldwork. For example, Sutton's dissertation centered Passamaquoddy language, like the Skutik, to resist colonial naming practices that restrict Indigenous knowledge relations. This centering and naming practice acknowledged how rivers shaped his movements in the field, including where he went, how he listened, and how he organized the dissertation itself.[2] Similarly, McGreavy's collaborative fieldwork in coastal communities grew into sustained relationships with clammers and diverse participants in municipal shellfish programs. By working to co-create knowledge with clammers whose livelihoods depend on their relationships with mud, tides, clams, and much more beyond, she began to learn how to practice an emplaced and embodied sense of tidal ethics. Finally, Hillyer, a graduate student in Ecology and Environmental Sciences at the University of Maine, brought an interest in interdisciplinary knowledge about pisipiqe and especially how collaborating with fishermen to study tidal flow within these places can support shellfish restoration as well as erode existing colonial knowledge structures within the shellfish comanagement system. Through in-depth dialogue and learning, we have come to an intimate understanding of the differences and incommensurabilities in forms of justice across these contexts.

In 2019, these relations coalesced in the formation of the Maine Shellfish Learning Network (MSLN), an organization whose evolving mission is to support learning, leadership, and equity in Maine and Wabanaki wild clam and mussel fisheries. As this mission signals, we have increasingly become aware of the need to avoid centering damage narratives in this work. Drawing from Eve Tuck's letter in which she cautions against damage-focused research, Michelle Murphy instead advocates for attending to "collectivities of life recomposed by the molecular productions of capitalism in our own pasts and the pasts of our ancestors, as well as into the future" (497). She terms such collectivities "alterlives," which is a distinctly ecological concept that draws attention to bodies' entanglements with "community, ecological, colonial, racial, gendered, military, and infrastructural histories that have profoundly shaped the susceptibilities and potentials of future life" (497). Staying with these kinds of entanglements becomes a way of dealing with the incommensurabilities in trying to create different relations out of colonial and capitalist ruins (Murphy, Tsing; see also la paperson). Importantly, our collaborations are not a search for common ground or mutual understanding. Drawing from Eve Tuck and K. Wayne Yang, Max Liboiron similarly notes that

"Incommensurability means that things do not share a common ground for judgement or comparison" (136). Instead, "an ethic of incommensurability [is] one that digs into difference and maintains that difference while also trying to stay in good relations" (137). In this orientation, tidal ethics have emerged as a way to stay with incommensurability, difference, and relations through rhythm.

Tidal Ethics

Across our engaged research efforts, tidal rhythms have impressed on our collective consciousness in different ways. Édouard Glissant's work helps us attune to tidal rhythms as ecological consciousness as he turns to tides and other watery formations as a means for loosening the grip of dominant ways of knowing. His orientation is inherently critical, in which ecological, relational poetics attunes to how racialization and colonization shape language and knowledge. Glissant's book *Sun of Consciousness* as well as his longer and more oceanic mediation in *Poetics of Relation* are philosophical discussions of complex, racialized, colonial, and ecological relationships between language, knowledge, and power. He characterizes these fraught relationships as a "tortured swarm of contradictions" (*Sun of Consciousness* 58) and stays with poetry as the art of crafting knowledge and language differently, errantly, from within such a swarm. Though Glissant's work is not typically read as an argument for collaborative and place-based research approaches, his poetic orientation continuously calls for distinctly applied orientations to knowledge and embodied engagement within one's home places. Of this commitment, Glissant argues, "One must become closed to the flux. Or, rather, listen carefully to it swell; but attach oneself at once to some square of earth, to problems of the everyday, to the strict measure of sight" (*Sun of Consciousness* 80). Poetic, embodied engagement, in this sense, "cannot guarantee us a concrete means of action. But a poetics, perhaps, does allow us to understand better our action in the world" (*Poetics of Relation* 199). We have been guided by Glissant's commitment to a poetic, embodied relationality within the ecological conditions of the times and places we inhabit.

Tidal ethics are based on a relational approach to knowledge that guides our actions in the world, from our small square of earth on an island in the Penobscot River just north of the head of tides at the edge of pisipiqe. Tides are a way of naming the recursive movements of oceanic water, as earth's rhythms emerge through circulatory relations with the moon and the sun. The tides themselves, as well as the stories we tell with tides, guide rhythmic movements as we make knowledge together. We have learned (and are still learning) how to listen to tidal voices in our home region and increasingly identified the need to seek out critical scholarship shaped alongside tides. In this search, we turned to a diverse set of tidal theories, starting with Glissant's poetics of relation and then tidalectics (Brathwaite), archipelagic rhetorics (de Onís, Glissant, Na'puti) and Black shoals (King). There are important differences in the histories, meanings, and subjectivities that these tidally influenced concepts articulate, and bringing them into conversation does not intend to collapse these differences into a singular framework. Yet these concepts all show how attuning to tides can help sense rhythms and work with language to disrupt the seeming fixity of dominant power. For example, Tiffany Lethabo King describes how shoals showed up through the rhythms of her daily commute in Florida, where shoals surround her.[3] Shoals offered themselves to King as a way to name "a place, a state of disruption, a slowing of momentum, and a process of rearrangement" (31). In what she describes as a methodology of listening, shoals are indeterminate spaces to "sculpt new epistemologies and sensibilities that shape the contours of humanness in more expansive ways" (King 29). Shoals, archipelagos, tides, and related watery formations offer attunements to ecological rhythms through which knowledge coalesces as we breathe, listen, and move together through time.

Tides and Time

One of the first and most significant lessons we learned from tides is about the rhythmic multiplicity of time. Tides create heterogeneous forms of time that also show how time and space are fundamentally connected and integral to the constitution of multiple worlds. For example, in engaged research when we are setting up times to go into the field or out on boats or for collaborative dialogues, we have learned how to tell time differently by consulting tide charts for a particular location and to schedule the trip accordingly for high, low, big, or small tide times. In doing so, we have also come to recognize the *errantry* in such multiplicity (Glissant, *Poetics of Relation*), as the difference in tidal times always escapes our grasp because tidal time in a particular region does not fit neatly onto tide charts. Low tide in the upper part of a bay may be later and longer than in the lower part as the water drains out and washes back in slower and later. Hillyer's bucket drifters have created a way of tracing these dynamics, of following tidal time by being out in its flows (see Figure 9.1). While tidal traces become a more fluid and dynamic way of telling tidal time, they are also incomplete records as these patterns shift seasonally, with changing benthic topographies, in the event of coastal storms, or with the use of different kinds of tracking technologies.

Still, the periodicity of tidal time productively disrupts the dominance of linear clock time, where tides create a rhythm to life that is impossible to control. Though tides are not a quantum phenomenon in the way western scientists describe, following their forces shows how tidal patterns are inherently recursive (Barad). Recursion is a way of naming movements that are circulatory and in which patterns demonstrate repetitions and errant connections. Recursion is less like the roots of a tree, where tracing assumes a material stability, and instead more like the dynamism of following tidal forces as they move into and out of a bay. As rhetoric, recursion names how symbolism and materiality flow together as memory, where the "present is a way of occupying time, not a specific moment. That ability to occupy time, to act within and from a sense of place, is recursive capacity" (Stormer 28). This orientation to recursion opens up the possibilities for tracing how rhetorics emerge as multiplicities and how these multiplicities are shaped ecologically.

This theoretical discussion of tides, time, and recursion raises the question: how does a tidal approach to time shape collaborative fieldwork and knowledge making? In addition to the iterative nature of scheduling fieldwork, orienting to tidal times within our collaboration means recognizing that our interactions

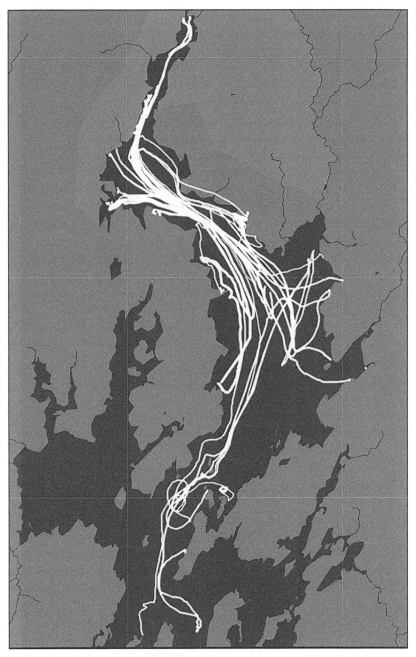

FIGURE **9.1.** *The map of all drifter tracks released in 2017 in the Medomak River Estuary, described in Hillyer et al.*

are also inherently recursive. Such recursive relationships have frequently been characterized as rhizomatic or rooted. Yet Na'puti calls attention to land-based metaphors, like rootedness, and argues for articulations that instead amplify movements when she says "*Belonging to* place, moving, and being both routed and rooted conveys open processes of movement while deepening important Indigenous relationships to land" (6). For Glissant, this approach constitutes a relation identity that "exults in the thought of errantry and of totality" (*Poetics of Relation* 144). Importantly, this totality is not a unified space but instead an action-oriented "gesture of giving-on-and-with" (192) that "works in a spiral: from one circularity to the next, it encounters new spaces and does not transform them into either depths or conquests" (199). Following tides become ways of tracing relational identities, of feeling and navigating the tensional forces that emerge through movement, resisting easy closures to instead embrace circulations, and giving oneself over to time as incommensurate difference and change.

This orientation redistributes capacities for rhetoricity in ways that decenter the human and acknowledge that abilities for symbolic-material actions in the world are distributed and not, in contrast, a unique human attribute. This shift introduces central problems for agency and choice making, where humans are no longer centered as rational actors, where loci for control are not individual but ecological, and where ecologies include ecosystems and forces, like tides, as well as oppressive forces such as neoliberalism, colonialism, genocide, and slavery. This shift requires addressing tensions in how rhetoric both capacitates and debilitates, as Yanar Hashlamon argues, where a "group's rhetoricity might be capacitated by the debility of others'— the distinction is meaningful in how it traces injustice within relations that rhetorical studies might seek to reveal and redress. Debility focuses attention to the way some forms of rhetorical empowerment require and depend on the inequitable distribution and production of rhetoricity" (8). Elizabeth Povinelli similarly reflects on capacities, debilities, and incommensurabilities that she learned to sense through partnerships with the Karrabing Film Collective (https://karrabing.info/).[4] Drawing from Brathwaite's concept of tidalectics, Povinelli describes "tidal forms of learning as becoming" that create embodied awareness of how "the purity of water for some is filtered through the toxicity of water for others, and the changing of those filtration systems will not be neutral to those who have and that which has benefitted from previous arrangements" (172). Thus, letting tides guide serves a non-innocent mode of ethical discernment for what it means to desediment (Glissant), or debilitate (Hashlamon), oppressive relations through rhythm, temporal and otherwise.

Listening, Breathing, and Standing with Tides

Tides remember rhythm as a primary condition of existence on earth, where time is multiplicity and where efforts to *know* temporalities are relational. Tides as formations of *water* is a significant detail in practices of remembering rhythms and relations. Sherri Mitchell, Penobscot writer, activist, and leader, describes how listening to water allows recursive forces to guide "people into right relationship with the earth and other people" (Mitchell 5). Attending to water acknowledges the recursive and quantum entanglements that Wabanaki and Indigenous peoples have long understood and that Western science has more recently come to recognize. Water can help guide because water, like winter, "stalks memory" (*Sun of Consciousness* 31) in its unique ability to weigh on ecological consciousness in ways that exceed awareness yet are still materially affective. Water, in this sense, is *heavy* in how it presses on memory (Bachelard, DeLoughrey) and when listening becomes a way of opening to this force (King).

Responding to Mitchell's call, we center listening to water and tides. Our early efforts to show up and listen to questions that were significant to partners became an opening for more ecological awareness of what listening means and what situated listening as rhetorical action can do for sensing rhetorics that have been buried—sedimented, debilitated—within dominant discourses. For example, in "Intertidal Poetry," McGreavy describes showing up for a community-based conservation event where clammers were transplanting clams from one mudflat that had been closed due to pollution to another where the clams would be able to expel the toxins so eventually clammers would be able to dig them up again for food and income. She was invited to attend this event to listen to concerns about water quality and shellfish conservation. As she paddled across a cove with a clammer who was leading this effort, he described how his attachments to clamming include but go far beyond earning an income. He described being out on this cove in a canoe late one summer night, watching the moon rise over the horizon, and how with every rhythmic dip of his paddle into the water, the ocean shimmered with phosphorescent plankton. At the time, this tidal perspective constituted a disruption in a space where dominant science devalues clammer knowledge and does not afford agency to the nonhuman world. This disruption also created an opening to begin recognizing the relationship between dominant science, colonialism, neoliberalism, and shellfish comanagement, as we describe more fully elsewhere (McGreavy, Ranco et al.). Listening created opportunities for disruption and ecological sensing of interconnected forces that were shaping rhetorical capacities and debilities for who was involved, where these activities took place, and for what ends.

Listening to water also points a way past dominant Western cultural understandings of listening, where listening is distinctly passive and ableist, made possible by "quieting voices and opening ears." This is not what we mean by listening. Instead, listening is rooted in embodied presence (Pezzullo), in which listening to water can occur through myriad enactments that may include sensing the sound vibrations of water as it spills over white rocks as they emerge just above the head of tides, sensing that can occur through ears as a sense organ but where this form of listening is not the only one available. Listening may also mean sensing vibrations not through ears but instead letting vibrations into our hearts; or slipping into the river and letting the water and whatever else swirl in those flows attach to our bodies; or taking in a drink and feeling how we become that water and everything therein. Listening can include smell, taste, and our bodies' relation to gravity. Smells shape movements, leading us toward the mudflat, similar to how siqonomeq (alewives), polam (salmon), and other anadromous fish find their home stream. The taste of water within a pisipiqe is also unique, a gathering place of fresh and salt water, creating a complex mixture of salt on the tongue.

Extending this approach to listening, other scholars offer breath as a related way to remember myriad relationalities. As a rhetorician with a poetic and ecological sensibility, Kenneth Burke recognized the power of biological metaphors, like listening and breath, which provide ways of sensing the "rock bottom" of human thought and expression (261). Taking a decolonial orientation to breath, Murphy invites readers to breathe as a way to remember coextensive relations that make breath both possible and risky. Breathing is a recursive remembering that the risks involved in breathing are not equal, especially for those whose air is laden with toxic chemicals. Breathing from where we reside on this island in the Penobscot River is a continual reminder of the colonial capitalist relations that have created a long legacy of polluting industries, with a paper mill that emits toxins into the air and has a contract with an upstream landfill to dump millions of gallons of leachate into the river every year ("Juniper Ridge"). And while we breathe in this awareness of how pollution is colonialism, in Max Liboiron's sense, we also recognize that the polluting effects of colonialism and capitalism have the potential to make their way into all lungs, transgressing bodily sovereignty in disparate ways. Attention to breath recognizes that the violence of chemical relations also create openings for life to become otherwise "which is not a nostalgic return, but instead the defending of sovereignty starting here, within oneself and each other, here in the damage now. There is no waiting for a better condition" (Murphy 501).

Breathing thus becomes a practice of recognizing connection across incommensurabilities. As Alexis Pauline Gumbs writes:

> Breath is a practice of presence. . . . The adaptations that marine mammals have made in relationship to breathing are some of the most relevant for us to observe, not only in relationships to our survival in an atmosphere we have polluted on a planet where we are causing the ocean to rise, but also in relationship to our intentional living, our mindful relation to each other. (21)

In this way, we use breath to move beyond boundaries between species, environment, and other to instead call attention to shared breath. This practice shapes relationality with the breath and movement of essok, tals (seaweed), kiwonkik (otter), cuspesok (harbor porpoise), and others within pisipiqe. It also broadens practices of listening to situated observations of these connections. As Jessica Hernandez's father describes how he was taught to fish, "I was always told by my elders when I would go ask them how one should fish to observe everything within this environment where the streams, rivers or oceans were located. To not just stare at the water where the fishes were, as this was not going to teach me how to truly catch fish" (Hernandez 120). In this way, our collaborations with each other, with a broader set of partners, and within this place intend to pursue this type of learning, in which listening and breathing guide observations and shape relations.

Listening and breathing thus become ways of trying to stay with and learn across difference when mutual or shared understanding is not the goal nor likely even possible. Instead, these rhythms invite mutual sensing of how the effects of dominant power can create new ways of gathering around shared concerns and the multiplicity of ways those concerns are expressed. Listening and breathing as embodied, collaborative praxis extend to myriad relations and become modes through which one may practice *standing with* each other and within communities, "human" and otherwise. Drawing a contrast between giving back and standing with, Kim TallBear argues that the latter frame invites researchers to change their respective subjectivities as a core part of the collaborative research process. She contends that an interdisciplinary orientation to knowledge can serve as a foundation for challenging dominant knowledge-power relations. In this approach, TallBear suggests that:

> It is also helpful to think creatively about the research process as a relationship-building process, as a professional networking process with colleagues (not "subjects"), as an opportunity for conversation and sharing of knowledge, not simply data gathering. Research must then be conceived in less linear ways without necessarily knowable goals at the outset. (2)

The emphasis here on interdisciplinarity, relationship-building, networking, ongoing dialogue, and where research is an open-ended process all demonstrate how "standing with" is also about moving with, writing with, and learning with, where knowledge is shaped through embodied rhythms of creating together.

What do listening, breathing, and standing/moving/writing/ learning with mean for our knowledge practices? We try to remember listening as a mode of openness to the world, to breathe together as a means for sensing interconnection in ways that also maintain difference, and we center learning as a continual process of responding to incommensurabilities as they arise and of changing through time. As part of this commitment, we are intentional about showing up in tidal spaces and opening ourselves to letting tidal forces guide, breathing in material histories and possibilities for disruption that emerge from these encounters. This started in our respective experiences as graduate students. Hillyer set buckets and inexpensive GPS units in the tides and followed their tracks to help clammers answer their own questions about tidal flows. Sutton listened to stories from elders about how tides shaped the construction of fish weirs and sustenance fishing practices. And McGreavy identified how working the tides offered a form of tidal governance for more collaborative approaches to coastal conservation and shellfish management.

Now we show up in tidal places together, visiting locations with no direct purpose aside from listening, breathing, and moving together to let the place shape us. For example, in the summer of 2021, we visited multiple colonial forts to strengthen our abilities to sense incommensurabilities that emerge through entanglements of ecosystems, oppressive forces like colonialism and neoliberalism, coastal inhabitation, and sustenance practices like fishing and clamming. For one of these trips, we visited a gathering place alongside pisipiqe, a location that in 1754 was (re)named Fort Halifax. At the entrance, a granite monument defines this place as one where "Native Americans inhabited this site at the confluence of the Kennebec and Sebasticook Rivers from at least 5,000 years ago, until 1692. A pilgrim trading post was also located on this site in the 1650s." This narrative provides a clear example of what Jean O'Brien refers to as firsting and lasting, where naming "Native Americans" is a rhetorical strategy to construct the disappearance of Wabanaki peoples from this land to make way for a series of colonial "firsts." In this case, the sign names the first construction of a pilgrim trading post and, by extension, the "best" use of this location for capitalist and economic development. Sensing this pattern here and elsewhere strengthened our ability to disrupt this narrative in our own writing, as we describe in the concluding section.

In addition to going places together, these attunements also mean constructing different types of interactions designed to amplify recursive rhythms of listening, breathing, and standing and moving together. This occurs within our core group, in which we listen to each other and make shared decisions about all aspects of this work including when and how we take on new commitments, what roles we can play in these efforts, as well as how to adjust those roles over time, what priorities deserve our attention, and how to discern what is right when forms of justice are incommensurate. As we describe below, listening to each other allows us to address unequal power among ourselves and continually work to establish more equitable relations to enable equity to recur as a pattern throughout our efforts. Importantly, this orientation to power is about our respective positionalities but where power is a constellation of forces. Said another way, this is a recognition of the complex forms of power that are constantly, inescapably shaping how we create knowledge as relation, which includes but is not limited to power associated with our respective roles within the academy and extends to the systems of power and oppression that inescapably shape our lives.

Critical attention to power as a constellation of forces acting upon us at a microlevel allows us to *listen* to each other to begin to identify *strategies* to transform how these patterns and forces *recur* more broadly. This includes material considerations of equity, where we seek to challenge low wages within the academy and build higher salaries into our grant budgets. We also include stipends for community participation that seek to value the expert knowledge our partners bring to these efforts and are on par with what lawyers, consultants, and related professionals would charge for their services. Working with partners whose knowledge has not been valued also means developing empathetic arguments to help challenge how they may undervalue their own knowledge. At the same time, we recognize the contradictions and incommensurabilities in this very approach to material equity, one that is inherently shaped in and through colonial and neoliberal relations. Working within and against academic institutions, la paperson recognizes the impossibility of this position. For them, this recognition means we must "theorize contingently" where "thinking is temporary; [our] right to think aloud is contingent on the apparatus of legitimated colonial knowledge production that ought to be abolished. Theorizing contingently is not to take an ultimate position but rather to commit to analyses that make space for Indigenous sovereign work, to commit to making space for Black and queer thought" (xxii). In language choices that are meant to problematize, they refer to such space making as occurring within layered worlds, nested within a "first world" university that accumulates, a second that critiques, and a third that *strategizes* as ways to open to a fourth. In these layered worlds, we can learn how to "attach a pacemaker to the heart of those machines [we] hate; make it pump for [our] decolonizing enterprise; let it tick its own countdown" (24). In short, we can learn to trust in the power of rhythms as guide and think contingently, like tides, for recursive, disruptive decolonial change.

Tidal Disruptions and Conclusions

Tides as rhythm disrupt temporal forces that construct knowledge as a linear process of discovery (forward progress, innovation, crossing frontiers) and where space and time are similarly figured as singular, separate, bound, and territorialized (Na'puti). In a relational orientation that amplifies rhythms, knowledge is no longer something graspable nor held by any single individual but is instead a poetic, creative process where writing offers unique possibilities. As Glissant describes, "Poetic knowledge is no longer inseparable from writing; momentary flashes verge on rhythmic amassings and the monotonies of duration. The sparkle of many languages utterly fulfills its function in such an encounter" (*Poetics of Relation* 84) and through which it becomes "necessary to renew the visions and aesthetics of relating to the earth" (*Poetics of Relation* 148). Taking Glissant's perspective to heart, we conclude by describing how intimate, poetic relations with tides shape our writing as praxis and ethics.

Tides disrupt how rhetorics become *sedimented* as history, where sedimentation refers to the process through which one world constructs material and symbolic dominance over many worlds (Glissant). For example, Moneskatik names a clam-gathering place that is *still* a place where clams and people gather each other. The names Bar Harbor and Frenchman Bay layer over this clam-gathering place, sedimenting colonial relationalities where this *also* becomes a place where French and British colonial ship captains, and now international cruise ships renamed this clam gathering place "Bar Harbor" to orient colonizers arriving by ship to the presence of a sandbar at low tide. As Na'puti describes, the ways in which these names become inscribed on maps construct colonial formations of territory, property, and landcentrism. And yet tidal concepts show how the persistence of names as relation is not absolute. Of this relationship, Na'puti describes how writing practices can attend to "place in creative and dynamic connections with land and ocean, providing a more expansive register of connections with and beyond landcentric configurations of space and time" (2). Thus, practices of (re)naming these places can disrupt this dominance.

Throughout this essay, working with Wabanaki languages seeks to desediment the seeming fixity of English and French as colonial naming and mapping practices. We agree with Stacey Sowards, who questions the dominance of English language and asks: "How might concepts in other languages besides English enhance our knowledge and understanding of multicultural rhetorical practices?" (477). For Wabanaki peoples, Esther Attean argues that the dominance of English language was an assimilation strategy used to eliminate Indigenous culture. We respond to these issues by recognizing how diversifying languages and writing practices we use in the context of clamming communities serve as modes of continual connection and disruption.

While we produce academic publications to support our own respective livelihoods, we also produce writing that is meaningful and accessible to diverse partners in a range of modalities, including grant proposals, technical documents and briefs, public presentations, infographics, an email listserve, multiple digital media archives and a series of collaborative of videos about clamming, podcasts and radio interviews, and more.

One of the more substantive efforts has been the development of a collaborative website that we currently call The Mudflat (themudflat.org) that also serves as an archive for many of these writing efforts. This website is an iterative and recursive process that responds to ongoing conversations with partners about their interests in communicating about clamming (Quiring et al.). The choices we make in composing The Mudflat are shaped through the rhythms of listening, breathing, and standing and moving with that have evolved into writing with and learning with to collaboratively compose this website.

Fully describing how tidal ethics have shaped our compositional choices on the website is beyond the scope of this chapter. However, we conclude by briefly highlighting four ways in which The Mudflat has become a gathering place, a strategic third space (la paperson), for writing into different relations than the ones that currently exist within coastal clamming communities. This is a contingent writing as theorizing effort, as we try to stay with the errant power of difference and the inherent incommensurabilities in what justice means in contexts where the interconnected forces of colonialism and neoliberalism intensify both rural poverty and Indigenous land dispossession. First, the writing is shaped through a recursive, tidal approach to time. In contrast to peer-reviewed publications, in which deadlines and publishing policies shape writing through a linear and progress-oriented temporality, writing in the strategic third space of a website allows the writing to tune to circular, nonlinear, and slower rhythms. Second, naming this website The Mudflat was a strategic choice to articulate intertidal mudflats as worthy of naming and to challenge the social biases directed toward those whose livelihoods are entangled with mud. This choice was also shaped by an ecological awareness of the power of tidal names to desediment dominant power. Third, as demonstrated in this chapter, we also (re)center Wabanaki languages as ways of knowing by appropriately recognizing the existing protocols for sharing and citing the use of these terms and by challenging English dominance and colonial naming by not providing justification for their inclusion and by letting language praxis speak for itself. As we started reintegrating Wabanaki languages into this space, our approach was also guided by Penobscot citizen Bonnie Newsom's approach that recognizes how Wabanaki language advances knowledge production in ways that normalize the use of Wabanaki languages for Indigenous people engaging in these spaces. Fourth and finally, working with a diverse group of students and community partners, we have developed a set of learning materials that are designed to amplify recursive commitments to listening and learning. One notable example of this approach includes a series of project profiles to describe efforts within Maine's shellfish comanagement system and within the Passamaquoddy Tribe at Sipayik to restore intertidal ecosystems. These profiles are crafted in partnership with those leading these efforts and are designed for access on the web but also as downloadable PDFs so that partners can share them in multiple ways and with their own audiences, too.

Calls for the need to change how rhetoricians create knowledge continue to intensify. Efforts to diversify and decolonize rhetorical scholarship, decenter dominant language praxis, and amplify voices that have been marginalized or debilitated are crucial responses to this call (Pezzullo and de Onís). In our experience, taking a collaborative approach to rhetorical fieldwork helps challenge dominant logics within research and, at the same time, requires an ecological, relational approach to ethics. Tidal ethics have emerged from this need. Letting tides guide is thus a commitment to showing up for what the world is asking us to do and to trust in collaboration for the discernment, learning, and embodied sense of ethics for knowledge that makes relations and difference.

Notes

1. We recognize that working with Wabanaki languages in the ways we do raises questions about cultural appropriation. We have talked with each other and with Penobscot and Passamaquoddy elders and mentors about how to demonstrate respect for cultural and language-based knowledge. Following their guidance, we appropriately credit and provide links to the original sources and amplify sources that Wabanaki Nations themselves are developing with the intent of promoting language revitalization. We are also making a concentrated effort to learn, be able to listen to, and, when appropriate, speak these languages in our conversations with each other and partners, which includes taking

language classes and doing self-directed study. Finally, consistent with tidal ethics, we keep coming back to the questions of what is right and our responsibilities and obligations to the language and Lands as we continue to learn together and change our practices through time. Our work with language is consistent with Penobscot scholar Bonnie Newsom's approach in which she integrates language into archaeology to amplify Wabanaki ways of knowing within academic spaces where they have not been allowed to function as knowledge, as well as to normalize language in everyday practices.

2. Wabanaki relations with the natural world are articulated through trust and reciprocity. In contrast, colonialism develops land-based relationships in one direction, where species are resources to support human development (Liboiron).

3. King, https://www.youtube.com/watch?v=IZxmnyc1GEY, starts at 10 minutes 35 seconds.

4. Karrabing is a place-verb that names "the point at which a tide is at its lowest and about to return to shore" (Povinelli 172).

Works Cited

Attean, Esther A., et al. "Truth, Healing, and Systems Change: The Maine Wabanaki-State Child Welfare Truth and Reconciliation Commission Process." *Child Welfare*, vol. 91, no. 3, 2012, pp. 15–30.

Bachelard, Gaston. *Water and Dreams: An Essay on the Imagination of Water.* Pegasus Foundation / The Dallas Institute of Humanities and Culture, 1983.

Barad, Karen. *Meeting the Universe Halfway: Quantum Physics and the Entanglement of Matter and Meaning.* Duke UP, 2007.

Brathwaite, Edward Kamau. "An Interview with Edward Kamau Brathwaite." Interview by Nathaniel Mackey. *Hambone*, vol. 9, 1991, pp. 42–59.

Burke, Kenneth. *Permanence and Change: An Anatomy of Purpose.* U of California P, 1954.

de Onís, Catalina. *Energy Islands: Metaphors of Power, Extractivism, and Justice in Puerto Rico.* U of California P, 2021.

DeLoughrey, Elizabeth. "Heavy Waters: Waste and Atlantic Modernity." *PMLA*, vol. 125, no. 3, 2010, pp. 703–12.

Francis, David A. and Robert M. Leavitt. *Passamaquoddy-Maliseet Language Portal*. Language Keepers, https://pmportal.org/terms-use. Accessed 24 Mar. 2024.

——. "Pisipiqe." *Passamaquoddy-Maliseet Language Portal*, https://pmportal.org/dictionary/pisipiqe. Accessed 6 Mar. 2022.

Glissant, Édouard. *Poetics of Relation*. Translated by Betsy Wing, U of Michigan P, 1997.

——. *Sun of Consciousness*. Translated by Nathanaël, Nightboat books, 2020.

Gumbs, Alexis Pauline. *Undrowned: Black Feminist Lessons from Marine Mammals*. AK Press, 2020.

Hashlamon, Yanar. "Rhetoricity at the End of History: Defining Rhetorical Debility under Neoliberal Colonialism." *Rhetoric Society Quarterly*, vol. 52, no. 1, 2022, pp. 18–31.

Hernandez, Jessica. *Fresh Banana Leaves: Healing Indigenous Landscapes through Indigenous Science*. North Atlantic Books, 2022.

Hillyer, Gabrielle, et al.. "Using a Stakeholder-Engaged Approach to Understand and Address Bacterial Transport on Soft-Shell Clam Flats." *Estuaries and Coasts*, vol. 45, no. 3, 2021, pp. 691–706.

Johnson, Jay T., et al. "Weaving Indigenous and Sustainability Sciences to Diversify Our Methods." *Sustainability Science*, vol. 11, no. 1, 2016, pp. 1–11.

"Juniper Ridge Landfill Megadump." *Sunlight Media Collective*, 14 Sept. 2020, https://www.sunlightmediacollective.org/juniper-ridge-landfill-megadump/. Accessed 6 Mar. 2022.

King, Tiffany Lethabo. *The Black Shoals: Offshore Formations of Black and Native Studies*. Duke UP, 2019.

——. "The Black Shoals: Offshore Formations of Black and Native Studies." *YouTube*, uploaded by ISSI, 2 Oct. 2020, https://www.youtube.com/watch?v=IZxmnyc1GEY.

la paperson. *A Third University Is Possible*. U of Minnesota P, 2017.

Liboiron, Max. *Pollution Is Colonialism*. Duke UP, 2021.

McGreavy, Bridie. "Intertidal Poetry: Making Our Way through Change." *Tracing Rhetoric and Material Life: Ecological Approaches*, edited by Bridie McGreavy, et al., Palgrave Macmillan, 2018, pp. 87–115.

McGreavy, Bridie, et al. "Science in Indigenous Homelands: Addressing Power and Justice in Sustainability Science from/with/in the Penobscot River." *Sustainability Science*, vol. 16, no. 3, 2021, pp. 937–47. *Springer Link*, https://doi.org/10.1007/s11625-021-00904-3.

Middleton, Michael K., et al. *Participatory Critical Rhetoric: Theoretical and Methodological Foundations for Studying Rhetoric In Situ*. Lexington Books, 2015.

Mitchell, Sherri. "Hearing the Waters: Indigenous Oral Tradition and the Sacred Science of Sound." *Orion: People and Nature*, vol. 37, no. 2, 2018, pp. 15–21,

Murphy, Michelle. "Alterlife and Decolonial Chemical Relations." *Cultural Anthropology*, vol. 32, no. 4, 2017, pp. 494–503.

Nadasdy, Paul. "The Politics of TEK: Power and the 'Integration' of Knowledge." *Arctic Anthropology*, vol. 36, nos. 1–2, 1999, pp. 1–18.

Na'puti, Tiara R. "Archipelagic Rhetoric: Remapping the Marianas and Challenging Militarization from 'A Stirring Place.'" *Communication and Critical/Cultural Studies*, vol. 16, no. 1, 2019, pp. 4–25.

Neptune, George. *Naming the Dawnland: Wabanaki Place Names on Mount Desert Island*. Bar Harbor, Abbe Museum, 2015.

Newsom, Bonnie. *Department of Anthropology and Northeast Archaeology Lab*. University of Maine, https://umaine.edu/anthropology/dr-bonnie-newsom/. Accessed 6 Mar. 2022.

O'Brien, Jean M. *Firsting and Lasting: Writing Indians Out of Existence in New England*. U of Minnesota P, 2010.

Pezzullo, Phaedra C. "Touring 'Cancer Alley,' Louisiana: Performances of Community and Memory for Environmental Justice." *Text and Performance Quarterly*, vol. 23, no. 3, 2003, pp. 226–52.

Pezzullo, Phaedra C., and Catalina M. de Onís. "Rethinking Rhetorical Field Methods on a Precarious Planet." *Communication Monographs*, vol. 85, no. 1, 2018, pp. 103–22.

Povinelli, Elizabeth. "The Kinship of Tides." *Tidalectics: Imagining an Oceanic Worldview through Art and Science*, edited by Stefanie Hessler, The MIT Press, 2018, pp. 165–76.

Quiring, Tyler, et al. "Affective Encounters with Tidal Livelihoods: Digital Field Rhetorics for Justice and Care." *Environmental Communication*, vol. 14, no. 3, 2020, pp. 416–29.

Rai, Candice, and Caroline Gottschalk Druschke, editors. *Field Rhetoric: Ethnography, Ecology, and Engagement in the Places of Persuasion*. U of Alabama P, 2018.

Simonds, Vanessa W., and Suzanne Christopher. "Adapting Western Research Methods to Indigenous Ways of Knowing." *American Journal of Public Health*, vol. 103, no. 12, 2013, pp. 2185–92.

Smith, Linda Tuhiwai. *Decolonizing Methodologies: Research and Indigenous Peoples*. Zed Books, 2012.

Sowards, Stacey K. "#RhetoricSoEnglishOnly: Decolonizing Rhetorical Studies through Multilingualism." *Quarterly Journal of Speech*, vol. 105, no. 4, 2019, pp. 477–83.

Stormer, Nathan. "Recursivity: A Working Paper on Rhetoric and Mnesis." *Quarterly Journal of Speech*, vol. 99, no. 1, 2013, pp. 27–50.

Sutton, Anthony. *From the St. Croix to the Skutik: Expanding Our Understanding of History, Research Engagement, and Places*. 2020. University of Maine, PhD dissertation. *Digital Commons*, https://digitalcommons.library.umaine.edu/etd/3204/.

Sze, Julie. *Sustainability: Approaches to Environmental Justice and Social Power*. New York UP, 2018.

TallBear, Kim. "Standing with and Speaking as Faith: A Feminist-Indigenous Approach to Inquiry." *Journal of Research Practice*, vol. 10, no. 2, 2014, pp. N17.

Tsing, Anna Lowenhaupt. *The Mushroom at the End of the World: On the Possibility of Life in Capitalist Ruins*. Princeton UP, 2015.

Tuck, Eve. "Suspending Damage: A Letter to Communities." *Harvard Educational Review*, vol. 79, no. 3, 2009, pp. 409–28.

Tuck, Eve, and K. Wayne Yang. "Decolonization Is Not a Metaphor." *Decolonization: Indigeneity, Education & Society*, vol. 1, no. 1, 2012, pp. 1–40.

van Kerkhoff, Lorrae, and Louis Lebel. "Linking Knowledge and Action for Sustainable Development." *Annual Review of Environment and Resources*, vol. 31, 2006, pp. 445–77.

Watts, Vanessa. "Indigenous Place-Thought & Agency amongst Humans and Non-Humans (First Woman and Sky Woman Go on a European World Tour!)." *Decolonization: Indigeneity, Education & Society*, vol. 2, no. 1, 2013, pp. 20–34.

Whitt, Laurie Anne. "Biocolonialism and the Commodification of Knowledge." *Science as Culture*, vol. 7, no. 1, 1998, pp. 33–67.

CHAPTER TEN

Mottainai *and Everyday Ecology at the Asian Rural Institute*

SAMANTHA SENDA-COOK

When visitors come to the Asian Rural Institute (ARI), they are immediately enfolded into a routine that reflects an agro-ecological mindset. ARI is a nonprofit located in Tochigi, Japan, and is founded on three principles: servant leadership, community advocacy, and sustainable agriculture. Rooted in Christianity, it has staff, participants, and volunteers from all over the world who contribute to running a sustainable farm that feeds the community and an education program to teach the practices of agro-ecology. Applying the concept of ecology to agriculture, agro-ecology is "both a science and a set of practices . . . [and] is deeply tied to movements of social justice against capitalism" (Montero 2). It is an approach to farming that challenges industrial methods and seeks to work in concert with rather than against the larger ecosystem. Visitors to ARI quickly get a sense of what this entails by joining in community exercises, doing chores to maintain the campus, and taking care of the farm. After eating a meal in Koinonia (the dining hall), they separate their food scraps into multiple buckets that will become pig feed and compost. Long after the visitors leave, the pigs will be slaughtered and the crops harvested. Pigs and crops will return to the plate, becoming fuel for workers to continue growing plants and animals in a pattern familiar to anyone interested in sustainable farming.

This case study, however, offers more than a chance to examine this typical sustainable farming cycle because ARI also teaches community members from around the world the Japanese concept of *mottainai*. Estuko Kinefuchi defines, "Mottainai—

'don't waste!' in a rough translation—is a mundane Japanese word. It is used in everyday conversation when a speaker wants to express a regret for wastefulness" (137). The term can apply to many things, but using it "emphasizes the appreciation toward food and the understanding of its finiteness" (Sirola et al. 8). ARI's holistic approach to environmentalism operationalizes the ecology-like cycles and consequences of food production while also recognizing the cultural factors that impact the decisions of farmers around the world. The concept and language of *mottainai* suggests that there is ecological thinking embedded in Japanese culture that ARI employs a foundation for its sustainable approach to farming.

Adopting an agro-ecology approach—which works with natural cycles instead of engaging in practices that will ensure high crop yields but leave the soil damaged or fattened animals that are prone to infection—is an act of resistance itself. People from all over the world already engage in such practices because they understand and have adapted to natural cycles (such as wet and dry seasons) to live. ARI embraces this approach and teaches this as a way to empower community members. These practices are not always easy; the short-term gains of chemical fertilizers, chemical pesticides, and growth hormones make them attractive options. But ARI's system shows people how to incorporate practices of ecology and *mottainai* into daily life so that they become habit, second nature, and can be done without too much extra effort. It makes actions like composting a normalized part of life. Therefore, I conceptualize these agro-ecological practices as habitual resistance. Building from Bourdieu's idea of the habitus, habitual resistance is not a protest or a trial run. It is not calling out others for their behaviors or accepting that environmentalism is asking too much. Instead, it means developing habits that go against the grain. It is not easy, but it is doable, and it exists in a lot of different places for groups of people who reject dominant values and practices. For this case study, I focus on how ARI's farm offers an example of ecological habitual resistance, in which ordinary acts that challenge dominant practices become part of the larger ecosystem (Senda-Cook and McHendry).

I argue that ARI demonstrates the complexity and advantages of an agro-ecological approach to farming through circularity and the dignity of labor, both of which are rooted in *mottainai* and habitual resistance. I begin this chapter by reviewing the concept of *mottainai* and discuss how it intersects with agro-ecology. Then, I advance an analysis that positions *mottainai* as manifesting through circularity and the dignity of labor. Finally, I explain how this project demonstrates the capacity of ecology to function through daily practices (as forms of habitual resistance) and combine with culturally meaningful concepts such as *mottainai*.

Mottainai as Everyday Ecology in Agriculture

Everyday actions create the world that we live in and function as expressions of ideology, culture, identity, and resistance as much as any speech. In the context of sustainable agriculture, ecological actions offer physical changes to the environment in addition to social constructions formed through rhetoric continuously. In the cyclical way that communication and culture operate—constructing one another—a cultural concept from Japan, *mottainai*, is especially relevant to my case study because ARI staff incorporate it into the everyday ecological operation of the sustainable farm. Bringing together the concepts of agro-ecology and *mottainai*, I emphasize how these can come together to form a habitual kind of resistance that functions on an everyday basis.

Ecology, as an organizing theory of biology and ecosystems, emphasizes interactivity, interconnection, systems, and cross-species influence; as an ontology, it has gained traction in rhetorical theory (see, for example, Edbauer), as this volume indicates. Ecology, then, has become a way of approaching other problems, attempting to see the interconnectivity of environmental issues along with agricultural, economic, scientific, educational, and religious ones, for example. Practices of economic justice and feminism join with environmental concerns to create new patterns of sustenance and support in agro-ecology. For example, Beatriz Cid Aguayo and Alex Latta write, "Agro-ecology combines aspects of local peasant knowledge with scientific knowledge gleaned largely by NGOs through transnational circuits of innovation and exchange around nonindustrial and organic agricultural technologies" (403). Connectivity and interdependence are cornerstones of agro-ecology because these methods depend on the cooperation of local people and nonprofits, information sharing, and transparency. Emmanuelle Reynaud, François Fulconis, and Gilles Paché emphasize the concept of circularity in agro-ecology: "the adoption of circular principles aims to decouple environmental pressure from agricultural productivism[, which] empower[s] local farmers to protect the environment and to fight against climate change" (66). Agro-ecology, in addition to being a set of practices, can also operate as a framework that recognizes the importance of the local physical world and culture, incorporating those elements to resist industrial agriculture processes, which can be wasteful.

Fighting against waste, ARI fully embraces the Japanese concept of *mottainai*. Kinefuchi unpacks the concept:

> The reference of mottainai is often a tangible object such as food, clothes, or other possessions, but it can be about nontangible phenomena such as time, opportunities, skills, and talents. Mottainai as an expression of regret for wastefulness reflects the etymology of the word; by not utilizing something fully to its potential, you are denying or not respecting its essence. (139)

It also represents a mindset and approach to daily life (Fujii). *Mottainai* can be part of a regional identity if the dominant practices in the area are associated with using things completely and saving them from being thrown out if they still have some life left in them (Ueda and Ooga). This concept has caught on outside of Japan with Wangari Maathai's use in her Kenyan campaign, one of the most well-known examples of its cross-cultural embrace (Mutua and Kikuko). *Mottainai* aligns with agro-ecology in its advocacy of avoiding waste; this goal can manifest as circularity, putting things that might be considered waste into use on a farm. Additionally, *mottainai* creates a space for thinking about the larger impacts of our actions on the environment around us. In this desire to not waste finite resources, ARI incorporates this cultural practice into most aspects of the farm, stressing an ecological approach every day.

From the habitus to prefigurative politics to my own articulation of rhetorical practices to Noora Sirola et al.'s definition of practice, scholars are increasingly interested in the ways that ideologies manifest habitually or as "an environmentalism of everyday life" (Schlosberg and Coles 161). Building on this concept, I seek to underline how resistance can be enacted on a daily basis when integrated with cultural concepts like *mottainai* and agro-ecology because they develop into habits. Instead of the easiest, unthinking practice being one that contributes to excess and waste, connecting (in an ecological way) a resonant cultural concept (*mottainai*) with everyday actions produces habits that are positive for the environment.

Background and Methodology

Understanding the roles of staff, participants, and volunteers at the Asian Rural Institute is helpful because it not only provides a sense of what ARI does, but it also demonstrates the range of diversity in community members' backgrounds and their different expectations while at ARI. Staff are permanent community members and run the farm, kitchen, office, and education program; they are from Japan, the US, the Philippines, and Ghana (when I was there). Participants come to ARI with a wealth of experience in one or more of the three principles and to learn more in depth about them. Coming from places that have been negatively impacted by colonization (e.g., Sierra Leone, Cameroon, and Myanmar), participants are at ARI for nine months and take on roles as students and team leaders. Finally, volunteers are there to support ARI's programs as farm, office, and kitchen workers. They typically come from privileged countries like Japan, the US, and Germany, and they make different time commitments with some coming just for a day or a few weeks to others who commit to service for a year or more.

I was interested in ARI because of its international, cross-cultural, environmental mission; those elements resonated with me most strongly. Being at ARI for five months, my volunteer time there allowed me to immerse myself in this community. As a white US American woman, I did not stand out in my role as a commuting volunteer—someone who volunteers but does not live on campus—but everyone on the farm knew I was conducting a research project, which differentiated me from others. I adopted a field methods approach to this research (Middleton, Hess, Endres, and Senda-Cook) and volunteered between 25 and 30 hours a week, making notes occasionally and writing them up more fully later, and conducted 45 interviews. ARI is a place that offers an opportunity to do as Phaedra Pezzullo and Catalina de Onís suggest and "make space for work that studies the center and the margins and those that trouble the rigid binaries of such distinctions" (5). ARI itself operates at the margins of Japanese society; largely, community members push against dominant Japanese values (e.g., by not conforming to dress standards, conventional gender roles, or a plastic package-heavy culture). While Christianity is one of the most dominant religions in the world, it is in the minority in Japan. However, many people at ARI, particularly volunteers, are economically privileged and can afford to donate their time and labor to ARI. In many ways, I occupied the center—I was privileged—while at ARI (in terms of race, economics, physical ability, and education); in other ways—mainly through my inexperience on a farm—I was at a disadvantage. This opened a space for me to be a learner, someone who could do unskilled but necessary physical work; it made sense for me to ask questions and follow others' lead.

Manifesting *Mottainai*

Daily environmental practices at ARI, which function as habitual resistance, work together as part of an ecological system and are rooted in the Japanese concept of *mottainai*. Staff members discussed *mottainai* specifically and early into the participants' nine-month program; there was a presentation about the meaning and spirit of *mottainai* to encourage community members to embrace it. A PowerPoint slide during that presentation said:

> On the surface, *mottainai* is an emotion directed at material loss. On the other hand, it also embodies an object with a Japanese spiritual worldview. How was it created? How long did it take

to get to this point? How many people were involved in making it? How many hours were spent? What is the story behind this object? It is the non-material "story" of any material object that is precious, irreplaceable, and most important to a Japanese.

The ways that *mottainai* manifests on ARI's campus are based on cultivating a mindset and habits that problematizes wastefulness. The daily practices at ARI reveal the integrated and cyclical processes of life on this sustainable farm; this is the first theme that I will address, and it is one that builds on agro-ecological theories. The second theme is correlated: the dignity of labor is based on equality and feminist ideals about sharing work and knowledge. These practices reflect ideological commitments as well as behavioral approaches to embodying those ideologies, ones that resist and promote change from industrial agriculture.

Circularity and "Waste"

What is waste when one approaches the world with *mottainai* in mind? At ARI, people embrace the idea that waste products can be inputs for farming. Waste is a socially constructed concept and things that might—under some circumstances—be considered waste can be reimagined as "resources" (Salliou and Barnaud). Without using the language of agro-ecology, ARI's inputs and outputs demonstrate the concept of circularity effectively. On ARI's campus, I observed this through the production of compost, *bokashi*, and rice husk charcoal. First, composting is widely known and adopted; food scraps are heaped with yard waste and turned with a pitchfork to promote decomposition. The product is nutrient rich and can be added to help plants grow.

 Bokashi is a super-charged version of this, breaking down tougher material faster and getting hot enough to kill weed seeds. Additionally, the product is more potent but can damage delicate new roots. When the farmers at ARI plant seedlings, they mix *bokashi*, compost, and rice husk charcoal—which I discuss below—together in the soil. One volunteer from the United States explained that learning *how* to make these materials gives participants a chance to adapt them to what is available in their climate and geographical region. ARI uses its food scraps to produce both compost and *bokashi*, and the farmers incorporate them into the planting rituals, measuring each by the handful per hole. One participant from the Philippines explained how this will impact her own farming, "We do not know about *bokashi*. We do not know about compost. . . . After ARI, I will teach compost and *bokashi* to my community." I followed up and asked if she thought people in her community would be open to using these materials instead of chemical fertilizers. She responded:

> I think they're very open to change, but sometimes these people, they want guarantee. Like, "We can try that, but we cannot afford to lose this cropping cycle, we're going to starve and everything." So, I think people understand if what you're doing will help them. But it's just that sometimes they hesitate because maybe a lot of people have failed them already. That hope that maybe this time it's going to work. They have that. And I hope that I don't waste it.

A participant from Ghana stated that that he and others are already using compost in farming but indicated that he is looking forward to introducing *bokashi* to the process because, "It's ready-made. Sometimes we think organic fertilizer don't release nutrient easily. But *bokashi* is ready-made. . . . It's an improved version of what we have." This unfamiliar product becomes attractive because people can use it to convert more "waste" products into resources.

What might be the most unfamiliar product that is also a soil additive is rice husk charcoal. ARI grows its own rice: separating seeds, nursing seedlings, planting them in patties, harvesting and drying the rice, and then dehulling and storing/eating it. The wasteful part of this process by the logic of *mottainai* is the dehulling because the hulls could be discarded. Instead, ARI burns them to produce charcoal, which in turn helps plants grow. While this by-product would usually be discarded or simply added to compost, the farmers at ARI make a special effort to transform it into something that will add new nutrients to the ground to grow additional food. Again, ARI teaches the technique and encourages community members to think about how, if they do not have rice

ECOLOGY AND THE IDEAS OF PLACE

husks, for example, they can employ this same thinking with what they do have available. A participant from Uganda said:

> ARI, of course, they teach us different things, but I have to make sure that what I learn here in ARI, if we don't have it in my country, what can I substitute it to have the same thing. I have to make sure to compare the resources that we have here at ARI, then I draw my picture back home in my country, that if we don't have this, can we replace this. For example, you have ARI uses rice husks, rice charcoal, and we don't have in my country. But I see we have cassava, we have charcoal, tree charcoal, so I make a connection, I see if I cannot have, what can I replace.

Compost, *bokashi*, and rice husk charcoal are soil additives and made on the farm to avoid additional costs and waste.

Although these circular practices are common on sustainable farms, ARI goes further to take advantage of waste regulations in Japan (explained below) and gather food waste from businesses and other organizations in the surrounding area to transform into animal feed. Each Monday afternoon, I drove around to do what they called "local resource." My route involved a local tofu maker for okara (leftover chunks of soybeans), a chain grocery store to pick up fish parts (e.g., heads, guts, and bones), and finally a central kitchen for the local schools to collect bags of carrot peels, the outer leaves of cabbages, and bags of white and wheat rolls, which students did not eat at lunch. All of this waste was turned into food for animals, complicating the idea that it is waste at all. More significantly, one staff member told me about a volunteer who missed bread and started taking these bags to his dorm room to eat. This was not acceptable, and they asked him to stop. But this does show the conceptual flexibility that can exist. For this volunteer, bread was food even if someone else had discarded it. For ARI, this was food but not for people. Additionally, this job could have been called "trash collection," but instead we called it "local resource." It illustrates the shift in mindset that ARI develops and that is informed by circularity, agro-ecology, and *mottainai*. Bringing an ecological perspective to this situation, ARI is broadening its food web. While it is still producing food locally, it has created and is relying on relationships with those near but not on its farm, which promotes connectivity and interdependence.

Participants are often inspired to replicate this system in their home communities. A volunteer explained why: "A lot of our participants come from communities where food insecurity's a major problem, where you don't necessarily have a guaranteed three meals a day, or even two, whether that be because of pricing issues, whether it be because of just unstable agricultural conditions, or just maybe a lack of knowledge of how to utilize local resources." Given these conditions, *mottainai* and local resource resonate for many participants. One person from Malawi was planning how to showcase this knowledge and said, "So, we will plan, with our local resources. No money. Maybe the problem will be, how to identify the [model] village, maybe to the land, but I know it will be possible after asking the chiefs." Another participant explained his own thinking:

> I know, in my country, we also have local resources there. So I believe this local resources I'll utilize in order to replace the resources because here also are ARI, they're using the same local resources. The only difference is the type, because we cannot have the same type in Sierra Leone that they are using here. So I think I just have to look at it and then I implement and then do my own experiments, which I will be able to utilize with my communities.

One Cameroonian participant was very enthusiastic. "The first thing is that I want to be able to improve all the farmers' techniques in agriculture. I want to use all our local resources, got a lot more resources than ARI by the way."

They see this knowledge as a path to better nutrition and of breaking free from dependence on companies and food imports. One participant from India stated, "I had this training on this nutrition. . . . We used to buy lots of these products from these companies, then give to the people. But we can utilize our local resources, so we healthy. We can grow by ourselves with different products." A Japanese staff member explained why this is important to their education curriculum, saying,

Sometime they don't utilize local resource well and they just throw [away] those by-products like sacks or cover and they never realize it. At same time, they believe the chemical, agrochemical, or some concentrate feed contribute their farm because of good advertisement. But they spend much money and sometime they lost their land, house, but even if they have rich resource around them, they don't realize. So, that why we show, want to show, you don't need to buy much feed. You don't need to rely on the feed outside so you can find something around you.

His comments emphasize the relationship between sustainable farming and empowerment because avoiding the debt incurred when people buy chemical fertilizers sometimes means that they do not have to sell their land to pay the companies back. By seeing waste as a resource, farmers can learn to use what they have in the right proportions to make strong crops.

For ARI, cultivating these relationships promotes circularity but also takes advantage of Japanese laws that require organizations and individuals to pay for everything they throw out. These laws function to create a context that rewards these practices, and yet they are still not dominant, operating as resistance to accepted industrial agricultural practices. For example, one Japanese volunteer who sold his business and retired from raising pigs industrially explained the difference in mindset: "If I need the pig [feed], just call the telephone. The pig company bring the feed into my main tank. But here, we are using local resource. Only few amounts of the grains we buy from outside. [Otherwise,] we are mixing by ourself." When approached, many people were eager to partner with ARI to provide their waste and avoid paying more to dispose of it. Anna Krzywoszynska writes, "What waste legislation affords is a uniquely powerful regulatory intervention into the spaces of agro-food production. [It] works by severing the socio-material connections linking excess materials with their local context, often by physically lifting these materials from the hands of their producers" (48). This allows ARI to not only promote circularity but also to produce locally fed and grown food. In another example, ARI gets leaves from the yard of a local school; they are bagged up and brought to campus. The rules (and cost) of waste disposal operate as external material structures that encourage, in this case, environmental innovation and impact our conceptualization of waste. The agro-ecology practices at ARI are not unique on a sustainable farm, but what is important is staff at ARI and the environment benefit from having a cultural concept—*mottainai*—that readily makes environmentally sound habits understandable to outsiders. With the grounding of *mottainai*, practices that might otherwise be rejected as strange, unsanitary, troublesome, or frustrating are instead accepted and sometimes even embraced.

The Dignity of Labor

Argo-ecological thinking recognizes that labor is a necessary part of growing food and unpacks how societies support their food systems by either highlighting sustainable, small-scale practices or critiquing industrial ones. ARI operates on the principle of the dignity of labor, meaning that everyone can contribute meaningfully to running a farm, no one's efforts go to waste, and no job is beneath someone. As one US volunteer stated, "everyone fills every role at one point or another," making it easy to have respect for work because one has done it before. By requiring everyone to do all kinds of work, ARI encourages people to have pride in their work and to understand how different people in society are the same. Producing food is not easy, but doing so in sustainable ways not only yields healthier food but also ensures a connection between people and their food. Another US volunteer was reflecting on this and said:

> This way of living is so different from the type of eating I'm used to doing, where in the United States the average plate of food comes from, like, 2,000 miles away. So to be able to know what I'm eating and how it's grown, to me, is really powerful. Also, just like recognize how much work it takes to produce the food I eat that I get so cheaply at the grocery store. It's humbling.

There were several days where everyone in the community was expected to help do some physical labor. For example, on Drain Cleaning Day, most people in the community redug trenches, shoveled out exterior drains where waste had collected, lifted heavy stones to clean the drains under them, and put everything back to ensure that water flowed smoothly. One volunteer said this was, "a very Japanese thing to do." She remembers going out with her family to join their neighbors in cleaning gutters in their neighborhood. This is another example of ARI incorporating culturally meaningful practices into the agro-ecological farm work, but it is also practical since this work needs to get done. In another example, they hand-planted an entire patty of rice to not only show people how to do this without machines but also to foster a community spirit. The work was preceded by special songs and prayers because this labor—planting rice—was part of Japanese heritage and identity; the day felt like a celebration. These are two short examples of unusual days. But two practices that happen daily illustrate the ordinariness of labor at ARI: *foodlife work* (FLW) and "cleaning chores." Everyone who lives on campus or works full-time at ARI is expected to pitch in to the labor of running a farm or accept less pay to essentially buy themselves out of this work.

After exercises and a short prayer at 6:30 each morning, community members divide up to do a cleaning chore, rotating to get different experiences. At various points, my morning chores were cleaning toilets, washing windows, tidying up newspaper piles, building a rock wall, raking cedar branches, and rebuilding the chapel garden. The staff, participants, and volunteers clean all the indoor spaces and maintain all of the grounds. They work together to cook food and clean dishes and floors (conceptualized by some as women's work) as well as dig out fire pits and turn the floor of a chicken coop (dirty work). There is nothing shameful about this work, and ARI regularly tries to combat sexist stereotypes about work being more suited to one sex or another, which in itself is a jarring act of resistance to some people on the farm.

The next task is what ARI calls foodlife work, which is defined as labor that helps everyone eat; this term intentionally links labor, food, and life. ARI wants to emphasize to everyone who comes through the door, even just for a day, that we all need to eat to live, and we all need to work to eat. ARI closes the distance between one's food and one's work by requiring that everyone contribute to FLW, which includes feeding, watering, and cleaning the living spaces of the pigs, chickens, and goats; planning and cooking nutritious meals; gathering and cleaning eggs; mixing animal feed; and planting, weeding, or harvesting crops. After FLW, everyone gets to eat breakfast. FLW happens again in the evening before dinner; the timing reinforces the relationship between the three concepts (work, food, life) because everyone must work with food-related products directly *before* they eat a meal.

In the United States, this work is often invisible, performed by marginalized workers who are poorly paid (see, e.g., Nishime and Williams). The work is physically challenging and sometimes risky, illustrated through news stories about the dangers of exposure to pesticides and exploitative bosses, practices allowed to continue because the context of the work is hidden and the people who perform it are not powerful (see, e.g., Ferguson, Rafter, et al. Union of Concerned Scientists). But ARI centers this work. It is in the open, and everyone takes turns leading and following. By doing different jobs, community members do not waste an opportunity to learn respect for this work and each other; they do not waste money by hiring someone else to do it. One participant from Indonesia said, "I still looking and learning about the culture in ARI, but the important thing is *mottainai*. So please keep something. Don't waste everything food, we can use everything. And respect others. It's very good here." Instead, they form a close relationship with their food, learn to trust one another to keep things clean and safe, and cultivate reverence for the labor that produces food, as the US volunteer's quote above indicates.

These practices function to normalize *mottainai*; they integrate it into a routine and make it an unquestionable part of everyone's life at ARI. Through a presentation to the community, the director explained the concept and importance of *mottainai*. This explicit reference helped situate the meaningfulness of their habitual actions. Moreover, ARI shows that everyone can do this work and that it is important, something to be valued. One Indian participant highlighted that the director participates in all of these same chores every day, which impressed many participants a great deal. He said, "I cannot say that Tomoko-san is Director, and she doesn't know how to take care of chicken. I cannot say.

She knows everything. She knows how to make *bokashi*. She knows how to make compost. How to apply those things." The staff model these behaviors and discuss the intentions behind them explicitly. For example, in the director's presentation about *mottainai*, she explained that not using one's talents—for example, by not doing work—harms their human dignity; it has negative moral and ethical implications.

For some, though, doing this work provides a physical understanding of why convenience food—prepackaged, microwavable, and industrially produced—catches on so quickly around the world. A volunteer from the US remarked that this amount of work is a potential barrier for people wanting to adopt "an intentional lifestyle." For US college student volunteers, the workload can seem particularly shocking. Many are accustomed to picking up food in the dining hall or heating up ready-made meals. Another long-term US volunteer struggled at ARI when she first got there because "convenience is what was my life before." However, for many people around the world, the option of easy food does not exist. After talking a little bit more with the first volunteer, she had changed her perspective and admitted, "yeah, these aren't chores, this is just living."

ARI demonstrates an agro-ecological mindset in which inputs and outputs are closely monitored and not to be wasted. They incorporate the principles of equality to emphasize that producing food is not only necessary work but work that ought to be recognized and celebrated. In short, we should respect those whose labor creates our food.

Contributions

Through circularity and the dignity of labor, the Asian Rural Institute embraces an agro-ecological ethos, which in itself is a form of resistance against industrial agriculture; what the organization adds to it is a cultural specificity. By recognizing and sharing the Japanese idea of *mottainai*, the Japanese staff members of ARI are able to encapsulate an environmental mindset. Moreover, this mindset, by being built into routines at ARI, has become part of everyday life, which makes these practices seem doable and desirable. They are ways of living that participants and volunteers can take with them when they leave ARI and incorporate into their own lives.

Putting *mottainai* in conversation with extant theories of habitual resistance deepens our current thinking about ecology by recognizing the ordinariness of it. We do not have to confine ecological thinking to specific places or situations. Nor do we have to wait for the correct circumstance to enact occasional ecological actions. Instead, ecological approaches can be incorporated as tactics of resistance by building on culturally meaningful concepts. Yuriko Sato states, "Wasting something means that its true nature or, one could say, its meaning of existence, is lost. This evokes a feeling of regret or concern in oneself, who is also inseparable from nature in the nexus" (149). For in-country Japanese volunteers who come to ARI for a few days or a week, the idea of *mottainai* is a familiar one. At ARI, they have the chance to see it in action. For those from other cultures, countries, and language systems, *mottainai* may resonate because it describes a feeling or way of being that they have experienced but did not have a word for. On the other hand, this may be a new idea and, taking a page out of Wangari Maathai's playbook, they can use it to introduce their community members to a way of being that will help them conserve their resources.

One way to build on the idea of everyday ecology is to understand how it is already happening. Samantha Senda-Cook and George F. McHendry, Jr. offer the concept of ecological habitual resistance: "We define [it] as rhetorical practices that consistently push against marginalizing structures . . . while also advancing alternative practices that allow people to act in accordance with a variety of political concerns. We examine the ways in which rhetorical acts of resistance become concomitant with everyday life" (225–26). Once incorporated into a routine, acts of agro-ecology become second nature. What might be viewed as a hardship by those who live a life of convenience becomes ordinary and unquestioned when enacted daily in a community where everyone is turning piles of compost or respecting labor of all kinds. The agro-ecological approach is enhanced through practice and through this culturally meaningful concept.

This approach to running a farm also emphasizes the relationship between the socially constructed world and the physical world and helps scholars articulate how they impact one another. For example, Nicolas Salliou and Cecile Barnaud argue, "whereas the relevant resources are often well known in most natural resource management situations, potential resources involved in this innovation (natural enemies and the landscape) are not necessarily considered as resources in the eyes of their potential users," because they are not socially constructed as such (1). By reconceptualizing "resources" through a process of social construction, the workers at ARI have to shift their thinking to figure out how to provide animal feed that relies on local waste rather than industrially produced, chemically formulated food. While in many ways ARI is self-sufficient, they are also dependent on the community. They are, ecologically speaking, part of the local food web, and so are the animals they raise. While they consume much of the food they produce, they also sell their food (e.g., eggs, soy sauce, and rice) to locals, again emphasizing the circularity of these physical relationships. In this way, ARI offers scholars a chance to rethink ecology from a community and cultural standpoint as well as a physical one.

Works Cited

Aguayo, Beatriz Cid, and Alex Latta. "Agro-Ecology and Food Sovereignty Movements in Chile: Sociospatial Practices for Alternative Peasant Futures." *Annals of the Association of American Geographers*, vol. 105, no. 2, 2015, pp. 397–406, https://doi.org/1 0.1080/00045608.2014.985626.

Bourdieu, Pierre. *Outline of a Theory of Practice*. Translated by Richard Nice, Cambridge UP, 1977.

Edbauer, Jenny. "Unframing Models of Public Distribution: From Rhetorical Situation to Rhetorical Ecologies." *Rhetoric Society Quarterly*, vol. 35, no. 4, 2005, pp. 5–24, https://doi.org/ 10.1080/02773940509391320.

Ferguson, Rafter, et al. *Farmworkers at Risk: The Growing Dangers of Pesticides and Heat*. Union of Concerned Scientists, 2019, www .ucsusa.org/sites/default/files/2019-12/farmworkers-at-risk-report-2019-web.pdf.

Fujii, Satoshi. "Environmental Concern, Attitude toward Frugality, and Ease of Behavior as Determinants of Pro-Environmental Behavior Intentions." *Journal of Environmental Psychology*, vol. 26, no. 4, 2006, pp. 262–68, https://doi.org/10.1016/j.jenvp.2006.09.003.

Kinefuchi, Etsuko. "Wangari Maathai and *Mottainai*: Gifting 'Cultural Appropriation' with Cultural Empowerment." *The Rhetorical Legacy of Wangari Maathai: Planting the Future*, edited by Eddah M. Mutua, et al., Lexington Books, 2018, pp. 137–56.

Krzywoszynska, Anna. "'Waste? You Mean By-Products!' From Bio-Waste Management to Agro-Ecology in Italian Winemaking and Beyond." *The Sociological Review*, vol. 60, no. S2, 2013, pp. 47–65, https://doi.org/10.1111/1467-954X.12037.

Middleton, Michael, et al. *Participatory Critical Rhetoric: Theoretical and Methodological Foundations for Studying Rhetoric In Situ*, Lexington Books, 2015.

Montero, Carla Guerrón. "Women Sustaining Community: The Politics of Agro-Ecology in Quilombo Tourism in Southern Brazil." *Bulletin of Latin American Research*, vol. 39, no. 2, 2018, pp. 191–207, https://doi.org/10.1111/blar.12884.

Mutua, Eddah, and Kikuko Omori. "A Cross-Cultural Approach to Environmental and Peace Work: Wangari Maathai's Use of *Mottainai* in Kenya." *The Journal of Social Encounters*, vol. 2, no. 1, 2018, pp. 22–36, https://digitalcommons.csbsju.edu/social_encounters/vol2/iss1/3.

Nishime, Leilani, and Kim D. Hester Williams, editors. *Racial Ecologies*. U of Washington P, 2018.

Pezzullo, Phaedra, and Catalina M. de Onís. "Rethinking Rhetorical Field Methods on a Precarious Planet." *Communication Monographs*, vol. 85, no. 1, 2017, pp. 103–22, https://doi.org/10.1080/03637751.2017.1336780.

Reynaud, Emmanuelle, et al. "Agro-Ecology in Action: The Environmental Oasis Projects." *Environmental Economics*, vol. 10, no. 1, 2019, pp. 66–77, https://doi.org/10.21511/ee.10(1).2019.05.

Salliou, Nicolas, and Cecile Barnaud. "Landscape and Biodiversity as New Resources for Agro-Ecology? Insights from Farmers' Perspectives." *Ecology & Society*, vol. 22, no. 2, 2017, pp. 1–10, https://doi.org/10.5751/ES-09249-220216.

Sato, Yuriko. "*Mottainai*: A Japanese Sense of *Anima Mundi.*" *Journal of Analytical Psychology*, vol. 62, no. 1, 2017, pp. 147–54, https://doi.org/10.1111/1468-5922.12282.

Schlosberg, David, and Romand Coles. "The New Environmentalism of Everyday Life: Sustainability, Material Flows and Movements." *Contemporary Political Theory*, vol. 15, no. 2, 2015, pp. 160–81, https://doi.org/10.1057/cpt.2015.34.

Senda-Cook, Samantha. "Rugged Practices: Embodying Authenticity in Outdoor Recreation," *Quarterly Journal of Speech*, vol. 98, no. 2, 2012, pp. 129–52, https://doi.org/10.1080/00335630.2012.663500.

Senda-Cook, Samantha, and George F. McHendry, Jr., "Embodying Resistance: A Rhetorical Ecology of the Full Cycle Supper." *Tracing Rhetoric and Material Life: Ecological Approaches*, edited by Bridie McGreavy, et al., Palgrave MacMillan, 2018, pp. 223–52.

Sirola, Noora, et al. "Mottainai!—A Practice Theoretical Analysis of Japanese Consumers' Food Waste Reduction." *Sustainability*, vol. 11, no. 23, 2019, pp. 1–14, https://doi.org/10.3390/su11236645.

Ueda, Akira, and Satoru Ooga. "The Culture of '*Mottainai*' Seen as Symbiosis between Japan's Ceramic-Producing Regions and the Natural Environment: Part I: The Tokoname Region of Aichi Prefecture." *The Science of Design: Bulletin of Japanese Society for the Science of Design*, vol. 57, no. 1, 2010, pp. 65–74, https://doi.org/10.11247/jssdj.57.65.

IV

WRITING WORLDS AND RELATIONS

CHAPTER ELEVEN

We Parentheses:
An Onto-Rhetorical Tale about
Circulating Visual Marks of Hate

(((LAURIE E. GRIES)))

Content warning: This paper discusses hurtful situations and regularly mentions violent acts, which might affect folks differently. It also includes hateful words, marks, and pictures that may trigger pain for some. Please proceed carefully and/or refrain from reading if it will be too traumatizing for you.

Introduction

This essay relies on four years of visual and textual data from studying visual rhetorics of hate via the method of iconographic tracking, a digital research method for tracking the circulation, transformation, and consequentiality of images across time and space (Gries). This data includes over 1,500 documentations of swastikas that have surfaced on social media and the streets of the United States as well white supremacist fliers and other slogans and signs adopted as of late by far-right and white-supremacist groups. Drawing on this data, I share an *onto-rhetorical tale* that demonstrates how the parenthesis—a seemingly innocent punctuation mark—has become entangled alongside the swastika and other visual marks in a highly distributed rhetorical ecosystem of white supremacy.[1] An onto-rhetorical tale, as I imagine and enact it here, is a critical-creative account of a single image's rhetorical life. In one sense, it is a biographical narrative that details both my own experiences with an image and the personal details of the image's experiences with others. In another sense, it is what Jane Bennett calls an onto-story that paints an ontological world in which all entities are "lively, affective and signaling" (117). Finally, it is an enactment of racial rhetorical criticism (Flores) that investigates and comments on the ways that visual marks generate ripples of white-supremacist consequences in collective life.

Throughout this telling, I attend to the interconnected intra-actions[2] through which a circulating visual mark not only engages with various bodies, discourses, and technologies but also transforms and contributes to culture-in-the-making. This new materialist visual rhetorical approach (see also Gries) is heavily informed by ecological notions of rhetoric that help attune scholars to the "amalgamations and transformations—the viral spread—of . . . rhetoric within [a] wider ecology" (Edbauer 19). As Jenny Edbauer's work has insisted and my own work has expanded upon, focusing on rhetorical situations is too static a move to gain a clear sense about rhetoric's unfolding eventfulness—the way rhetoric transforms across time and space via distribution, circulation, and consequentiality. Such focus also does not capture the complexity of affective-persuasive dimensions that, in addition to concrete entities such as authors, audiences, and media, contribute to such eventfulness nor how each is mutually transformed through the unfolding and often unpredictable process that constitutes rhetoric itself. No framework, of course, can ever do complete justice to the multiplicity of elements that contribute to any given rhetorical affair, especially a highly distributed one. However, new materialist visual rhetorical approaches heavily informed by ecological notions can help to "more fully theorize rhetoric as a public creation" (9) and disclose how such creation unfolds with time and space.

For this particular research project, I draw on theories and philosophies from rhetoric, new materialism, cultural studies, and hate studies to investigate how visual marks contribute to the racial politics of circulation in the contemporary US—a phenomenon previously described by Gries and Bratta as the ways in which discourse, bodies, and race are wrapped up in a reciprocal feedback loop of (re)production and (re)circulation (418). While cultural and new materialist studies are not new to rhetorical studies, hate studies is a relatively untapped shared inquiry for the field. The Bard Center for the Study of Hate identifies hate studies as "Inquiries into the human capacity to define, and then dehumanize or demonize an 'other,'" as well as the "processes which inform and give expression to, or can curtail, control, or combat, that capacity." A new materialist perspective challenges us to recognize that hate—as a force of action that is constitutive of multiple -isms and oppressions—is not triggered by human capacities alone. As Nathan Stormer and Bridie McGreavy note, capacities always emerge from intensities of relationality in which all involved entities are transformed through their intra-actions. As the following onto-rhetorical tale discloses, when it comes to white supremacy, circulating marks are constantly catalyzing new rhetorical intra-actions that map onto histories of past rhetorical intra-actions, generating a highly distributed ecosystem that functions to uphold residual values and beliefs within and across particular cultures. Here, I thus zoom in on a visual mark's contemporary rhetorical intra-actions, as well as out on the broader ecologies of which they are apart, to help disclose how hate, as a means of systemic injustice, gets distributed and amplified, even as it may wax and wane across time and space. I specifically track the parenthesis as it becomes embroiled with other signs of hate such as the swastika in order to give antisemitism[4] more due in rhetorical study.

Antisemitism, according to my understanding, is a mechanism of white supremacy[5] that is constituted by perceptions, discourses, and practices that often manifest in acts of prejudice, low-level incidents of hate, and various high-level acts of violence toward Jews (and non-Jews). It is also an affective economy (Ahmed) that is largely fueled by what I call *rhetorical distortions*—in this case, false beliefs, paranoias, and claims about Jewish nature and power that reverberate across communities and have throughout history resulted in a spectrum of consequences—from visual and verbal assaults to institutional equities to murder, extermination, exile, and other oppressive and deadly behaviors. While some recent rhetorical scholarship has addressed antisemitism in significant ways,[6] antisemitism—as it is currently being enacted—demands further attention. While often relegated to a historical past, recent horrific events such as the massacre at Pittsburgh's Tree of Life synagogue in the United States and the recently thwarted attack on a synagogue in Hagen, Germany, make evident that antisemitism is running rampant in the United States and across Europe. Such on-the-ground incidents are only being exasperated by an uptick in online antisemitic incidents as reported by the Anti-Defamation League as well as the Institute for Strategic Dialogue—a think tank for the European Commission. How does hate and antisemitism spread in our contemporary media environment in which viral circulation enables such phenomena to often go undetected? While it is widely recognized that visual marks such as the swastika play an instrumental role in such phenomena, this onto-rhetorical tale inductively demonstrates how hate and antisemitism, in a highly saturated media environment, are co-constituted by even the most unexpected of visual marks.

An Onto-Rhetorical Tale[7]

The only philosophy which can be responsibly practiced in the face of despair is the attempt to contemplate all things as they would represent themselves from the standpoint of redemption.
—THEODOR W. ADORNO

How do we think ontologically about a punctuation mark?

Punctuation marks are more than just mere signs—marks of grammar that indicate relations between other words on the page. Gertrude Stein articulates how punctuation marks possess different personalities and conjure different feelings. Was Stein just waxing poetic here, or are we missing something when we relegate punctuation marks to simply signs on the page? What if, instead, we thought of them as lively marks—visual impressions with complex rhetorical lives that manifest serious consequences in the world as they circulate and engage in various instances of rhetoric activity? What would we learn about them, about rhetoric, about ourselves?

I first fell in love with punctuations marks in the poems of E. E. Cummings. I especially grew fond of the parenthesis. I liked the way it resembled little slivers of moons and smiles of happy faces, only bent sideways. But mostly, I admired how the parenthesis acted in Cummings's poems—the way it whispered the narrator's most intimate feelings toward his lovers, the way it amplified his romantic pleas to them, the way it even tried, in some cases, to bring them back to life.

(eliena, my dear)[8]

Punctuation marks are slippery, of course; circulating to and fro, they slide in and out of rhetorical intra-actions that have different spatio-temporal configurations, stimulating even more intra-actions in their wake.

For much of its rhetorical life, the parenthesis simply marked off needless asides or "throwaway information"—a signal of "dead text" for readers to merely skim over.[9] From Greek *parentithenai*, it signified "a putting in beside." This is why E. E. Cummings was so important to the parenthesis. Cummings rescued the parenthesis from a life of rhetorical monotony, showing how it could do emphatically much more.

Up into the silence the green
Silence with a white earth in it
You will(kiss me)go....[10]

In my younger days, I believed the parenthesis was at its best in Cummings's poems. Those little slivered moons made my teenage mind linger. Refusing to rush past, I read their insides over and over to decipher what they wanted me to know. They made me yearn not only for future lovers but for words and poems and style.

(I write (read me) because of poetic devices like them.)

But the parenthesis is more than a poetic device just as it is more than a signifier. As a mark able to simultaneously manifest in different versions with different functions, it has much more rhetorical and distributed power than that. In one, it is a rhetorical intra-action, a deliverer of intimate longings; in another, a bearer of conceptual opposition; in still another, a means of verbal deconstruction.

(Do you (dis)identify?)

The parenthesis, too, is vitally active, cogenerating, through its encounters, ripples of affective-persuasive sensations that circulate and bleed across publics[11] and hit bodies differently. It is diffractive, in this sense, stimulating patterns of difference constituted by diverse rhetorical resonances and dissonances that themselves make a difference.[12]

Many critics, I learned in college, were outraged at the parenthesis in E. E. Cummings's poems for his production of an oft-considered antisemitic epigram:[13]

> *a kike is the most dangerous*
> *machine as yet invented*
> *by even yankee ingenu*
> *ity (out of a jew a few*
> *dead dollars and some twisted laws)*
> *it comes both prigged and canted.[14]*

Cummings insisted he meant no malintent with such lines, of course, but the parenthesis was already caught up in a controversial scandal from which even Cummings could not escape. Rhetorics of blame and shame popped up across the globe in books, at conferences, in magazines. Forever stained, the parenthesis in Cummings's epigram would be cited over and over as evidence of his antisemitic portrayals.

(The parenthesis with a scarlet A.)

In the second decade of the twenty-first century, the parenthesis has become once again embroiled in an antisemitic affair. Tripled to create an (((echo))) that reverberates across social media, this mark began to intentionally identify and threaten Jewish bodies.

Etymologically, a mark is a trace, an impression in Old English. But it is also in Old Norse and German languages, a boundary enforcer, a line of division that indicates what or who is on the margins. And in Middle English, a target.[15]

Sometimes, the belly of a triple echo is a general term such as (((banker))), the parentheses here calling attention to the term's stereotypical Jewish affiliation. But more often than not, a specific (((person))) or (((organization))) is called out, signaling others where to target their hatred and harassment.

This triplet version of the parenthesis became popularized on a right-wing blog called *The Right Stuff*, where it was intended to take on tripartite representational meaning and demonize the Jewish body[16]:

> The inner parenthesis represent[s] the Jews' subversion of the home [and] destruction of the family through mass-media degeneracy. The next [parenthesis] represents the destruction of the nation through mass immigration, and the outer [parenthesis] represents international Jewry and world Zionism.[17]

The inventor, Michael Peinovich, has been designated by the Southern Poverty Law Center as one of the most vociferous and recognizable white-nationalist figures. Known in alt-right circles as Mike Enoch, he is a recognizable figure at white-supremacist rallies across the country where he spews warnings of white genocide:

> *Diversity means you're next white people. Your heads are on the chopping block.*
> —Freedom of Speech rally,
> Washington, DC, June 25, 2017

> *We're here to talk about white genocide, the deliberate and intentional displacement of the white race. Have we heard this conspiracy theory of white privilege? This is a concept that was brought to us by Jewish intellectuals, to undermine our confidence in ourselves.*
> —Unite the Right Rally,
> Charlottesville, VA, August 12, 2017[18]

The echo in relation to white supremacy actually began as a sound effect, a sonic, resonant vibration. During a 2014 segment of *The Right Stuff*'s affiliated podcast *The Daily Shoah*, an echo reverberated across the airwaves every time a Jewish name was mentioned. It started, according to Enoch, as a "funny pun."[19] But in representing the echoes of damage that Jewish people have supposedly created throughout history,[20] the echo became a rhetorical distortion—both in the etymological sense of a twisted perversion and in the sonic sense, a change in wave-form, catapulting affective-persuasive frequencies of hate across the airwaves.

It transformed into the visible impression of a triple parenthesis on *The Right Stuff* blog in 2016. There it comingled among allusions to gas chambers and ovens and grew in popularity to become the blog's "signature meme,"[21] proving especially useful for launching antisemitic attacks against journalists and popular figures such as Amy Schumer.[22]

The echo did not stop there, however. It thereafter circulated as a meme on Twitter and 4chan and other social media, marking Jewish bodies and organizations as targets for symbolic (((and embodied))) annihilation.

Jonathan Weisman, a target of this visual mark, shared his experience with the triple echo in the *New York Times* this way:

> THE first tweet arrived as cryptic code, a signal to the army of the "alt-right"...: "Hello ((Weisman))." @CyberTrump was responding to my recent tweet of an essay by Robert Kagan on the emergence of fascism in the United States.
>
> "Care to explain?" I answered, intuiting that my last name in brackets denoted my Jewish faith.
>
> "What, ho, the vaunted Ashkenazi intelligence, hahaha!" CyberTrump came back. "It's a dog whistle, fool. Belling the cat for my fellow goyim." With the cat belled, the horde was unleashed.
>
> The anti-Semitic hate, much of it from self-identified Donald J. Trump supporters, hasn't stopped since. Trump God Emperor sent me the Nazi iconography of the shiftless, hooknosed Jew. I was served an image of the gates of Auschwitz, the famous words "Arbeit Macht Frei" replaced without irony with "Machen Amerika Great." Holocaust taunts, like a path of dollar bills leading into an oven, were followed by Holocaust denial. The Jew as leftist puppet master from @DonaldTrumpLA was joined by the Jew as conservative fifth

columnist, orchestrating war for Israel. That one came from someone who tagged himself a proud future member of the Trump Deportation Squad.[23]

And, of course, Weisman was not the only target. A Google Chrome plug-in was even invented to automatically track Jews and brand prominent Jewish figures with an echo.[24] Apparently, the extension—ironically called "The Coincidence Detector"— had a suggestions tab to submit Jewish names to be added to the algorithm and at one point, over 8,700 names had been listed.[25]

The plug-in has since been deactivated, but the echo did not stop moving. As Anthony Smith and Cooper Fleishman report,[26] it circulated throughout much of 2016 as coded hate speech, the epitome of the alt-right's secret corners of anti-Semitism. And on 4chan, it widened its rhetorical targeting to become a means of "nebulous othering," a catalyst for what Marc Tuters and Sal Hagen call "memetic antagonism" against anyone who was deemed a "suspicious actor."[27] ((Media)). (((Hollywood))). And, quite frequently, the ill-defined but pointed (((they))).[28]

As I trace such transformation across a highly distributed variety of rhetorical intra-actions, I can't help but think of the parenthesis's troubling rhetorical fate—its unpredictable entanglement in a longstanding history of white supremacy. Adorno has argued that "History has left its residue in punctuation marks, and it is history, far more than meaning or grammatical function, that looks out at us, rigidified and trembling slightly, from every mark of punctuation."[29] From this perspective, yes, the echo is coded hate speech; yes, it is a symbol of antisemitism, but, again, the triple parentheses is also more than that. As a residual of white supremacy, it is a vital actant[30] in a highly distributed rhetorical ecosystem of cultural racism still-in-the-making.

(We are the punctuation marks that we leave on the page as much as they are us out there circulating and co-constituting a shared world. We injure through and with the marks that punctuate us all.)

In Raymond Williams's terms, the residual can be understood as dominant cultural practices and/or beliefs that have been effectively formed in the past but still play an active role in cultural processes of the present.[31] Especially because of shifting social conditions, the residual, often times, does not manifest in the exact ways of the past; as such, it might appear to be altogether different. But the residual carries forth dominant meanings, values, and expressions, such as beliefs about racial superiority, that have been effective in the past to manifest similar effects and affects in the contemporary moment.

The parenthesis, if not definitively before, now bears the residual weight of white supremacy. Sitting there among the SS Bolts, the Aryan fist, and the swastika, the echo resides in the database of hate symbols generated by the Anti-Defamation League.[32] Some of these symbols like the swastika itself have a longstanding history in a rhetorical ecosystem of white supremacy that unfolds on local, national, and global scales as an unrelenting phenomenon. But others, like the triple parenthesis and the not-equal sign (≠) have emerged anew—the latest example of how right-wing extremists invent, appropriate, and weaponize various symbols and cultural memes to generate a new spectrum of iconography for their white supremacist purposes.[33]

(Think of Pepe the Frog with a Hitler mustache and his signature feel goods message replaced with "Kill the Jews Man.")[34]

In his own work with the swastika, graphic design historian Steven Heller has asked if the swastika is beyond redemption due to its longstanding contributions to Nazi oppression and violence. For thousands of years, after all, the swastika has spread across the globe via Hindu, Jain, Buddhist, and Sikh faiths where it was considered sacred, issuing good luck and fortune. And still today, it emits positive vibrations for many as it lingers here and abroad, on tombstones and temples, on tiled floors and tapestries hanging above altars with candles lit beneath. Does it deserve rehabilitation?

The answer, of course, depends on who is entering into the conversation, how their own cultural histories and traditions and/ or experiences have impacted their own perspectives, who they want to most empathize with and how. Rhetorical ecosystems are dynamic, ever-shifting as bodies, emotions, beliefs, and values clash in tension with the flux and flow of bodies, discourse, technologies, affects, and actions.

In 2016, the neo-Nazi group, the Daily Stormer, hacked copy printers on several college campuses across the US to distribute fliers with swastikas and a highly disturbing message: "White man are you sick and tired of the Jews destroying your country through mass immigration and degeneracy. Join us in the struggle for global white supremacy."[35] Due to a perceived lack of just administrative response to these and other swastika incidents, some students are claiming civil rights violations for "allowing a hostile environment" in which antisemitism is rampant.[36] Thus far, most college administrations are denying culpability and thus are not taking strict action to ban the proliferation of harmful marks on their campuses. But in K–12 districts in Maryland and Oregon, administrators are starting to institute bans against swastikas, confederate flags, nooses, and other marks of violence on school premises.

In the meantime, both in the United States and abroad, an organized group called the Pro-Swastika Alliance is trying to resurrect the swastika and reclaim its original meaning. "The word swastika," as they explain on their website homepage, "comes from the Sanskrit *svastika. Su* meaning well, *asti* meaning 'to be,' and *ka* as a suffix. The swastika literally means 'to be well.'"[37] It is one of the oldest symbols on Earth, discoverable in some version in most religions and traditions around the globe. Thus, they publish articles, get petitions signed, lobby politicians, and hold annual Swastika Rehabilitation Day rallies across the world. The swastika's appropriation by Aryan groups in Europe and later the Third Reich is just one small moment in its long mostly benevolent history, they point out. They want to honor their cultural histories, religions, and traditions. It's a matter of freedom of religion; it's a matter of cultural respect.

In light of such a divergent developments in the swastika's ongoing rhetorical life, Heller himself notes that the swastika is a really quite a "tragic case."[38] But despite its oft-benign functions across time and space, the swastika, he ultimately concludes, should not be rehabilitated in mainstream Western cultures.[39] We need to make sure we don't forget the terror that fascist regimes can manifest, he insists, the horrors that can stem from politics grounded in racism and ethnic cleansing. There seems to be a heartfelt sorrow attached to his answer, even as he cannot forgive the swastika for all the violence it has done.

As a white, non-Jewish scholar of visual rhetoric with an invested interest in honoring and studying diverse cultural rhetorics, I empathize with the Pro-Swastika Alliance; indeed, as Mukti Jain Campion notes, the swastika has been traced back 15,000 years ago to a Paleolithic settlement near the Russian border where it was found carved on a small ivory figurine believed to be a fertility symbol. In ancient Greece, it adorned pots and vases; in the twelfth century, the dress of a Slav princess, believe to ward off evil. It hangs now in the homes of one of my colleagues, on a banner over an altar to bring good fortune. This is not a benevolent rhetorical history that is easy to let go of.

Still, as someone who has been tracking the uptick of swastikas as they surface on the streets of America for the last four years, Heller's position is hard not to support. Unsurprisingly, due to its longstanding history with antisemitism, swastikas here in the US have been targeting Chabad houses, synagogues, and the dorm doors of Jewish students. But the swastika has also spread its tendrils of hate to target non-Jewish Latinx immigrants, Muslims, Black Americans, transgender activists. In New York last year, a Black American couple's home was tagged with a swastika and then burned down. An immigrant-owned restaurant was smeared with swastikas in red paint, a note left on the door telling the owners to go back home. As if hate against a few minorities were not enough, the swastika seems to be fomenting more distributed hate than ever. Its rhetorical stain stretches out like red ink splattered across a pseudo-white canvas. It's hard to forgive something when it continues to perpetuate harm and violence.

I do wonder, however, about the parenthesis's own potential for redemption. A dissonant rhetorical intra-action quickly emerged in 2016 as the triple parenthesis began to rebel against its own sordid actions. In attempt to "bea[t] the far-right, two brackets at a time,"[40] Jewish figures and their allies took to appropriating the echo in their social media handles, perpetuating its circulation via self-ascription until it loses all rhetorical power. As one reporter signed in her name to an investigation of this phenomenon, "(((Zoe Williams)))."[40]

Gay activists, of course, have done such things to some success with the pink triangle. Once a mark of hate emplaced on the sleeves of Holocaust prisoners to mark the male non-normative (aka, corrupting[41]) body, it was appropriated by the group Act Up! in the 1980s as an act of defiance and activism. It now looms largely over the Castro District in San Francisco. Envisioned as a memorial to the thousands of homosexual men killed during the Nazi regime, for many, it also screams, yes, we are still here, and we are proud and unified, and we will not be intimated.[42]

The triple echo attempted a similar turn of fate, as Jewish journalists and allies began to use Twitter handles as opportunities to diminish the ontological anti-Semitic weight of the triple parenthesis. Still, it's clear that such targeting by this visual mark has shaken the Jewish community. Weisman even went so far as to use the tactic in the title of his 2018 book that documents how the Jewish experience has changed under the Trump administration:

(((Semitism))): Being Jewish in America in the Age of Trump

These concerns, of course, were only exacerbated as white nationalists, in a defiant move, fought back with figures such as)))Lana Lokteff(((flipping the triple parenthesis to signal their non-Jewish heritage.[43]

The Punctuation mark is the message.[44]

Conclusion

Since this intense moment in 2016, the rhetorical battle entangling the parenthesis has seemed to die down, giving the parenthesis a chance, perhaps, to recoup some of its less harmful ethos for the long term. But the implications for both our communities and visual rhetorics of hate are clear. As I draw on Hess as well as Zannettou et al. to argue, under the guise of humor and creative sign play, the alt-right has clearly figured out how to use social media, visual tactics, and harassment to incite a fresh wave of antisemitism to sustain an ongoing rhetorical ecosystem of white supremacy. In a new materialist sense, an ecosystem is a complex assemblage with an identifiable and felt presence that grows and morphs as intra-acting entities, with differing degrees of power, move in and out of relations and not only mutually impact one another but the entities and environments around them. A rhetorical ecosystem of white supremacy, as I define it here, consists of diverse intra-actions of bodies, marks, words, infrastructures, practices, policies, and technologies from which affective-persuasive sensations of hate radiate, circulate, and reverberate throughout and across communities to uphold white power. Antisemitism and other -isms of oppression that contribute to white supremacy have never been enacted in a singular fashion across time and space. The enactment of hate morphs with the transformation of strategies and tactics and the invention and uptake of digital technologies and social platforms that afford new mechanisms of rhetorical influence. Especially troubling is how this ecosystem is being exacerbated as antisemitism and hate proliferate rapidly online and often go unchecked due to the mass scale and high speed that circulating coded words and visual marks are now able to achieve (See also Zannettou et al. 795).

Due to this ongoing morph and perpetual, oft-unchecked consequentiality, I want to move toward closure by advocating for more research into how members of the alt-right are able to infiltrate social media by weaponizing visual marks to amplify and perpetuate antisemitism and hate, more generally. In this chapter, I have tried to disclose how even a seemingly innocent punctuation mark such as the parenthesis can be deployed to bolster a rhetorical ecosystem of white supremacy that has been historically constructed and continues to exist and evolve, even as it may wax and wane in terms of visibility and felt violence. I have also tried to elucidate how, in an age of social media, the power of hate comes to be amplified as a publicly circulating affective, persuasive force with pressing embodied and cultural ramifications.

As the onto-rhetorical tale above discloses, hate comes to take on affective and persuasive force in a few different ways. In one sense, hate takes on force through paranoia. For white Aryans, "the Jew," Adorno notes, "evokes a neurotic fear of being Other" (as cited in Wheeler 117). We saw such evocation in the rhetorical spews of Mike Enoch when, among other warnings, he reminds white people that their "heads are on the chopping block." The triple echo exasperates such paranoia by marking, harassing, and threatening Jewish bodies (journalists, bankers, rabbis) who are perceived to have power to contribute to the longstanding denigration of the white race.

Hate also comes to take on force as a rhetorical distortion of blame, functioning as both and simultaneously a fracturing force and a unifying one. As Ahmed explains, white Aryans share a "love for the nation that makes the white Aryans feel hate towards others who, in 'taking away' the nation, are taking away their history, as well as their future" (43). Hate, then, works to oppress and take away perceived power from Jews and non-whites while simultaneously binding whites in a collective vision for a white nation. In such circumstances, hate does function as a singular, directed emotion (49) toward specific individuals, organizations, institutions, etc., as this onto-rhetorical tale about the triple echo has made visible. Yet hate also generates, in Ahmed's words, an affective economy—a (re)organizing machine that fuels the engines of white-supremacist logics, identities, and discourses that constitute a broader rhetorical ecosystem of white supremacy. Visual marks circulating across social media play an important role in such contemporary formations. Yes, they often work toward resistance as we saw when Weisman, other Jewish figures, and many allies appropriated the triple echo to disrupt its venomous power. However, as evident in the viral targeting of Jewish bodies by the triple echo, visual marks also feed the emotions, logics, identities, and rhetorical distortions that unfold across the World Wide Web to help solidify and sustain collective efforts of white control and power.

Lastly, and especially when weaponized via visual marks such as the triple parenthesis, hate also comes to take on force as sanctioned violence. In *Toward a Theory of Peace*, Forseberg argues that "sanctioned forms of violence are associated with particular problems in a given form of social organization; and that the moral beliefs which justify given forms of socially-sanctioned violence concern not merely the actual or perceived utility of the practice as a means to certain ends, but the perceived significance of the ends themselves" (128). Typically, when thinking of sanctioned violence, many conjure acts of physical violence condoned by local or national governments; however, sanctioned violence is also enacted and perpetuated by various groups who justify the vehement use of powerful emotions as an important means of preserving power. Such actions, as this onto-rhetorical tale discloses, often become enacted through visual assaults, which accumulate force through a combination of symbolism, direction, frequency, and scale (see Lozano). In the case of the parenthesis, we saw, for instance, how it gathered force as hate, as violence, when it was tripled, repeatedly and broadly circulated, and deployed to directly target and threaten Jewish bodies—actions sanctioned by alt-right figures such as Mike Enoch to help prevent "white genocide" and thus preserve white dominance and control.

As scholars continue, then, to study white supremacy in an era when visual rhetorics of hate are often able to virally circulate often under the radar across the web, let me close with a few questions to drive future research. For it is not just the alt-right who operationalize visual marks as hate in the borderless spaces of the web nor geographical spaces across the globe. Based on my research for a public humanities project I am working on right now called the Swastika Monitor, it is, in fact, quite clear that swastikas and other visual marks of hate are in high circulation both in Europe and abroad, and they are surfacing with new slogans aimed to launch a fresh wave of antisemitism. In 2020 in Paris, for instance, syringes in the shape of swastikas surfaced in signs at protests over France's coronavirus health pass where they circulated alongside a new but increasingly concerting antisemitic slogan "Mais qui" (Willsher). It is too soon to tell if this "veiled accusation" (Dessi, par. 1) that Jews are responsible for the global COVID pandemic will become a powerful new anti-Semitic slogan. But for those interested in addressing the racial politics of circulation in and across the globe, it does point to the urgent need for scholars to keep pace with emerging visual and textual, digital and material rhetorics that become entangled, often right under our nose, with bodies, organizations, technologies, and other discourse in antisemitic and white-supremacist affairs. As visual rhetoric scholars, we especially need to ask: What other visual marks besides the parenthesis and the swastika are circulating in conjunction with diverse slogans to which we need to pay closer attention in order to help make sense of how antisemitism and white supremacy are still in the making? And why, in our contemporary moment, are these being turned to by the far right and other white-supremacist groups? What do they afford in an era not only of ongoing white supremacy but also slow creep of contemporary fascism? While asking such questions may not help us halt the circulation and consequentiality of visual rhetorics of hate, rhetoric scholars can at least do our part to expose how the highly distributed affair of white supremacy and its various threads of hate proliferate in an intensely networked globalized world.

Notes

1. See page 260 of this essay to see how I define *rhetorical ecosystem of white supremacy.*

2. Intra-action is a term deployed by K. Barad (2007) to note how entities that come into an encounter are mutually transformed through the process and that it is through such encounters that agency emerges.

3. As I have described elsewhere (2015), rhetorical transformation refers to the ways in which images become affective and persuasive with time and space as they circulate, enter into diverse collective activities, and catalyze a multiplicity of consequences.

4. In this paper, I adhere to the spelling of antisemitism as such suggested by the International Holocaust Remembrance Alliance Committee on Antisemitism and Holocaust Denial. I have not changed the spelling of this word in titles published by other authors or in quoted material.

5. Many white supremacists blame Jews for the possible extinction of the white race. As explained in "White Supremacy" by the Anti-Defamation League (n.d.), this extinction is perceived to be caused by "a rising 'flood' of non-whites, who are controlled and manipulated by Jews . . ." (par. 1). In addition, as A. Myers (2019) notes, white nationalists often pit Jews against other minoritized communities, perpetuating a narrative that Jews, who control financial power, are the ones that oppress others by locking them in systems of poverty (par. 4).

6. As just two recent examples, see Kiewe, 2020; Fernheimer 2016.

7. In this onto-rhetorical tale, I deviate from MLA citation format guidelines and use endnotes in order to generate a fluent, affective narrative. The endnotes document all cited sources, which have also been included in the bibliography.

8. See Cummings, E. E. *Complete Poems,* 825.

9. Cummings 215–47.

10. Cummings 529.

11. See Edbauer. Also Stewart.

12. See Dolphijn and van der Tuin interview with Barad.

13. See Miller 13–22.

14. See Cummings 644.

15. See entry for "Mark" on the Online Etymology Dictionary.

16. By *body* here, I mean to indicate both the individual and collective.

17. Quoted in Smith and Fleishman, "(((Echoes)))," par. 11.

18. Quoted in "Michael 'Enoch' Peinovich," Southern Poverty Law Center, par. 2 and 3.

19. Quoted in Marantz, par. 38.

20. Quoted in Yglesias, par. 8.

21. Marantz, par. 39.

22. See Smith and Fleishman, "(((Echoes)))" for a picture of the triple echo targeting Amy Schumer on *The Right Stuff* blog.

23. Weisman 2016, par. 1–4.

24. See Fleishman and Smith, "'Coincidence Detector.'"

25. See JTA.

26. See Smith and Fleishman, "(((Echoes)))."

27. See Tuters and Hagen 2220 and 2230.

28. See Tuters and Hagen 2230.

29. Adorno, Theodore. "Punctuation Marks," 300–305.

30. An actant is term used by Latour (2004) to signify interactions between human and material entities that ". . . modif[ies] other actors through a series of . . ." actions (75).

31. Williams, pp. 121–6.

32. See Anti-Defamation League, "ADL to Add (((Echo))) Symbol," n.d. See also Tiven, 2016.

33. See Hess.

34. See the collage of antisemitic remixes of Pepe the Frog offered by the Philadelphia Holocaust Remembrance Foundation. https://www.philaholocaustmemorial.org/antisemitism-explained/.

35. See Cuthbertson.

36. See "UIUC Jewish Students," ABC 7 Chicago Digital Team, 2020.

37. See proswastika.org.

38. Heller 169.

39. Heller 165.

40. See Williams, Zoe.

41. Ibid.

41. See United States Holocaust Museum.

42. See Fehely.

43. See Hess, par. 17.

44. Hess writes that "the message is in the punctuation," but we might also draw on Marshall McLuhan to say the punctuation mark is now the message.

Works Cited

"ADL to Add (((Echo))) Symbol, Used by Anti-Semites on Twitter, to Online Hate Symbols Database." *Anti-Defamation League*, 6 June 2016, www.adl.org/news/press-releases/adl-to-add-echo-symbol-used-by-anti-semites-on-twitter-to-online-hate-symbols. Accessed 15 Mar. 2020.

Adorno, Theodor. *Minima Moralia: Reflections on a Damaged Life.* Translated by E. F. N. Jephcott, Verso, 2006.

———. "Punctuation Marks." *Notes to Literature.* Translated by Sherry Weber Nicholsen, Columbia UP, 1993, pp. 91–97.

Ahmed, Sara. *The Cultural Politics of Emotion.* 2nd ed., Routledge, 2014.

Barad, Karen. *Meeting the Universe Halfway: Quantum Physics and the Entanglement of Matter and Meaning.* Duke UP, 2007.

Bennett, Jane. *Vibrant Matter: A Political Ecology of Things.* Duke UP, 2010.

Campion, Mukti Jain. "How the World Loved the Swastika—until Hitler Stole It." *BBC News*, 23 Oct. 2014, https://bbc.com/news/magazine-29644591. Accessed 10 Jan. 2020.

Cummings, E. E. *Complete Poems, 1904–1962,* edited by George J. Firmage, Liveright, 1991.

Cuthbertson, Anthony. "Hacker Hijacks Thousands of Printers to Disseminate Nazi Propaganda." *Newsweek,* 30 Mar. 2016, www.newsweek.com/hacker-hijacks-thousands-printers-disseminate-nazi-propaganda-442263. Accessed 10 Oct. 2020.

Dessi, Giulia. "How Qui? (Who?) Became the New Anti-Semitic Slogan of the Far Right and Conspiracy Theorists in France." *Media Diversity Institute*, 27 Sept. 2021. www.media-diversity.org/how-qui-who-became-the-new-antisemitic-slogan-of-the-far-right-and-conspiracy-theorists-in-france/. Accessed 15 Oct. 2021.

Dolphijn, Rick, and Iris van der Tuin. "Interview with Karen Barad." *New Materialism: Interviews & Cartographies.* Open Humanities Press, 2012, pp. 48–70, https://quod.lib.umich.edu/o/ohp/11515701.0001.001/1:4.3/—new-materialism-interviews-cartographies?rgn=div2;view=toc. Accessed 15 Jan. 2020.

Edbauer, Jenny. "Unframing Models of Public Distribution: From Rhetorical Situation to Rhetorical Ecologies." *Rhetoric Society Quarterly*, vol. 35, no. 4, 2005, pp. 5–24.

Fehely, Devin. "Pink Triangle above SF Castro Symbolizes LGBTQ Pride and Resilience." *CBS News*, 24 June 2017, https://sanfrancisco .cbslocal.com/2017/06/24/pink-triangle-twin-peaks-sf-castro-pride/. Accessed 15 Jan. 2020.

Fernheimer, Janice W. "Confronting Kenneth Burke's Anti-Semitism." *Journal of Communication & Religion*, vol. 39, no. 2, 2016, pp. 36–53.

Fleishman, Cooper, and Anthony Smith. "'Coincidence Detector': The Google Chrome Extension White Supremacists Use to Track Jews." *Mic*, 2 June 2016, www.mic.com/articles/145105/coincidence-detector-the-google-extension-white-supremacists-use-to-track-jews#.ND6w4ZgBM. Accessed 15 Jan. 2020.

———. "The Neo-Nazi (((Echoes))) Symbol Is Officially Hate Speech." *Mic*, 6 June 2016, www.mic.com/articles/145459/the-neo-nazi-echoes-symbol-is-officially-hate-speech. Accessed 15 Sept. 2019.

Flores, Lisa A. "Towards an Insistent and Transformative Racial Rhetorical Criticism." *Communication and Critical/Cultural Studies*, vol. 15, no. 4, 2018, pp. 349–57.

Forsberg, Randall Caroline Watson. *Toward a Theory of Peace: The Role of Moral Beliefs*, edited by Matthew Evangelista and Neta C. Crawford, Cornell UP, 2019.

"Gay Men under the Nazi Regime." *United States Holocaust Memorial Museum*, https://encyclopedia.ushmm.org/content/en/article/persecution-of-homosexuals-in-the-third-reich. Accessed 10 Jan. 2021.

"Hate Studies." *Bard Center for the Study of Hate*, https://bcsh.bard .edu/hate-studies/. Accessed 15 Sept., 2019.

Heller, Steven. *The Swastika: Symbol beyond Redemption?* Allworth Press, 2000.

Hess, Amanda. "For the Alt-Right, the Message Is in the Punctuation." *The New York Times*, 10 June 2016, www.nytimes.com/2016/06/11/arts/for-the-alt-right-the-message-is-in-the-punctuation.html. Accessed 15 Jan. 2020.

JTA. "Google Removes Anti-Semitic App Used to Target Jews Online." *The Jerusalem Post*, 4 June 2016, www.jpost.com/Diaspora/Google-removes-anti-Semitic-app-used-to-target-Jews-online-455902. Accessed 15 Jan. 2020.

Kiewe, Amos. *The Rhetoric of Antisemitism: From the Origins of Christianity and Islam to the Present.* Lexington Books, 2020.

Latour, Bruno. *Politics of Nature: How to Bring the Sciences into Democracy.* Translated by Catherine Porter, Harvard UP, 2004.

Lazroe, Beth. "Visual Assault on the Streets of Prague." *In Our Faces,* https://bethlazroe.com/inourfaces/authorstatement. Accessed 15 Oct. 2021.

Marantz, Andrew. "Birth of a White Supremacist." *The New Yorker,* 9 Oct. 2017, www.newyorker.com/magazine/2017/10/16/birth-of-a-white-supremacist. Accessed 13 Mar. 2020.

"Mark, N. (1)." *Online Etymology Dictionary,* www.etymonline.com/search?q=mark. Accessed 15 Jan. 2020.

"Michael 'Enoch' Peinovich." *Southern Poverty Law Center,* www.splcenter.org/fighting-hate/extremist-files/individual/michael-enoch-peinovich. Accessed 15 Jan. 2020.

Miller, Marc. "Jews and Anti-Semitism in the Poetry of E. E. Cummings." *Spring,* no. 7, 1998, pp. 13–22.

Myers, Alex. "White Supremacy Is the Root of Violence against Jews." *YES!* 31 Dec. 2019, www.yesmagazine.org/opinion/2019/12/31/attack-monsey-antisemitism. Accessed 22 June 2021.

"Pro-Swastika." *Pro-Swastika,* www.proswastika.org/. Accessed 16 June 2020.

Smith, Anthony, and Cooper Fleishman. "(((Echoes))), Exposed: The Secret Symbol Neo-Nazis Use to Target Jews Online." *Mic,* 1 June 2016,, www.mic.com/articles/144228/echoes-exposed-the-secret-symbol-neo-nazis-use-to-target-jews-online. Accessed 15 Sept. 2019.

Stormer, Nathan, and Bridie McGreavy. "Thinking Ecologically about Rhetoric's Ontology: Capacity, Vulnerability, and Resilience." *Philosophy & Rhetoric,* vol. 50, no. 1, 2017, pp. 1–25.

Tartakovsky, Roi. "E. E. Cummings's Parentheses: Punctuation as Poetic Device." *Style,* vol. 43, no. 2, 2009, pp. 215–47.

Tiven, Lucy. "White Supremacists Are Using a Google Chrome Plugin to Target Jews." *ATTN:,* 13 June 2016, https://archive.attn.com/

stories/8796/white-supremacists-are-using-google-chrome-plugin-to-target-jews-online. Accessed 15 Jan. 2020.

Tuters, Marc, and Sal Hagen. "(((They))) Rule: Memetic Antagonism and Nebulous Othering on 4chan." *New Media & Society,* vol. 22, no. 12, 2020, pp. 2218–37.

"UIUC Jewish Students File Complaint Alleging University Allows for Anti-Semitic Hostile Environment." *ABC 7 News,* 25 Oct. 2020, https://abc7chicago.com/uiuc-jewish-students-file-complaint-anti-semitic-harassment-university-of-illinois-urbana-champaign/7304226/. Accessed 15 Dec. 2020.

Welsch, J. T. "Gertrude Stein: Poetry & Grammar." *The Portable Poetry Workshop,* edited by Nigel McLoughlin, Red Globe Press, 2016, pp. 195–200.

Wheeler, Brett R. "Antisemitism as Distorted Politics: Adorno on the Public Sphere." *Jewish Social Studies: History, Culture, Society,* vol. 7, no. 2, 2001, pp. 114–48.

"White Supremacy." *Anti-Defamation League,* www.adl.org/resources/glossary-terms/white-supremacy. Accessed 15 June 2020.

Williams, Raymond. "Dominant, Residual, and Emergent." *Marxism and Literature,* Oxford UP, 1977, pp. 121–277.

Williams, Zoe. "(((Echoes))): Beating the Far-Right, Two Triple-Brackets at a Time." *The Guardian,* 12 June 2016, www.theguardian.com/technology/shortcuts/2016/jun/12/echoes-beating-the-far-right-two-triple-brackets-at-a-time. Accessed 15 Jan. 2020.

Willsher, Kim. "Hate Speech Inquiries Launched in France over Antisemitic Protest Banners." *The Guardian,* 16 Aug. 2021, www.theguardian.com/world/2021/aug/16/hate-speech-inquiries-launched-in-france-over-antisemitic-protest-banners. Accessed 22 Sept. 2021.

Zannettou. Savvas, et al. "A Quantitative Approach to Understanding Online Antisemitism." Fourteenth International AAAI Conference on Web and Social Media (ICWSM 2020), 8–11 June 2020, online.

CHAPTER TWELVE

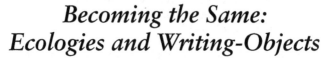

Becoming the Same:
Ecologies and Writing-Objects

JOHN H. WHICKER

When Richard Coe introduced *eco-logic* to writing studies, he did so as a means of attending to how "meaning is relative to context" (233). Since then, *ecology* in writing studies has become a more radical concept, attending not only to socio-cultural influences on meaning but also the inherent ecology of writing itself that emerges from the material and social interplay of human and nonhuman entities (Boyle; Cooper; Dobrin; Hawk). In the broader field of composition, *ecology* has become commonplace, a broader more dynamic model of context that replaces well-critiqued concepts like *discourse community* and which is accepted as a means of acknowledging the role of nonhumans in writers' development and identity (see Wang) and their processes (see Rule). This increasingly common use of ecology, however, often strips the concept of its more disruptive, posthuman, and postcompositional force. For most of the field, ecologies, like communities, remain places into and through which writing subjects, however situated, travel, like tourists stopping in to encounter the local culture, wildlife, and landscapes.

One reason for this resistance to posthuman ecological theory is likely that while, as Raúl Sánchez notes, "our field's image of the scene of writing is more detailed than ever before, allowing us to see invention as a distributed property rather than as the work of a singular intentional agent . . . singular agents remain a part of the landscape, even if we no longer give them ontological or epistemological pride of place" (17). While it is certainly the case that the subject lingers in writing studies, Sánchez accurately notes here that part of the reason why it lingers is that no matter how distributed, ecological, entangled we understand writers to be, there remains "a reserve of agency that is not necessarily exposed to the ecological economy" (90). Or, in other words, ecological theories have not theorized writing in a way that entirely renders individual writers and their choices impotent or unnecessary, nor have they, in the end, really attempted to do so, nor should they. As Sánchez argues, "the idea that some notion of Cartesian sovereignty might remain, even in such thoroughly ecological metaphors for writing, is not necessarily a theoretical problem that needs to be solved. Rather, the problem we should focus on is what to make of that sovereignty" (76). The task, in other words, is not to arrive at ecological theories that do finally elide any sense of the individual agent but instead to theorize that agent in a way that complements ecological accounts of writing as entangled, distributed, dynamic, fluid, and embodied.

As Sidney I. Dobrin argues, we need an understanding of ecology "that looks to the whole of the agent/system relation, privileging neither above the other" (130). Most recent theories that do address or have implications for agents (see Boyle; Gries; Hawk; Pflugfelder; Rickert), as Marilyn Cooper argues, "have either retained some form of this [socially constructed postmodern] subject, or tacitly assumed the transcendental subject by referring to volition and intention, or simply stopped talking about subjects or agents at all" (128). Ecological writing theories can and need to do more. It is possible and important to articulate a theory that can truly balance both agent and system, individual and collective, part and whole, being and becoming, neither reducing relationality to the actions of a subject nor robbing objects of their agency. Articulating such a theory has been the focus of my theoretical thinking for a while now (Whicker), and Cooper also continues to attempt to find such a balance. Where Cooper, however, attempts to recuperate individual agents from a radical account of relationality, I argue that such a balance is better found through a radical defense of the individual agent borrowing from object-oriented ontology (Bryant; Harman; Maciel; Mickey). In this chapter, I will attempt to articulate the outlines of my theory with a focus not on critique but on complementarity and harmonization with Cooper and other posthuman relational accounts in a way that shows how such a defense of individual agents might usefully reimagine what writing is and how human experience of agency is a function of writing. More importantly, I will show that close attention to the question of individuality reveals that rather than writing being a product of thinking, thinking is a function of writing.

Accounting for Agency

Contemporary theorists have tended to take one of two approaches to the remainder of individual agency and agents: begin with some sense of a subject and attempt to chip away at subjectivity, eliminating transcendence and autonomy, volition and intention, to articulate a situated, or entangled, quasi-subject (Hawk; Rickert), while others argue that agency is not a quality of individuals but emerges from interaction in and is distributed among networks of humans and nonhumans (Boyle "Writing"; Gries; Hawk; Pflugfelder; Stormer and McGreavy). It is worth noting that in both cases, the focus is on writing, rhetoric, and action as an emergent function of ecologies, but while some explain individual agency, primarily human agency, through some alternate, quasi-subject, like Heideggerian Dasein, others elide or neglect the question of the individual's remaining agency. The first, as Cooper notes, risks directly or tacitly reifying elements of the subject that epistemologically or ontologically privilege the role of humans; the second risks dispensing with agents altogether, making it very difficult to usefully explain individual actions. As Sánchez argues, "the idea of distributing invention across ecological components and across space and time . . . does not—and in a sense cannot—speak to the exigencies that move an individual writing subject to make certain decisions rather than others, decisions that result in one text rather than another" (96). If we agree that it is important to both fully entangle the writer as one actor among many but still theorize writers' remaining agency in a way that leaves room for consequential decisions, we seem to be confronted with a dilemma, which scholars so far seem to have struggled to overcome.

Beginning with a human subject and then attempting to limit subjectivity seems likely to fall short. Any figure that in any way reifies something like a subject reifies a sense that humans, as subjects, even in very limited ways, stand apart, outside, the entangled interactions of ecologies, interpreting a world presented to and for them. This is likely why the increasingly dominant approach is to argue that agency should be redefined as a product of interaction within networks of humans and nonhumans. Such theories do seem to offer a useful way of accounting for the complex dynamic nature of interacting social and material systems. They also, however, seem, as Sánchez argues, to leave no way to explain any meaningful individual agency. Without some way to recuperate individual agency, the choices and decisions of writers become determined, what we might call *contingent determinism*, since the determining factors become entirely the contingent intra-actions of the system.

Cooper, recognizing this possible determinism, works from a relational perspective to recover individual agency. She argues that "cutting agency off from any kind of actor is more mystifying than helpful" (129). She also, however, "envisions individuals as entangled in intra-active phenomena from which they co-emerge contingently in an ongoing process of becoming" (9). In much of her account, Cooper sounds very much like other relational theorists, while at other times, especially when discussing writers or students, she seems committed to individual agents that sometimes even begin to sound like subjects. She argues, "Writers are affective and kinetic as well as cognitive bodies that learn about and participate in their worlds" (5). This strong sense of writerly agency, however, is usually mitigated by downplaying the role of consciousness in agency and writing. Cooper states, "I argue that agents are individuating entities who act and make a difference, but whose actions are not consciously intended and do not determine the difference they make" (131). The end result is somewhat of a paradox in which at the same time "everything is made new in every moment" (9), but agents "do act and make a difference through their intra-actions" though they "do not act with conscious intentions, and their actions cannot determine the difference they make" (13–14). It seems that by conceiving the world entirely as becoming, it becomes very difficult to articulate an agent that endures.

Cooper draws on an impressive diversity of thinkers from many fields, but more than others she turns to the works of Alfred North Whitehead and, to a lesser extent, those of Gilbert Simondon, to try to resolve this paradox or rather to reconceive "the relation of permanence and change as complementary rather than dialectical and individuals as emergent within metastable complex systems" as "individuating entities" (126). These sources, however, do not seem to ultimately supply an enduring agent. Cooper notes, "Whitehead's actual entities . . . neither precede nor persist after the moment of concrescence" (135). Simondon's theories are even more dependent on a fleeting actor that individuates from an undifferentiated pre-individual milieu. As Otávio S. R. D. Maciel argues, paraphrasing Graham Harman, for such philosophies, "discontinuity is a mystery, since everything is supposed to be metaphysically continuous—be it the continuity of *durée* (Bergson), the Deleuzian virtual plane, the radical empiricism of James, or the Simondian pre-individual realm that has not yet been carved up into specific individuals" (339). Cooper's reading of Whitehead equates his philosophies with those of Simondon and Karen Barad, which seems to impede her attempt to recover an agent to balance the "shift from focusing on objects to focusing on phenomena or events of becoming" (36). The individual agent becomes simultaneously ephemeral and assumed.

Sánchez, in contrast, attempts to grab the other horn of the dilemma and to "emphasize the individual act, to focus on the supposed interiority of the writer, to try to isolate a moment that is deeply integrated with and inextricably related to things around it" (2–3). He notes that "the metaphors of relation we use to describe writing's entwinement in the world cannot help us answer the question of where texts come from. Neither can they help us know what goes on in individual acts of writing" (111). He also highlights that, as is evident in Cooper's need to theorize an individual agent, "our more recent descriptions of writing as distributed, enmeshed, and ecological retain some sense of isolation or separation, the black box" (85). This "black box" is the interior of the individual, and Sánchez looks to "make a way for a theory of how texts come to be, a way to think about agents as the boundaries of interiority and exteriority" (36), which, if it can't open up that black box, can at least help us to explain "how texts come to be," including the contribution of individual writers who, for Sánchez, are human writers (26), and part of such an explanation must be "a newly theorized writing subject" (26). To avoid reifying the modernist or postmodernist subject, however, Sánchez proposes a theory of identity that allows for agency that "is neither sovereign nor constricted but, rather, functional or symptomatic" (72). On the one hand, Sánchez correctly shows that any ecological theory of writing is incomplete if it cannot account for "the core question of what happens when a text is made by an agent" (13), a question that is inextricably linked to "an account of the relation between interiority and exteriority" without which writing theory "cannot really capture writing's complexity" (74). For posthuman ecological theories of writing, on the other hand, any theorization of the agent limited to human identity is unworkable.

It becomes clear that a fully realized ecological account of writing requires an alternative agent to account both for individual action and posthuman ecological entanglement without reifying some sense of an ontologically privileged human subject. This alternative is available in the as yet unexplored individual agency of objects sans humans. Cooper acknowledges that "discussions in rhetoric and composition have rarely if ever focused on the new nonhuman agents, whether living or material" (129). Instead, even Cooper's own account focuses on intra-actions among "humans and other entities" (30). What is missing in both Cooper and Sánchez's attempts to theorize individual agents, and all other posthuman ecological theories, is a theory of things in themselves, without us.

I do not want to turn to objects, however, as an alternative, critique, or counter to posthuman relational theories but, rather, as a complement to relationality, to the flow of becoming. Beings, objects, after all, emerge from becoming, but in emergence much of becoming is not becoming *different* but an ongoing *becoming the same.*

A General Theory of Object(ive) Agency

My theory of objects is primarily influenced by Object-Oriented Ontology (Harman; Bryant), but I find insights for objects in Maciel's reading of Whitehead, Sam Mickey's object-oriented integration of Jean-Luc Nancy, Bruno Latour's Actor-Network Theory, and in previous posthuman ecological writing theories. In the end, I depart very little from the premises of Cooper's enchantment ontology in particular, and I find harmony in even more relational theories like Casey Boyle's account of posthuman practice. The only real break I have to make with relational accounts is a radical defense of individual objects that necessarily requires I assert that, while everything is entangled, everything is not entangled with everything else; there are gaps. The fact of individual action and choice itself, which both Cooper and Sánchez acknowledge, point to this conclusion. Object-oriented theories help to explain why this is.

Object-Oriented-Ontology (OOO; "triple-O") defines objects as "any unified entity" that is "irreducible to its component pieces or to its effects on the surrounding environment" (Harman, *Bells and Whistles* 60, 39). In other words, objects are those things that unify their parts, *become the same*. It is in this relation of parts to whole that OOO both radically defends individual objects and complements relationality or, in Maciel's terms, "*admits* both [an object's] independency *and* its connectivity" (334). Objects are what unify their parts, even if those parts are spatially and temporally distributed, so every object "is simultaneously a totality and a community" (Bryant 108). Because the unification of an object's parts exceeds those parts, every object remains an individual object, as does every part. In Maciel's terms, an object "is not reducible to its parts—neither is the part reducible to its 'towards-the-whole' systemic feature . . . both gaps and linkages need to be explained" (336). This endurance of objects that produces enduring gaps between things is derived from the fact that, despite the constant flow of the world, some things *don't change*. A water molecule, whether it is frozen in ice, boiled as steam, or flowing down a river, remains the unification of one oxygen and two hydrogen ions. This same endurance extends to all objects, including humans and societies, even if such objects are constantly replacing their parts, because it is the continued unification of parts and not the particular parts unified that defines the object. The Ship of Theseus is still the same object even though all its parts have been replaced because of the continuation of its unity. We *can* step into the same river twice. It is this endurance or invariance of qualities that relational theories cannot sufficiently explain in individual action and agency. For agents to be responsible for their actions and whatever differences they make, they have to be the *same* agents that acted.

Whitehead also explains endurance this way in *Process and Reality*, he notes that "an ordinary physical object, which has temporal endurance, is a society . . . an 'enduring object' . . . These enduring objects and 'societies' . . . are the permanent entities which enjoy adventures of change throughout time and space" (35). Enduring objects as societies, or later on the same page "corpuscular societies," contrast with "actual entities" that "perish, but do not change; they are what they are" (35). Cooper focuses primarily on these actual entities, but as Maciel explains, "An actual entity is perpetually perishing, indeed, but the corpuscular society/real object can withstand change, for it is not dependent on their relations to everything else all the time" (339). Whitehead, in Maciel's reading, thus arrives at another key feature of objects, which OOO explains as the relationship between the sensual objects of experience (actual entities for Whitehead) and the withdrawn object or the remainder by which objects exceed both the sum of their parts and their participations, or relations as parts to larger objects. Objects are both enduring societies not reducible to either their parts or their relations with invariant qualities that emerge through ongoing processes of *becoming the same* and sensual objects "enjoying adventures of change" in inter-action with the world, equally active in *becoming different*.

The concept of withdrawal is central to Harman's (*Quadruple*) conceptualization of the four-fold object, which divides the inner core of objects (which Harman emphasizes as the "real object") from the invariant qualities of that core as well as both from the sensual objects and their qualities of relation. Harman often seems to push this concept of withdrawal and the real object too far, creating a duality between reality, hidden "real" objects, and

WRITING WORLDS AND RELATIONS

objects in experience, sensual objects, that he admits he views as unreal (*Bells and Whistles* 77). As Harman himself notes, this radical conception of withdrawal and its implications are what most other OOO thinkers "are most willing to abandon even when they agree with other aspects" (*Bells and Whistles* 175). This is because Harman's account of withdrawal not only makes the objects of relation—sensual objects, Whitehead's actual entities—fictional but also because it creates an esoteric ontology in which the reality of objects are hermetically sealed from contact. As Maciel argues, "The thesis of discontinuity [between withdrawn and sensual objects] is not as absolute as Harman views it" (336). I follow Sam Mickey's integration of OOO with Jean-Luc Nancy's "concept of touch" that "accounts for the sensual intertwining of bodies as well as the withdrawal of bodies from any relation" (293). As Mickey explains, "All entities touch while remaining withdrawn from contact, touching without touching" (294). In other words, withdrawal, rather than being a total exit from touch, is both touching but also holding something back; what withdraws is not the entirety of the "real" object or of the core of qualities that emerge in the unification of parts, the processes of becoming the same, but always *a remainder*, the part of the object that is not participating in every relation. As Maciel states, objects "do not . . . integrally control what will be hidden and in which way it will connect with or be appropriated by others" (335). The *real* object is the whole object. The real object is the unification of all the object's parts, including the sensual objects, actual entities, it participates in when it relates. Objects do withdraw, do always have a remainder of reality because of the way they unify their parts, their processes of *becoming the same*, that yield invariant qualities that always elude any attempt to catalog them in relation. This is how objects endure as systems, and this is how objects are also agents.

Agents, in this sense, however, are in no way reducible to human agency. As Levi R. Bryant argues, "Humans, far from constituting a category called 'subject' that is opposed to 'object,' are themselves one *type* of object among many" (*Democracy* 249). This insistence, however, doesn't deny that humans may be unique among objects, but it does deny that this uniqueness elevates human beings in the world to a place of ontological or epistemological privilege. As Harman notes, "The fact that humans seem to have more cognitive power than shale or cantaloupe does not justify grounding this difference in a basic ontological dualism" (*Guerrilla* 83). Ontologically, there are only objects that differ from each other in myriad ways. Cooper echoes this sentiment when she notes, "Rational conscious thought, language, and technology are all involved in writing, but they do not account for what is most important about writing nor does possessing them distinguish humans from other living beings" (46). Not only is this concept of agency prior to any conception of human agency, it is not even limited to living things—a concept that should not be strange in ecological theories of writing since all follow Latour in agreeing to the fact that "kettles 'boil' water, knifes 'cut' meat, baskets 'hold' provisions, hammers 'hit' nails on the head, rails 'keep' kids from falling, locks 'close' rooms against uninvited visitors, soap 'takes' the dirt away . . . and so on" (71). The only difference here is that the non-living agents I am discussing so far are agents even without humans in the picture at all. This means there is no real danger that, as Casey Boyle fears, "a focus on an individual's agency returns practice to a humanist . . . frame for rhetoric" (50). If anything, this account of agency is even more posthuman than relational theories because it describes agency sans humans—though I fully intend to explore how the unique agency of humans arises from this general theory of agency.

One aspect of a general theory of objects as agents that may prove challenging is its reliance on the universalization of perception inherent in OOO. Harman argues that "*all* objects must come to terms with each other, translating or caricaturing one another's reality whether humans are in the vicinity or not" (*Guerrilla* 227). This, however, is merely another way of noting that objects never exhaust all of their reality in any or even all of their relations. Something is always withdrawn, so the object that any other encounters is experienced as a caricature of its whole reality, its whole agency. This view of perception is not limited to OOO. Boyle similarly argues, quoting Brian Massumi, that "perception should not be linked only to human activity since, for example, an electron perceives or 'takes account' of an electromagnetic field in its movements or that trees perceive or 'take account' of their surrounding terrains by the ways they gather water and sunshine" (51). Perception is universal, though such perception is not reducible to human perception or anything derivative of it. As Mickey notes, "Object-oriented philosophy is more of 'polypsychism' than a panpsychism. There is not one kind of interiority to rule them all, neither a human cogito nor a cosmic psyche" (297). This universalization, of course, leads to the conclusion that everything is an object, including humans, but in Harmans terms, since "the term 'objects' is not opposed to 'subjects' . . . it is not such a bad fate to be an object" (*Bells and Whistles* 38–9). For OOO, everything from water molecules to international institutions like the United Nations are objects as long as they continue to unify their parts and thus are also agents.

Object-oriented or *object(ive) agency* is a function of the processes through which objects become the same, unify their parts, and the way unification determines how objects can and cannot act and be acted on. Levi R. Bryant, drawing on Niklaus Luhmann, provides the fullest articulation of how such agency operates. Important for my project here, this account also provides a way to address the particular agency of living beings and thus a starting point for how an object(ive) agency might account for writing. The end result of this endeavor leads to a, perhaps, radical conclusion: that *writing is the selective creation of meaning through inscription in patterns of neurons, and it is through the function of writing that objects become conscious and then create texts in the world.*

Luhmann argues that systems, or objects, "maintain themselves by creating and maintaining a difference from their environments" (65). Objects or systems determine their own boundaries by what they do or do not integrate as a part of the system, through their processes of becoming the same, unifying their parts. As Bryant notes, "this distinction is not a distinction between two entities in their own right, but is rather a distinction that arises from *one side* of the distinction. In short, it is the *system* itself that 'draws' the distinction between system and environment" (*Democracy* 146). An object's environment is the objects with which it can relate. The way objects unify their parts and draw their boundaries in their ongoing processes of *becoming the same* forecloses the system to some relations. Bryant, following

Luhmann, refers to objects being *selectively open* to objects in their environment. As Bryant notes, neutrinos can pass through most objects without perceiving them or being perceived at all, so neutrinos are not included in most objects' environments (*Democracy* 154). Bryant uses the term *perturbations* for the contact between objects when they can relate.

Objects, however, do not experience perturbations, being foreclosed. Instead, perturbation stimulates the production of *information* on the interior of the system. Luhmann draws his sense of information from Maturana and Varela, for whom information is related to energy or activity. When I press the keys of my keyboard, perturb them, the contact creates information in the computer, but the information is not the appearance of the letters on the screen but the initial electronic signal that ultimately stimulates the computer to produce the type I see. In my own system, information is the initial firing of nerve cells when I type or the initial impact of light waves on the cone cells in my eyes.

This account of information is also compatible with Boyle's Simondon-derived concept of information, which always involves *transduction* "the process in which energy is transformed from one kind of signal to another" (79). In this case, the action of one object perturbs another open to it, which is transformed into information on the inside of the second object's system.

When information is produced, in Bryant's account, it then evokes *system states*, which are the actualization of the object's capacities to act or, in other words, the object's response. Bryant notes that "all objects are defined by their affects or their capacity to act and to be acted upon" ("The Ontic Principle" 274). These qualities and capacities, however, "can only ever be *inferred* from [their] local manifestations in the world" (Bryant, *Democracy* 88). Agency here is the activation of system-states in response to information transduced from the perturbations of objects in the environment of the object. Objects are agents because of the unique ways they unify their parts, which determines their boundaries and the objects in their environment as well as the infinite ways they can and cannot act or be acted on. Objects are agents because they endure in the unification of their parts; agency is their actions in the world. Agents can only be "known" through inference from their effects, just as subatomic particles can only be identified by what they do. As Cooper argues, "agency is unavoidable: what one does always makes a difference" (139). Agents, here, include all objects.

While it is useful to recover a truly posthuman agent in an object(ive) general agency, since what I want to theorize is writing, I need to find a way to explain consciousness while maintaining that "agency is the basic mode of interiority, with cognition being one special way in which agency is configured" (Mickey 297). Agency is also, here, in no way intentional, volitional, or something the agent *has*. Agency is the agent's being in the world. For objects that think, being in the world is more complicated.

The Agency of Writing-Objects

For Luhmann and Bryant, thinking objects, or psychic systems, are those that become aware of their own processes of drawing boundaries or distinctions. Bryant notes that "this awareness is made possible by reproducing the distinction in the interior of the system. Sentient, or self-aware, systems or objects, then, are self-aware because they filter information through a second distinction" (*Democracy* 164–65). This second distinction, this interior reproduction of the self/environment distinction as awareness, allows sentient objects to draw further distinctions, to notice further difference, but it also indicates that rather than experiencing information directly, sentient objects filter information selectively through this second distinction, selecting some information while discarding the rest. This selection of information and its recording in memory produces not information, which the system already produces, but *meaning*. This is the means by which sentient beings can separate the information transduced from some perturbations, such as words, from all the other information produced in the system by other sounds. As Bryant argues, for conscious objects "it is always possible for perturbations to which a system *is* open to nonetheless produce no event of information such that the perturbation is coded merely as background noise" (*Democracy* 154). This is largely possible because the internalization of the object environment distinction that produces awareness cuts that awareness off from the processes of information production. Some information is *unconsciously* selected as important or meaningful and other information is *unconsciously* not, allowing objects to act more efficiently. As Bryant illuminates, this filtering can suppress the selection of system-states by information screened or filtered out as meaningless.

I am only conscious of information my system selects as meaningful already screened from among the innumerable bits of information my system unconsciously produces, the vast majority of which I simply can't consciously experience at all, like the creation of vitamin D when sunlight strikes the melanin in my skin. I can only focus on things my system is already filtering as meaningful. This process is both preconscious and involuntary, which is evident in the fact that I can't voluntarily screen out information I don't like such as pain or grief. The process of screening and recording information in my nervous system leaves my consciousness on the other side of my neural processes experiencing only meaning—the meaning unconsciously filtered through and recorded in my neurons—and not information directly. Cooper comes to the same conclusion through the neuroscience of Walter Freeman. She states, "Nonconscious cognition is inaccessible to awareness but supports conscious cognition in integrating bodily representations and sensory inputs" (55) and that "emotions, intentions, actions, meanings, memories, dispositions, and narratives emerge from the complex system of the nervous system through processes of which the agent is mostly not aware" (144). Further, Cooper, paraphrasing Freeman, notes,

> neurons interact to create a *pattern* that is not a representation of an odor or color, but rather a response unique to each sensing individual, shaped by each individual entity's history and shaped anew in every *iteration*. In response to recurrent stimuli, synapses between neurons are strengthened, forming neuron assemblies that respond as a whole to input coming from any of the neurons in the assemblies. (142, emphasis added)

The qualities of this process, then, are the physical *marking* of neuro-systems in the selective processing of information that *produces* meaning and consciousness itself. Consciousness, then, is a function of writing.

Writing, as Derrida asserts, "creates meaning by enregistering it, by entrusting it to an engraving, a groove, a relief, to a surface" (*Writing and Difference* 12). Establishing that, as Michael Carter also notes, "What makes writing is that it leaves . . . marks. Even with all the technological changes that have brought us from bark to computer screens, writing is still conceptually bound up in the scars left on the face of bark or stone. Writing is those marks and the acts of marking" (102). The development of written marks, however, is not from bark to computer screens but from neural systems to computer screens and includes the ephemeral marking of the air by sound waves in sonorous texts and all other such marks. The marking of neurons is the first writing. Derrida, though lacking an object(ive) account of agency to prevent humanist assumptions, still similarly concludes, "Writing supplements perception before perception even appears to itself. 'Memory' or writing is the opening of that process of appearance itself. The 'perceived' may be read only in the past, beneath perception and after it" (*Writing and Difference* 224). Writing is what allows for consciousness of information through marks and caesura in memory. Derrida furthers this in "Signature Event Context," arguing "that the recognizable traits of the classical and narrowly defined concept of writing are . . . valid . . . for the entire field of what philosophy would call experience, that is, the experience of Being" (92), at least for conscious objects. Derrida thus concludes, as I do, that thought is writing, and it is through writing that sentient beings experience the world. *Writing is the production of meaning through the selection and recording of information in and through neural systems.*

The implications of these findings are immense but also, I think, perfectly complementary to posthuman ecological writing theory. It dramatically shifts the frame of reference through which we might take up Sánchez's assertion that "a fleeting and ill-fitting relationship between the *outside* and the *inside* characterizes every act of writing" (33). It is writing that, for conscious objects, *writing-objects*, creates an awareness of an outside and an inside. Writing emerges prior to any development of language and occurs, initially, entirely on the interior of writing-objects, though neither consciously nor under the control of any writing subject. Regardless of the modality of languages or even pre-linguistic making like painting and sculpture, neural texts are written with and in the brain itself as a marked surface. Even the "oral tradition" depended on inscribed neural texts. Certainly then, writing is, as Sánchez argues, "the context in which such notions as *communication* and *representation* become intelligible in the first place" (14). The processes through which the writing that produces consciousness lead to the making of material objects on the exterior of objects, however, require further theorization.

Levi Bryant notes that "autopoietic machines [conscious writing-objects] can both be actualized in a particular way through information and can actualize themselves in particular ways through ongoing operations internal to their being" (*Democracy* 163). Bryant allows, then, that writing-objects can act through meaning generated from information on the interior of a sentient object's system even in the absence of perturbations and the information they stimulate. This operation that draws connections between neural texts and current experience on the interior of writing-objects is *imagination*, invention, creativity, altering and producing new neural patterns, texts. In this way, imagination allows for the production of additional neural texts that alter the writing ecology of the mind, producing additional imaginative meanings. This imaginative neural-writing, thinking, is the source for further, more sophisticated interactions with writing. While system states, or actions, in most writing-objects occur because of perturbations from the environment, information produced imaginatively allows sapient objects to act more complexly. This complements Cooper's account of the entertaining of Whiteheadian propositions when she notes, "Speculation marks the entrance of conscious thought into the entertainment of propositions" (41). Even this writing, however, remains pre-linguistic and decidedly not a matter of representation. Even in imagination or speculation, writing activates neural patterns that produce meanings as a response and in no way as a representation of something else. Whether meaning comes from perturbations from the exterior of the object that produces information or from the self-activation of neural patterns on the interior of the object, these texts produce direct experience. In the same way, the neural texts activated by being directly perturbed by a thing are activated in the same way by any other means, including language.

The awareness writing produces of the distinction between the writing-object and its environment allows writing-objects, as Bryant notes, to "develop new distinctions, thereby enhancing their capacity to be irritated or perturbed by other objects" (*Democracy* 173). It is this development that gives rise to technologies: ways of writing into the environment systematically to create new objects in order to affect events more extensively than was previously possible. As Harman explains, "we continue to increase our bodily organs with the external proxy of mechanical and electrical devices, and the day may come when these proxies are no longer external" (*Guerrilla* 247). This supports Cooper's conclusion that "language is the tool of writing" that "participates in making meaningful entities" (102). As writing-objects experience being in the world as the processes of information and meaning production, as Boyle argues, "we practice, we exercise our tendencies—our relations and affinities— to generate greater capacities to affect and be affected" (53). This includes the production of increasingly sophisticated objects in the environment that do not externalize internal neural texts but rather allow the technology to produce new objects that perturb us, and potentially others, in ways that alter events in the environment as part of our ongoing being, or rather *writing*, in the world.

The implications of this object(ive) ecological theory of writing and writing-objects for the interactions of wider ecologies will need to be further explored. Here, it is enough to acknowledge the agency of writing-objects.

Works Cited

Boyle, Casey. *Rhetoric as a Posthuman Practice*. Ohio State UP, 2018.

Bryant, Levi R. *The Democracy of Objects*. Open Humanities Press, 2011.

———. "The Ontic Principle: Outline of an Object-Oriented Ontology." *The Speculative Turn: Continental Materialism and Realism,* edited by Levi R. Bryant, et al., re.press, 2011, pp. 261–78.

Carter, Michael. *Where Writing Begins: A Postmodern Reconstruction.* Southern Illinois UP, 2003.

Coe, Richard M. "Eco-Logic for the Composition Classroom." *College Composition & Communication*, vol. 26, no. 3, 1975, pp. 232–37.

Cooper, Marilyn M. *The Animal Who Writes: A Posthumanist Composition.* U of Pittsburgh P, 2019.

Derrida, Jacques. "Signature Event Context." *A Derrida Reader: Between the Blinds*, edited by Peggy Kamuf, Columbia UP, 1991, pp. 80–111.

———. *Writing and Difference.* Translated by Alan Bass, U of Chicago P, 1978.

Dobrin, Sidney I. *Postcomposition.* Southern Illinois UP, 2011.

Gries, Laurie E. *Still Life with Rhetoric: A New Materialist Approach for Visual Rhetorics.* Utah State UP, 2015.

Harman, Graham. *Bells and Whistles: More Speculative Realism.* Zero Books, 2013.

———. *Guerrilla Metaphysics: Phenomenology and the Carpentry of Things.* Open Court Publishing, 2005.

———. *The Quadruple Object.* Zero Books, 2011.

Hawk, Byron. *Resounding the Rhetorical: Composition as a Quasi-Object.* U of Pittsburgh P, 2018.

Latour, Bruno. *Reassembling the Social: An Introduction to Actor-Network-Theory.* Oxford UP, 2005.

Luhmann, Niklas. *Social Systems.* Translated by John Bednarz, Jr. and Dirk Baecker, Stanford UP, 1995.

Maciel, Otávio S. R. D. "A Case for the Primacy of the Ontological Principle." *Open Philosophy*, vol. 2, 2019, pp. 324–46, https://doi.org/10.1515/opphil-2019-0025.

Maturana, Humberto, and Francisco J. Varela. *The Tree of Knowledge: The Biological Roots of Human Understanding.* Rev. ed., Shambhala, 1998.

Mickey, Sam. "Touching without Touching: Objects of Post-Deconstructive Realism and Object-Oriented Ontology." *Open Philosophy*, vol. 1, 2018, pp. 290–98.

Pflugfelder, Ehren Helmut. "Is No One at the Wheel? Nonhuman Agency and Agentive Movement." *Thinking with Bruno Latour in Rhetoric and Composition,* edited by Paul Lynch and Nathaniel Rivers, Southern Illinois UP, 2015, pp. 115–34.

Rickert, Thomas J. *Ambient Rhetoric: The Attunements of Rhetorical Being.* U of Pittsburgh P, 2013.

Rule, Hannah J. *Situating Writing Processes.* WAC Clearinghouse / UP of Colorado, 2019.

Sánchez, Raúl. *Inside the Subject: A Theory of Identity for the Study of Writing.* National Council of Teachers of English, 2017.

Simondon, Gilbert. "The Genesis of the Individual" translated by Mark Cohen and Sanford Kwinter. *Incorporations,* edited by Jonathan Crary and Sanford Kwinter, Zone Books, 1992, pp. 297–319.

Stormer, Nathan, and Bridie McGreavy. "Thinking Ecologically about Rhetoric's Ontology: Capacity, Vulnerability, and Resilience." *Philosophy & Rhetoric,* vol. 50, no. 1, 2017, pp. 1–25.

Wang, Zhaozhe. "Relive Differences through a Material Flashback." *College Composition & Communication,* vol. 70, no. 3, 2019, pp. 380–412.

Whicker, John H. *Object-Oriented Writing Theory: Writers, Texts, Ecologies.* 2015. Ohio University, PhD dissertation.

Whitehead, Alfred N. *Process and Reality.* The Free Press, 1978.

CHAPTER THIRTEEN

Environmental Communication in a Polluted Ecosystem: Challenges in the Age of Social Media

DENISE TILLERY

Environmental rhetoric has always been enmeshed in multiple networks. From early on, groundbreaking work in technical communication, including Killingsworth and Palmer (14) and Herndl and Brown (11), have traced the networks between science, science writing, technical and regulatory writing, and nature writing. To tell compelling stories, present clear evidence, and convince multiple stakeholders, environmental rhetors have to be fluent in multiple discourses. As more environmental discourse has moved to digital platforms, writers have also learned to be conversant in new media, from early blogs and websites to complex, intertwined social media platforms. But as recent political events have unfolded, it is becoming evident that the current social media landscape is extensively polluted, perhaps even hopelessly toxic. Algorithm-driven networks such as Facebook and Twitter have created a digital ecosystem that is potentially inimical to the kind of lengthy, participatory deliberation required to engage in equitable environmental decision making. Furthermore, contemporary research on technology and social media has demonstrated that new digital technologies, despite early promises to be forces for equality, often serve to further marginalize already disadvantaged groups (Sackey 37), and bad actors can use platforms' affordances to enable hostile and abusive activism (Trice and Potts 2).

The information ecosystem in which environmental rhetoric resides has transformed dramatically over the last four decades. My goal in this chapter is to reflect on this transformation, to understand how we got to this perilous moment when record-breaking temperatures in the Antarctic and the Arctic hardly make headline news while prominent political leaders continue to deny the reality of global warming. While our planetary system is in actual danger, the information ecosystems in which environmental discourses must flourish are also unstable, unhealthy, colonized by bad actors, and invaded by competing lines of misinformation. As I will show in this chapter, several trends happening within and around environmental discourses offer some insight into how we got to this moment. This transformation has caused environmental groups to gradually lose ground as social media has become both more divisive and a greater source for the circulation of misinformation. The narrative I'm developing here rests in part on a reflection of my own work: possibilities I saw in online environmental discourses early in the internet age and how some of that initial promise withered away.

In his "Counterhistory of Rhetorical Ecologies," Jones notes that ecology typically connotes "relational systems" (339). Jones shows how the conceptual history of ecology is implicated in the effects of nuclear colonialism, arguing that rhetorical ecology needs to "come to terms with the theoretical, material, and practical constraints that this spatiotemporal inheritance places on contemporary rhetorical ecological inquiry" (340). Jones urges us to combine place-based fieldwork with historiography (348) as a way to engage with disciplinary history. I've made a similar call to emphasize the local (Cagle and Tillery, "Climate Change Research" 158). In this chapter, however, I'm taking a longer view, putting some of my earlier locally based work into a larger perspective to reflect on how environmental discourses have been shaped in response to the changing context of emerging digital platforms. In this sense, I am using rhetorical ecology as a metaphor, in a way that Druschke critiques; nevertheless, I find the traditional and ancient metaphor of argument as the marketplace of ideas bankrupt and totally incapable of accounting for the ways that new digital platforms have profoundly challenged how environmental discourses circulate. I suggest we take the systems thinking inherent to ecological rhetoric and join it to recent "rhet-ops"-style scholarship that incorporates work on social media platforms and their affordances; this approach might offer a fuller picture of how environmental discourses might continue to survive, and perhaps flourish, in the digital discursive landscape.

The story I want to relate starts in the late twentieth century with the passage of milestone environmental legislation including the National Environmental Policy Act, which shaped environmental rhetoric for decades. I will first trace key developments that I see as crucial to understanding our current context; these developments seem to have evolved in tandem or closely following each other and have shaped both environmental rhetoric and its scholarly studies. The three developments are first, the emergence of significant genres of environmental writing in the late twentieth century; second, the development of a critical lens in science and technology studies; and third, and coincident with the first two, the evolution of the internet and digital rhetoric. After presenting this brief historical context, I will reconsider two of my earlier studies of online environmental rhetoric, which will illustrate why we need to include an understanding of "rhet ops" in our accounts of our current context. I join an overview of "rhet-ops"-style scholarship on social media with recent work on circulation of conspiracies to give a fuller illustration of the information ecosystem in which current environmental discourses must exist. Finally, I'll offer some examples of environmental activists using social media effectively to suggest some potential pathways forward.

A Brief History of Late Twentieth-Century Environmental Rhetoric and Its Contexts

The Environmental Protection Act passed in 1970, transforming the landscape of environmental rhetoric. In Miller's groundbreaking consideration of Environmental Impact Statements (EIS), a report form defined by the legislation, she defined genre as a typified action in response to a recurrent rhetorical situation (Miller 151) and argued that at the time of her writing (1984), EISs did not meet the definition of genre because they did not achieve a rational fusion of elements (164), in part because "the probabilistic judgments that are the substance of environmental science conflicted with the formal requirements of objectivity and quantification," and the "pattern of thinking in the context of administrative bureaucracies created a set of values at variance with the environmental values invoked by the legislation requiring impact statements" (164). Similarly, Killingsworth and Palmer's *Ecospeak*, first published in 1992, argued that the EIS did not fulfill its potential or intended purpose (170). The tension between the dependence on scientific evidence and the requirement for a fully public, democratically engaged system for debate is exemplified in much of the early work on public engagement in environmental debates, including Waddell (144), Killingsworth and Palmer, and Stratman et al. (6).

Bazerman et al. reconsidered the EIS as a genre in 2003, arguing that "the EIS genre and the kind of work facilitated by it in turn have spawned a constellation of related genres, created a large informational market to fulfill the requirements of the genre and its extended family of related genres, and led to a proliferation of information" (Bazerman et al. 457). Tracing the impact of the National Environmental Policy Act and its mandate of the new genre of the EIS, Bazerman et al. describe how the EIS was intended to provide greater public access to information in order to pressure government agencies and act politically (464). The genre "has provided a mechanism that has helped advance and proliferate a large market in information to monitor the environmental and human actions affecting the environment" (466). While Bazerman et al. address the growth of information online, including the expansion of the EPA's website and the Web of Science, they do not investigate either the design or the delivery aspects of the sudden expansion of easily available information whose essential existence depends on the internet. Publicly available documents such as EISs have in many ways been shaped by the online environment that was never envisioned in the early days of the genre created by NEPA.

As the later decades of the twentieth century saw positive momentum in legislative victories for environmental protections, there was also a trend toward greater cultural suspicion of scientific authority, for understandable reasons. While scholars including Miller, Bazerman, and Rude (2004) broadened our understanding of the ways that environmental discourses operated in this highly regulated technical context, work in risk communication throughout this same period of time (1990s through early 2000s) took aim at the power imbalances embedded in the processes of risk assessment and risk communication. Studies including Katz and Miller's "Low-Level Radioactive Waste Siting Controversy" (1996), Waddell's "Saving the Great Lakes" (1996), and Grabill and Simmons's "Toward a Critical Rhetoric of Risk Communication" (1998) all foreground the power dynamics at work in assessing and communicating risks and in the process of incorporating public responses to risks. Katz and Miller describe a "seeming contempt for the public" that arose from the Low-Level Radioactive Waste Management Authority's control of the risk communication process and its restricted understanding of communication as a one-way process (123). Both Katz and Miller and Waddell note the ways that technical experts were able to dismiss public concerns by dictating that the public was required to use technical language (Katz and Miller 125) or framing public responses as emotional rather than rational (Waddell 149) instead of being based in appropriate science or technical evidence. Grabill and Simmons critiqued the "positivist positioning of most risk communication studies," arguing that risk communication should attend to the ways that hierarchies of power are established and exercised in its foundational disciplines (417). Much of this work was influenced, directly or indirectly, by the arguments laid out in Ulrich Beck's *Risk Society: Towards a New Modernity* (1992), particularly his assertion that "some people are more affected than others by the distribution and growth of risks" (23). These critical investigations revealed the ways that institutions wielded the epistemic authority of science and technology to the detriment of those without power. They also brought a critical rhetorical lens to the discipline of risk communication, arguing for the social construction of risk and the fundamentally rhetorical nature of risk analysis as well as risk communication.

These scholarly critiques of science did not occur in a vacuum, of course, and this quick overview leaves out a mountain of work by feminist critics of science such as Harding (1986), as well as scholars of race (Roberts 2011). This work also occurred in the context of the rapid expansion of the internet. The decades between Miller's initial study of the EIS and Bazerman's reconsideration were characterized by the rapid expansion and evolution of the internet. Environmental activists have been active in online spaces from the early days of the internet (Tillery 409; see Elgesem, Steskal, and Diakopoulos for an overview of blogs on climate change). In the 1990s, early internet spaces such as bulletin boards, listservs, and chat rooms served as gathering spaces for progressive groups (Warf and Grimes 263). At a time of rapid growth in the early days of the World Wide Web, Warf and Grimes cataloged internet links to progressive causes (264), a project that would be virtually impossible now. In the early 2000s, the wide availability of blogging platforms offered individuals and small groups still easier access to a medium that could potentially reach around the globe, causing a second wave of explosive growth of online authors, communities, and resources for online activists, and climate change and environmental activists were active participants (Elgesem, Steskal, and Diakopoulos 21). This rapid growth occurred hand in hand with the development of early social media, such as platforms including LiveJournal (launched in 1999) and Friendster (2001) even before the purchase of Blogger by Google (2003).

The co-evolution of these three trends over the last several decades has meant that environmental rhetoric has had to grapple with constant change. This is the scholarly and cultural context in which my earlier work appeared. In the early 2000s, I completed two studies of online environmental discourse: the first (Tillery, "Radioactive Waste") focusing on anti-nuclear waste activist websites and the second (Tillery, "The Problem of Nuclear Waste") focusing primarily on government websites and responses to that newly publicly available information. The primary focus of these studies was on the ways that activist groups made use of scientific and technical arguments, sometimes even data from sources that they were criticizing. Here, I want to briefly revisit that work with the aim of seeing changes over time in the ways that online discourses about the environment have transformed in relation to each other and in relation to changes in the overall online environment.

My 2003 study focused on challenges to nuclear waste disposal sites and considered early genres of online technical information created by online activist groups including Nuclear Watch New Mexico. Even after more than twenty years, the fact sheet about the Waste Isolation Pilot Project (WIPP) in New Mexico is still available on Nuclear Watch New Mexico's website (see *Fact* Sheet), although only accessible directly through the URL. The nukewatch.org website has grown extensively and remains a robust source of information regarding all things nuclear relevant to the state of New Mexico. Fact sheets on each relevant topic, including the WIPP site, plutonium pit production, and the Los Alamos National Laboratory, are easily accessible. One notable difference is that more contemporary fact sheets are extensively linked, in comparison to the old, static PDFs that have traditional reference lists but no links. A second difference is the sources used; in the early version, I discussed the tension I perceived between the extensive reliance on sources from the Department of Energy and the strong distrust of the DOE's claims about safety. With the exception of one group, the Southwest Research and Information Center, most of the citations in the 2002 fact sheet refer to DOE publications. By contrast, the most recent fact sheets have links and references to activist sites such as the Center for Public Integrity and the Union of Concerned Scientists and news outlets such as the *Albuquerque Journal* and NPR with fewer links directly to government sources such as the National Nuclear Safety Administration. This shift in links and citations is most likely a result of much easier access to online journalism (including the ability to provide stable links that readers can follow), but it also indicates that Nuclear Watch New Mexico has become thoroughly embedded in an online ecosystem of environmental and anti-nuclear activist sites. Of course, from the very beginning, activist groups have always been connected with cross-links and resource and information sharing. More significantly from the perspective of the information ecosystem, however, the citations in the more recent fact sheet keep the reader within this system instead of directing them to government or library resources. Naturally, another shift in the features of this website is its embedded links to social media handles, including Facebook, Twitter, and Snapchat, none of which were available twenty years ago, and all of which serve to keep readers within a community of like-minded groups and individuals.

The 2006 article focused on one particular controversy at the Yucca Mountain Project site, a proposed storage facility for high-level nuclear waste. This article focused on how scientific authors craft appeals to ethos in ways that extend and sometimes violate the scientific norms of objectivity (Tillery 327) in favor of directly addressing uncertainty and policy topics (327–32), a strategy I categorized as part of Aristotle's description of "practical wisdom," one of his three types of appeals to ethos (Aristotle 121). I also addressed the ways that certain scientific documents were more easily accessible through online searches (Tillery 332), which I argued was an aspect of the traditional rhetorical canon of delivery, as suggested by Rude (271) as well as an ethos-building strategy. One important lesson in this article was the ability to access a scientific study (published by the government, thus not behind a paywall) that directly addressed a critique discussed in newspapers and local media. Google searches at the time did not redirect searchers to social media or to the information echo chamber of like-minded critics, so at the time, access was a highly important ethos-building tool. While misinformation was available, it was not driven to the top of search results. The shift from an information ecosystem relying on publicly vetted sources to a more contained ecosystem referring to motivated sources is an important development that has had far-reaching consequences, especially given the emergence of the social web.

Much of the scholarly work I've traced here addresses the ways that scientific evidence is used in arguments about environmental topics. Critiques of science resulted in significant correctives for an unquestioning faith in expertise; however, serious tensions have arisen in response to a seeming rejection of scientific expertise. In 2004, Latour raised the question of whether the spirit of critique "might not be aiming at the right target," (225), that "while we spent years trying to detect the real prejudices hidden behind the appearance of objective statements, do we now have to reveal the real objective and incontrovertible facts hidden behind the illusion of prejudice?" (227). Latour saw how the critiques of science articulated by prominent scholars in science and technology studies have been appropriated by bad actors, including climate change deniers, but in 2004, he did not anticipate the way these trends would accelerate and amplify in the age of social media. In 2013, Condit called attention to "a newly powerful array of social forces and alliances to which any astute rhetorician should attend" (3) and argued that "the oppositional emotions of rhetoricians should not currently be directed primarily at scientists" (3). In particular, she suggests "that the predominance of 'science bad' studies is ill-considered and probably disadvantageous to our own interests, as well as those of humanity more generally" (4). Specifically, the crisis of faith in science that Condit and Latour both described here can be summed up in this way: in the twenty-first century, humanity faces multiple, overlapping, reinforcing crises that will not be solved without reliable scientific and technological expertise, at a time when the public's ability and willingness to rely on that expertise has been undermined, and continues to be undermined, for reasons that are understandable as well as reasons that are meretricious. Both Latour and Condit argue that scholars—the rhetoric of science scholars in particular, according to Condit—need to stop emphasizing critiques of science, as those critiques are picked up and used by bad faith actors to undermine scientific certainty. And, I argue, the pace at which those arguments have been deployed has rapidly accelerated thanks to social media.

Rhet-Ops-Style Information Warfare and the Environment

The crisis in misinformation seemed to become urgent in 2016 with the unexpected election of Trump. His ascension into the presidency ushered in four years during which prominent officials proved willing to circulate misinformation, if not outright deceptions, through social media accounts with tremendous numbers of followers. The urgent crisis became catastrophic when the COVID-19 pandemic hit in early 2020, as the Trump administration's contempt for expertise ratcheted up amid resistance to recommendations for masks and shutdowns.

But in fact, this crisis of misinformation has intersected with a skepticism, even contempt, for expertise long before the Trump administration and even before widespread adoption of social media. Misinformation has long been a serious challenge in healthcare and health communication (Wang et al.; Kolodziejski 172). The Wakefield article on vaccines and autism, published in 1998 and retracted in 2010, contributed significantly to the misguided idea that vaccines cause autism. Kolodziejski showed how Wakefield et al. used hedging strategically to introduce ambiguity and "make the article seem to simultaneously declare and deny a causal link between the MMR vaccine and autism" (172). Kolodziejski's analysis showed how Wakefield made use of hedges in the scientific sphere to bolster a strong causal claim that he made in a public press conference, a non-technical sphere, to promote the article's findings. Subsequently, the media amplified Wakefield's claims that vaccines caused autism (Kolodziejski 177). And once the narrative was established as a commonplace, it has proven extremely resistant to refutation, even more than a decade after the *Lancet* retracted the original paper, and study after study has failed to establish a link between vaccines and autism. And while scientific expertise on vaccines was being undermined, the wellness community was using the long history of biases in biological and medical sciences to foster increased skepticism about medical expertise.

In my book (2018), I discuss how commonplaces such as "follow the money" are used as typical lines of argument to undermine scientific claims (Tillery, *Commonplaces* 29–30). Such commonplaces have emerged over decades in environmental discourses, starting with work of mid-twentieth-century conservationists such as Rachel Carson, who first suggested that this dynamic operated as the agricultural industry influenced information available about pesticide safety (Tillery 55). With trust in government resources such as the USDA and the Department of Energy destabilized, and actions such as the *Lancet* first publishing, then retracting, articles suggesting that vaccines were unsafe, these lines of argument about how to determine the reliability of scientific evidence became increasingly important. As Oreskes and Conway show in great detail in *Merchants of Doubt* (170), technical "experts" directly funded by the fossil fuel industry had great success in the late twentieth and early twenty-first centuries sowing doubt on what should have been seen as settled science. However, it is important to note that disinformation and misinformation occur on all sides of the political spectrum. Unfortunately, the conjunction of the sudden proliferation of information with a growing distrust of technical expertise has had some dramatic consequences. Here, I want to draw connections between some specific "rhet ops"-style events to make explicit the extent to which our information ecosystem has become an unwelcoming place for environmental discourses. I take the term "rhet ops" from Ridolfo and Hart-Davidson (2019), who use it to describe "rhetorical operations that make use of the latest digital and social networking technology to append, enhance, and amplify state and non-state conflicts" (p. vii). Ridolfo and Hart-Davidson refer specifically to the 2016 presidential campaign and how it was shaped by the story of Russian hacking, but I want to go back to an earlier "rhet ops" event that is inextricably linked to the trajectory of climate change discourse.

In addition to the broad disinformation campaigns of the sort described by Orestes and Conway, in the last fifteen years, there have also been highly targeted disinformation campaigns that have successfully used platforms such as blogs and social media to further destabilize trust in once commonly accepted sources of information. A hallmark of these targeted disinformation campaigns is that, increasingly, their goal seems to be to destabilize public trust rather than working to sow doubt or resist consensus on a particular topic. One of the early incidents of this nature was the 2009 hack of the East Anglia's Climate Research Unit and subsequent publicizing of highly cherry-picked communications, an incident sometimes referred to as "Climategate." The very "stickiness" of this label, which implies the presence of a scandal and cover-up along the lines of the Watergate scandal, has been one of the triumphs of climate change denialists. While it is still unclear who was responsible for the initial hack, the process set a blueprint for future climate change denialists, as well as other bad actors seeking to circulate conspiracy theories that undermine trust or destabilize sources of knowledge. The hackers were able to create a media event by mining through a trove of thousands of emails and other files and selecting a small number of emails between scientists, carefully quoting communications in a way that suggested these scientists were using "tricks" to manipulate data or arguing with scientific outlets in order to quash dissent about climate change. These carefully selected communications were then released strategically to climate skeptic blogs run by public skeptics such as Steve McIntyre of the blog Climate Audit. The apparent coordination and release of the hacked, cherry-picked emails to multiple outlets allowed the skeptics to drive media attention toward the distorted story of nefarious scientists manipulating data rather than the actual story of the coordinated hack and public disinformation campaign. In 2012, Leiserowitz and Maibach concluded that this event had a measurable impact on public trust in science (824), although their study showed that conservative Americans were most likely to have lost trust in climate scientists (827).

Because this event occurred relatively early in the evolution of social media, the information was circulated primarily on blogs such as Climate Audit and Watts Up with That. Five years later, with platforms like Twitter and Facebook fully established, a movement initiated and prolonged by what Trice would label "online knowledge disruptors" (106) used similar strategies but more sophisticated understanding of the affordances of social media platforms, most especially Twitter, to undermine faith in journalism under the guise of promoting "ethics in journalism." This 2014 event, now known by the label "Gamergate," is difficult to describe in a clear narrative, but it can be summed up as an ongoing harassment campaign directed against feminists or women gamers who were seen as transgressing into a space dominated by men. Trice describes it as a movement that involved "low accountability governance that would allow Gamergate to operate in parallel as a salacious rumor mill and as a populist outcry for a certain class of consumers feeding off grievances related to feminism, political correctness, and the media" (107). According to Trice, "this new activism of dissenting knowledge work, or dissentivists, represents one of the most significant dangers to online communication because it champions an ethos of conspiracy and paranoia that makes consensus impossible, even within the activist community itself" (108). Once again, the mainstream media was unable to grapple effectively with the event as it unfolded, as Gamergate participants succeeded in the short term in propelling the narrative about "ethics in gaming journalism" forward while the ongoing, directed harassment and doxing of prominent women gamers and feminist critics was largely unreported on by the media while it happened. As with the East Anglia climate hack, the narrative about the event was largely written by the main culprits behind it, and a conspiratorial mindset proved to be effective in both generating arguments and in persuading a largely sympathetic audience. The two events also resulted in highly personalized and disruptive harassment campaigns directed at individuals, a pattern that has become increasingly common.

The dangers of an ethos of conspiracy were also foreseen by Latour in 2004 when he asked, "what's the real difference between conspiracists and a popularized, that is a teachable version of social critique inspired by a too quick reading of, let's say, a sociologist as eminent as Pierre Bourdieu . . . ? In both cases, you have to learn to become suspicious of everything people say because of course we all know that they live in the thralls of a complete *illusio* of their real motives" (229). Latour, like Condit, anticipated the weaponization of these critical investigations of science but did not connect that weaponization to the affordances suddenly made available by social media. Trice shows how activists working from a framework of populist grievances used those affordances to propel a movement that undercuts public faith in the knowledge work of journalism. We can see similar trends in vaccine misinformation as well as climate change denial.

Conspiracy rhetoric, like critical approaches, is characterized by commonplaces of questioning motives and drawing conclusions based on lines of power and authority. However, the patterns of argument over conspiracy rhetoric are distinct. In *Awful Archives*, Rice argues that the very abundance of evidence of conspiracies, regardless of its quality, takes on a weight of its own, noting that "proliferation is a hallmark of conspiracy theory in general" (66). She describes the "awful archive" of 9/11 "truthers" as being characterized by "hyperevidentia," suggesting that "proliferation and magnitude generate rhetorical impacts of their own, aside from the contents being prolifically communicated" (69). Rice notes that this proliferation has long been a feature of conspiracy rhetoric, going back to conspiracies about the moon landing being faked. She does acknowledge the contemporary flavor of conspiracies on social media: like Trice, and Trice and Potts, Rice discusses the roles of social media platforms such as 4Chan and Reddit in circulating misinformation and conspiracy theories.

Spaces like climate change denialist blogs and subreddits dominated by gamers are sites where you might expect to find flourishing misinformation and distrust of scientific expertise. There is no doubt the destabilization of knowledge, or even a distorted shared reality, that originates in these spaces can spill into reality, as in the PizzaGate QAnon conspiracy that Rice considers (163) or the East Anglia climate hack. However, there is another influential channel through which misinformation flows and conspiracy rhetoric flourishes, a channel that should share many ideological frames and assumptions with environmental movements: the online wellness sphere. The proliferation of misinformation, and undercutting of expertise, in the online wellness community is a troubling development over the last two decades.

Vaccine refusal is a well-studied phenomenon that has been increasing over the past twenty years (Carrion 311). Carrion's study revealed that vaccine-refusing mothers are often well educated and apparently scientifically literate, as they "acknowledged the inferiority of anecdotal evidence" (314) and focused on the validity of the scientific research on vaccines. They focus on the lack of double-blind, randomized studies or point to conflicts of interest with studies funded by pharmaceutical companies (315), both of which are tropes that emerge in environmental arguments (Tillery "*Commonplaces*"). At the same time, these women also argued that maternal intuition was an alternative form of knowledge production that could override scientific knowledge claims, making claims about the value of lived experience in contrast to technical evidence that parallel the arguments made by standpoint epistemology theorists such as Harding (Carrion 220). In this way, the mothers Carrion studied are carrying out the same critique that Latour (2004) described, calling into question scientific evidence for reasons that are valid on their face but ultimately leading to a closed-off discursive space that is resistant to all evidence claims to the contrary. Worse yet, these discursive spaces are not metaphorical but literal, actual online spaces such as Facebook groups.

A pandemic-era *Washington Post* article describing vaccine misinformation in the wellness community (Maloy and De Vynck) reveals the links between anti-vaccine messages and groups that embrace alternative health practices and overall health and wellness topics like vegetarianism and yoga. In the past, such groups would have an ideological affinity with environmental causes; in particular, groups with New Age-adjacent practices such as meditation and natural healing would seem to have a natural alignment with a "Nature-as-Spirit," deep ecology perspective described by Herndl and Brown (11). The ways that scientific authority is contested and the centering of lived experience over technical evidence can be seen in both communities. But the way that wellness groups have evolved on platforms like Facebook and Instagram has transformed many of these spaces into nodes in a larger network that links wellness community participants to conspiratorial outlets (Johnson et al.). Johnson et al. show how during the pandemic, alternative health communities on Facebook acted as conduits between parenting communities and non-COVID conspiracy theories including chemtrails and 5G. Because Facebook and Instagram reward engagement, the more extreme links are pushed up automatically and are rewarded with more likes, clicks, and follows, in a vicious cycle that continues in spite of Facebook's stated commitment to combating vaccine disinformation. Thus, the aphorism "do your research," embraced by the mothers Carrion studied, becomes a one-way ticket to a conspiratorial rabbit hole like those described by Rice (46–47). Individuals who start out with a critical worldview, whether left-leaning or right-leaning, are then corralled into spaces where "critical" tips over into "conspiratorial," and those spaces are almost always inimical to progressive worldviews, in part because the resistance to consensus that Trice describes undercuts efforts to organize collective action.

Conclusion: Holding Space for the Local

It's worth questioning whether progressive, collective-oriented worldviews are always disadvantaged on social media platforms.

Certainly there are left-wing extremist groups that are highly conspiratorial in nature that would seem to be mirror images of right-wing extremist groups. But over the past decade, a peculiar phenomenon of prominent leftist embracing openly anti-science stances has emerged. The most significant avatar of this phenomenon is probably Robert F. Kennedy, Jr., who rose to prominence as an environmental lawyer working for the Natural Resources Defense Council but who is now a highly active anti-vaccine proponent embraced by the political right. The transformation was gradual, starting with a 2005 article published in *Rolling Stone* and the online outlet *Salon*, which has since been retracted. However, over the ensuing decades, his output has veered from critiques of George W. Bush's anti-environmentalism to, most recently, a book-length tirade against Anthony Fauci and Bill Gates, one praised by Tucker Carlson. Other once-prominent leftists have followed similar paths: Jill Stein, the 2016 Green Party presidential candidate, has likewise embraced vaccine skepticism. Although conspiracy thinking has always existed on both sides of the political spectrum, the emergence of right-wing conspiracies in the discourse of once prominent environmentalists and the acceleration of this trend post-2005 suggest something particular about our current media and social media ecosystem might be driving this trend. Conspiracy-minded ideas, in these cases, have supplanted and outcompeted critical thinking, and public thinkers who value the currency of attention find conspiracy thinking rewarded in far-right online spaces.

Of course, many scientists have embraced social media and use it as a vehicle for promoting science communication (Cagle and Tillery, "Tweeting" 131); in the early 2010s, environmental groups quickly embraced opportunities afforded by Facebook and other social media platforms to create an online presence without expertise in web design. But as the sequence of events I've delineated here shows, there is a clear trajectory of vetted scientific information being overrun by misinformation on social media.

There are some conclusions we might draw about the ability of environmental discourses to flourish in the current information ecosystem. First, it is clear to me that rhet ops-style information warfare, conducted using social media affordances such as hashtags, interconnections of platforms, and engagement of highly motivated and highly online populations, will not favor environmental causes or problem-solving on global issues such as climate change. These movements rely simultaneously on conspiratorial thinking and on quick reactions to hashtags or other rapidly circulating artifacts, and while there may be nothing inherently conservative about either of these elements, they are inimical to the kind of large-scale collaboration and centralized decision making that will be necessary to envision and carry out solutions to climate change. While conspiratorial thinking might often be characterized as resistance to authority, the culmination of the Trump administration in the January 6 riots most visibly characterized by a figure known as the "QAnon Shaman" shows how easily such conspiracy thinking can be co-opted by bad actors willing to indulge in conspiracy thinking to forward selfish ends.

Second, the admonition to "act locally" and focus on specific locations, as exemplified by the best work in rhetorical ecology (including Jones and Druschke), remains meaningful and important but requires a different approach in engaging digital platforms. I have seen this in my own work, as the group I investigated and have followed on social media since 2011 has been less and less prominent in my own Facebook feed, as constant changes to Facebook's algorithm has continued to disadvantage small groups with few controversial posts that are rewarded with excited engagement. Writers who want to use social media to promote environmental activism are also increasingly cautious on platforms like Twitter, where gaining the wrong kind of attention can lead to determined attacks intended to drive activists off the platform. But it's still possible to create synergies with local groups by engaging social media strategically. The local groups I've studied still tend to use Facebook, and the posts with most engagement involve invitations to and photo albums about work projects. Such content tends to encourage a sense of self-efficacy, an important quality that measures the extent to which we feel we can take meaningful action (Cagle and Tillery, "Climate Change Research" 151). Focusing on highly local activities that bring users out to engage with other people with specific actions can be the best way to ensure that online environmental engagement converts to real-world consequences.

Works Cited

Aristotle. *On Rhetoric: A Theory of Civic Discourse.* Translated by George Kennedy, Oxford UP, 1991.

Bazerman, Charles, et al. "The Production of Information for Genred Activity Spaces: Informational Motives and Consequences of the Environmental Impact Statement." *Written Communication,* vol. 20, no. 4, 2003, pp. 455–77, https://doi .org/10.1177/0741088303260375.

Beck, Ulrich. *Risk Society: Towards a New Modernity.* Translated by Mark Ritter, SAGE Publications, 1992.

Cagle, Lauren E., and Denise Tillery. "Climate Change Research across Disciplines: The Value and Uses of Multidisciplinary Research Reviews for Technical Communication." *Technical Communication Quarterly,* vol. 24, no. 2, 2015, pp. 147–63.

———. "Tweeting the Anthropocene: #440ppm as Networked Event." *Scientific Communication: Practices, Theories, and Pedagogies,* edited by Han Yu and Kathryn Norcut, Routledge, 2018, pp. 131–48.

Carrion, Melissa L. "'You Need to Do Your Research': Vaccines, Contestable Science, and Maternal Epistemology." *Public Understanding of Science,* vol. 27, no. 3, 2018, pp. 310–24.

Condit, Celeste. "'Mind the Gaps': Hidden Purposes and Missing Internationalism in Scholarship on the Rhetoric of Science and Technology in Public Discourse." *Poroi,* vol. 9, no. 1, 2013, pp. 1–9.

Druschke, Caroline Gottschalk. "A Trophic Future for Rhetorical Ecologies." *Enculturation: A Journal of Rhetoric, Writing, and Culture,* 20 Feb. 2019, https://enculturation.net/a-trophic-future.

Elgesem, Dag, et al. "Structure and Content of the Discourse on Climate Change in the Blogosphere: The Big Picture." *Climate Change Communication and the Internet,* edited by Nelya Koteyko, et al., Routledge, 2019, pp. 21–40.

Fact Sheet on the Waste Isolation Pilot Plant. Nuclear Watch New Mexico, 2002, https://nukewatch.org/oldsite/facts/nwd/WIPP FactSheet.pdf.

Grabill, Jeff T., and Michele W. Simmons. "Toward a Critical Rhetoric of Risk Communication: Producing Citizens and the Role of Technical

Communicators.*" Technical Communication Quarterly*, vol. 7, no. 4, 1998, pp. 415–41, https://doi.org/10.1080/10572259809364640.

Harding, Sandra G. *The Science Question in Feminism*. Cornell UP, 1986.

Herndl, Carl G., and Stuart C. Brown, editors. *Green Culture: Environmental Rhetoric in Contemporary America*. U of Wisconsin P, 1996.

Johnson, Neil F., et al. "Mainstreaming of Conspiracy Theories and Misinformation." *arXiv*, 2021, https://doi.org/10.48550/arXiv.21 02.02382. Preprint.

Jones, Madison. "A Counterhistory of Rhetorical Ecologies." *Rhetoric Society Quarterly*, vol. 51, no. 4, 2021, pp. 336–52.

Katz, Steven, and Carolyn Miller. "The Low-Level Radioactive Waste Siting Controversy in North Carolina: Toward a Rhetorical Model of Risk Communication." *Green Culture: Environmental Rhetoric in Contemporary America*, edited by Carl Herndl and Stuart Brown, U of Wisconsin P, 1996, pp. 111–40.

Killingsworth, M. Jimmie, and Jaqueline Palmer. *Ecospeak: Rhetoric and Environmental Politics in America*. 1st ed., Southern Illinois UP, 1992.

Kolodziejski, Lauren R. "Harms of Hedging in Scientific Discourse: Andrew Wakefield and the Origins of the Autism Vaccine Controversy." *Technical Communication Quarterly*, vol. 23, no. 3, 2014, pp. 165–83, https://doi.org/10.1080/10572252.2013.816487.

Latour, Bruno. "Why Has Critique Run out of Steam? From Matters of Fact to Matters of Concern." *Critical Inquiry*, vol. 30, 2004, pp. 225–48.

Leiserowitz, Anthony A., et al. "Climategate, Public Opinion, and the Loss of Trust." *American Behavioral Scientist*, vol. 57, no. 6, 2013, pp. 818–37.

Maloy, Ashley F., and Gerrit De Vynck. "How Wellness Influencers Are Fueling the Anti-Vaccine Movement." *The Washington Post*, 12 Sept. 2021, www.washingtonpost.com/technology/2021/09/12/wellness-influencers-vaccine-misinformation/.

Mehlenbacher, Ashley. *Science Communication Online: Engaging Experts and Publics on the Internet*. Ohio State UP, 2019.

Miller, Carolyn R. "Genre as Social Action." *Quarterly Journal of Speech*, vol. 70, no. 2, 1984, pp. 151–67, https://doi.org/10.108 0/00335638409383686.

Oreskes, Naomi, and Erik M. Conway. *Merchants of Doubt: How a Handful of Scientists Obscured the Truth on Issues from Tobacco Smoke to Climate Change*. Bloomsbury Publishing, 2011.

Rice, Jenny. *Awful Archives: Conspiracy Theory, Rhetoric, and Acts of Evidence*. Ohio State UP, 2020.

Ridolfo, Jim, and William Hart-Davidson, editors. *Rhet Ops: Rhetoric and Information Warfare*. U of Pittsburgh P, 2019.

Roberts, Dorothy. *Fatal Invention: How Science, Politics, and Big Business Re-Create Race in the Twenty-First Century*. The New Press, 2011.

Rude, Carolyn. "Toward an Expanded Concept of Rhetorical Delivery: The Uses of Reports in Public Policy Debates." *Technical Communication Quarterly*, vol. 13, no. 3, 2004, pp. 271–88.

Sackey, Donnie J. "One-Size-Fits-None: A Heuristic for Proactive Value Sensitive Environmental Design." *Technical Communication Quarterly*, vol. 29, no. 1, 2020, pp. 33–48.

Stratman, James F., et al. "Risk Communication, Metacommunication, and Rhetorical Stases in the Aspen-EPA Superfund Controversy." *Journal of Business and Technical Communication*, vol. 9, no., 1, 1995, pp. 5–41.

Tillery, Denise. "Radioactive Waste and Technical Doubts: Genre and Environmental Opposition to Nuclear Waste Sites." *Technical Communication Quarterly*, vol. 12, no. 4, 2003, pp. 405–21, https://doi.org/10.1207/s15427625tcq1204_4.

———. "The Problem of Nuclear Waste: Ethos and Scientific Evidence in a High-Stakes Public Controversy." *IEEE Transactions on Professional Communication*, vol. 49, no. 4, 2006, pp. 325–34, https://doi.org/10.1109/TPC.2006.885868.

———. *Commonplaces of Scientific Evidence in Environmental Discourses*. Routledge, 2018.

Trice, Michael. "GamerGate: Understanding the Tactics of Online Knowledge Disruptors." *Rhet-Ops: Rhetoric and Information Warfare*, edited by Jim Ridolfo and William Hart-Davidson, U of Pittsburgh P, 2019, pp. 105–24.

Trice, Michael, and Liza Potts. "Building Dark Patterns into Platforms: How GamerGate Perturbed Twitter's User Experience." *Present*

Tense: A Journal of Rhetoric in Society, vol. 6, no. 3, 2018, www
.presenttensejournal.org/volume-6/building-dark-patterns-into-
platforms-how-gamergate-perturbed-twitters-user-experience/.

Waddell, Craig. "Saving the Great Lakes: Public Participation in
Environmental Policy." *Green Culture: Environmental Rhetoric in
Contemporary America*, edited by Carl Herndl and Stuart Brown,
U of Wisconsin P, 1996, pp. 141–65.

Wang, Yuxi, et al. "Systematic Literature Review on the Spread of
Health-Related Misinformation on Social Media." *Social Science
& Medicine*, vol. 240, 2019, pp. 1–12.

Warf, Barney, and John Grimes. "Counterhegemonic Discourses and the
Internet." *Geographical Review*, vol. 87, no. 2, 1997, pp. 259–74,
https://doi.org/10.1111/j.1931-0846.1997.tb00074.x.

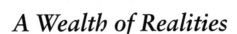

CHAPTER FOURTEEN

A Wealth of Realities

CASEY BOYLE

A swerve to clear the . . . asteroid . . . took us off our course.

At this moment, a 2010 cherry-red Tesla Roadster is cruising through outer space in an arc that, unless the car collides with a celestial body, will orbit the galaxy for millions of years. Inside that top-down convertible sits a humanoid figure wearing a white jumpsuit and matching helmet with a visor reflecting the stars toward which the car approaches. Against the blackness of space, the white-suited human form stands out in sharp contrast as something that, despite potentially millions of years and billions of miles awaiting, may never settle into anything that resembles belonging.

Starman, as it is called, was an experiment that doubled as a publicity stunt. As a test payload for a rocket delivery service/travel company (SpaceX), it joins myriad other shocking and spectacular, fortunate and failed, envisioned and enacted forays designed to render space accessible while exercising human capacities to travel into the stars and toward planets to which we might begin to migrate. The proposals that characterize what many are calling the era of NewSpace fuse the potential of astro-engineering to fantastic fictions of interplanetary colonization as the culminating achievement of a species, refiguring and reconstellating our ecological reality. These projections of spacefaring privateers habituate everyday citizens to a daily dose of spectacle, an aesthetic of world-building rhetoric that—via Tweets, news headlines, and sketches of capsule architectures—

remind us that human's self-appointed stewardship of this world has failed, demanding we create other worlds to inhabit. Yet the case for a planetary exit strategy builds *from* environmental facts *toward* fictional fabulations that over-determine concerns about the natural world, exploit the limitations of dominant environmental imaginaries, and enmesh rhetorical systems with the realities and fictions of existing and imaginary planetary ecologies.

These circumstances present rhetoric and writing studies an imperative for returning to and expanding on its ecological orientations to attune to how dominant environmental imaginaries collapse the very complexity that systems thinking pursues. Especially in its embrace of ecological conceptions, our scholarship offers numerous ways to help understand how the conquest of space is embodied and enacted, especially through aesthetics. Indeed, efforts to conceive of both "space" and "place" are at the heart of writing's turn to ecological conceptions of relationships. Such address how we relate to our natural world but also gravitate into complex technical systems and layered cultural interactions through which our writing composes. Few works in writing studies, however, leverage those conceptions toward the stars to look out on our increasing forays into space. How do ecologies of writing contribute to "new" frontiers (sic) of space exploration and colonization? How do spectacles and other imaginaries participate in shaping our *natural* worlds? How many realities are we ignoring?

This essay responds to those questions by understanding that to engage in rhetorical ecologies, and the ecological rhetorics therein, offers not only our world new imaginations but offers imaginings as worlds to inhabit. Where we might understand writing and its technologies as merely representing the world they orbit, this essay will try to understand the reality of texts and imaginative compositions as worlds in and of themselves. Indeed, even modes of existence as immaterial as imagination and fiction offer a *wealth of realities* for which to promote or against which to contend or in which to abide.

We now suspect that what we say is space / and glassy-dear around Aniara's hull / is spirit, everlasting and impalpable . . .

It is hard to know where to start. The unending collapse of ecosystems, the ongoing failure of institutions, the non-stopping erosion of shared aims toward which to orient human action accumulate many more crises than we can identify and far more than those in which we can intervene. Given the interlaced and interlocking relations that permeate each of these places, ecological orientations are necessary to even partially contend with the multiplicity of crises that confront us. Perhaps, then, *anywhere* is a good place to start, considering any place is always and already constellated in a relational matrix. *An ecology.* Nathan Stormer and Bridie McGreavy propose any rhetoric that can be seen ecologically is one that considers qualities of relations between entities, not just among humans, that then "enable different modes of rhetoric to emerge, flourish, and dissipate" (3).

Margaret Syverson's orientation of ecological models of composition toward thinking about complex processes and systems is a particularly formative influence. In the *Wealth of Reality*, Syverson foregrounds a definition of ecology as "a set of interrelated and interdependent complex systems," defined, roughly, as phenomena that are self-organized, adaptive, and dynamic (3). Occurring at any scale from the granular to the galactic, such systems are further characterized by being *distributed*, structured across space and time; *emergent*, self-organized arising in networks of connected components; *embodied*, contained in systems that include bodies and the practices that instantiate those bodies; and *enacted*, interpreted as activities and experiences through an ongoing process. Syverson's articulation of complexities previously flattened by approaches lacking "theoretical consideration of the psychological, social, temporal, or physical dimensions of writing" provides crucial grounding for the proliferation of composing's ecological thought (14). The transformative ideas that writing consists, as Marilyn Cooper writes, "of a complex web of ideas, purposes, interpersonal interactions, cultural norms, and textual forms" (8–9) has moved through the work of scholars who part with causal and linear analyses to consider constellations of writers in and of systems, from Rice to Rivers, Hawk to Dobrin.

As her title forecasts, what animates Syverson's explication of self-organizing, adaptable ecological systems is desire to get at the "richly complex, interdependent, and emergent" nature of reality—its *wealth* (xiv). Tacit in most of the text, the phrase is treated explicitly only in an epigraph taken from Ilya Prigogine and Isabelle Stengers's *Order Out of Chaos*: "The real lesson to be learned from the principle of complementarity, a lesson that can perhaps be transferred to other fields of knowledge, consists in emphasizing the wealth of reality, which overflows any single language, any single logical structure" (225). It's no strain to see how the cited work, which approaches the famous dialogue between Albert Einstein and the Indian philosopher Rabindranath Tagore as an archetypal confrontation between two competing conceptions of reality, inspires Syverson's own. Here, Prigogine and Stengers lament the ascension of Einstein's view of reality as independent from the subject of knowledge and human existence as the dominant ideal of scientific discovery. For them, Tagore's insistence that reality is always relative to the human spirit opens a path to reclaiming the relevance of *who describes the world*, disrupting the myth of omniscience with recognition that knowledge is constructive and creative of a reality that is never given. Nature "speaks with a thousand voices" (131), necessitating a quantum principle like complementarity to attune us to all that cannot be measured at once. For them, the "irreducible plurality of perspectives on the same reality expresses the impossibility of discovering a comprehensive perspective from which the whole reality is simultaneously visible" (313).

Instantiating a thoroughly ecological search for "the various possible languages, the different points of view" (Prigogine and Stengers 313), Syverson makes an aside I want to take up as a key point of departure for this chapter's exploration of NewSpace. As a brief illustration of emergence, she mentions how popular fictional characters acquire "genuine force and momentum" (13) via movement along a trajectory that is at once self-organizing and undetermined. In essence, such beings achieve an escape velocity, bolting from the gravitational pull of their origins and bursting into common vernacular with their own animate life. These might include terms that spring forth from novels (such as Catch-22 or Kafkaesque) or characters that find existence outside pages (such as Don Quixote or Walter Mitty). What Syverson hints at, then, is not only how intricately interwoven fictional forces are in the textual ecologies that determine what we think of as real, but also how imaginary beings can gain a *real* existence of their own.

Moving this idea from side to center, we might further elaborate it through the work of French philosopher Étienne Souriau. Currently being rapidly recovered in media studies, sociology, and other fields, the work of this aesthetician first and foremost involves recasting reality through "different modes of existence," multiplying reality infinitely. As he writes in *The Different Modes of Existence*, the question is not if anything exists but how to make it *more real*. Reclaiming as Luce de Vitry Maubrey says "a knowledge rooted in being" (325), Souriau rewrites traditional ontology as "a matter of inventing (as one 'invents' a treasure)" (162) that enables what he calls *instauration*, the creative labor through multiple and multiplicitous modes to bring a thing into existence. Instauration, despite the labor one gives to it, has no guarantee of success. Indeed, as Bruno Latour and Stengers write, the possibility that "everything, at every moment, can fail, the work as well as the artist. . . . For yes, with Souriau, the world itself might fail" (18).

Along with its pluralist and aesthetic attunements, perhaps the deepest appeal of Souriau's philosophy is its disruption of ways of thinking that force either/or perceptions of reality. Indeed, we may assume Souriau would gently challenge the notion that Einstein and Tagore can represent two opposing approaches to reality, one of which may defeat the other. What he names as the two "genres" that bring existence into being—*aseity*, "existence in and of itself, independent, absolute in its mode" and *abaleity*, "referential existence"—can neither be ordered as stronger and weaker forms nor functionally separated. Rather, each carries meaning, and their ratio to each other shifts the balance of being. As Catherine Noske explains, "we understand our own human existence as aseitic, biologically independent, in responding to our empirical experience of reality. But these experiences and the world around us have their own abaleitic existence, which supports ours in our relations to them" (4). Souriau's terms resonate with another conceptual pairing at play in ecological discourse fields: *autopoiesis*, a biological and potentially social and political goal of systemic self-maintenance and the less referenced but no less meaningful *autopoiesis*, coined by biologists Humberto Maturana and Francisco Varela to describe system goals that surpass self-maintenance. Mapping Souriau to these ecological concepts suggests seeing them not in opposition but rather in dynamic tension of a *more/less* relationship.

The unique capacity of the abaleitic existence to instaure beings that inhabit their own reality even as they offer to our aseitic lives comes clear in Souriau's treatment of works of art. Indeed, Syverson's hint toward fictional emergence is richly articulated in this theorization, which explains how aesthetic beings are constituted within and by assemblages that must first emerge from the arrangements that found their mode of existence. To borrow from literary theorist Stephen Muecke:

> A novel "takes shape" or the image of Mickey Mouse "gels" and "captures" the imagination of the public, but not before a lot of work is put into the technical and institutional means for the dissemination of this being. Once Mickey Mouse is "out there" and has achieved the kind of immortality only available to fictional beings, he is very hard to unmake, because his existence is cradled in networks of devotion.

These more-than-representations cannot be de-represented once instaured or re-contained once they reach escape velocity. What we see is an emergent reciprocity among realities and imaginaries. *We constitute fictional beings from our factual existences, theirs reconstitute ours, and our reconstituted existences maintain their circulation.* As this chapter will further rehearse, these dynamics are complex systems in and of themselves. Tipped in balance toward *autopoiesis*, they promote emergence against entropy, but, locked into autopoetic mode, they become overly self-referential and calcify, restricting an ecology's capacities to perceive and imagine new realities.

The relevance of a vibrantly aesthetic approach that encompasses, at once, the ever-present possibility of failure; the need for multiple modes of existence; and the role of the fictional in constituting those modes can hardly be understated at this environmental and ecological juncture. Arguing in *Chaosmosis* for a "new aesthetic paradigm," Felix Guattari posits that such a paradigm holds "ethico-political implications because to speak of creation is to speak of the responsibility of the creative instance to the thing created, inflection of the state of things, bifurcation beyond pre-established schemas, once again taking into account the fate of alterity in its extreme modalities" (107). We can easily pull this into composition's ecological thinking, which faces a heightened challenge to complicate the reigning dichotomies of the environmental imaginary and invigorate possibility beyond the extremes of chaos, crisis, and collapse. Advanced further in the next section, my claim is that attending to fictional aesthetics helps move us from boundless multiplicities as they "all deal with the same reality" (e.g., Prigogine and Stengers 313) to such multiplicities as they deal with *different* realities, a move that itself opens our ability to grasp more than *the wealth of reality* but *a wealth of realities.*

> *That was how the solar system closed . . . and severed [us] . . . from all the bonds and pledges of the sun.*

In his case for a new paradigm of aesthetic thought, Guattari argues that it has never been so important to "shed our mechanist visions of the machine and promote a conception which encompasses all its aspects" (107), a conception that for him unfolds through an expanded field of practices both thought of and not thought of as art. Indeed, the "aesthetic machine" offers the richest potential to lay the underseen aspects of the mechanist machine bare, "the finitude relative to its life and death, the proto-alterity in the register of its environment and of its multiple implication, its incorporeal genetic filiations" (107). More than anything, it is the "extraordinary techno-scientific mutations" that lock us in a breakneck, no-alternative race for "ruin or radical renewal" that make developing what he calls an *ecology of the virtual* just as pressing as attending to the ecologies made visible to us by the natural world (91).

Guattari died long before the NewSpace imaginary metastasized, but one can easily imagine him holding these fabulations in view while making this case. The grandiose plans for human colonization of Mars rely centrally on the idea that Earth's fragile ecosystem, failed by human self-appointed stewardship, make it urgent to *realize* technological capacity to reach other planets. If the consensus assumption of this platform is, as Jeff Bezos put it, "We will have to leave this planet, and we're going to leave it, and it's going to make this planet better," its points of dissent are only *how* we leave, in terms both of *in what state* and *by what means.* Infused with the language of freedom and exploration, enabled by the rich wealth of recent tech booms, the vast scope of these proposals to escape this atmosphere foresee the most aspirational experiments of astro-engineering. But that is not all. Alongside the tech, the most utopian envisionings of arcology actualize through a vast array of spectacular assemblages that will seal us into cabin and capsule structures necessary to sustain interstellar survival. Writing off this world even as it writes us off this world, this rhetoric invents the genres and habituate the aesthetics of imminent departure, masterfully harnessing, as Eva Diaz writes "[t]he power of space exploration to organize earthbound desires" ("Art" 147).

For Souriau, the world-making potential of imaginaries holds profoundly compelling consideration for multiple existences. "Imaginaries, suspended within a base phenomenon, participate in the conditioning of reality that belongs to the latter, whether those be distinct or vague, intense or weak" (153). For him, attending to the "transitive and transitory character" (153) of the possible or virtual, a mode of existence that offers sketches or starts through which any number of other existences are built, highlights how all can be imagined, from fictional characters to "the beings of dreams" (152), may gain or fail to gain a foothold. Whether "a plan that is realized, the construction of a building, the filming of a screenplay, the performance of a musical score," virtuals, as David Lapoujade explains, share the exigence to "change their plane of existence in order for their reality to grow" (3). For Souriau, allocating to the virtual its own mode recognizes *all* that aims for realization—all bridges, built or broken or only hopefully conceived. For instance, "The bridge that no one thinks to build ... exists with a virtual existence that is more positive than the one that was begun, but whose completion was rendered impossible by a flaw or a faulty design" (157). Instauration always inheres the risk of failure, but the real failure is not *not to be instaured*: rather, it is in collapsing failure to that which is not yet or cannot be achieved, closing ourselves to the multiplicity of existences by adhering to any sole plan.

Techno-utopian vision of interplanetary colonization erects such a virtual bridge. Not yet realized and potentially never to be, perhaps for the good—its supremely inhospitable conditions make Mars, as Shannon Stirone put it recently in the *Atlantic*, a "hellhole"—they nevertheless coalesce a discursive universe that *feels* real. And feeling matters, for as Williams James proposes, "every kind of thing experienced must somewhere be real" (83), and as Martin Savransky further elaborates, "everything that feels and is felt anywhere in the universe" must be seen as a reality (8). Yet what do we make of a virtual that *realizes* the conditions for its own ecological emergence on the ontological certainty of a wholly exhausted earth? Of one that bases its *becoming more real* on amplification of the very modes of existence from which it seeks to escape, one that augments its rich imaginary by impoverishing our reality? Writing for *The Conversation*, historian Ted McCormick explains how the reigning visionaries of the planetary exit strategy, deploying a logic of competitive survival, confabulate a worldview that contracts by purporting to expand:

> They offer colonialism as a panacea for complex social, political, and economic ills, rather than attempting to work toward a better world within the constraints of our environment. And rather than facing the palpably devastating consequences of an ideology of limitless growth on our planet, they seek to export it, unaltered, into space. They imagine themselves capable of creating livable environments where none exists. But for all their futuristic imagery, they have failed to imagine a different world.

As art critic Eva Diaz writes, this vision enacts the "astonishing work of repression involved in pretending that a technologically governed capsule existence can surpass the plentitude of ecologies on Earth, or that space travel will foster freedoms, both bodily and political, when it will above all be determined by scientific instruments applied with capitalist means" ("Art" 147). In short, its particular eco-aesthetics constitutes a *poor* reality. Yet arguably, what vexes most about this imaginary is its paradoxical capacity to convince of its own richness.

Certainly in developing composition's attunement to complex ecological systems around the emergence of new technological visions, thinkers in rhetoric and writing have made important space for considering how aesthetics, no mere surface feature, figure deeply in the imaginative structuration of what we take as given. Specifically, we might look back at possibilities offered by two influential texts: Charles Bazerman's 1999 *The Language of Edison's Light* and John Law's 2002 *Aircraft Stories*. Surveying *the* moment of the light bulb invention as an extended effect of "heterogeneous engineering," Bazerman discovers a rhetorical process involving the "coordination and application of many kinds of knowledge and practice, all of which are united and instantiated in the final product" (335). His essential point is that the "invention" of incandescent illumination required coordination of a vast array of different modes of relation to imbue that existence with allies in other modes, including symbolics references, values, meanings, instruction, etc. Light bulb moments are not merely the flipping of a switch; imagination itself has to be made to exist alongside the thing one might imagine. Law echoes this point but with a twist. Where Bazerman shows how Edison and his team had to coordinate a myriad of modes to substantiate and make the light bulb *more* real, *Aircraft Stories* shows us that reality can be made and performed without even the technical object—the aircraft that did not yet physically exist but still bore reality through a wealth of documents, promotional materials, government procurements, and other genres and written imaginaries. Modeling a way to "take [the aesthetic] seriously" (118), these stories, he says, also offer a choice to either "imagine that they tell about and thus represent a version of reality" or "imagine, reflexively, that telling stories about the world also helps to perform that world" (6).

Law pinpoints the latter approach as essential to understanding that writing is not standing outside of the world capturing it objectively, but writing is always staging a performance. Relevantly, he notes that "such a staging ensures that, everything else being equal, what is being performed is thereby rendered more obdurate, more solid, more real than it might otherwise have been" (8). To further this chapter's exploration of the aesthetics of the imaginary and their effects on ecological thought, the following section aims to deepen understanding of how the NewSpace staging of a virtual bridge to interplanetary colonization doubles down on the most restrictive conditions of what Souriau calls "absolute" possibility, a "stylistics particular to the imaginary" that habituate "gratuitous and excessive conformity to a given ontic and cosmic conditioning" (155). To do so, it dives into close analysis of the particular fabulations of tech entrepreneurship but, in contrast, of artistic performance as well. In considering this eco-aesthetics especially in its "performance or performative modalities" (91), I take a cue from Guattari, whose ecology of the virtual insists that such attention, more than preserving existing cultural ecologies, develops extraordinary new ones through vigorous imagining, pushing us closer to finding the treasures buried in the wealth of realities.

> . . . *now that we realize what our space-ship is: / a little*
> *bubble in the glass of Godhead / In any glass / that stands*
> *untouched for a sufficient time, / gradually a bubble in*
> *the glass will move / infinitely slowly to a different point*

If textual ecologies always play a role in the emergent realities of technological advance, this role seems amplified in the era of Muskism, what Jill Lepore in a recent *New York Times* op-ed defined as a "capitalism rooted in science fiction stories and animated by fanciful plans to conquer." Nearly every day, we are cajoled to "Read What Musk Reads" with headlines like, "Elon Musk Recommends 12 Books That Changed His Life" or even "68 Books Recommended by Elon Musk." While these medleys often also include texts on popular science, entrepreneurial achievement, and self-discipline, they perhaps most importantly often feature world-building fiction; for instance, Robert Heinlein's *The Moon Is a Harsh Mistress*, Isaac Asimov's Foundation series, or J. R. R. Tolkien's Lord of the Rings saga. From one angle, the exhortation to read like Musk is just one more iteration of an everyday prompt to model ourselves after successful capitalists. Yet there would seem to be more in this hyping of self-styled

NewSpace visionaries as avid readers. Certainly their favored fictions promise us access to their visions, but more, we seem to need to believe that they read, that these fictional devotions are real. That the reality of their transhumanist fictions matter because they are rapidly becoming our realities is a point Lepore makes cuttingly: "Billionaires, having read stories of world-building as boys, are now rich enough, as men, to build worlds. The rest of us are trapped in them" (Lepore).

The plans that Musk began touting as early as 2006 gesture to an allopoietic fictional ecology within the autopoietic refrain of the planetary exit strategy. The crux of his insistence that colonizing Mars is an "incredibly important thing for the future of life itself" is an either-or choice: "Either we spread Earth to other planets, or we risk going extinct." Mars is a "fixer-upper of a planet," he has said, but workable as the "next natural step" toward "Making Humanity a Multi-Planetary Species" before inevitable catastrophe brings about its end. Yet his warnings that it is "uncertain how much time is left" to achieve interstellar inhabitation are regularly offset by the idea that "becoming a space-faring civilization is one of those things that makes you excited about the future." Indeed, he has contended, it would be "cool to die on Mars." For disciples of this would-be prophet that one journalist called "the ultimate doomsday prepper" (Shieber), the certainty that space *will be* the place is suffused with more enthusiasm than despair. The gambit to reproduce existing ecological structures in interstellar terrain is arguably an escape from culpability, since now that one portion of the species has extracted and pillaged the majority, all must be saved, including the culprits. Rebooting Manifest Destiny for forays into the stars, the rhetoric of frontier expansion and conquest unselfconsciously replicates while also further obscuring a long history of settlers appropriating lands from Indigenous cultures. Yet it whitewashes its own disinterest in challenging racial and social inequity with performative claims of a world rebuilt. Further, a point that bears repeating, its goal of conquest for "life" and "all humanity" makes prior conquests of human and all other life a means through which, as an end, interstellar migration justifies.

The fascination of this distinctive eco-aesthetics pulls heavily on prolific deployment of fictional figments. For one cluster of examples, consider Musk's public hype on the orbital grabbing arm that, if construction is successful, could help launch SpaceX's new Starship Rocket to Mars. On Twitter in April 2021, he postulated that if this launch tower had legs, it would resemble "Mechazilla"—an apparent reference to the Mechagodzilla character of the Godzilla movie franchise. In another Tweet the same year, his announcement that "SpaceX will try to catch the largest ever flying object with robot chopsticks" included a video clip from *The Karate Kid.* "Success is not guaranteed," the post concluded, "but excitement is!" Even as towering fantastical monsters augment the impressive feats of astro-engineering, more realistic fictions endear an enthusiastic pursuit that oscillates between metacognition confrontation with potential failure and insistence on sure success. Beings of fiction help constitute an aesthetics of imminence that pull distant and imagined temporalities into realistic proximity. Thus, alongside the anticipatory rhetoric that hails the successful completion of Mechazilla, we hear sure-sounding predictions that SpaceX could "achieve its most ambitious targets, like launching the same Starship three times per day. That, in turn, means it has a chance of achieving its goal of a city on Mars by 2050" (Brown).

We find another lens, or method, for this aesthetic performance by returning once more to Souriau. In his theory of the "Cube and the Sphere," he offers two conceptions of staging theatrical space that also present as ways of rendering a world through imagination. The cube is a contained world and works by "cutting out a predetermined fragment in the world that is going to be set up." Staging a performance within "preestablished architectural constraints," it orients a "face-to-face relationship, that arrow-like function of the actor with reference to the spectator" (15). In contrast, the sphere, a slightly carved out and partial world, "seeks out [the world's] dynamic center, its beating heart, the spot where the action is emotionally at its keenest and most exalted" (13). To put this in terms rhetorical scholars would understand, the former offers a complete logic of a syllogism while the latter delivers the opportunity for an audience to participate in something akin to an enthymeme. Drawing on the "absolute availability . . . of every manifestation momentarily needed, of every dimension to be traversed or conquered," it maximizes the unconstrained freedom of improvisational theatrical movement (15). If as Shakespeare once said "all the world's a stage," this bit of Souriau adds that each stage is itself a world, sketching two approaches that we, moving into rhetorical language, might call architectural composing and ecological composing to highlight the distinction in more constructive versus circulatory modes. Musk's rhetoric would seem to draw on the aesthetical arrangements of the cubical style to play out his enthralling plot of planetary departure. Invoking "the All or Nothing, i.e., really present or completely absent" ("The Cube and the Sphere" 16), his promising construction of space colonies relies dually on the *presence* of strong claims of planetary failure and the absence of recognition that those who have capitalized from the processes of that failure now stand again to benefit.

Should we seek a universal worldview that perhaps more closely models a spherical production style? If yes, we might turn to the space imaginaries of the musician and band leader Sun Ra. An avant-garde polymath whose interests ranged across experimental music, cosmic philosophy, and theatrical performance, Sun Ra claimed from the start to have been from space. In fact, despite frequent association with the NewSpace platform, Ra is arguably due credit for the phrase *Space Is the Place*, the title of his 1972 science fiction film about Sun Ra leading an exodus of Black Americans from Earth to an unnamed planet. Depicted by biographers as an avid reader for his whole life, Ra's socially conscious rhetoric reflects worries that were front and center when, decades ago, some of humanity started heading to new interstellar contexts while others were suffering the weight of Earth life. Or as Gil Scot-Heron memorably put it, "No hot water, no toilets, no lights . . . but Whitey's on the moon." Ra's visions helped forge "the aesthetic blueprint" foundational to an Afrofuturism that, as Nettrice Gaskins writes, "sought visions of the future based on engagements with science and historical fiction, fantasy, Afrocentricity, and magic realism with non-Western cosmologies in order to critique not only the present-day dilemmas of Black people, but also to revise, interrogate, and re-examine the historical events of the past" (152).

Asserting that people would need to "realize that there's an unknown that they need to know in order to survive," Ra's fundamentally, ontologically uncertain projection of interstellar existence is fashioned around a central contention that *we are all aliens*. Channeling the cultural treatment as a Black man growing up in Alabama in the earliest decades of the twentieth century, he took no ownership of its earthly context, saying curtly but sympathetically: "I'm glad this is not my planet. I am so sorry it's yours." Pushing back on transcendent truth and objectivity based in rationality, Sun Ra emphasized the need to judge ourselves and to figure out how to live regardless of—indeed, in opposition to—the prevailing order. Where whiteness configures space as an opportunity for resolute continuation, for Ra, space opens as "a utopian outside to segregation and white supremacy, a parallel dimension in which to model a life beyond discriminatory histories of colonization and injustice on Earth" (Diaz, "We Are All Aliens" 4). There, "those of the reality have been bruised and beaten by the truth" can realize that they had "been slaves of a bad truth" and turn instead toward the unlimited potential of myth. Ra is often theorized as a progenitor of Afrofuturist escapism, but this word may actually undermine his determination to cease vesting in oppressive authoritative structures. Unlike Musk's virtual play to replicate existing structures, Ra's exodus consciously differentiates his story from "HIS-story" and divorces himself from history, offering his self-presentation as "part of the mystery, which is my story" as virtual for living otherwise.

We can easily read Musk and Ra's aesthetics as respectively cubical and spherical of their worldviews. Simply in contrasting their adopted ethos, we may be struck by the resonance of this distinction:

> One producer, essentially Apollo-like, will prefer by far an assignment that permits him to play the clever architect; he will lay out in advance the dramatic or spectacular action of his team-mates upon the stage, through the strong and ingenious structure he creates in Olympian fashion at the very start, by the very act of cutting out his block of reality. Another, more Dionysian, will yield to the intoxication of being the sum and substance of all the forces seething on the stage; he will seek to amplify the rhythm of such forces, to set in motion the beat of a freely expanding universe, and to direct a great evocatory rite in which theoretically he has control even over the public. (16)

Staging a fabulist technocapitalist theater, Musk appears to organize a representative model of universal life for the consumptive viewing of a mono-directionally oriented audience. Stylized for maximum realism, performances like launching a Tesla into space enact spectacles of aesthetic arrangement and confinement that prefigure eventual colonial life in the SpaceX Mars City. They are overtly territorial in the familiar sense but perhaps also in the sense formulated by Vinciane Despret in her Souriau-inspired writing of songbirds, which speculates that while we tend to think of songbirds taking territory "as a site for display and spectacle" (23), perhaps it is more that "territory provides them with a stage for songs and displays" (24). If Musk maximizes the theatrical resources that are already provisioned by a techno-utopian vision of life directed and organized by astro-engineered systems, Ra's inhabitation of territory arguably declines any strictly ordered arrangement into which his ecological context would by default place him. Rather, his "demand to diversify access to space and space fantasies" (Diaz, "We Are All Aliens" 14) is directly inspired by an effort to capture and transport the universe's "dynamic center," composing a fictional world "limited only by the limits of the creators' vision" (Souriau 13).

Given that Souriau offers this ambivalent lens for two "equally authentic although antithetical" modes of reality-creation (16), perhaps setting them in opposition is not problematic. Yet arguably, a more productive intervention against binary thought would ask how contrasting Musk and Ra disturbs the cube/sphere configuration. In fact, seeking the spectrums and multiplicities in the alterity of these rhetorics brings Souriau back into alignment with his preferred framing of *more/less* in place of *no/yes*. A "more cube/more sphere" framing invites us to see both as performers who have dispositions but not absolutes, recalling that the point of this analysis is not to advance one cosmic worldview over another but rather to juxtapose two rhetorics that array our engagement with eco-aesthetic imaginaries. For me, thinking of composing in terms of "more cube/more sphere" suggests a turn back to *Aircraft Stories*, which begins by moving quickly from the question "How should we write?" to "How might we write about multiplicity in a way that also produces the effects of singularity? Or about singularity in a way that does not efface the performances of multiplicity?" (4). Key to his approach is what he calls *fractional coherence*. A moment in composing's ecological thought that captures much of this chapter's argument, Law pinpoints habits of dominant Euro-American thought that move us smoothly from desiring a consistent whole to assuming that which cannot form a consistent whole cannot be coherent to thinking in binaries that re-satisfy coherence craving. This, put differently, is the path to the death of pluralism and, for our purposes here, un-ecological thinking. Against the reduction to a choice between "something that is a singularity because it holds together coherently" and "something that is broken and scattered," fractionality enables a generative grappling "with the idea that objects, subjects, and societies are both singular and multiple, both one and many. Both/and" (4).

Supercharging an environmental imaginary of irreversible disaster, NewSpace fabulations redouble longstanding challenges faced by rhetoric's engagement with ecological thought. These challenges beg further enrichment of rhetorical capacities through aesthetic and ontological attunements that spring the traps of singularities and dichotomies without being ensnared by them. Rhetoric's response needs to take seriously the formulations of given powerful rhetors without losing their groundedness in complex systems of assemblage that themselves emerge, Guattari reminds us, from unstable ontological grounding. While Souriau's cube and sphere formulation enjoins that, of course, the character and choices of composers matter, Stormer and McGreavy rightly rejoin that the "aesthetic, creative, performative affordances of a rhetoric are the concern more so than who or what activates its potential" (7). Certainly, even the richest of these affordances may contain contradictions that cannot be easily escaped—as Law notes ruefully, even as his own narrative "tells about fractionality, it also performs singularity" (194). The work of this aesthetic is to develop the capacity for attending to these seemingly mutually exclusive modes of existences. Law, for instance, offers the pinboard with its logics of "juxtaposition, of pastiche" as a locus of inventive rhetorical resources for "living with the tension of unknowable ends" (194). The need is just as bad, Law himself would no doubt concur, for resources that leverage against ends *presenting as known*. From poking holes in the "impeccable" plans of billionaires to proliferating the kind of thinking modeled by futurist Amy Webb, whose recent *The Genesis Machine* with Andrew Hessel diversifies the narratives of groundbreaking biological advancement to repair against the existential threats of *this* world, the foregone conclusion of a technocapitalist exit strategy that drives "demand for lifeboats to flee Earth, rather than investing in an egalitarian quality of life for all" (Diaz, "Art" 159) adjures us to *pin more*.

> *. . . and one of them who quietly went mad / stepped up magniloquent on verbal ladders / to lecture on the human race's travels*

In a dystopian fictional future of Harry Martinson's poem "Aniara" (and through subsequent versionings of its narrative through film, theater, opera, and a graphic novel), an enormous, richly appointed spaceship cruises the vastness of space, shuttling passengers on a routine three-week voyage from a dead and dying Earth, ravaged beyond repair by climate change, to their new home on a colonized Mars. What is, at the time of this writing, one of many potential ends for Starman's interstellar foray—collision with space debris—befalls this vessel, and the *Aniara* is forced to jettison fuel as it is knocked off course. What the captain initially announces will be two years adrift before the ship encounters a celestial body with the gravity to restore its course will stretch well on, but life aboard the ship shifts almost instantly. The first technology to fail is the Mima, an AI machine that induces a drug-like trance as she transmits idyllic, individually tailored visions of Earth's lost nature. Initially a little-used luxury, Mima quickly becomes life support, sustaining an endless line of passengers against panic and despair. Yet Mima does not only disburse the fictions of living nature to humans but also absorbs their realities of its traumatic dying. Poisoned by this imbalance, Mima breaks down, incanting in human language as human dread becomes hers: "How terror blasts in, how horror blasts out." Her last message as she self-destructs is both paean for Earth's loss and censure of humanity: "My conscience aches for the stones. . . .

I've heard them cry their stonely cries, seen the granite's white-hot weeping. . . . There is protection from nearly everything, but there is no protection from mankind."

That the fate of the ship's humans is sealed when their fiction machine dies upholds a key contention in this chapter: autopoiesis out of step with allopoiesis leads not only to entropy but to a divestment from the abundant realities that make up our worlds. The message of "Aniara" that we are all adrift warns of clinging to any isolated set of fictions, no matter how vivid—of ensconcing a solitary imaginary as the only reality, a single reality as the only imaginary. Martin Savransky poignantly articulates the necessity of thinking toward multiple realities, writing "Pluralizing the present, these other stories, these other worlds in this world, precipitate a pragmatics of collective imagination against ongoing desolation" (1–2). Enthymematically, what awaits the failure of this pragmatics is desolation. Instead of collectively imagining against desolation, Mima's patrons feed their collective desolation into her imagination. More repercussions for ecological thinking come clear in another of the *Aniara* film's narrative's plotlines, when the ship's leaders discover a missive of unknown origin or meaning moving directly toward them. They proclaim that a rescue fuel probe is en route, for a short time reigniting hope in recovering an orbit thought lost forever. Yet when a recovery mission succeeds, no one can figure out what to do with the probe—how to open it, whether it contains fuel or instructions, or even its origin. This moment in the movie, arguably, models the total failure of ecology, the utter loss of complex systems of thought that should have written imaginative reference for the missive's recovering parties. If, as Syverson and others have argued, ecological systems leverage emergence against the pull of entropy, here we see how autopoiesis reverses the flow, enervating emergence against an entropy that wins out.

The key elements of what I want to call Late Humanity are captured by what the humanity of "Aniara" had become: isolated, lacking ecologies, and solely invested in one over-exhausted mode of existence. Ecological thinking in rhetorical studies no doubt helps illuminate the apparent aims of the technocapitalist movement that calls us to abandon a wasted Earth—wasting it fully, no doubt, along the way—and become interplanetary colonialist settlers. Yet technocapitalist fabulations call us to more actively leverage *imagining* against *the imaginary* to multiply reality against singular realities and root out fictions of ontological certainty that embed themselves in our critical aims. Consider Thomas Rickert, in his case for an ecosophy with spacecraft: "For life to maintain itself in space, bubbles of lifeworld must be constructed. To construct a bubble of lifeworld requires a profoundly rich explication of an ecological background we take for granted on earth, where our lifeworld is simply given" (77). If this quote speaks to the rich potential in existing ecological orientations to capture *a wealth of realities*, then it also hints toward the risk of becoming too enamored of our constructive capacities; too convinced in one end, one plan to reach it; too persuaded that any lifeworld is given. We find stark contrast in Martinson's original "Aniara" with the line that appeared earlier in this chapter, an enactment of the poem threaded through its running headings, "O would that we could turn back to our base / now that we realize what our space-ship is: / a little bubble in the glass of Godhead." Dwelling in the more/less ratios in the shifting mutual dependencies of the fictive and the real, the autopoietic and the allopoietic, the abaletic and aseitic, rhetoric's aesthetic sensibilities would be made more affective by multiplying the realities through, in, and by which it participates. Without that work, we may satisfy ourselves by completing the story of us and our travels; without that labor, we lose the joy in rendering ourselves, and multiple modes of existence, to be incomplete.

Works Cited

Bazerman, Charles. *The Languages of Edison's Light*. The MIT Press, 2002.

Brown, Mike. "SpaceX Starship: How the Mechazilla Grabbing Arm Will Enable a Mars Rocket." *Inverse*, 31 Aug. 2021, www.inverse .com/innovation/spacex-mechazilla-starships-giant-orbital.

Cooper, Marilyn M. "The Ecology of Writing." *College English*, vol. 48, no. 4, 1986, pp. 364–75.

Despret, Vinciane. *Living as a Bird*. Translated by Helen Morrison, Polity Press, 2022.

de Vitry Maubrey, Luce. "Etienne Souriau's Cosmic Vision and the Coming-into-Its-Own of the Platonic Other." *Man and World*, vol. 18, 1985, pp. 325–45.

Díaz, Eva. "Art and the New Space Age." *New Left Review*, vol. 112, 2018, pp. 144–60.

———. "We Are All Aliens." *e-Flux*, vol. 91, 2018, pp. 1–11.

Dobrin, Sidney I., editor. *Ecology, Writing Theory, and New Media: Writing Ecology*. Routledge, 2011.

Edbauer, Jenny. "Unframing Models of Public Distribution: From Rhetorical Situation to Rhetorical Ecologies." *Rhetoric Society Quarterly*, vol. 35, no. 4, 2005, pp. 5–24.

Gaskins, Nettrice. "Cosmographic Design: A Cultural Model of the Aesthetic Response." *Aesthetics Equals Politics: New Discourses across Art, Architecture, and Philosophy*, edited by Mark Foster Gage, The MIT Press, 2019, pp. 151–68.

Guattari, Félix. *Chaosmosis: An Ethico-Aesthetic Paradigm*. Translated by Paul Bains and Julian Pefanis, Indiana UP, 1995.

Johnson, Doug. "Decolonizing the Search for Extraterrestrial Life." *Undark*, 4 Apr. 2022, https://undark.org/2022/04/04/decolonizing-the-search-for-extraterrestrial-life/.

Lapoujade, David. *The Lesser Existences: Étienne Souriau, an Aesthetics for the Virtual*. Translated by Erik Beranek, U of Minnesota P, 2021.

Law, John. *Aircraft Stories: Decentering the Object in Technoscience*. Duke UP, 2002.

Lepore, Jill. "Elon Musk Is Building a Sci-Fi World, and the Rest of Us Are Trapped in It." *The New York Times*, 4 Nov. 2021, www.nytimes.com/2021/11/04/opinion/elon-musk-capitalism.html.

Martinson, Harry. *Aniara*. Translated by Hugh MacDiarmid and Elspeth Harley Schubert, Avon Books, 1976.

McCormick, Ted. *The Conversation*. https://theconversation.com/profiles/ted-mccormick-791744

Muecke, Stephen. "Motorcycles, Snails, Latour: Criticism without Judgement." *Cultural Studies Review*, vol. 18, no. 1, 2012, pp. 40–58.

Noske, Catherine. "Towards an Existential Pluralism: Reading through the Philosophy of Etienne Souriau." *Cultural Studies Review*, vol. 21, no. 1, 2015, pp. 34–57.

Prigogine, Ilya, and Isabelle Stengers. *Order Out of Chaos: Man's New Dialogue with Nature*. Bantam, 1984.

Rickert, Thomas. "Toward Ecosophy in a Participating World: Rhetoric and Cosmology in Heidegger's Fourfold and Empedocles' Four Roots." *Tracing Rhetoric and Material Life: Ecological Approaches*, edited by Bridie McGreavy, et al., Palgrave Macmillan, 2018, pp. 59–83.

Rivers, Nathaniel. "Tracing the Missing Masses: Vibrancy, Symmetry, and Public Rhetoric Pedagogy." *Enculturation: A Journal of Rhetoric, Writing, and Culture*, 17 Mar. 2014, https://enculturation.net/missingmasses.

Savransky, Martin. *Around the Day in Eighty Worlds*. Duke UP, 2021.

Shieber, Jonathan. "Elon Musk Is the Ultimate Doomsday Prepper." *TechCrunch*, 12 Mar. 2018, https://techcrunch.com/2018/03/12/elon-musk-is-the-ultimate-doomsday-prepper/amp/.

Souriau, Étienne. "The Cube and the Sphere." *Educational Theatre Journal*, vol. 4, no. 1, 1952, pp. 11–18.

———. *The Different Modes of Existence*. Translated by Erik Beranek and Tim Howles, U of Minnesota P, 2015.

Stengers, Isabelle, and Bruno Latour. "The Sphinx of the Work." *The Different Modes of Existence*, by Étienne Souriau, U of Minnesota P, 2015, pp. 11–87.

Stirone, Shannon. "Mars Is a Hellhole." *The Atlantic*, 26 Feb. 2021, www.theatlantic.com/ideas/archive/2021/02/mars-is-no-earth/618133/.

Stormer, Nathan, and Bridie McGreavy. "Thinking Ecologically about Rhetoric's Ontology: Capacity, Vulnerability, and Resilience." *Philosophy & Rhetoric*, vol. 50, no.1, 2017, pp. 1–25.

Syverson, Margaret A. *The Wealth of Reality: An Ecology of Composition*. Southern Illinois UP, 1999.

Webb, Amy, and Andrew Hessel. *The Genesis Machine: Our Quest to Rewrite Life in the Age of Synthetic Biology*. PublicAffairs, 2022.

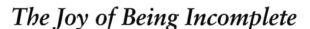

The Joy of Being Incomplete

MARILYN M. COOPER

In their introduction, Dobrin and Jones declare that this collection does "not seek to outline a complete map of rhetorical ecologies as a unified concept" but rather to understand ecologies as "*plural, . . .* multiple, divergent, and highly situated knowledge-making practices." Still, the rhetorical ecologies discussed here do display what Wittgenstein calls family resemblances (*Philosophical Investigations,* 67). All are complex systems emerging in relationality; they are ethical, cultural, material practices that make not only knowledge (in the scholarly sense) but rather lifeworlds, Uexküll's umwelten. As Karen Barad argues, "Knowing is not a play of ideas within the mind . . . knowing is a physical practice of engagement." Almost all include humans, but, as Ingraham and Halm observe, humans are no longer uniquely the agents. They state that agency is "always both the work of an individual human and the work of something else." As they and other contributors acknowledge, this "anthro-decentrizing" of rhetoric is an "extreme" and "radical . . . shift in what one takes rhetoric to be and to do." Instead of understanding rhetoric as a conscious and willful act of the good man speaking well, it is understood as emerging from entangled intra-active relations among agents of all kinds: inorganic, climatic, biological, digital, fictional. In his ecology of ethics, Guattari refers to "a 'futurist' and 'constructivist' opening up of . . . animal-, vegetable-, Cosmic-, and machine-becomings" (quoting Guattari). Some contributors to this collection also include important others as agents, such as nitrogen (Grant), land (Collins, Arola, and Seigel), tides (McGreavy, Sutton, and Hillyer), symbols (Gries), fictions (Boyle). The purview of rhetoric has been vastly increased from *vir bonus* and the rhetorical triangle to include innumerable others that languished unnoticed in what was reluctantly mentioned, if at all, as context.

And rhetorical ecologies are not necessarily good; in many, toxic systems or even entropy emerge, as in the disappearance of chimney swifts described by Clary-Lemon, or Gries's rhetorical ecosystem of white supremacy, or the NewSpace fantastic fictions of interplanetary colonization described by Boyle. Boyle's analysis is particularly insightful in pointing out that such "bad" ecologies do not fail to emerge but instead fail to "leverage imagining against the imaginary to multiply reality against singular realities and root out fictions of ontological certainty." In many chapters, the rhetorics of anthropocentrism, whiteness, colonization, and environmental disaster are called out as the antithesis of rhetorical ecologies, but it is important to recognize that they are also powerful complex systems rooted in entangled relationships.

Conceiving rhetorical ecologies as lifeworlds with many diverse agents is a significant shift in what rhetoric is. Also of significance is the shift to conceiving what rhetoric does: in creating lifeworlds, it embodies highly situated values of specific cultures. It follows, then, that an important part of what rhetoricians do is to be mindful of and respect the disparate values embodied in rhetorical ecologies. Not recognizing—or not caring—that the ethical values of a culture that is not your own differ in ways that have profound effects on rhetorical practices is, as Boyle says, to fall into the dead end of ontological certainty. It has led to the various forms of injustice criticized in chapters in this collection. But even when unfamiliar cultural values are recognized, they still too often fall prey to simplification, distortion, and misunderstanding. So, an even more important part of what ecological rhetoricians do is to develop ways of relating to and learning from other rhetorical ecologies. All the contributors to this collection engage in this work at least tacitly; others do so more explicitly and spectacularly.

Senda-Cook describes in detail how the Asian Rural Institute (ARI) employs the Japanese concept of *mottainai* to develop practices of habitual resistance to industrial methods of farming such as chemical fertilizers, chemical pesticides, and growth hormones. A common, everyday word in Japan, *mottainai* means simply "don't waste." Referring to food or clothes or intangibles such as time, opportunities, skills, and talents, it expresses regret: "by not utilizing something fully to its potential, you are denying or not respecting its essence" (quoting Kinefuchi). But it also refers to the Japanese spiritual value placed on the time and effort invested in the creation of an object or skill that makes it precious and irreplaceable. Sustainable agriculture practices such as processing agricultural wastes like manure or rice husks into compost or charcoal, along with Japanese laws that require individuals and businesses to pay for everything they throw out, complement *mottainai*: waste becomes instead a "local resource" that saves money and the environment. ARI also addresses waste in the realm of work by promoting the dignity of labor: "no one's efforts go to waste, and no job is beneath someone." All workers participate in cleaning chores and "foodlife" work: cooking, caring for animals, and crop-raising chores. By drawing on a situated cultural value, ARI renders practices of sustainable agriculture and equality understandable and practical habits.

Because workers at ARI come from countries that have felt the impact of colonization and have come to ARI learn more about the sustainable agriculture that it espouses, they are also amenable to adapting these practices in their own countries, even in the face of the dominance of industrialized agriculture there. It is more difficult to gain acceptance of unfamiliar cultural values that conflict with the values of the dominant industrialized, Anglo-Eurocentric rhetorics of Western cultures. The Indigenous and Native American rhetorical ecologies discussed by Collins, Arola, and Seigel can be challenging for most Western rhetoricians to understand or embrace or even to recognize.

One key to understanding the rhetorical ecologies of Indigenous and Native American cultures is "recognizing land, and land-people relations, as an agent that shapes rhetoric." Collins, Arola, and Seigel use the term "land-people" to refer to a "living agential land that educates, organizes, informs, and persuades people through the stories that it tells." Understanding land-people as a relationship of "co-constitutive shaping" requires accepting land as really, not metaphorically, agential, able to tell informative and persuasive stories, not fictions, to people who respond to and learn from them. It requires, as Collins, Arola, and Seigel say, not separating ontology and epistemology, instead maintaining "realism toward *phenomena* and the entangled material practices of knowing and becoming" (Barad, 56). Land is not an abstract concept, but "a physical, actual, material relationship to 'an ecosystem present in a definable place' that has been cultivated throughout my short life, and for much longer by those relations who came before me" (quoting Brooks). Brooks here refers to several important aspects of the land-people relationship. The relationship is one of kinship; what people learn from the land is "how to be human" (quoting Schelly). The relationship is not only material but specific: in the Anishinaabe language, *ayaa* "means to be *in* a certain place." And the relationship is an intergenerational praxis, one that means living life "in a way that promotes rebirth, renewal, reciprocity, and respect" (quoting Simpson), "making choices and actions with the seventh generation in mind." I have tried here to just briefly remind readers, through abundant quotation, of the values embodied in the term land-people in the more complete presentation in the chapter. I hope I have represented them faithfully; if not, this exemplifies the challenges of fully grasping the spirit of cultures not one's own.

Consequential misunderstandings of Native American cultural values have been rife in federal treaties. Collins, Arola, and Seigel cite Article 13 of an 1836 treaty that ceded Anishinaabeg lands in Michigan: "The Indians stipulate for the right of hunting on the lands ceded." Freeland, based on his research in the Anishinaabe worldview and language, explained that for the Anishinaabeg in the nineteenth century, this stipulation would not imply that hunting was the right of an individual Indian. Instead, "the right of hunting" would be understood to refer to land-people which "includes the hunter, the hunter's community, and the land itself." And the relationship would not be considered to be one of rights but of responsibility for maintaining the flourishing of the whole hunting ecology. "The right to hunt would've meant, according to Freeland, that the land on which one would hunt will be cared for so that the animals continue to prosper." As all the relations, including the land, are agential participants in the practice of hunting, this stipulation articulates an ecological and culturally specific value, one foreign to the federal treaty-makers. Collins, Arola, and Seigel comment, "Separating out 'the right to hunt' from a concept of understanding the land and her resources as kin, as agential, is inconceivable. . . . This land-people way of being and knowing is always in relation."

Collins, Arola, and Seigel's project was to study the values underlying the strategic energy action plans of two communities in Michigan: the Keweenaw Bay Indian Community (KBIC) and Traverse City. They originally planned to interview KBIC members using a method which "entails 'going walkabout' with informants in the places that they consider to be important, and collecting social, historical and ecological data *in situ.*" The method would highlight the values of the land-people relationship as well as enabling the community to co-constitute the goals of the project. Because "researchers and community members would have been standing together on the land, a land-people relationship . . . would be very apparent—the land would be agential in shaping and drawing forth stories that would have been told about energy use in this context." Unfortunately, the COVID-19 pandemic intervened, and the researchers had to fall back on document collection and analysis, "looking for traces of water, rock, and tree."

In comparing the vision sections of the Traverse City and KBIC plans, they noted that while both discuss economic outcomes, the Traverse City plan focuses entirely on economic benefits and makes no mention of the land, while the KBIC's plan aims "to provide a healthy and productive resources base to sustain the members of KBIC far into the future, as well as to enhance and perpetuate all of the traditional, cultural, and spiritual values that tie members to the land." KBIC's plan also subordinated economic goals to supporting tribal sovereignty: "Tribal Nations . . . are increasingly focused on energy sovereignty as an assertion of self-determination" (quoting Bessette, et al.). "For the Ojibwe, and in the SEP itself, the land isn't merely a territory to be owned; it is an actor that ties people to tradition, to land, and to language." The KBIC Strategic Energy Plan, by reasserting control over decisions about the local ecology, also returns decisions about the land to the Anishinaabe land-people as a form of environmental justice.

The challenges of research that focuses on rhetorical ecologies of non-Western cultures are very real. In their conclusion, Collins,

Arola, and Seigel comment on the histories of colonization entangled in academic spaces and offer a warning: "if these worldviews and rhetorics go unchallenged, they will continue to influence who and what we think of when we consider issues of race and technological literacy and expertise" (quoting Haas). The five-year project they describe in their chapter was funded by the National Science Foundation's Growing Convergence Research Program. When it was reviewed by an NSF panel at the end of the second year, it was not renewed. The reasons offered by the panel included "that our science wasn't adding any new knowledge to existing research, and that our technological component wasn't seen as innovative." They comment, while it "bears note that 'centering of Indigenous knowledge' would never be given as an explicit reason for nonrenewal of any project. . . . What counts as science, technology, and as knowledge itself within academic spaces is still very much defined by a colonial, imperialist orientation, even (or maybe especially) in spaces that are explicitly looking for innovation and new approaches to knowledge creation."

Damaging misunderstandings arising from ignoring divergent cultural values are, unfortunately, common, and are not limited to interactions between Indigenous and Western cultures. While still noting these problems, some contributors in this collection take up the challenge to develop ways of relating to and learning across differences without perverting or erasing them. They employ cross-disciplinary practices and scholarship to create different relations that unearth and challenge anthropocentric understandings of place, agency, and ontology and move toward more ecological understandings. McGreavy, Sutton, and Hillyer's crafting of a tidal ethics based on a relational approach to knowledge is a good example of this approach. Inspired by Glissant's "commitment to a poetic, embodied relationality within the ecological conditions of the times and places we inhabit," they have learned "how to listen to tidal voices" in "our small square of earth on an island in the Penobscot River just north of the head of tides, at the edge of pisipiqe." In their research on the local ecology of the Maine and Wabanaki wild clam and mussel fisheries, their intent is to challenge dominant systems of power that marginalize or limit access to and use of clammers' knowledge and the knowledge of long-term Wabanaki inhabitants. They assert, "We have observed, asked questions about, and sought to co-create knowledge with pisipiqe, elomocokek, intertidal ecosystems, shellfish harvesters, and many other partners." The collaborative practices they describe here also challenge the "standard" concept of researchers as the core agents; they reconceive research "as a professional networking process with colleagues (not 'subjects'), as an opportunity for conversation and sharing of knowledge, not simply data gathering" (quoting TallBear).

They describe their research practices of listening, breathing, and standing with as not "passive and ableist" but "rooted in embodied presence" with each other and with partners both human and otherwise. These practices are all modes of multisensory apprehension of patterns of time and place formed and reformed by tidal-like rhythmic, recursive movement. They posit that rhetorical ecologies, like tidal patterns, form and reform over time and place and, also like them, leave buried traces of earlier or other rhetorical ecologies, all of which can be sensed by "showing up in [rhetorical] spaces and opening ourselves to letting tidal forces guide, breathing in material histories and possibilities for disruption that emerge from these encounters." For an example, McGreavy, Sutton, and Hillyer recount their visit to a location that was (re)named Fort Halifax. They noticed a monument at the entrance that informed visitors that the site was inhabited by Native Americans "from at least 5,000 years ago until 1692. A pilgrim trading post was also located on this site in the 1650s." Standing with the monument and each other, they sensed a narrative pattern of "firsting and lasting": "a rhetorical strategy to construct the disappearance of Wabanaki peoples from this land to make way for a series of colonial 'firsts'. . . and, by extension, the best use of this location for capitalist and economic development." They conclude, "Sensing this pattern here and elsewhere strengthened our ability to disrupt this narrative in our own writing."

McGreavy, Sutton, and Hillyer describe this rhetorical recursive forming and reforming through history as sedimentation: "the process through which one world constructs material and symbolic dominance over many worlds." But tidal rhythms can disrupt and desediment these patterns, as in the example of the monument at Fort Halifax. Their deliberate inclusion of Wabanaki languages, especially in renaming places, can also disrupt this dominance, as it works "to desediment the seeming fixity of English and French as colonial naming and mapping practices." For example, the Wabanaki name for what is currently known as Bar Harbor was Moneskatik, which "names a clam-gathering place that is *still* a place where clams and people gather each other." Colonial ship captains renamed the place to alert other ships to the sandbar that blocks the harbor at low tide, "sedimenting colonial relationalities" and making it *also* a place for international shipping. "And yet," McGreavy, Sutton, and Hillyer comment, "tidal concepts show how the persistence of names as relation is not absolute." In a footnote, they explain their deliberate inclusion of Wabanaki languages is as well an effort to amplify Wabanaki ways of knowing within academic spaces, and they note that their commitment to learning and using the languages is not superficial but ongoing (footnote 1).

Tidal ethics, like the Indigenous ecologies described in Collins, Arola, and Seigel, value relations and place and recognize the agency of nonhumans as partners in the co-creation knowledge. But McGreavy, Sutton, and Hillyer do not appropriate these Indigenous values and concepts; they develop them from the specific values of their home cultures. Their understandings reflect what they have learned in their intra-actions with tides and the other human and nonhuman entities that compose the ecology of the Maine coast and from their immersion in scholarship from a broad array of disciplines. For them, knowledge is relational in that it emerges from relations with partners (not kin) of various kinds. Places are specific locations that shape how they live and do research; they are not property nor are they central to the sovereignty of a nation.

Tidal ethics have emerged from an effort to change how rhetoricians create knowledge, from androcentric, colonial practices to relational ones. These alternate practices of listening, breathing, and showing up enable McGreavy, Sutton, and Hillyer "to move beyond boundaries between species, environment, and others" and to recognize "connections across incommensurabilities." Eschewing a search for common ground or mutual understanding, they instead engage more deeply in an effort "that digs into difference and maintains that difference while also trying to stay in good relations" (quoting Liboiron). "Letting tides guide," they conclude, "is thus a commitment showing up for what the world is asking us to do and to trust in collaboration for the discernment, learning, and embodied sense of ethics that are required in engaged, difference-making research."

In emphasizing the agency of tides that guide and a world that asks us to do something, McGreavy, Sutton, and Hillyer draw attention to the resistant anthropocentrism of Western rhetoric. That things are agents is a linguistic commonplace, memorably noted by Latour ("knifes 'cut' meat"; "soap 'takes' the dirt away" [Whicker, quoting Latour]), but the concept of humans as the ultimate conscious, willful agents of change pops up everywhere, even in work by scholars committed to posthumanist ecologies. Engaging the tides and other entities as partners in their research, McGreavy, Sutton, and Hillyer instead breathe in possibilities for disruption of settled patterns that emerge from these encounters.

In his chapter, Whicker combats anthropocentrism directly: "for posthuman ecological theories of writing . . . any theorization of the agent limited to human identity, is unworkable." He proposes instead a "radical" theory of "the as yet unexplored individual agency of objects sans humans." Whicker notes a crucial gap in relational theories of becoming: they cannot account for the endurance of objects and thus of agents. And he argues, "for agents to be responsible for their actions and whatever differences they make, they have to be the *same* agents that acted." He offers his emendation as a complement to relational theories (Cooper's enchantment ontology, Boyle's posthuman practice) with the caveat that "while everything is entangled, everything is not entangled with everything; there are gaps." He turns to Harman's and Bryant's Object-Oriented-Ontology (OOO), which defines objects as "those things that unify their parts, become the same . . . even if those parts are spatially and temporally distributed": a water molecule, for example, or the Ship of Theseus, which "is still the same object even though all its parts have been replaced because of the continuation of its unity." Such objects are what Whitehead calls "enduring objects": "the permanent entities which enjoy adventures of change throughout time and space" (quoting Whitehead). Whitehead's example is

Cleopatra's Needle, which is recognizable because it thus "sustains a character" (*Process and Reality*, 35): "there it is again" (*The Concept of Nature*, 144). Enduring objects contrast with "actual entities" that "perish, but do not change; they are what they are." Whitehead posits as the ontological principle "the decision amid 'potentiality'" that constitutes the actual entity, commenting that "the point to be emphasized is the insistent particularity of things experienced" (*Process and Reality*, 43). Harman's conception of the object is based on a withdrawal within the object: "the inner core of objects (which Harman emphasizes as the 'real object')" withdraws "from the invariant qualities of that core as well as both from the sensual objects and their qualities of relation." Whicker argues (and I agree) that Harman pushes withdrawal too far, rendering sensual objects and their qualities of relation (Whitehead's actual entities) fictional and the reality of objects cut off from contact. Whicker argues instead that "what withdraws is not the entirety of the 'real' object or of the core of qualities that emerge in the unification of parts . . . but always a *remainder*, the part of the object that is not participating in every relation" (emphasis added). Objects always have a remainder because "their processes of becoming the same . . . yield invariant qualities that always elude" relations. This allows objects to endure over time and place and be recognizable as the same agents that acted.

Whicker concludes, "objects are both enduring societies not reducible to either their parts or their relations with invariant qualities that emerge through ongoing processes of *becoming the same* and sensual objects 'enjoying adventures of change' in inter-action with the world, equally active in *becoming different*." Having established how objects both endure and create novelty through complementary modes of becoming the same and becoming different, Whicker then lays out accounts of agency and of writing that closely accord, as he often remarks, with my account in *The Animal Who Writes*. By explicitly including "things in themselves, without us," he can boast a theory of agency that "is even more posthuman than relational theories." Indeed, he says that not only is agency not unique to humans, it is simply the object's actions in the world as it responds to perturbations. Agency is action that is not conscious and "in no way intentional, volitional, or something the agent has." "Agency is the agent's being in the world." Latour's knives cutting meat and soap taking dirt away qualify as agential equally with the actions of humans, who are "one type of object among many" (quoting Bryant). Humans are "writing-objects."

Whicker's theory of writing would also seem to allow sentient animals other than humans to be writing-objects. In animals with a nervous system, perturbations stimulate the production of information through the firing of nerve cells which, in turn, evoke the animal's response. Information is unconsciously selected as meaningful and recorded in memory as neurons create patterns and interact to form assemblies that are unique to each individual. "This process is both pre-conscious and involuntary"; the animal experiences only meaning, not information. Whicker follows Derrida's understanding of writing: writing "creates meaning by enregistering it, by entrusting it to an engraving, a groove, a relief, to a surface" (quoting Derrida). Writing leaves marks, and "the marking of neurons is the first writing." Whicker concludes, "writing emerges prior to any development of language and occurs, initially, entirely on the interior of writing-objects, though neither consciously nor under the control of the writing subject . . . neural texts are written with and in the brain itself as a marked surface." In a further step, Whicker notes Bryant's contention that writing-objects can draw "connections between neural texts and current experience" in the process of "*imagination, invention, creativity*," producing "additional neural texts that alter the writing ecology of the mind." He likens this step, which "marks the entrance of conscious thought" into writing, with Whitehead's account of entertaining propositions, but notes that "even this writing, however, remains pre-linguistic and decidedly not a matter of representation." The entrance of conscious thought about neural texts, like speculation in the entertaining of propositions, perhaps brings Whicker closer to a kind of writing that excludes more, though not all, sentient animals other than humans. But as Harman says about his conclusion that everything is an object, including humans, since "the term 'objects' is not opposed to 'subjects' . . . it is not such a bad fate to be an object" (quoting Harman).

Boyle engages imaginative texts in an equally radical challenge to Western rhetorical ecologies as he argues that instead of "merely representing the world they orbit . . . imaginative compositions [are] worlds in and of themselves," offering "a wealth of realities." He critiques the dominant environmental imaginaries of NewSpace that "fuse the potential of astro-engineering to fantastic fictions of interplanetary colonization as the culminating achievement of a species," thus collapsing "the very complexity that systems thinking pursues." Ecological conceptions of relationships are central to systems thinking, and it is the nature of such relationships that Boyle pursues in this chapter. McGreavy, Sutton, and Hillyer gestured toward it when they described eschewing a search for common ground or mutual understanding and instead engaging more deeply in an effort "that digs into difference and maintains that difference while also trying to stay in good relations." Conceiving of differences as equally viable and of equal interest opens new possibilities for thinking. Whicker characterizes the relationship of modes of becoming as complementary, as both/and, when he describes how objects both endure and create novelty. Boyle, considering the entangled relations among imaginative and independent realities, says they are more/less, and asks, "How many realities are we ignoring?"

All of these relations—differences, modes of becoming, imaginary and independent existence—are ecologically necessary, as Whitehead avers in describing permanence and change not as contradictions but as contrasting processes: "both are in the grip of the ultimate metaphysical ground, the creative advance into novelty," each as "the instrument of novelty for the other" (*Process and Reality*, 349). Whitehead was especially interested in how mental habits of thinking were transmitted either as "'living values,' values that incite curiosity, the appetite for contrasts . . . or as 'dead values,' usually inciting compliant submission and the inhibition" of doubt (Stengers, *Thinking with Whitehead*, 333). Stengers writes that Whitehead was "terrified" by the power of commonplaces of the industrial revolution over the "best men" of the time, who submitted with a "stone-blind eye" to conceptions of workmen as "mere hands, drawn from the pool of labour." "These honorable men . . . held fast only by inhibiting, in them and around them, that which would make them doubt" (333). Whitehead refers to such situations as "the trick of evil," not as personal failures but as a cosmic event. As

Stengers describes it: "evil must be overcome, that is, that what was felt as intolerable be accepted, canalized, admitted to infect its social environment, making it capable of original responses" (333–34). Such commonplaces are rife in rhetorical ecologies; they are what everyone knows. They are not always and at all times dangerous—Whitehead also says that "insistence on birth at the wrong season is the trick of evil" (*Process and Reality*, 223)—but the inhibition of imagination and doubt is a bad cosmic habit.

Boyle cites Stormer and McGready's proposal that "any rhetoric that can be seen ecologically is one that considers qualities of relations between entities, not just among humans, that then enable different modes of rhetoric to emerge, flourish, and dissipate" (quoting Stormer and McGready), a requirement that is hampered by the trick of evil. Boyle takes a tip from Syverson and elaborates it through Souriau's theory of instauration to consider how NewSpace fabulations of interplanetary colonization, like the commonplaces of industrial revolution cited by Whitehead, enact the trick of evil—and how they may not. Syverson notes in passing how fictional characters like Mickey Mouse acquire real existence through the work of their dissemination in multiple media. Boyle notes that "for Souriau, the worldmaking potential of imaginaries" was compelling: "a mode of existence that offers sketches or starts through which any number of other existences are built, highlights how all can be imagined, from fictional characters to 'the beings of dreams,' may gain or fail to gain foothold" (quoting Souriau). Souriau rewrote traditional ontology as instauration, a process that accounts for Syverson's wealth of realities. Instauration is "a matter of inventing": "the creative labor through multiple and multiplicitous modes to bring a thing into existence" (quoting Souriau). Boyle suggests that such things, "referential realities," not be considered in opposition to "independent realities" "but rather in dynamic tension of a *more/ less* relationship," as they actually depend on one another just as do Maturana and Varela's conceptual pairing of autopoiesis and allopoiesis.

But instauration can fail, and fictional productions like those of Musk do fail, at least for some readers. Boyle levies a stinging critique:

The gambit to reproduce existing ecological structures in interstellar terrain is arguably an escape from culpability, since now that one portion of the species has extracted and pillaged the majority, all must be saved, including the culprits. Rebooting Manifest Destiny for forays into the stars, the rhetoric of frontier expansion and conquest unselfconsciously replicates while also further obscuring a long history of settlers appropriating lands from Indigenous cultures. Yet it whitewashes its own disinterest in challenging racial and social inequity with performative claims of a world rebuilt. Further, a point that bears repeating, its goal of conquest for "life" and "all humanity" makes prior conquests of human and all other life a means through which as an end, interstellar migration justifies.

And he asks, "what do we make of a virtual that realizes the conditions for its own ecological emergence on the ontological certainty of a wholly exhausted earth?" On what everyone knows? This is true of other NewSpace fictions whose "points of dissent are only *how we leave*, in terms both of *in what state* and *by what means*." "They have failed to imagine a different world" (quoting McCormick). The real failure of instauration, Boyle observes, "is not *not to be instaured*: rather, it is in collapsing failure to that which is not yet or cannot be achieved, closing ourselves to the multiplicity of existences by adhering to any sole plan."

Souriau also conceived of two performative styles that can describe ways of imagining realities: cubic and spherical. Boyle renames them architectural composing (imagining a contained plot) and ecological composing (imagining improvised movement). Souriau's aesthetic, like McGreavy, Sutton, and Hillyer's research practices, asks for the work of developing "the capacity for attending to these seemingly mutual exclusive modes of existences" as contrasts, as in the relation of more/less. Boyle observes, "a 'more cube/more sphere' framing invites us to see both as performers who have dispositions but not absolutes, recalling that the point of this analysis is not to advance one cosmic worldview over another but rather to juxtapose two rhetorics that array our engagement with eco-aesthetic imaginaries." Boyle cites Law's argument that telling stories is always staging a performance that renders "what is performed . . . more obdurate, more solid, more real than it might otherwise have been" (quoting Law). Law offers a way of attending to contrasting realities by thinking of bulletin boards as a site for "inventive rhetorical resources for living with the tension of unknowable ends" (more sphere) and for "poking holes in the 'impeccable' plans of billionaires" (more cube). Law's example also illustrates how the trick of evil can be translated: by accepting, rather than disputing, "what was felt as intolerable" (the foregone conclusion of a technocapitalist exit strategy) can be rerouted, rethought, "canalized, admitted to infect its social environment," thus "making it capable of original responses." Focusing attention on technocapitalists' presumption of a wholly exhausted earth, Webb's "narratives of groundbreaking biological advancement . . . repair against the existential threats of *this* world . . . [by] investing in an egalitarian quality of life for all." This is the role for such fabulations, Boyle says; they "call us to more actively leverage imagining against the imaginary to multiply reality against singular realities and root out fictions of ontological certainty that embed themselves in our critical aims." But the same lure of ontological certainty threatens referential realities. Referring to Rickert's presumption of the need to re-create in any spaceship a "background we take for granted on earth, where our lifeworld is simply given." Boyle notes "the risk of becoming too enamored of our constructive capacities; too convinced in one end, one plan to reach it; too persuaded that any lifeworld is given." Still, multiplying the realities within which rhetorical ecologies contend and working with more/less relations of contrasting processes is the way to go, cosmically speaking. Boyle concludes: "Without that work, we may satisfy ourselves by completing the story of us and our travels; without that labor, we lose the joy in rendering ourselves, and multiple modes of existence, to be incomplete."

Works Cited

Barad, Karen. *Meeting the Universe Halfway: Quantum Physics and the Entanglement of Matter and Meaning.* Duke UP, 2007.

Cooper, Marilyn M. *The Animal Who Writes: A Posthumanist Composition.* U of Pittsburgh P, 2019.

Stengers, Isabelle. *Thinking with Whitehead: A Free and Wild Creation of Concepts.* Translated by Michael Chase, Harvard UP, 2011.

Whitehead, Alfred North. *The Concept of Nature.* Prometheus, 2004.

———. *Process and Reality: An Essay in Cosmology.* edited by Donald Ray Griffin and Donald W. Sherburne, Corrected ed., The Free Press, 1978.

Wittgenstein, Ludwig. *Philosophical Investigations.* Translated by G. E. M. Anscombe, Macmillan, 1953.

INDEX

physical mechanics as
  persuasions in, 83–84
purview of, 332–33
relationshipping, 69–73, 75
requirements of, 87
sedimented as history, 218
types of, 69
Rhetoric (Aristotle), 47–48
"Rhetoric 2001" (Coe), 9–10
rhetorical, basis for the, 68
rhetorical act, the classic, 67
rhetorical ecologies
  act locally, admonition to, 305
  boundaries, 16–17
  counter-traditions, 17
  history of, 5–14, 15*f*, 16–18,
    19*f*, 20*f*
  interest in, 18, 20*f*
  as lifeworlds, 333
  as metaphor, 290
  Native Americans, 334–35
  toxic, 333
  unified theory of general,
    21–26
rhetorical studies, 67, 75–76
rhetorical triangle model, 12
Rhetoric as a Posthuman Practice
  (Boyle), 96
*On Rhetoric: A Theory of Civic
  Discourse* (Kennedy),
  92–93
rhetoricians, functions of, 333
rhythm, 48–53
The Rhythmic Event
  (Ikoniadou), 50
Rice, Jenny, 301–03, 313
Rickert, Thomas, 329, 346
Ridolfo, Jim, 299
The Right Stuff (blog), 253–54
Rìos, Gabriela Raquel, 25
risk communication, 293
*Risk Society: Towards a New
  Modernity* (Beck), 293
Rivers, Nathaniel, 87, 313
Roane, J. T., 25
Roderick, Noah, 5

Roorda, Randall, 13
Rude, Carolyn, 292, 296
Rundle, Chester, 135–36
Russell, George, 51

Salliou, Nicolas, 242
Sánchez, Raúl, 270–73, 275–76,
  284–85
saneism in design, 116
sanity, boundaries for, 114–15
Sato, Yuriko, 241
"Saving the Great Lakes"
  (Waddell), 293
Savransky, Martin, 318, 328
Schumer, Amy, 254
science
  critiques of, 293, 296–97
  misinformation crisis, 297–98
  public trust in, 296–98, 300,
    302–03
  rhet-ops style information
    warfare and the, 297–305
  weaponization of critical
    investigations of, 301
Scot-Heron, Gil, 323
Seigel, Marika, 334–37
*(((Semitism))): Being Jewish in
  America in the Age of
  Trump* (Weisman), 259
Senda-Cook, Samantha, 17, 23,
  241
seventh-generation thinking, 190,
  191
Shakespeare, 323
Shaviro, Steven, 85–86, 90
shoals, 207
"Signature Event Context"
  (Derrida), 284
Silent Spring (Carson), 1
Simmons, Michele W., 293
Simondon, Gilbert, 274, 281
Simpson, Leanne, 190
Sirola, Noora, 230
situations, rhetorical, 74
Sky Woman, 185
Smith, Anthony, 255

writing
  components of, 312
  defined, 284–85
  emergence of, 342
  marks of, meaning created by, 284
  as staging performance, 319–20
  teaching, 94
  in third space of a website, 219–20
  thought as, 284
"Writing and Knowing: Toward Redefining the Writing Process" (Reither), 10
writing-objects, 282–86, 342
"Writing Offshore" (Haynes), 40
writing programs. *See also* stretch composition program (UW)
  antiracist and culturally sustaining, 160–66

ecological attributes of, 151–55
ecologies of, 148
equity and social justice, envisioning and creating with in, 148–50, 152
place-based, transformational equity work, doing, 148–50, 152
writing spaces for clamming communities, 219–20
writing studies, 270–71

Yang, K. Wayne, 205
Young, James, 137–38
Young, Vershawn Ashanti, 148
Yucca Mountain Project, 295–96
Yusoff, Kathryn, 130, 136–37, 143–44

Zannettou, Savvas, 259

EDITORS

Sidney I. Dobrin is a professor and chair in the department of English at the University of Florida. He is the founding director of the Trace Innovation Initiative. He is the author and/or editor of numerous books, most recently *Blue Ecocriticism and the Oceanic Imperative* (Routledge 2021) and *AI and Writing* (Broadview Press 2023). He serves as a Digital Thought Leader for Adobe.

Madison P. Jones is an assistant professor of Professional & Public Writing and Natural Resources Science at the University of Rhode Island, where he directs the Digital Writing Environments, Location, and Localization (DWELL) Lab, is a Senior Fellow at the Coastal Institute, and coordinates the Science Writing & Rhetoric graduate certificate program. His research intersects the rhetoric of science and technology and environmental communication. His digital projects combine spatial rhetorics with locative media for community-engaged science communication, social justice, and environmental advocacy. His articles have appeared in journals such as *Kairos, Communication Design Quarterly, Rhetoric Review,* and *Rhetoric Society Quarterly* and have garnered recognition from ARSTM and CCCC/NCTE's Best Article Awards. For more, visit: madisonpjones.com.

CONTRIBUTORS

Kristin L. Arola is an associate professor in Writing, Rhetoric, and American Cultures, and American Indian and Indigenous Studies at Michigan State University. Arola's research and teaching focus on the intersections between American Indian rhetoric, multimodal pedagogy, and digital rhetoric. She believes best practices for research, teaching, and teamwork must acknowledge and honor all relations that afford and affirm our making. As such, her work is rooted in Anishinaabe community practices, histories, and futures.

Casey Boyle is an associate professor of rhetoric and writing and director of the Digital Writing & Research Lab at the University of Texas-Austin. At present, he is either in the middle of writing a book about aesthetics, rhetoric, and Late Humanity, or he will soon be starting a book project about failing to write a book about aesthetics, rhetoric, and Late Humanity.

Jennifer Clary-Lemon is associate professor of English at the University of Waterloo. She is the author of *Planting the Anthropocene: Rhetorics of Natureculture and Cross Border Networks in Writing Studies*. Her research interests include environmental and material rhetorics, theories of affect, critical discourse studies, writing and location, and research methodologies. Her current research examines infrastructural entanglements of humans and nonhumans as material rhetorical arguments, focusing on mandated recovery strategies for species at risk.

Jason Collins is a PhD candidate in the English RCL program at the Ohio State University. His research focuses on the ways climate researchers engage with Indigenous people's Traditional Ecological knowledge. Working through decolonial theories, he asks how these engagements shape the researchers and their research and how they care for the knowledge they engage with.

Marilyn M. Cooper is a past editor of *College Composition and Communication* and author of *The Animal Who Writes: A Posthumanist Composition* (2019). She is currently chair of the publications committee of the Isle Royale and Keweenaw Parks Association, where she edits and oversees production of books such as *How the Rock Connects Us: A Geoheritage Guide to Michigan's Keweenaw Peninsula and Isle Royale* and is now working on a book of transcriptions of the first volume of the logbooks of the Menagerie Island Lighthouse on Isle Royale, 1875–1893. In the ever-warming UP summers, she enjoys walking with her border collie Scout observing eagles, loons, and mergansers catching fish in the cold waters of Lake Superior.

David M. Grant is associate professor at the University of Northern Iowa where he teaches courses in technical writing, rhetorics of science, and writing studies. His work at the intersection of new materialisms and decolonial rhetorics has appeared in *College Composition and Communication*, *Rhetoric Review*, and *enculturation*. He is also working on a NASA-funded space grant to develop an online, interactive game for STEM information literacy.

Laurie Gries is an associate professor with a joint appointment in the Program for Writing and Rhetoric and the Department of Communication at the University of Colorado-Boulder. Her research focuses on visual rhetoric, circulation studies, new materialisms, and digital research methods. She is author of *Still Life with Rhetoric: A New Materialist Approach for Visual Rhetorics* (2015) and coeditor of *Circulation, Writing, and Rhetoric* (2018). More recently, she has published in *College English*, *College Composition and Communication*, and *Rhetoric Review*. Her forthcoming coedited collection with Computers and Composition Digital Press (CCDP) is *Doing Digital Visual Studies: One Image, Multiple Methodologies*.

Matthew Halm is a Marion L. Brittain Postdoctoral Fellow in the Writing and Communication Program at Georgia Tech, where he teaches technical communication and studies new materialist theories of rhetoric and media.

Byron Hawk is a professor of English at the University of South Carolina. His primary research interests are histories and theories of composition, rhetorical theory and technology, sonic rhetorics, and rhetorics of popular music. He is the author of *Resounding the Rhetorical: Composition as a Quasi-Object* and *A Counter-History of Composition: Toward Methodologies of Complexity*, which won JAC's W. Ross Winterowd Award in 2007 and received honorable mention for MLA's Mina Shaughnessy Prize in 2008. Hawk is also senior editor of the online journal *enculturation*, which he founded in 1996.

Leah Heilig is an assistant professor of professional and public writing at the University of Rhode Island. Her research focuses on technical communication, accessibility, and disability studies, with a focus on inclusion for those with psychiatric or mental disability. Her work can be found in *The Palgrave Handbook for Disability and Communication, Journal of Business and Professional Communication Quarterly, Technical Communication Quarterly, Communication Design Quarterly,* and *Tinfoil Hats: Mad Stories for an Insane World.*

Gabrielle Hillyer recently received her doctorate from the University of Maine Orono in ecology and conservation sciences. Her work embodies themes of engaged and collaborative research, coastal resilience, oceanography, and co-managed fisheries. She is continuing this work as a Sea Grant Knauss Fellow, serving with the Office of Oceanic and Atmospheric Research at NOAA as a member of their congressional policy team in 2024.

Chris Ingraham is an assistant professor of communication at the University of Utah, where he is also a core faculty member of the Environmental Humanities graduate program. He has been a Fulbright fellow in digital culture at the University of Bergen, Norway; and, in addition to publishing widely in rhetorical theory and media studies, is the author of *Gestures of Concern* and coeditor of *LEGOfied: Building Blocks as Media.*

Bridie McGreavy is an associate professor in the Department of Communication and Journalism at the University of Maine. Her research and teaching use collaborative and decolonial methods to co-create knowledge focused on water and environmental justice. She is co-lead of the Maine Shellfish Learning Network and affiliated with the Mitchell Center for Sustainability Solutions.

Anselma Widha Prihandita is a PhD candidate in language and rhetoric at the University of Washington. Her research explores the intersections between writing pedagogy, decoloniality, and transnationalism. She is interested in questions such as how the university, academic discourse, and global production of knowledge can uphold epistemic racism; how writing and language education can be leveraged to undo this; and how students and teachers who come from marginalized social and geopolitical locations navigate teaching and learning that are often not culturally sustaining for them.

Candice Rai is an associate professor of English at the University of Washington. She recently co-wrote *Rhetorical Climatology* (with Chris Ingraham, Jennifer LeMesurier, Bridie McGreavy, Nathan Stormer, and John Ackerman) and coedited *Writing across Difference: Theory and Intervention* (with James Rushing Daniel and Katie Malcolm) and *Field Rhetoric: Ethnography, Ecology, and Engagement in the Places of Persuasion* (with Caroline Gottschalk Druschke). She is the author of *Democracy's Lot: Rhetoric, Publics, and the Places of Invention*. Her work focuses on education justice and engages place-based inquiry to study public rhetoric and writing, political discourse and action, and argumentation.

Nolie Ramsey currently works as a lead strategist on the Education practice at Intentional Futures, where she collaborates with clients working to create equity in higher education. Previously, Nolie served as a writing instructor and writing program administrator at the University of Washington. She holds a BA in English from Mississippi College and an MA in English Language and Literature from the University of Washington. She is also currently an English PhD candidate at the University of Washington, completing her dissertation that explores the intersections of colonialism, religion, and poetic form in the work of Toru Dutt, Sarojini Naidu, and Gerard Manley Hopkins.

Marika Seigel is dean of the Pavlis Honors College and associate provost for Undergraduate Education at Michigan Technological University. Her primary areas of research include educational innovation, writing program administration, and the rhetoric of health and medicine—particularly as it pertains to women's reproductive health and pregnancy. In addition to two books with the University of Chicago Press—*The Rhetoric of Pregnancy* and *Expecting: A Brief History of Pregnancy Advice*—Seigel's work has appeared in scholarly journals such as *College Composition and Communication*, *Rhetoric Review*, *Studies in Engineering Education*, and *Sustainability*.

Samantha Senda-Cook is an associate professor in the Department of Communication Studies and an affiliated faculty member with the Environmental Science and Sustainability programs at Creighton University. She studies rhetorical theory and analyzes environmental communication and materiality in the contexts of social movements, outdoor recreation, and urban spaces/places. She was awarded a Fulbright Fellowship to study in Japan in 2019. Her work has been published in the *Quarterly Journal of Speech*, *Environmental Communication*, and *Argumentation and Advocacy*. When she's not researching or teaching, she's probably reading a mystery novel, cooking, or riding the hills of Omaha on her bike.

Contributors

Anthony Sutton is Passamaquoddy from Sipayik. He is an assistant professor of Native American Studies and Food Systems at the University of Maine and Faculty Fellow at the Mitchell Center for Sustainability Solutions. Sutton's work focuses on historical and contemporary aspects of Wabanaki foodways, unpacking the histories that have shaped lands, waters, and species central to Wabanaki foodways to the present by centering Wabanaki visions for the restoration of foodways and fisheries.

Denise Tillery is a professor of English and associate dean in the College of Liberal Arts at the University of Nevada, Las Vegas. She has published multiple articles and book chapters on environmental rhetoric, gender and rhetoric, and technical communication program administration, as well as a book, *Commonplaces of Scientific Evidence in Environmental Discourses,* and an edited collection, *The New Normal: Pressures on Technical Communication Programs in the Age of Austerity.* Her work focuses on the uses of scientific evidence in environmental rhetoric in a variety of contexts and media, including Facebook and other digital formats.

John H. Whicker is an independent scholar living in the four-corners area of the southwest United States. His work has appeared in *JAC, Composition Studies, Composition Forum,* and *Across the Disciplines.*

This book was typeset in Sabon LT Pro.
Typefaces used on the cover include Garamond Premr Pro and Cera Pro.
The book was printed on 50-lb. white, offset paper.